The Social History of Health and Medicine in Colonial India

AF655804

The Social History of Health and Medicine in Colonial India

Edited by

Biswamoy Pati
and Mark Harrison

PRIMUS BOOKS

First published 2009
by Routledge
2 Park Square, Milton Park, Abingdon, Oxon OX14 4RN

*Routledge is an imprint of the Taylor & Francis Group,
an Informa business*

© Editorial selection and matter, Biswamoy Pati and Mark Harrison;
individual chapters, the contributors, 2009, 2011

Typeset in Times New Roman by
Keystroke, 28 High Street, Tennenhall, Wolverhamptom

All rights reserved. No part of this book may be reprinted or reproduced or utilized in any form or by any electronic, mechanical, or other means, now known or hereafter invented, including photocopying and recording, or in any information storage or retrieval system, without permission in writing from the publishers.

First published in India 2011
Reprinted 2013, 2015

Published by **PRIMUS BOOKS**
An imprint of Ratna Sagar P. Ltd.
Virat Bhavan
Mukherjee Nagar Commercial Complex
Delhi 110 009

Offices at CHENNAI KOLKATA LUCKNOW
AGRA AHMEDABAD BENGALURU COIMBATORE DEHRA DUN
GUWAHATI HYDERABAD JAIPUR KANPUR KOCHI MADURAI
MUMBAI PATNA RANCHI

Published by kind permission of Routledge, an imprint of
the Taylor & Francis Group, an Informa business

ISBN: 978-93-80607-85-6

Printed at Sanat Printers, Kundli, Haryana

This edition is for sale only in India, Bangladesh, Bhutan, Nepal, Pakistan and Sri Lanka.

This book is meant for educational and learning purposes. The author(s) of the book has/have taken all reasonable care to ensure that the contents of the book do not violate any existing copyright or other intellectual property rights of any person in any manner whatsoever. In the event the author(s) has/have been unable to track any source and if any copyright has been inadvertently infringed, please notify the publisher in writing for corrective action.

Contents

Figures

Tables

Contributors

Partho Datta teaches undergraduate history in Zakir Husain Evening College, Delhi, and is currently Fellow at the Nehru Memorial Museum and Library, New Delhi.

Achintya Kumar Dutta is Professor of History at the University of Burdwan, West Bengal, India. His publications include *Economy and Ecology in a Bengal District: Burdwan 1880–1947* (2002) and he also co-edited *History of Medicine in India: The Medical Encounter* (2005).

Sanchari Dutta is an historian of medicine and works on modern South Asia. She completed a D.Phil. at the University of Oxford in 2007. Her research focuses on prisons and medicine in colonial India.

Waltraud Ernst is Professor of the History of Medicine and Director of the Centre for Health, Medicine and Society: Past and Present, at Oxford Brookes University. She has published widely on the history of psychiatry in South Asia and edited *Race, Science and Medicine* (1999; with B. Harris), *Plural Medicine, Tradition and Modernity, Histories of the Normal and the Abnormal* (2002) and *India's Princely States: People, Princes and Colonialism* (2007; with B. Pati).

Mark Harrison is Professor of the History of Medicine and Director of the Wellcome Unit for the History of Medicine at the University of Oxford. He has written extensively on the history of medicine, disease and imperialism, particularly with respect to India.

Amar Farooqui is Professor of History, University of Delhi, Delhi. His publications include *Smuggling as Subversion: Colonialism, Indian Merchants, and the Politics of Opium, 1790–1843* (2005); and *Opium City: The Making of Early Victorian Bombay* (2006).

Amna Khalid did a D.Phil. at the University of Oxford in 2008. Her thesis focuses on the connection between pilgrimage and epidemic diseases in colonial northern India. She is currently a postdoctoral research fellow at the Cultural Studies Centre, University of Sussex, and is working on aspects of Muslim identity in Britain and North America. Her research interests include Sufi shrines in South Asia as syncretic spiritual spaces.

Saurabh Mishra completed a D.Phil. at the University of Oxford in 2008 on the social history of the Haj from colonial India. At present he is researching aspects of colonial medical policies and their interaction with indigenous forms of knowledge. His publications include 'Politicization of a Holy Act: The Haj from the Indian Subcontinent during Colonial Times' in the *Journal of the Royal Asiatic Society of Bangladesh* (2005).

Projit Bihari Mukharji is Lecturer in Modern History at Newcastle University. He was educated at Presidency College, Calcutta, Jawaharlal Nehru University, New Delhi, and the School of Oriental and African Studies, London. His main research interests relate to studying the processes of modernization of healing practices in colonial South Asia. He has published work on imperial cultural history and the history of sport.

Chandi P. Nanda is Reader at the Academic Staff College, Utkal University, Bhubaneswar. He authored *Vocalizing Silence: Political Protests in Orissa, 1930–42* (2008).

Biswamoy Pati is Associate Professor in Modern Indian History, Department of History, University of Delhi. His latest publications include *South Asia from the Margins: Echoes of Orissa, 1800–2000* (2012); an edited book, *Invoking Ambedkar: Contributions, Receptions, Legacies* (2014); and a co-edited book, *Colonial and Contemporary Bihar and Jharkhand* (2014).

Samiksha Sehrawat is the John Anderson Research Lecturer in History at the Centre for the Social History of Health and Healthcare, Glasgow. Her recent research and publications focus on the history of hospitals, the colonial army, medical professionalization, gender and healthcare in India. She is currently engaged in finalizing a monograph on the social history of hospitals in colonial north India, which is funded by the University of Strathclyde Research Excellence Fund.

Madhuri Sharma completed her doctoral research on colonial medical advertisements from the Jawaharlal Nehru University, Delhi, in 2007. She has taught history in some colleges of the University of Delhi and was a Visiting Fellow of the British Academy in the Department of History, University of Strathclyde, Glasgow, in 2007–8.

Acknowledgements

The contributors to the volume stood by and extended their full cooperation, which we deeply appreciate. Dorothea Schaefter and Suzanne Chilestone at Routledge were a welcome source of encouragement. Maggie Lindsey-Jones and Emma Wood have been of invaluable help as project managers. Thanks are also due to Saurabh Mishra for helping out with the index.

1 Social history of health and medicine

Colonial India

Mark Harrison and Biswamoy Pati

When writing the introduction to a previous volume of essays in 2001, we remarked on the rapid growth of the history of medicine as it relates to India under British rule. Since that time, the growth has continued apace, with more local studies helping us to set the peculiarities of place against the broad brushstrokes of pioneering early works. Entirely new dimensions of health and medicine have also been revealed, often by younger scholars working at doctoral level. It is therefore pleasing to report on the vitality of a subject which we feel to be important, from both a historical and a contemporary point of view. And yet much of this new research is unknown or barely known to historians working in cognate areas – a problem that this volume attempts to resolve. In bringing together these essays, we hope to showcase the work of younger scholars researching on health and medicine in colonial India, albeit with one or two contributions from more established ones. Our main aim is to highlight some of the newer themes that have emerged over recent years, and in what remains of this introductory chapter we identify these and set them against the background of previous scholarship. Our survey of secondary literature, however, is indicative rather than exhaustive and readers seeking a fuller review of secondary works should consult some of the recent publications cited below.

Public health

The subject of 'public health' has been very much to the fore in the historiography of medicine in India over recent years. Broadly speaking, there are two tendencies in the literature to date. The first is concerned with questions of the colonial legacy in public health, and whether or not the British made much progress in this regard. Opinions on this matter have differed widely, from claims that public health flourished only under British agency,[1] to claims that successive British administrations sought merely to protect the health of colonial enclaves.[2] Some scholars have even questioned the appropriateness of the term 'public health' in the Indian context, preferring to employ the term 'state medicine' instead. Hence the second tendency in the historiography – much indebted to the writings of Michel Foucault – which has examined 'public health' measures in the light of colonial power, as a means by which the state aimed to know and control its subjects.[3] These two tendencies are not necessarily opposed to one another, and, as Partho Datta notes in his chapter in this volume, the notion of 'public health' emerged from a reformist mode of governance which was part and parcel of British imperialism. Fashioned out of new administrative practices and conceptions of social order, this notion of the public was rather different from the 'reasoning public' familiar to readers of Habermas. This notional public was constituted by the state and was simultaneously defined and transformed through state action.

Early nineteenth-century Calcutta is the ideal beginning for a set of essays which examine various facets of public health and medicine in India. As the imperial capital, it saw the first major initiatives in sanitary reform, in urban planning and in the creation of hospitals and dispensaries. It was the location of the first school of Western medicine and witnessed the early flowering of the Indian medical profession. Many features of the history of public health from this period will already be familiar to readers of this volume,[4] but recent work has highlighted important new dimensions and has suggested ways in which the subject can be invigorated. One way in which this may be possible is to broaden our frame of analysis. Much, though by no means all, work on public health in British India has considered the country in isolation, ignoring the fact that some of the most important colonial interventions came about in response to external pressure. More often than not, the pressure came in the form of quarantine and other restrictions on Indian shipping. Anyone who has read the proceedings of the sanitary branch of the Government of India's Home Department cannot but be struck by the enormous amount of material concerning quarantine. Quarantines in the Red Sea, the Suez Canal and the Mediterranean damaged colonial trade, interrupted mail, and caused great inconvenience, whether for Europeans on leave or pilgrims on the Haj. These difficulties struck at the heart of colonial government and created friction between it and its Muslim subjects, as we see in Saurabh Mishra's chapter. In order to reduce disruption to a minimum, the Government of India was forced to comply, often unwillingly, with international demands to regulate its shipping, clean up its cities, and establish domestic quarantine in ports under its control.

As Mishra argues, the response to international pressure, especially after the Constantinople Sanitary Conference of 1866, created a great deal of tension within the British Empire. The Government of India had rather different priorities from those of the home government, being more concerned about the political effects of quarantine domestically, while provincial governments did not always see eye to eye with the authorities in Calcutta.[5] Nevertheless, reluctantly or not, health measures inside India were affected by these developments. The establishment of port health trusts in cities such as Bombay and Calcutta was one direct result of this, as, of course, was the flurry of activity that resulted from the importation of plague into Bombay in 1896. The government was compelled to moderate the draconian measures introduced initially in Bombay Presidency, but the epidemic left an important legacy for health and medicine in India. Partly in order to reassure international opinion, new legislation was enacted in the form of the Epidemic Diseases Act (1897) and spending on public health was substantially increased. Other initiatives, such as the establishment of city improvement trusts and medical laboratories, also followed in the wake of plague. As Amna Khalid reminds us in her chapter, international scrutiny led the Government of India to intervene in highly sensitive matters such as the pilgrimage of Hindus to sacred sites along the Ganges. Gatherings of pilgrims at Hardwar and Allahabad were identified at international sanitary conferences as focuses from which cholera disseminated within India and, hence, as the reservoirs of pandemics that periodically afflicted the rest of the world.

The Mediterranean states, such as France and Italy, tended to call loudest for measures against Indian shipping at times of cholera and plague because they were likely to be among the first European countries affected if either disease spread west of Suez. Austria-Hungary, which had long been concerned about the spread of plague from the Ottoman Empire, was also alarmed by the prospect of plague spreading from Mesopotamia and the Persian Gulf to Europe via Indian ports such as Bombay. These states leant heavily on the Egyptian and Constantinople boards of health, threatening sanctions against Egyptian and Ottoman shipping if their boards did not take measures against Indian vessels. However, the latter governments also used quarantine restrictions to further their own interests, for example to protect their near monopoly of trade in Turkish Arabia and the Red Sea. This serves as a reminder that there was always a political dimension to quarantine and such measures were rarely determined by geographical location alone.[6] States moderated or increased their demands for quarantine to gain commercial and territorial advantage, not least in the 'Great Game' between Britain and Russia, as Sanchari Dutta shows in her chapter.

The chapters written by Dutta, Khalid and Mishra demonstrate the importance of placing the historiography of public health in British India within a wider frame of analysis that pays close attention to an emerging, albeit unstable, internationalism in the field of health.[7] The same could be said to some extent for all states – colonial or otherwise – but it is perhaps especially true of British India, which was identified as the source of 'Asiastic' cholera and thus subjected to close international scrutiny. Nor should we forget that British India was effectively an empire in its own right, exercising control over ports such as Aden and having an expanding sphere of influence that extended into the Persian Gulf and Central Asia. This meant that the purview of the Indian state was necessarily a large one; geographically, at least. However, the chapters in this volume show that the colonial state was a complex institution; or, more accurately, a set of institutions, with subtly differing priorities that sometimes led to material differences over policy. Generalizations have their place, and one ought not to lose sight of common themes and interests, but the new emphasis on the fractured nature of colonial power has generated important insights into the process of policy making and the implementation of policies. In particular, it has highlighted the vital role of Indian agency – the subordinate medical staff responsible for implementing measures such as smallpox vaccination, for example.[8] In Amna Khalid's chapter on health measures introduced at pilgrimage sites, we also learn of the key role played by the subordinate police and of the problems that arose from this. Such studies demonstrate the extent to which colonial policies could be modified locally: sometimes through a process of constructive negotiation, sometimes through corruption and maladministration. Scholars of India have been slower to pay attention to the vital role of subordinate staff than have some of those who have examined other colonial contexts, where they often played a somewhat more prominent role,[9] and Khalid's examination of non-medical agencies like the police appears to be unique.

Another neglected feature of colonial health policy emerges from Achintya Kumar Dutta's chapter: the role of therapeutics. Again, this is a subject in which scholars of other colonial contexts have led the way, especially those working on tropical Africa. One of the reasons for the greater prominence of therapeutic interventions in African colonies is that medical work there more often took the form of disease-specific campaigns than it did in India. State intervention in matters of health came later in these newer colonies and coincided with the emergence of therapies based on the new sciences of bacteriology and parasitology.[10] British India, by contrast, had an older sanitary infrastructure which had evolved – with certain modifications – on the lines of that in Britain itself. Disease-specific campaigns – like that against malaria, for example – thus tended to be absorbed into other areas of public health work. However, during the twentieth century, therapeutics did become a more established feature of public health work in India. The discovery that kala-azar could be treated effectively with antimonial medicines such as tartar emetic created new possibilities for intervention based partly upon treatment. A programme of mass treatment was backed by government, in conjunction with the Indian Tea Association, kala-azar being very much a disease of plantations. But the grants provided to fund treatment and sanitary measures at local level fell far short of what was required.

The growing importance of treatment to public health programmes during the twentieth century is also evident in Biswamoy Pati and Chandi Nanda's study of leprosy in Orissa. They show how a supposedly effective treatment in the form of Hydnocarpus oil became the linchpin of a new attempt to control leprosy which combined treatment with confinement in asylums. A great deal of political and professional pride was invested in this form of treatment and it persisted despite growing doubts over whether it was effective; indeed, a considerable industry developed around supplying the oil to leprosy asylums in India and elsewhere. Commercial extraction of the oil continued long after the treatment was found to be effective, and it was used in the manufacture of ayurvedic soap and other such products.

Pati and Nanda's chapter also highlights a recurring theme in the history of public health, not only in India but internationally. It has long been observed that public health measures have been used to remove or control the movement of sections of the population considered undesirable, and more often than not it is the poor who have been identified as the source of infection.[11] Measures to control leprosy in colonial Orissa were no exception. The authors argue that the desire to incarcerate leprosy sufferers amounted almost to a class offensive by the Oriya middle class against the poorest sections of society: it supported colonial medical initiatives in order to remove the beggars – many of them afflicted by leprosy – who congregated in this important centre of pilgrimage. Similar motives appear to have been behind initiatives to incarcerate victims of leprosy elsewhere in India and, indeed, were the main force behind the All-India Lepers Act of 1898.[12]

Institutions

Asylums for the confinement of the leprosy-afflicted and the mad – European and Indian – have provided historians of British India with fertile subject matter over the last two decades.[13] While all are agreed that there was no 'great confinement' in India, either of the insane or of leprosy sufferers, it has been argued that asylums were nevertheless significant because they allowed the removal of dysfunctional individuals and because they were relatively controlled environments in which doctors could attempt to fashion colonial subjects. But as Waltraud Ernst reminds us, the relationship between medicine and colonial power was by no means straightforward. In her chapter in this volume, she shows how the function of colonial asylums shifted markedly over time from the incarceration of violent and intractable persons to more determined attempts at cure. Similarly, by the end of the nineteenth century, doctors came to exercise greater control over the running of these institutions than hitherto, which leads Ernst to the conclusion that were was a 'medicalization' of colonial power.

Whatever the nature of the regime in colonial mental asylums, it is clear from existing work that measures were often contested by the patients themselves.[14] Much the same can be said of leprosy asylums, as we learn from the work of Jane Buckingham and Sanjiv Kakkar, and in this volume, from the chapter by Pati and Nanda.[15] It is clear that there was widespread dissatisfaction with the regime imposed in Orissa's leprosy asylums, and numerous attempts to escape.

Leprosy and lunatic asylums were among the first medical institutions to receive attention from historians of India but there has been a recent spurt of interest in maternal health care – especially the hospitals of the Dufferin Fund (the National Association for Supplying Female Medical Aid to the Women of India) – and in missionary institutions.[16] These studies provide important insights into the nature of official and non-official mentalities and more generally into the interplay of race and gender. The spotlight on Indian women was intended to highlight the benevolence and liberality of Western culture which sought to protect the most vulnerable, to the callous indifference of Hinduism and Islam. Mission hospitals and initiatives like the Dufferin Fund were also vitally important to female doctors trained in the West, a high proportion of whom left Britain in an attempt to escape the restrictions of a rigidly patriarchal profession.

However, asylums and missionary institutions comprised a very small proportion of the hospitals and dispensaries established in British India. Hospitals for European soldiers, sailors and civilians were established from the seventeenth century in an attempt to reduce the high death rate suffered by the East India Company's employees. These institutions were often makeshift affairs but they played an important, though largely unacknowledged, role in the development of Western medicine, being important sites of innovation in morbid anatomy and therapeutics, for example.[17] In such hospitals, European practitioners found much more freedom to experiment than they did at home.

By the early nineteenth century, these old establishments had given way to more permanent institutions located in the larger towns. The turn of the century also saw the establishment of hospitals for Indians, following the example set by Calcutta in the 1790s.[18] The typical hospital of the early nineteenth century was an institution for the Indian poor, funded partly by government and partly by private subscription.[19] As the century progressed, larger hospitals began to develop around the medical colleges established in the presidency and other large towns, as well as many smaller institutions. This expansion occurred alongside a rapid growth in the number of dispensaries providing out-patient care, which generally proved more popular than treatment within the hospital. However, in 1910, the Government of India frankly admitted that most of the Indian population still did not have access to any Western medical institution, especially in rural districts. In that year, the government gave up all pretence of providing comprehensive medical relief, declaring that it would never have the means to provide the necessary coverage.[20] Instead, it was decided to rely on training more private practitioners and nurturing the development of what was referred to as the 'independent' (Indian) medical profession.

The scope of hospital care in British India was clearly limited but those who choose to study the history of hospitals will be rewarded with a rich archive that will enable them to answer important questions about the scope and influence of Western medicine. The hospital may well have played a rather different role in India from some Western countries, but it is clear that it became increasingly important as a location for medical education, clinical innovation and research. In India, no less than in Britain, the hospital became the key to the development of medical careers, and access to consultancy posts became one of the main objectives of Indian doctors, such as those represented by the Bombay Medical Union.[21] Philanthropic donations to hospitals and the creation of private caste and religious institutions are also likely to constitute a fruitful area for study,[22] while attendance at hospitals and dispensaries provides a crude index of their popularity with certain sections of the community. Preliminary indications are that demand for hospital and dispensary care increased massively from the middle of the nineteenth century, although with notable differences among classes, castes, genders and religions.[23] Indeed, the most interesting studies are likely to be those which take account of the peculiarities of place and which examine hospitals as institutions intertwined with the history of the communities they serve. Apart from the large general hospitals, many smaller hospitals and dispensaries were established for particular communities, ranging from institutions for textile and plantation workers to hospitals catering exclusively for particular castes or religious groupings.[24] Detailed studies of hospitals in Bengal and Bombay are already in progress but have yet to be published; however, in this volume, Samiksha Sehrawat's chapter shows the great potential of British India's vast military archive for the study of hospital and medical arrangements. Indeed, as in other European colonies, the experiences of Indian soldiers serving overseas may have led to increased expectations of medical care, both within the army and in civilian life.

Race

In one way or another, race was never far below the surface in colonial health policy. It was sometimes present in explicit ways, in medico-bureaucratic categories and in segregated medical institutions, but just as often in unspoken assumptions about the needs of the Indian people, their liability to different forms of illness, and the role of their habits in the production of disease. Medical manuals written by and for Europeans working in the tropics constantly stressed the dangers posed by the habits of Oriental peoples and often blamed them for their failure to make progress in matters of public health. However, there was nothing peculiarly 'Indian' about this, and colonial discourse in India reflected assumptions made in the colonies of other Western powers.[25] To some extent, also, it mirrored the prejudice displayed towards the working class at home, categories of class, caste and race being mutually reinforcing.

Racial divisions also kept Indians at the margins of medical policy. Although attempts were made to 'Indianize' the Indian Medical Service in the early twentieth century, the majority of top government positions continued to be occupied by Europeans.[26] Similarly, the role of Indians as policy makers in government was confined mostly to the municipal arena, although extending to provincial administrations following devolution in 1919. Thereafter, medical relief and sanitary reform came increasingly to attract the attention of nationalist politicians and the Indian press, who berated the British for their failure adequately to fund health care. Indian doctors – often working in state employment – highlighted the lack of priority given to such areas as nutrition and tuberculosis, for example.[27] Although Indians had rather more impact on policy making than subjects in most other colonies, they had substantially less than their counterparts in Ceylon, where rapid progress towards democracy and in health care went hand in hand.[28]

In one or other of these aspects, race features in all the chapters in this volume, but in some it is a major theme. In Mark Harrison's chapter we learn more about the construction of race as a category in medical thought and practice. This chapter develops some of the author's earlier work, looking in more detail at how notions of race began to be constituted within the framework provided by morbid anatomy.[29] It argues that questions of racial difference fascinated British and Indian medical practitioners equally and formed an important part of the activities of the Calcutta Medical College in its early years. Perceived differences between races and the way they manifested disease were also reflected in different forms of treatment advocated for Indians, Europeans and persons of mixed race.[30] One may perhaps mention here the importance of race in the classification and aetiology of mental disorders, especially in the middle years of the nineteenth century.[31] Crude racial stereotyping became less apparent towards the end of the century, as greater professionalism accentuated the difficulties experienced by individual patients. However, some of the ideas developed in earlier medical texts lingered on in popular and political discourses, being particularly evident in calls for national renewal.[32] As Madhuri Sharma shows in her chapter, the fear of racial degeneration was adroitly exploited by advertisers who played on concerns about health and virility.

Advertisements equated health and progress with adoption of Western-style medicinal products, though often in a reassuringly traditional guise.[33]

Gender, medicine and health care

Along with race, the relationship between gender and health was a major theme in colonial politics. Nevertheless, it was ignored by historians of colonial India until as recently as the 1980s, even in studies that focused exclusively on gender.[34] This was true not only of social historians in general, but also of those who looked particularly at issues around health and medicine.[35] However, it is no longer the case. From the 1980s, scholars have delved into questions related to the medicalization of childbirth and motherhood,[36] and some have examined curative care.[37] Research has also begun on female sexuality and on debates surrounding birth control.[38] However, most of the scholarship on health and gender over the last two decades has examined the work of women medical missionaries and its connections to the so-called 'civilizing mission' of the churches and the colonial administration.[39] Aptly described as the 'white woman's burden',[40] these activities have been traced to the agendas of 'maternal imperialists' who sought to legitimize colonial health policies in India.[41] Some attention has also been paid to the health concerns of the white woman in colonial India. The focus here has been largely on areas such as mental health and neurasthenia, which have highlighted the specificities of the colonial context.[42]

Studies of the nursing profession in India are still very much in their infancy.[43] To date, most attention has been directed to one specialist aspect of nursing – midwifery – rather than the broader issues of professionalization, status and recruitment, which loom large in the literature on nursing in Britain and its African colonies. In particular, scholars have examined colonial efforts to undermine traditional 'midwives' (*dais*), who appeared to symbolize ignorance and superstition.[44] Another subject arising from recent research is the life and work of women who were practitioners either of traditional medicine[45] or of what is normally referred to as Western medicine.[46] Both areas offer great potential for research, including the use of oral history to recover the voices of practitioners who are, still today, often overlooked in official discourse. The education of medical women has also suggested itself as a fruitful area for research, as has the treatment of women in hospitals and mental asylums.[47] There is, however, already a considerable body of scholarship on one aspect of the medical treatment of women – the forcible treatment of women within 'lock' hospitals which were strategically linked to the colonial army. Indeed, the history of prostitution and sexually transmitted diseases is perhaps the most developed area of scholarship on the health of women in colonial India.[48]

Indian medical traditions

The indigenous medical traditions include unani, siddah and ayurveda. Scholars like Neshat Quaiser, Claudia Liebeskind and Guy Attewell have examined some aspects related to unani, for example. Quaiser focuses on the effort to trace the 'ancient' Greek origins of unani, which situated unani as the basis for the birth of 'modern' medicine. Cast in the form of an anti-colonial discourse, this was positioned as a device to resist the colonial state's efforts to marginalize unani (as well as other Indian medical systems of medicine). Liebeskind throws light on the arguments made to prove that the unani system was scientific. Together they delineate the reformative and modernizing features of the unani system in north India that resulted from this debate with the colonial health establishment. Attewell extends their argument by focusing on south India.[49]

Until the early nineteenth century, British attitudes were marked by tolerance and some British practitioners were even appreciative of Indian 'systems' of medicine, such as ayurveda. Until about 1800, Western medicine and ayurveda shared many common features, including a basis in humoral pathology. This permitted an appreciation of Indian drugs on terms not dissimilar to those of Western medicine. Indeed, at this time, Western medicine possessed little evident advantage in the treatment of many of the most common diseases of India, including malaria, cholera and dysentery.[50] This early 'openness' was later accompanied, in the early nineteenth century, by more systematic efforts to study ayurveda.[51] Originally the inspiration of British Orientalists, these studies later became part of a nationalist project to construct an ayurvedic canon based on a corpus of ancient Sanskrit texts. The projected identity of ayurveda in this period was that of an ancient, Sanskritized and overwhelmingly 'Hindu' system. Some recent scholarship has explored the ayurvedic tradition on the basis of these texts,[52] although as David Hardiman has recently argued, ayurveda and other Indian medical 'traditions' have been invented as nationalist alternatives to biomedicine.[53] In reality, as a number of eminent scholars have shown, Indian medical 'traditions' have been characterized by diversity and by their formative interactions with both colonialism and nationalism.[54] Seen from within the colonial world of India, ayurveda has been located as a part of 'subaltern' science in relation to 'Western' science.[55] This is perhaps essentially true for the period after the 1820s, when the earlier openness towards ayurveda was replaced by an antiquarian interest on the one hand and a search for cheap and effective herbal simples on the other, without much regard for its theoretical principles.

These studies have enriched our understanding of regional cultures and diversities associated with ayurveda and have helped us to situate the pluralities of what has often been constructed as a monolithic system of 'Hindu' medicine. Projit Mukharji's chapter in the present collection needs to be seen against this background. He explores the interactions between colonial botany and the political and economic order of colonialism. Mukharji seeks to unpack the constitution of a discourse on indigenous drugs by early Orientalists, which was later inherited and refracted through nationalist deployments.

Madhuri Sharma's chapter explores the history of ayurveda in relation to another important theme which has scarcely been examined in relation to India: the growing commercialization of medicine and, in particular, the role of advertising.[56] Through advertisements in the print media, she shows that attempts were made to create a space for both indigenous and 'Western' medicine. The method of securing legitimacy for these products saw serious drives by entrepreneurs associated with both varieties of medicine. Here one can refer to the indigenous treatment of leprosy organized at Keonjhar (a princely state in Orissa) by its chief. This was publicized as an 'ancient' cure and was promoted in such a way as to enable the durbar to secure legitimacy for itself.[57] Similarly, an Oriya newspaper carried an advertisement for a 'Marvellous Remedy' for cholera, diarrhoea and dysentery made by Kabiraj Babu Laxminarayan (Kendrapada, Cuttack), that carried testimonials to support its claim from Waris Ali, the Headmaster, and Ganesh Chandra Mahapatra, the Police Inspector.[58] In fact, Madhuri Sharma's chapter in this collection grapples with advertisements in Hindi and English newspapers and journals which aimed to market medical and health products in colonial north India. Her study illustrates the way in which cultural complexities and communication techniques were drawn upon to attract the consumer. Sharma compares the English and the Hindi advertisements to delineate complexities associated with the world of advertisements.

Although the last two chapters concentrate on ayurvedic medicine, the broader themes of medical pluralism, the dialogue between modernity and tradition, and growing commercialization are also evident in the work of Attewell, Sivaramakrishnan and some other scholars. As more local and regional studies add complexity to what was once a rather simplistic picture of the decline of indigenous medical traditions under British rule, we can expect more unpacking of these rigidly defined 'medical systems'. Looser configurations are beginning to emerge in which medical 'traditions' are seen to have evolved in response to one another and the changing nature of Indian society. A great deal of work remains to be done in respect of both Indian and Western medicine but it is to be hoped that the chapters in this volume may provide the stimulus to further enquiry.

Notes

1 H.R. Tinker, *The Foundations of Local Self-Government in India, Pakistan and Burma*, London: Athlone Press, 1954.

2 R. Ramasubban, *Public Health and Medical Research in India: Their Origins and Development under the Impact of British Colonial Policy*, Stockholm: SAREC 1982; idem, 'Imperial Health in British India, 1857–1900', in R. MacLeod and M. Lewis, eds, *Disease, Medicine and Empire: Perspectives on Western Medicine and the Experience of European Expansion*, London: Routledge, 1988, 38–60; D. Arnold, 'Medical Priorities and Practice in Nineteenth-Century British India', *South Asia Research*, 5: 1985,167–83.

3 D. Arnold, *Colonizing the Body: State Medicine and Epidemic Disease in Nineteenth-Century India*, Berkeley: University of California Press, 1993.

4 For an overview of the historiography of public health in India, see: M. Harrison, *Public Health in British India: Anglo-Indian Preventive Medicine 1859–1914*, Cambridge: Cambridge University Press, 1994; M. Harrison and B. Pati, 'Introduction', in B. Pati and M. Harrison, eds, *Health, Medicine and Empire: Perspectives on Colonial India*, Delhi: Orient Longman, 2001, 1–3; D. Kumar, ed., *Disease and Medicine in India: A Historical Overview*, New Delhi: Tulika, 2001.

5 See also M. Harrison, 'Quarantine, Pilgrimage and Colonial Trade: India 1866–1900', *Indian Economic and Social History Review*, 29: 1992, 117–44; idem, *Public Health*, chap. 5.

6 For a largely geographical interpretation, see P. Baldwin, *Contagion and the State in Europe 1830–1930*, Cambridge: Cambridge University Press, 1999.
7 Valeska Huber, 'The Unification of the Globe by Disease? The International Sanitary Conferences on Cholera, 1851–1894', *The Historical Journal*, 49: 2006, 453–76.
8 S. Bhattacharya, M. Harrison and M. Worboys, *Fractured States: Smallpox, Public Health and Vaccination Policy in British India 1800–1947*, Hyderabad: Orient Longman, 2005.
9 For example, 'The Age of the Tribal Dresser', in John Iliffe, *East African Doctors: A History of the Modern Profession*, Cambridge: Cambridge University Press, 1998, 34–59; George O. Ndege, *Health, State, and Society in Kenya*, Rochester: University of Rochester Press, 2001, chaps 3–4.
10 This is especially true of campaigns against sleeping sickness. See Jean-Paul Bado, *Médecine Coloniale et Grandes Endémies en Afrique*, Paris: Kathala, 1996; Wolfgang U. Eckart, *Medizin und Kolonialimperialismus: Deutschland 1884*–1945, Paderborn: Ferdinand Schöningh, 1997, 340–9; Maryinez Lyons, *The Colonial Disease: A Social History of Sleeping Sickness in Northern Zaire, 1900–1940*, Cambridge: Cambridge University Press, 1992.
11 In colonial contexts, this feature of public health policy has perhaps been more evident in Africa than in India. See the classic study by Swanson and the more recent study by Echenberg for comparison: M. Swanson, 'The Sanitation Syndrome: Bubonic Plague and Urban Native Policy in the Cape Colony, 1900–1909', *Journal of African History*, 18: 1977, 387–410; M. Echenberg, *Black Death, White Medicine: Bubonic Plague and the Politics of Public Health in Colonial Senegal, 1914–1945*, Oxford: Heinemann, 2002.
12 S. Kakkar, 'Leprosy in British India, 1860–1940: Colonial Politics and Missionary Medicine', *Medical History*, 40: 1996, 215–30.
13 e.g. W. Ernst, 'The Establishment of "Native Lunatic Asylums" in Early Nineteenth-Century British India', in G.J. Meulenbeld and D. Wujastyk, eds, *Studies on Indian Medical History*, Groningen: Egbert Forsten, 1987; idem, *Mad Tales from the Raj: The European Insane in British India 1800–1858*, New York and London: Routledge, 1991; J. Mills, *Madness, Cannabis and Colonialism: The 'Native-Only' Lunatic Asylums of British India, 1857–1900*, London: Macmillan, 2000.
14 Mills, *Madness, Cannabis and Colonialism*, esp. chap. 6.
15 S. Kakkar, 'Medical Developments and Patient Unrest in the Leprosy Asylum', in Pati and Harrison, eds, *Health, Medicine and Empire*, 188–216; J. Buckingham, *Leprosy in Colonial South India: Medicine and Confinement*, Basingstoke: Palgrave, 2002.
16 See S. Hodges, ed., *Reproductive Health in India: History, Politics and Controversies*, Hyderabad: Orient Longman, 2006; G. Forbes, 'Medical Careers and Health Care for Indian Women: Patterns of Control', *Women's History*, 3: 1994, 515–30; M. Lal, 'The Politics of Gender and Medicine in Colonial India: The Countess of Dufferin's Fund, 1885–1888', *Bulletin of the History of Medicine*, 68: 1994, 29–66.
17 Pratik Chakrabarti, ' "Neither meete nor drinke but what the Doctor Alloweth": The Hospital amidst War and Commerce in Eighteenth-Century Madras', *Bulletin of the History of Medicine*, 80: 2006, 1–38.
18 D.G. Crawford, *A History of the Indian Medical Service*, Vol. 2, London: W. Thacker, 1913, 424–31.
19 For example, the Native Hospital at Benares was founded following the collection of Rs50,000 in private subscriptions and government assistance in the form of a recurring monthly grant of Rs600. See Bengal Public (Home) Proceedings, F/4/364, OIOC, British Library.
20 Proceedings of the Government of Bombay, Home (Medical), No. 1/1324, 1913.
21 Proceedings of the Government of Bombay, Home (General), No. 604, 1913, 'Appointment of Consulting Staff for Government Hospitals in Bombay City for the Year 1913–14', Government of Bombay, Maharashtra State Archives. On hospitals in

non-Western contexts more generally, see M. Harrison, M. Jones and H. Sweet, eds, *From Western Medicine to Global Medicine: The Hospital Beyond the West* (Hyderabad, forthcoming).

22 The philanthropic work of the Parsi businessman Sir Jamsetjee Jejeebhoy and the Kutchi merchant Goculdas Tejpal, among others, is discussed in Arnold, *Colonizing the Body*, 268–74; M. Ramanna, *Western Medicine and Public Health in Colonial Bombay 1845–1895*, Hyderabad: Orient Longman, 2002, 48–82. Patronage was not confined to Western hospitals either: the Nizam of Hyderabad created hospitals for both unani and Western medicine, for example. See G. Attewell, 'Authority, Knowledge and Practice in Unani Tibb in India *c.* 1890–1930', University of London Ph.D. thesis, 2004.

23 Arnold, *Colonizing the Body*, 271–3; Harrison, *Public Health*, 88–90; Ramanna, *Western Medicine*, chap. 2.

24 See Subho Basu, 'Emergence of the Mill Towns in Bengal 1880–1920: Migration Pattern and Survival Strategies of Industrial Workers', *The Calcutta Historical Journal*, 18: 1995, 97–134.

25 For a recent insightful analysis of colonial hygienic discourse, see Warwick Anderson, *Colonial Pathologies: American Tropical Medicine, Race and Hygiene in the Philippines*, Durham, NC, and London: Duke University Press, 2006.

26 Harrison, *Public Health*, chap. 1.

27 Mark Harrison, 'Towards a Sanitary Utopia? Professional Visions and Public Health in India, 1880–1914', *South Asia Research*, 10: 1990, 38–40.

28 Margaret Jones, *Health Policy in Britain's Model Colony: Ceylon (1900–1948)*, Hyderabad: Orient Longman, 2004, chap. 8.

29 M. Harrison, *Climates and Constitutions: Health, Race, Environment and British Imperialism in India 1600–1850*, Delhi: Oxford University Press, 1999.

30 Arnold, *Colonizing the Body*; M. Harrison and P. Chakravarti, *British Medicine in an Age of Commerce and Empire: India and the West Indies 1660–1830* (in preparation).

31 See Waltraud Ernst, *Mad Tales from the Raj. The European Insane in British India, 1800–1858*, London and New York: Routledge, 1991, 130–63; and Waltraud Ernst, 'Colonial Policies, Racial Politics and the Development of Psychiatric Institutions in Early Nineteenth-century British India', in W. Ernst and B. Harris, eds, *Race, Science and Medicine, 1700–1960*, London and New York: Routledge, 1999, 80–100.

32 D. Arnold, ' "An Ancient Race Outworn": Malaria and Race in Colonial India, 1860–1930', in W. Ernst and B. Harris, eds, *Race, Science and Medicine, 1700–1960*, London and New York: Routledge, 1999, 123–43.

33 M. Sharma, 'Western Medicine and Indian Responses: A Case Study of Banaras Region, *c.* 1890–1947', Jawaharlal Nehru University Ph.D. thesis, 2006.

34 One can cite here Kumkum Sangari and Sudesh Vaid, eds, *Recasting Women: Essays in Colonial India*, New Delhi: Kali for Women, 1989.

35 In fact, Maneesha Lal puts it across rather aptly through the very title of her article, ' "The Ignorance of Women in the House of Illness": Gender, Nationalism and Health Reform in Colonial North India', in Bridie Andrews and Mary Sutphen, eds, *The Politics of Identity*, London: Routledge, 2003, 14–40.

36 One has in mind here P. Jeffrey, R. Jeffrey and A. Lyon, *Labour Pains and Labour Power: Women and Childbearing in India*, London: Zed Books, 1989; see also Dagmar Engels, 'The Politics of Childbirth: British and Bengali Women in Contest, 1890–1930', in Peter Robb, ed., *Society and Ideology: Essays in South Asian History*, Delhi: Oxford University Press, 1993, 222–46; Geraldine Forbes, 'Managing Midwifery in India', in Dagmar Engels and Shula Marks, eds, *Contesting Colonial Hegemony: State and Society in Africa and India*, London: British Academic Press, 1994, 152–72; Supriya Guha, 'The Unwanted Pregnancy in Colonial Bengal', *Indian Economic and Social History Review*, 33:4, 1996, 403–35; Anshu Malhotra, 'Of Dais and Midwives: "Middle Class" Interventions in the Management of Women's Reproductive Health: A Study from Colonial Punjab', *Indian Journal of Gender Studies*,10:2, 2003, 229–59; and Sarah

Hodges, ed., *Reproductive Health India: History, Politics and Controversies*, New Delhi: Orient Longman, 2006.

37 One can cite here Samiksha Sehrawat, 'Curative Care in Delhi and Haryana, c. 1911–1921', University of Oxford D.Phil. thesis, 2006.

38 See, for example, Barbara Ramusack, 'Embattled Advocates: The Debate over Birth Control in India, 1920–1940', *Journal of Women's History*, 1:2, 1989, 34–74; and S. Anandhi, 'Reproductive Bodies and Regulated Sexuality: Birth Control Debates in Early Twentieth Century Tamilnadu', in Mary E. John and Janaki Nair, eds, *A Question of Silence? The Sexual Economies of Modern India*, New Delhi: Kali for Women, 1998, 139–66.

39 Maneesha Lal, 'The Politics of Gender and Medicine in Colonial India: The Countess of Dufferin's Fund, 1885–1888', *Bulletin of the History of Medicine*, 68:1, 1994, pp. 29–66; and Antoinette Burton, 'Contesting the Zenana: The Mission to Make "Lady Doctors for India", 1874–1885', *Journal of British Studies*, 35:3, 1996, 368–97; Maina Chawla Singh, *Gender, Religion and 'Heathen Lands': American Missionary Women in South Asia (1860–1940s)*, New York: Garland, 2000.

40 Antoinette Burton, 'The White Woman's Burden: British Feminists and the "Indian Woman", 1865–1915', in Nupur Choudhuri and Margaret Strobel, eds, *Western Women and Imperialism: Complicity and Resistance*, Bloomington: Indiana University Press, 1992, 137–57.

41 We borrow this term from Barbara Ramusack, 'Cultural Missionaries, Maternal Imperialists: Feminist Allies: British Women Activists in India, 1865–1945', in Choudhuri and Strobel, *Western Women and Imperialism*, 119–36.

42 Waltraud Ernst has been a pioneer in this field; see, for example, her 'European Madness and Gender in Nineteenth Century British India', *Social History of Medicine*, 9:3, 1996, 357–82; Indrani Sen, 'The Memsahib's "Madness": The European Woman's Mental Health in Late Nineteenth Century India', *Social Scientist*, 33: 5–6, 2005, 26–48.

43 Rosemary Fitzgerald, ' "Making and Moulding the Nursing of the Indian Empire": Recasting Nurses in Colonial India', in Avril A. Powell and Siobhan Lambert-Hurley, eds, *Gender and the Colonial Experience in South Asia*, New Delhi: Oxford University Press, 2006.

44 See especially Supriya Guha, 'Defaming the *Dai*: The Medicalization of Childbirth in Colonial India', paper presented at the Fifth National Conference of the Indian Association for Women's Studies at Jadavpur University, 9–12 February 1991; and Sean Lang, 'Drop the Demon Dai: Maternal Mortality and the State in Colonial Madras,1840–1875', *Social History of Medicine*, 18:3, 2005, 357–78.

45 Charu Gupta, 'Procreation and Pleasure: Writings of a Woman Ayurvedic Practitioner in Colonial North India', *Studies in History*, 21:1, 2005, 17–44.

46 Geraldine Forbes, 'Introduction to Memoirs', in Tapan Raychaudhuri, trans. and ed., *The Memoirs of Dr Haimavati Sen: From Child Widow to Lady Doctor*, Delhi: Roli Books, 2000, 152–72.

47 Maina Chawla Singh, 'Gender, Medicine and Empire: Early Initiatives in Institution-building and Professionalisation (1890s–1940s)'; and Samiksha Sehrawat, 'The Foundation of the Lady Hardinge Medical College and Hospital for Women at Delhi: Issues in Women's Medical Education and Imperial Governance', in Shakti Kak and Biswamoy Pati, eds, *Exploring Gender Equations: Colonial and Post Colonial India*, New Delhi: Nehru Memorial Museum and Library, 2005, 93–115 and 117–46 respectively; Waltraud Ernst, 'Feminising Madness – Feminising the Orient: Madness, Gender and Colonialism in British India, 1860–1040', in Kak and Pati, eds, *Exploring Gender Equations*; 57–91.

48 Arnold P. Kaminsky, 'Morality Legislation and British Troops in Late Nineteenth-Century India', *Military Affairs*, 43, 1979, 78–83; David Arnold, 'Sexually Transmitted Diseases in Nineteenth and Twentieth-Century India', *Genitourinary Medicine*, 69: 1993, 3–8; Philippa Levine, 'Venereal Disease, Prostitution and the Politics of Empire:

The Case of British India', *Journal of the History of Sexuality*, 4: 1994, 579–602; idem, *Prostitution, Race and Politics: Policing Venereal Disease in the British Empire*, London: Routledge, 2003; Judy Whitehead, 'Bodies Clean and Unclean: Prostitution, Sanitary Legislation and Respectable Femininity in Colonial North India', *Gender and History*, 7:1, 1995, 41–63; for details related to the Indian legislation, Kenneth Ballhatchet, *Race, Sex and Class under the Raj: Imperial Attitudes, and Policies and their Critics, 1793–1905*, London: Curzon, 1980.

49 Neshat Quaiser, 'Politics, Culture and Colonialism: Unani's Debate with Doctory', in Pati and Harrison, eds, *Health, Medicine and Empire*, 317–55; Claudia Liebeskind, 'Arguing Science: Unani Tibb, Hakimma and Biomedicine in India, 1900–50', in Waltraud Ernst, ed., *Plural Medicine, Tradition and Modernity, 1800–2000*, London: Routledge, 2002, 58–77; Guy Attewell, *Refiguring Unani Tibb: Plural Healing in Late Colonial India*, Delhi: Orient Longman, 2007.

50 David Arnold, *The New Cambridge History of India: Science, Technology and Medicine in Colonial India, III–5*, Cambridge: Cambridge University Press, 2000, 66, highlights the early British attitudes and the inadequacies of biomedicine vis-à-vis epidemics.

51 William Ward, *A View of the History, Literature, and Mythology of the Hindoos*, Vol. II, London: publisher not mentioned, 1822; T.A. Wise, *Commentary on the Hindu System of Medicine*, London: publisher not mentioned, 1845; F.J. Mouat, 'Hindu Medicine', *Calcutta Review*, VIII: 1847, 379–433; Kissory Chand Mitter, '*Hindu Medicine and Medical Education*', originally published in the *Calcutta Review*, 1865, and reprinted by the British Library as an electronic resource.

52 Notably Meulenbeld and Wujastyk, *Studies on Indian Medical History*, and Francis Zimmerman, *The Jungle and the Aroma of Meats: An Ecological Theme in Hindu Medicine*, Berkeley: University of California Press, 1987.

53 David Hardiman, 'The Invention of Indian Traditions', *Biblio*, 12: September-October 2007, 24–5.

54 See, for example, Charles Leslie, ed., *Asian Medical Systems: A Comparative Study*, Berkeley: University of California Press, 1976, especially Brahmanand Gupta, 'Indigenous Medicine in Nineteenth and Twentieth Century Bengal', 368–82; Poonam Bala, *Imperialism and Medicine in Bengal: A Socio-Historical Perspective*, New Delhi: Sage, 1991; K.N. Panikkar, 'Indigenous Medicine and Cultural Hegemony' in *Culture, Ideology, Hegemony: Intellectuals and Social Consciousness in Colonial India*, New Delhi: Tulika, 1995, 145–75; Jean M. Langford, *Fluent Bodies: Ayurvedic Remedies for Postcolonial Imbalance*, Durham, NC: Duke University Press, 2002; Charu Gupta, 'Procreation and Pleasure: Writings of a Woman Ayurvedic Practitioner in Colonial North India', *Studies in History*, 21:1, 2005, 17–44; and Kavita Sivaramakrishnan, *Old Potions, New Bottles: Recasting Indigenous Medicine in Colonial Punjab, 1850–1945*, New Delhi: Orient Longman, 2006.

55 David Arnold, *The Tropics and the Travelling Gaze: India, Landscape and Science 1800–1856*, New Delhi: Permanent Black, 2005.

56 The pioneering study in this field has been by Charles Leslie, 'The Ambiguities of Medical Revivalism in Modern India,' in Leslie, *Asian Medical Systems*, 356–67.

57 For details, see Chapter 7 by Pati and Nanda.

58 *The Orissa Student*, 1:1, October 1886, cited in Biswamoy Pati, *Situating Social History: Orissa, 1800–1997*, New Delhi: Orient Longman, 2001, 18.

2 Ranald Martin's *Medical Topography* (1837)

The emergence of public health in Calcutta

Partho Datta

Calcutta: changing representations

In 1809 the surveyor C.G. Nicholls scribbled the following in his notebook on a tour of Calcutta:

> The near approach to Calcutta, amply compensates for past disappointment, and he, whose eye had been hitherto fatigued with gazing on uncultivated and barren shores, is equally surprised and delighted at the luxuriancy of the scene as he approaches this famed city. Gardens tastefully laid out and houses more resembling the Palaces of Princes. . . . The abodes of private Gentlemen, certainly contribute to give the stranger a most favorable idea of the metropolis of the British Empire in the East. Here the windings of the River greatly tend to increase the pleasurable sensations, which the sight of a populous Town is everywhere calculated to excite after a voyage of some months duration; and when by a sudden turn, the Fort, the Town, Shipping & co. burst for first time on the sight of the enraptured stranger, the coup d'oeil is magnificent beyond description.[1]

In the first few decades of the nineteenth century, the British view of Calcutta changed dramatically for the worse, however. Far from the idyllic accounts of Calcutta, an oasis of Western calm surrounded by fierce tropical country, the city came increasingly to be imagined as a hotbed of tropical diseases, subject to the vagaries of tropical weather, a dangerous arena where precious English lives were lost. For the expatriate English and sundry other Europeans at the turn of the eighteenth–nineteenth century, the values most associated with colonial Calcutta's charm had a lot to do with social climbing. This included leading the life of the English upper classes in look-alike Palladian buildings, replicating their frenetic social activity in balls, perambulations and parties and always being assured of a well-laden table. But the shadow of epidemics, especially the spread of cholera from lower Bengal after 1817, threw a pall over the city, giving rise instead to a wary scepticism towards its famed splendours. How different from C.G. Nicholls does James Kennedy sound in the following account penned two decades later:

> The stranger who visits Bengal, alive to the 'splendour of the East', discovers little to gratify his expectations. . . . Weighing anchor at day-break, he leaves the treacherous 'Sand Heads' behind him, and enters the estuary of the River Hooghly. . . . The sun is now gathering strength, and the malarious vapours are seen coiling themselves up from the surface of the land, which presents the unbroken aspect of an endless swamp, covered with low, black, impenetrable jungle. . . . Having reached Diamond Harbour, scarcely five and thirty miles from Calcutta, the current of observation flows in a new channel. The pilot points to this as the place where thousands of our countrymen have been sacrificed to marsh fever. The Company's ships, in delivering their cargoes here, send many a gallant tar never to return. The malignant cholera, also soon after its ravages were begun, travelled through the shipping at the anchorage, and carried off many victims. These remarks in passing fill the stranger with a tide of mournful emotions, and evil anticipations: his home and the expectant faces of parents, brothers and sisters, on the one hand; his own untimely death, and their unutterable sorrow, on the other.[2]

Approaches to public health

As its grip over North India increased, the mercantilist government centred in Calcutta refashioned itself as a full-fledged colonial state with many new concerns. One abiding theme in the archival documents from this period was the prolix discourse about public health and this was reflected in the changing representations of the city in the nineteenth century.

The history of this public health has been addressed in many accounts, the most prominent being S.W. Goode's official and very thorough *Municipal Calcutta* published almost a hundred years ago and still highly regarded by historians of the city.[3] The book is a detailed if rather Whiggish history of sewers, water supply, road building, slum clearance, electrification and so on. Goode's narrative is about municipal progress and the legacy of good works from the nineteenth century. Keshab Chaudhuri's scholarly monograph published nearly fifty years later covered much the same period as Goode, but with the emphasis more on nineteenth-century municipal government.[4] Chaudhuri showed how municipal policy developed in tandem with the vigilante role of early Bengali nationalists who were adept at exposing the race and class bias of municipal 'progress'. Both these standard works assume, however, that there existed a given 'public' whose 'health' needed to be addressed, the proper task of all modern and worthy governments.

Mark Harrison's more recent book has also grappled with similar themes, i.e. the complex politics of public health in India as it developed with the introduction of Western medical practice.[5] Drawing on Harrison's important work, this chapter instead of assuming that 'public' and 'health' were inherent givens, argues that these concepts reflected a new way of governance that highlighted the reformist nature of the colonial state in India.[6] While on the one hand municipal progress or the lack of it can be read for its racist and imperialist limitations, on the other hand 'public health' can also be expanded to reveal themes like improvement, public good and reformism. Public health may have had a limited reach but it can be deconstructed to understand the imperatives of rule, creation of authority, ruling ideology and consensus. The notions of public health and public good were certainly attractive to the Indian elite who implicitly absorbed some of these precepts and, as the experience of the nineteenth century shows, helped to create that elusive thing called colonial modernity.

The notion of the public owes much to Jurgen Habermas's celebrated definition of the public sphere as that realm of public opinion that was constituted by a 'reasoning public'.[7] However, historians have argued that the authority wielded by the state was directed at another kind of public, constructed usually of urban populations that were the target and sphere of state-directed action.[8] It was often in this sphere that consensus by the state was sought out and negotiated. Thomas Metcalfe has shown that in colonial India the realm of this public was codified by law, the colonial state drawing on an authoritarian version of utilitarianism to implement modern education, public works and public health.[9] Sudipto Kaviraj has also written about the development of a 'protopolitical' public in colonial India which was highly restricted and regulated.[10] Gyan Prakash has shown how the introduction of public sanitation was imposed by the colonial state since it believed that the 'backward' Indian public was incapable of self-regulation.[11] Similarly the interlinked categories of health and hygiene have been theorized not only as an objective category of people who are sick but also as a discourse of the normal and the pathological. Michel Foucault's classic essay on public health in eighteenth-century Europe points out that the 'emergence of . . . physical well-being of the population in general [was] one of the essential objectives of political power', the other being 'order, enrichment and health'.[12]

The discourse of the 'public' and what became 'public health' was brought about through state policy from the beginning of the nineteenth century in Calcutta city. The two extracts quoted at the beginning of this chapter demonstrate how the colonial revaluation of Calcutta underwent a dramatic change due to the threat of epidemics. Thomas Metcalfe has pointed out that the early experience of Calcutta, the formal capital of empire from the late eighteenth century, had congealed as a prototype of the perils of tropical weather and disease.[13] That is why the range of activities known as public health in Calcutta becomes important as a precedent for colonial policy in the ensuing decades throughout India. In Calcutta, public health encompassed a wide range of activities from setting up committees at the initiative of the colonial government and European merchants to formulate public policy to road building, slum clearance and regulation of markets.

Another significant initiative was hospitals. In Calcutta, hospitals were modern institutions, very much a Western import. They attested to the gradual importance of Western medical practice to state policies. Calcutta had many hospitals set up by the governing British. Records show that from the late eighteenth century there existed the General Hospital and Sanatorium, a Lunatic Asylum, a Leper Asylum, a Native Hospital (*c.* 1794, for the establishment of which Lord Cornwallis donated some money), and a Police Hospital (*c.* 1789) attached to the Office of the Police. Hospitals assume a 'public' and it is certainly worth asking if an undifferentiated population constituted this 'public'. While the General Hospital and the Lunatic Asylum were exclusively for Europeans, the Native and the Police hospitals catered to the Indian populace. The Police Hospital, for instance, received 'poor wretches . . . those who are perfectly destitute and found lying about in the streets'.[14] Many of the destitute who found their way into Calcutta were migrants forced to flee from the countryside by lack of work, flooding and famine.[15] While the racial segregation of hospitals for Europeans and Indians was apparent, from the early decades of the nineteenth century another kind of segregation became important, that between the abandoned and destitute on the one hand and the sick but potentially productive and useful labourers on the other.

This distinction or sifting of the Indian populace becomes more marked with the spread of epidemics, which threatened the economic activities of the East India Company's government in Bengal. A momentum gathered to regulate this productive section of the Indian population in the city. In another essay Michel Foucault has warned that this 'precocious' interest of the state in Europe before the second half of the nineteenth century in public health administration, or what he calls 'state medicine', should not necessarily be read as a regulation of labour power for the economy but as an interest in 'bodies of individuals insofar as they combined to constitute the state'.[16] By the 1830s, however, the economic imperative of the colonial state in India was more than apparent. Its own personnel, European doctors in Calcutta attached to the Police and Native hospitals who articulated the need for the state to regulate labour, underscored the overwhelming nature of this 'state medicine'. They urged the setting up of another new 'Fever' Hospital to deal with the menace of uncontrollable epidemics. Testimonies by doctors such as Dr Vos, Surgeon in the Police Hospital, reveal that they wanted the new hospital not for 'beggars and destitutes, but for a better class, such as the servants of the Baboos and other wealthy natives, also for Musselmen and Hindoos, and the servants of European families in general'.[17] Dr J. Ranald Martin testified that the abandoned and the destitute should be handled by the 'medical police' who were properly in charge of regulating street life, implying that the real task of catering to the labouring sick should be taken up by a new hosptial.[18] Ranald Martin had in fact already written a small tome elaborating his ideas and they give us a glimpse into notions of the public and public health that gradually became the norm in the coming decades. His account is significant in ways that make it an important source for subsequent historians.

The contexts of medical topography

Ranald Martin's *Notes on the Medical Topography of Calcutta* published in 1837 was one of the first important surveys done of Calcutta in the nineteenth century.[19] Martin, who was a surgeon in the Native Hospital,[20] wrote his account to draw the attention of the government to the increasing threat of disease arising from the deteriorating conditions in Calcutta and the urgent need for medical institutions for the labouring poor. A wide-ranging account of 'native', i.e. Indian, life and its defects, it encompassed not only topography, ecology and architecture but even observations on music. Martin's views make fascinating reading today for they reveal a great deal about official and unofficial views of the British in Calcutta. It is possible, for instance, to piece together from his report a fairly detailed urban profile of the city. It is thanks to Martin that we know something of the kind of building that was found in north (i.e. Indian) Calcutta, the condition of the suburbs, and the mortality and pathologies of the working population. Yet Martin's views were typical and fell into a well-defined pattern.

Medical topographies were a genre of their own. Mark Harrison has shown that the production of medical topographies was similar to botanical and military cartographic surveys begun in the late eighteenth century, closely linked to the imperatives of British rule and dominance.[21] Francis Buchanan's famous account of the topography and natural history of South India, for instance, begun in 1799, was commissioned by Lord Wellesley following his military conquest of Mysore.[22] Surveys of a similar kind throughout the nineteenth century were intended to render the Indian environment 'habitable and bountiful for Europeans'.[23]

In European medical practice, medical topographies were fairly typical and had grown out of the neo-Hippocratic tradition which stressed the importance of environmental conditions, i.e. air, water and light, to the understanding of disease. Historically they represented a middle ground between ancient and modern forms of theorizing health. Medical topographies usually presented a graphic picture and a record of the degenerative influence of environment on human habitations. In his *Notes*, Martin wrote 'that a slothful squalid-looking population invariably characterizes an unhealthy country'.[24]

By the 1830s, however, the principles underlying medical topography had come to be challenged in Europe, with the growth of more sophisticated theories of disease and a better understanding of social conditions. In India medical topographies persisted, however,[25] and often lent a critical edge to theories of racial superiority, especially in the context of British territorial expansion which was encountering military resistance from Indian rulers and rival European colonial powers in the eighteenth and nineteenth centuries. Martin's was one of many accounts produced about India throughout the nineteenth century, part of the discourse justifying conquest, a report on the vulnerabilities of newly conquered regions. Mark Harrison has argued that 'such ideas were convenient in the sense that they boosted Europeans' confidence in their ability to rule parts of the globe with climates very different from their own'.[26] Interestingly, while Martin's book followed the norm in dwelling on climate, the terrain and human habits (these are discussed below), a certain shift is also noticeable. In grappling with Calcutta, Martin was addressing problems of an already conquered and settled area, in this case a burgeoning town. It was for this reason that Martin was less preoccupied with justifying the conquest of a place than with regulating spaces within the city.[27] Emergent from his topography was an early notion of what constituted the public.

Utilitarian reformism

Medical topographies built on the idea that the superior civilizational values of Europe had their roots in temperate climate and geography. Martin wrote, 'it was climate which made the Hindu heedless and slothful' while it 'forces the native of Holland [here the Dutch example probably stood in for all European peoples] to be careful, laborious and attentive to excess'.[28] In the eighteenth and nineteenth centuries, a period of ascendant nation-states in Europe, this was of course a great boost to national vanity. During the period of colonial rule it only consolidated imperial and racial superiority. Furthermore, a climatic and topographic condition not only explained individual human nature and habits but also forms of government. India, which did not fit the classic European norm, had produced instead 'despotic' oriental governments.[29] Closely echoing the views of James Mill, Martin's were also influenced by utilitarianism.[30] Perhaps this explains the judgemental rhetoric about Bengalis and his impatience with Indian society and culture. Strongly reformist in tone, utilitarianism in its colonial context was all about asserting power, marking out cultural differences between the rulers and the ruled where the latter were seen as inferior.[31] Bengalis in Calcutta particularly came very low down on the Indian social scale:

> The Bengalee, unlike the Hindoo of the north, is utterly devoid of pride, national or individual. His moral character is a matter of history; and I think it unworthy now, when we are looking forward with such well founded hope to the improved results of European knowledge and example diffused amongst the natives, to bring into relief their worst qualities, or those engendered by ages of atrocious tyranny, civil and religious. Let those who like it, follow the Bengalee in his practice of falsehood and perjury – his insensibility to the feelings of others – his 'perfection in timidity' – his cruelty and ferocity – his litigiousness – his physical uncleanliness and obscene worship.[32]

Bengali culture too reflected this degeneration. Martin wrote of Bengali music as 'the noise made by cows in distress, with an admixture of the caterwaulings of a feline congregation and the occasional scream of an affrighted elephant'.[33]

This moral stridency and superiority in Martin's tone and the denunciation of Bengali culture thus not only reflected prejudice but also constituted a necessary part of the discourse on reform. If Bengali life was defective then there was ample opportunity to improve it. Martin, like many officials, was reflecting the very modern temper of his time, and his rhetoric implying the optimism and confidence to transform society. Full of admiration for Governor General William Bentinck's attempt at legislating social reform, he hoped that a similar English influence on medical practice would set up a *norm* for improvement. He wrote.

> The abolition for ever of the barbarous rite of the Suttee, will doubtless hand the name of Lord William Bentinck to the grateful remembrance of remote ages in India; but the foundation of an *English* School of Medicine (the success

> of which is no longer doubtful) will prove of far greater importance in as much as the diffusion of European medical science, with its collateral branches, must prove one of the most direct and impressive modes of demonstrating to the natives, the superiority of European knowledge in general and that they must cultivate it actively, if they would rise in the scale of nations.[34]

In Martin's scheme the proposed improvements could only be brought about by the government since its proper appreciation was beyond the understanding of native society 'with the exception to a few educated Baboos'.[35] Bengal, according to him, had no enduring tradition of such initiatives. He wrote loftily: 'there are no remains of great public works in any of [the] eastern dominions – none certainly of utility belonging to the Hindoos; and most of those that belonged to their more civilized conquerors of the Mahomedan faith, have fallen into decay.'[36] He noted, however, that in Calcutta European education and example were influencing the 'moral character of the more enlightened classes of natives in a surprising manner and in a thousand ways'.[37] Martin assumed that the bait of economic benefit from property – a basic utilitarian virtue – would suffice as an appeal to Calcuttans. He wrote that,

> from the natives we cannot expect any great aid, *until they are shewn* the *usefulness* of *public work*, when I am confident, they will readily comprehend how the clearing and proper draining will certainly make the value of landed property in certain quarters, incalculably greater than it is now, by rendering what is at present useless, fit for building and similar purposes; so that what *we* know to be most conducive to *health*, they may at the same time be led to perceive as greatly conducive to their pecuniary interests.[38]

Martin's plea for improvement thus took the novel form of public health and hygiene. He wrote that,

> the natives have yet to learn, in a public and private sense, that the sweet sensations connected with cleanly habits, and pure air, are some of the most precious gifts of civilization, and a taste for them tends to give a distaste to degrading and grovelling gratifications.[39]

Martin's recommendations, anchored in the prevailing medical consensus of his time, were crucial in mapping the emerging public arena. Indeed the notion of the 'public' was strategically important in the way the state justified its intervention in this sphere. 'Were I to mention all the customs of the Hindoos that are injurious to health, I should write a respectably sized book. The institution of caste is of itself an enormous injury to public health, because prejudicial to public happiness,' he wrote.[40] Martin's topographical investigations of Calcutta had turned into a judgement on indigenous society.

Explorations of Calcutta

Martin's book was based on his own experiences as a doctor and the diligent survey that he carried out in various parts of Calcutta. But his book also reflects the influential work of the Lottery Committee in building roads and drains in Calcutta that preceded his own account.[41] The Lottery Committee had produced an informal bank of knowledge and a certain way of evaluating the city. Martin systematized this knowledge and his account was more sophisticated, grounded in Western medical wisdom tempered by local administrative imperatives. His book addressed three intertwined themes whose basic concern was the threat to public health in Calcutta. The first was a detailed evaluation of the city's natural habitat. The second was an investigation of Indian habits and living conditions. And third, scattered throughout his book were recommendations for reform.

Martin's assumptions drew on familiar and well-grounded neo-Hippocratic principles. His concern with miasmas reflected a new evaluation of smell, seen as an active risk to healthy living. 'Miasmas' or bad air were thought to be produced by decaying vegetation or animal matter and putrid atmospheric exhalations like the odour from earth, water, excrement and corpses as well as living bodies. Carlo Cipolla has written that the 'clarity, logic and consistency of the humoral-miasmatic paradigm' was in fact sanctioned by long practice.[42] This increased recognition of smell in its turn produced guidelines for reordering urban spaces. Alain Corbin has shown that health or sickness came to be determined by olfactory imperatives.[43] In fact public health during this time translated into policies for 'deodorization and ventilation' of the city.[44] Ten miles below Calcutta, Martin wrote, 'the rapidity and rankness of vegetation is suffered to infect the air, the jungle or violent bilious fever is sure to attack any one who comes for a time within its atmosphere.'[45] To the east the annual subsidence of the salt-water lake left a marshy bank exuding the stench of rotting fish exposed to the 'vertical sun'.[46] In the city proper the stagnation due to lack of sufficient fall in the drains gave rise to 'deleterious exhalations'.[47] The banks of the newly built canals in Boitakhana and Entally in the suburbs had rendered these areas unhealthy as they stopped the natural drainage towards the east.[48] The tanks dotting the city were 'in an impure and neglected condition, from the annual accumulations of the vegetation . . . until at length they become the half-dried, green and slimy puddles, which so contaminate every portion of the native town'.[49]

The European areas had some advantages compared to the Indian settlements but the design of the houses based on European models was defective as the lofty Grecian pillars admitted too much sun, which was harmful to health.[50] Because these houses were situated geographically to the south they benefited from the wind that flushed out the miasmas. This was a fortunate choice of location by Job Charnock, the founder of the city, noted Martin ironically, for 'had it been ordered otherwise . . . and we had the black town to windward during the south-west monsoon, then must the Europeans have tried their fortune somewhere else.'[51] The vast open space around Fort William, he remarked, made it the 'lungs of Calcutta' and the continuous flow of the river Hooghly flushed away the filth and was therefore the natural 'great scavenger'.[52] For Martin, such accidental advantages of nature underlined even more strongly the need for more decisive and interventionist public health planning in Calcutta.

Indian living conditions, especially buildings, merited special attention since the latter acted as repositories of filth and helped to breed disease. Martin's account contained one of the first detailed surveys of Indian Calcutta, which had historically developed to the north. There was a long tradition of seeing north and south as 'native' and 'British' respectively although it was not uncommon for Indians to settle in the south. There were, however, few instances of Europeans venturing beyond the central areas of the city. Martin was convinced that the two areas exhibited different characteristics and that 'they have few points in common'.[53] Although such a characterization reflected a racist stereotype, it was handy since it helped Martin fix blame on the 'natives' whom he held responsible for the problems of Calcutta.

Martin's investigation of the public in the city threw up a much more varied picture. Certainly his schematic division of the city into Indian (north) and European (south) became more complicated. Martin reported that the commercial hub of the Europeans between Dharmatalla and Bow Bazar was 'thickly inhabited' with both Europeans and 'country born Christians' (i.e. Indian Christians), forming a sort of intermediate zone.[54] To the south the more exclusive Chowringhee was thinly populated and the European houses widely scattered. Mostly Indians servicing the English inhabited pockets in this area like Colinga.[55] Indian Calcutta concentrated between Bow Bazar and Machuabazar Street contained 'the most dense part of the . . . population of Calcutta'. The efforts of the Lottery Committee had been to stamp out the sinuosities of organic Indian settlements and instead encourage habitation along spacious rectilinears such as the newly built Cornwallis Road, so that better access to north Calcutta could be obtained. However, Indians only reluctantly took to this kind of town planning and in the initial years the laying out of the new areas to the north did not prove to be a conspicuous success. Areas to the north and east of the city, Martin observed, were still characterized by 'extensive gardens, large half dried tanks and ruinous tenements'. Martin could not help being surprised at 'how much the condition of the native portion of the town has been neglected in this great city and its suburbs . . . in an affair of so much importance to the public health', thereby unwittingly pointing a finger at government lack of initiative and apathy.[56] Villages and outlying areas between and around the New Circular Canal and the Circular Road (which formed the boundary of Calcutta), like Chitpur, Nundenbagh, Bahir Simlah, Komarpara and Sealdah, all exhibited uneven development and haphazard urban growth. Filth had accumulated along the banks of the old canal of Beleghata. Fever was common in these areas and Martin blamed the irregularity of the ground for the bad drainage. Belts of jungle obstructing ventilation and the lack of good water also contributed to this state of affairs. His suggestion was to use the earth dug up to create the new canal to fill up the uneven patches of ground.[57]

The suburbs too were painted in bleak colours. Martin wrote that, 'it was useless to attempt any great improvement within the city: while every square acre of the circumference is left in a state worse than nature, it were in vain to work in the centre'.[58] During the 1833 epidemic of 'remittent fever', according to Martin, eight out of ten people died in the suburbs to the east and the south.[59] Entally (beyond Circular Road to the east and below the Eastern Canal), with its large population of Indian Christians, and Ballygunge further south, where a cantonment was located, needed proper drainage. Martin claimed to have effected some improvements in the cantonment with the support of the Governor General, the Marquess of Hastings.[60] Bhowanipur, the 'most populous native suburb' in the south, had no supply of fresh water and its inhabitants had to walk all the way to Chowringhee for their supply.[61] Areas near the river like Garden Reach and Khidirpur were no better. Khidirpur, famous for its docks and the most populous suburb after Bhowanipur, looked like 'one entire jheel' for lack of proper drainage.[62] Alipur was very exclusive and European, on higher and somewhat better-drained ground.

The labouring poor, Martin's investigations revealed, were scattered throughout the town and the official 1822 city census confirmed that they had only makeshift housing.[63] He wrote:

> The mass of labouring classes live in huts, the walls of which are of mud, or of matted reed or bamboo, roofed with straw or tiles according to the means of the occupant; these would not be so bad, but they are uniformly placed on the bare ground, or on damp mud, but little raised, which continually emits injurious exhalations.

He added that, 'nine-tenths of the population sleep on the bare ground. In this important matter [the] Bengallee is behind many savage tribes.'[64] Elsewhere in his report he noted that temporary huts had been erected by Indian landlords on 'their own plans, at the cheapest rates, and for the mere purpose of letting to the highest profit: no wonder then, that they should be constructed without reference to locality, climate or convenience.'[65] This was an alarming picture of a working population at risk from poor living conditions, for some of which Indian landlords could be held accountable. Martin was certainly perceptive in pointing to the familiar scenario of Indian slum landlords haphazardly settling poor immigrants for their own monetary benefit, a practice that remained widespread throughout the nineteenth century. Martin's observations added momentum, however, to the regulation of landlords and slum areas in the following decades, indeed all those 'public' areas that were gradually being delineated as fit for intervention.

Martin's curiosity took him to Calcutta's richest Indian business district. One early morning before sunrise in the narrow lanes north of Barrabazar, Martin confronted the 'rankest compound of villainous smells that ever offended the nostril'.[66] In Barrabazar itself, 'the want of water courses, and means of facility for removing accumulations of filth . . . would stand as insuperable bars to the best devised regulations of medical police.'[67] Martin was more admiring of the houses of the rich 'Baboos' (landlords and merchants) in this area.

> They are uniformly built in the form of a hollow square, with an area from 50 to 100 feet each way, which, on occasion of Hindoo festivals, is covered

> over, and when lighted up, looks very handsome . . . altogether, this form of building, if placed on open ground and made more roomy, would not appear ill calculated for the climate.[68]

In this most densely populated centre of the city, Martin wanted 'all masses of buildings . . . opened out, old walls and decayed houses removed; for even under ordinary circumstances these are fertile sources of fever'.[69] Streets, he recommended, 'should be as much as possible in the direction of the prevailing winds'.[70]

Public health and town planning

Martin's prescriptive zeal anticipated later nineteenth-century municipal policy regarding drainage, sewage and drinking water. The persistent problem of Calcutta, he surmised, was faulty drainage since the city was in the deltaic region and prone to inundation. On sewers, he commented, 'there is probably no subject connected with public health and comfort . . . of more consequence than the state of sewers'. He recommended a planned network of great sewers built of solid masonry that would also be arched. Houses were to be connected by smaller lines to these main sewers which in turn would debouch in the river at a point well below the ordinary low water mark. Open smaller sewers were to be made 'in the direction of prevailing winds, and wide, so as to admit of exposure to the sun and free ventilation'.[71]

Martin wanted the use of water from the open tanks to be regulated in the Indian parts of the city, and bathing and washing of clothes at tanks used for drinking water to be prohibited. He even urged the policing of tanks on private properties of 'Baboos'. His justification was that 'no person ought to have exclusive property or right in what is injurious to the public health'.[72] The intrusion into the private/personal domain was entirely consistent with the bent of Martin's earlier observations on 'natives', be it the pervasive institution of caste, style of domestic living, etc. This viewpoint showcases an early expression of what later became administrative wisdom, gaining wide currency in the later part of the nineteenth century. In the first instance it was the government that came to determine what was 'public' even if this meant the violation of sacrosanct rights to private property. Second, in the interests of the 'public' it assumed the right to regulate and intervene if necessary. James Holston has argued that in Europe from the 1830s such a move which restricted rights to property ownership in the cities was in fact one of the early examples of modern urban planning. He has shown that such an intervention by urban governments, together with emerging knowledges generated on the city, helped consolidate 'centralized administrative and political powers in these European states'.[73] In Calcutta too, throughout the nineteenth century, the ownership of land became accountable to government on sanitary grounds. Although this view was challenged and a tussle followed, some educated Indians were persuaded by the improving idea of greater public good. 'Improvement', as Ranajit Guha has argued, was a political strategy to persuade the indigenous elite to 'attach' themselves to the colonial regime and to make imperial rule acceptable, even desirable, to Indians.[74] It is interesting that Martin's *Medical Topography* was welcomed 'with delight' (Bengali: *aalhadpurbak*) in a book notice published in a contemporary Bengali journal as showing the way to lessen the 'ills' (Bengali: *pira hras*) of the city. The reviewer's enthusiasm was all the more extraordinary for it was in the face of Martin's severe strictures and lampooning of contemporary Bengali society.[75]

Some conclusions

Martin's confidence in modern sanitary reform persuaded him that existing settlements in Indian Calcutta were an impediment to public health. His mapping of the city reveals a discernible pattern in which beginning with a description of general topography, the focus narrows down on 'native' Calcutta, moving inwards into 'native' buildings, creating a passage for the 'public' into the 'private'. Martin's view that a combination of smell, dirt and dense building were somehow incompatible with civilizational values was a reflection of the deep current of reformism popular among the governing classes in England and increasingly in Calcutta. One outcome of this view was that Indians were typified as unchanging, passive and helpless, needing to be worked upon to raise them from their moribund state. In a sense Martin's ethnography of Calcutta was an attempt to search for a public, but what he found he rejected. Instead he wanted to create a new notion of the public, that of 'public health' in Calcutta. Paul Rabinow has argued that surveys similar to that of Martin in Europe in the nineteenth century had initiated 'new scientific discourses, new administrative practices, and new conceptions of social order, and hence ushered in a long period of experimentation with spatial/scientific/social technologies'.[76] The experience in Calcutta was no different.

On his own initiative and before it came out as a book, Martin had sent a copy of his *Topography* to the Governors of the Native Hospital in 1835. This in its turn motivated the Governors to set up with government help what became known as the Fever Hospital Committee, consisting of administrators and doctors who initiated a massive enquiry into Calcutta. The detailed investigations of this Committee led to the setting up of what eventually became Medical College Hospital in Calcutta in 1852.[77] This new hospital epitomized a certain vision of government in Calcutta city. It needs to be pointed out that the pressure for investment in institutions like hospitals brought about a transition whereby the state withdrew from philanthropy and charity to engage in new reformist measures like public health. Needless to say, this utilitarian approach to poverty had a devastating impact on the general populace, which found that traditional relief measures no longer had the support of the state.[78]

Acknowledgements

I would like to thank Biswamoy Pati, Shakti Kak and G.P. Sharma for inviting me to present this paper in Jamia Hamdard and Jamia Millia Islamia, Delhi, and to Radhika Chopra and Ananya Vajpeyi for their detailed comments and suggestions.

Notes

1 C.G. Nicholls, 'Field Book of Survey of a Part of Calcutta', 1809, Manuscript in Rare Book Collections, National Library, Calcutta.

2 James Kennedy, *History of the Contagious Cholera*, London, 1831, quoted in Mark Harrison, *Public Health in British India, Anglo-Indian Preventive Medicine, 1859–1914*, Cambridge: Cambridge University Press, 1994, 44.

3 S.W. Goode, *Municipal Calcutta, Its Institutions in their Origin and Growth*, Edinburgh: T. and A. Constable, 1916. P. Thankappan Nair's *Calcutta Municipality at a Glance*, Calcutta: Municipal Corporation, 1989, updates Calcutta's municipal history and statistics to the 1980s.

4 Keshab Chaudhuri, *Calcutta, Story of its Government*, Calcutta: Orient Longman, 1973.

5 Harrison, *Public Health*.

6 Colonialism in India has always had a reformist streak running through its history, from the influence of the Physiocrats in revenue management in the eighteenth century to that of Utilitarians on state policy in the nineteenth. The classic study is Eric Stokes, *English Utilitarians and India*, Delhi: Oxford University Press, 1959, rpt 1982. The reformist nature of the British colonial state has recently been highlighted by Richard Drayton in his *Nature's Government: Science, Imperial Britain and the 'Improvement' of the World*, New Haven, Conn., and London: Yale University Press, 2000. Drayton wrote that ' "Improvement" was a concern shaping activity at the empire's periphery as well as center' (113).

7 Jurgen Habermas, 'The Public Sphere', *New German Critique* 1:3, 1974, 50.

8 In his commentary on Habermas, John B.Thompson has located the 'public sphere' between 'public authority' and 'civil society'. He defines 'public authority' as 'state-related activity, that is, to the activities of a state system which had legally defined spheres of jurisdiction and which had a monopoly on the legitimate use of violence', (*Ideology and Modern Culture*, Cambridge: Polity Press, 1992, 110).

9 Thomas Metcalfe, *Ideologies of the Raj*, Delhi: Cambridge/Foundation Books, 1998, 37, 187–8.

10 Sudipto Kaviraj, 'Filth and the Public Sphere: Concepts and Practices about Space in Calcutta', *Public Sphere* 10:1, 1997, 95–6.

11 Gyan Prakash, 'Body and Governmentality', *Another Reason: Science and the Imagination of Modern India*, Princeton, NJ: Princeton University Press, 1999, 130–1.

12 Michel Foucault, 'The Politics of Health in the Eighteenth Century', *Power/Knowledge: Selected Interviews and Other Writings 1972–1977*, Brighton: Harvester Press, 1977, 169–70.

13 Metcalfe, *Ideologies of the Raj*, 171.

14 'Printed Proceedings of the Governors of Native Hospital dated 20th May 1835, with notes and proceedings of the General Committee from 18th June 1835 to 12th November 1840', bound manuscript volume, Vol. I, West Bengal State Archives, hereafter Fever Hospital Committee, 23–4; W.J. Buchanan, 'The First Hospital in Calcutta', *Bengal Past and Present* 1, July-December 1907, also has some information on the early hospitals in Calcutta. I would like to thank Manu Sehgal for drawing my attention to this essay.

15 Government of India, Home Public, No. 28, 9 June 1834, National Archives of India.

16 Michel Foucault, 'The Birth of Social Medicine', in *Power, Essential Works of Foucault*, Vol. 3, ed. James D. Faubion, London: Penguin Books, 2002, 141.

17 Fever Hospital Committee, Vol. 1, 24.

18 Fever Hospital Committee, Vol. 1, 12, 24. The term 'medical police' is frequently used in Calcutta documents for this period. Michel Foucault has explained:

> Down to the end of the *ancien regime*, the term 'police' does not signify, at least not exclusively, the institution of police in the modern sense; 'police' is the

> ensemble of mechanisms serving to ensure order, the properly channeled growth of wealth and the conditions of preservation of health 'in general'.
>
> ('The Politics of Health', 170)

19 James Ranald Martin, *Notes on the Medical Topography of Calcutta*, Calcutta: Bengal Military Orphan Press, 1837.

20

> James Ranald Martin, 1793–1874, was the son of a minister in the Isle of Skye. He was admitted as a student to St George's Hospital, London, in 1813 and became a member of the Royal College of Surgeons in 1817, whereupon he joined the Bengal Medical Service. After three years in Orissa as a military surgeon, Martin began civil practice in Calcutta, leaving India in 1843 to become president of the East India Company's Medical Board. In the same year, he became a Fellow of the Royal College of Surgeons, and was elected a Fellow of the Royal Society in 1845. Martin was knighted in 1860 and served on the Army Sanitary Commission established in 1857.
>
> (Harrison, *Public Health*, fn. 52, 259)

21 Mark Harrison, *Climates and Constitutions, Health, Race, Environment and British Imperialism in India, 1600–1850,* Delhi: Oxford University Press, 1999, 114.

22 Marika Vicziany, 'Imperialism, Botany and Statistics in Early Nineteenth-century India: The Surveys of Francis Buchanan, 1762–1829', *Modern Asian Studies* 20:4, 1986, pp. 628–9.

23 Harrison, *Public Health,* 101.

24 Martin, *Medical Topography,* 45.

25 F.P. Strong, *Topography, and Vital Statistics of Calcutta*, published later in 1849, in a similar vein continued the established tradition of producing topographies. Strong's account has been reprinted in Alok Ray ed. *Calcutta Keepsake*, Calcutta: Riddhi India, 1978.

26 Harrison, *Public Health*, 38.

27 Michel Foucault has commented on this shift in the following manner:

> Whereas the medical topographies of regions analyze climatic and geological conditions which are outside human control, and can only recommend measures of correction and compensation, the urban topographies outline, in negative at least, the general principles of a concerted urban policy.
>
> ('The Politics of Health', 175)

28 Martin, *Medical Topography*, 48.

29 Martin, *Medical Topography*, 49.

30 Mark Harrison, *Public Health*, 47–8.

31 Mark Harrison, *Public Health*, 51.

32 Martin, *Medical Topography,* 46.

33 Martin, *Medical Topography,* 51–2.

34 Martin, *Medical Topography,* 60, emphasis in the original.

35 Martin, *Medical Topography,* 49.

36 Martin, *Medical Topography,* 49.

37 Martin, *Medical Topography,* 47.

38 Martin, *Medical Topography,* 15, emphasis in the original.

39 Martin, *Medical Topography,* 24.

40 Martin, *Medical Topography,* 49.

41 The Lottery Committee, 1817–36, so called because profit from public lotteries helped finance its activities, was one of the first systematic attempts by the colonial government in Calcutta to give shape to the city through schemes of road building and removal of huts.

42 Carlo M. Cipolla, *Miasmas and Disease, Public Health and the Environment in the Pre-Industrial Age*, New Haven, Conn., and London: Yale University Press, 1992, 4–5, 7.
43 Alain Corbin, *The Foul and the Fragrant, Odor and the French Social Imagination,* Cambridge, Mass.: Harvard University Press, 1986, 5–7.
44 Warick Anderson, 'Excremental Colonialism, Public Health and the Poetics of Pollution', *Critical Enquiry* 21, Spring 1995, 642.
45 Martin, *Medical Topography,* 13.
46 Martin, *Medical Topography,* 69.
47 Martin, *Medical Topography,* 24.
48 Martin, *Medical Topography,* 35.
49 Martin, *Medical Topography,* 28.
50 Martin, *Medical Topography,* 61.
51 Martin, *Medical Topography,* 18.
52 Martin, *Medical Topography,* 68.
53 Martin, *Medical Topography,* 18.
54 Martin, *Medical Topography,* 18.
55 Martin, *Medical Topography,* 18.
56 Martin, *Medical Topography,* 18–19.
57 Martin, *Medical Topography,* 30–1.
58 Martin, *Medical Topography,* 30.
59 Martin, *Medical Topography,* 34.
60 Martin, *Medical Topography,* 32–3.
61 Martin, *Medical Topography,* 33.
62 Martin, *Medical Topography,* 36.
63 Martin was referring to 'The Population of Calcutta', *Government Gazette*, 8 August 1822, reprinted in Alok Ray ed. *Nineteenth Century Studies*, Calcutta: Bibliographical Research Centre, 1974, 4–6.
64 Martin, *Medical Topography,* 21.
65 Martin, *Medical Topography,* 63.
66 Martin, *Medical Topography,* 23.
67 Martin, *Medical Topography,* 19.
68 Martin, *Medical Topography,* 20.
69 Martin, *Medical Topography,* 19.
70 Martin, *Medical Topography,* 23.
71 Martin, *Medical Topography,* 24.
72 Martin, *Medical Topography,* 28.
73 James Holston, *The Modernist City, An Anthropological Critique of Brasilia*, Chicago and London: University of Chicago, 1989, 47.
74 Ranajit Guha, 'Dominance without Hegemony and its Historiography', in Ranajit Guha ed. *Subaltern Studies VI*, Delhi: Oxford University Press, 1989, 240–43.
75 'Kolikata Medical Topography', *Jnanannesan*, 21 October 1837, rpt. in Suresh Chandra Moitra ed. *Selections from Jnanannessan*, Calcutta: Prajña, 1979, 57, Bengali section. However, it is important to remember William J. Glover's recent qualification that 'British and Indian voices for reform did not speak with a single voice of authority, even if their concerns sometimes overlapped' ('Objects, Models and Exemplary Works: Educating Sentiment in Colonial India', *Journal of Asian Studies* 64:3, 2005, 555).
76 Paul Rabinow, *French Modern: Norms and Forms of the Social Environment*, Cambridge, Mass.: MIT Press, 1989, 15.
77 Binaybhushan Ray, 'Native Haspatal Theke Fever Haspatal', in Debashish Basu ed. *Kolkatar Purakatha*, Calcutta: Pushtak Bipani, 1992, in Bengali.
78 In 1834, the government refused help to the District Charitable Society, Calcutta, for famine victims from Balasore, Orissa, arguing that 'most of the indigent families referred

to will have returned to their villages and found a livelihood in the ordinary employments of the Season' (Government of India, Home Public, No. 31, 9 June 1834, National Archives of India). This theme has been developed in detail by Sanjay Sharma, *Famine, Philanthropy and the State: North India in the Early Nineteenth century*, Delhi: Oxford University Press, 1991.

3 Beyond the bounds of time?

The Haj pilgrimage from the Indian subcontinent, 1865–1920

Saurabh Mishra

> Time has affected the very environment of Haj. It has brought many changes to the city of Mecca, the surrounding holy areas and to Ka'aba itself. Yet the functions and the rituals of Haj are unchanged for their character is immutable.[1]

The pilgrimage to Mecca is a subject of overwhelming importance for Islamic scholars. A supreme symbol of unsullied faith, it soars above mere materialities in their writings. Indeed, their copious ruminations upon the spiritual wonders of the Haj seem to have left a mark on other academic works too. Thus F.E. Peters, in his detailed multi-volume treatment of the subject, appears to take this immateriality and timelessness to be one the features of the pilgrimage.[2] Many anthropologists too, due to their rather broad approach towards pilgrimages in general, do not attempt to situate the phenomenon within a temporal framework.[3] Within the European treatment of Islam in general, there appears a distinct lack of temporal awareness, so that the seventh century rubs shoulders with the present in a flat and unchanging landscape. European interest in the Haj was born partly out of a suspicion that the pilgrimage was a vehicle for breeding fanaticism. In widely read accounts of the pilgrimage, travellers and chroniclers from Europe testified to the open intrigue breeding at Mecca. Such accounts were so popular that many of them ran into several editions, while some of them were also serialized in leading newspapers.[4]

The Haj also occupied pride of place within nationalist accounts discussing the 'Muslim question', where it was identified as being reflective of broader transnational currents. The congregation of Muslims from all over the world at Mecca, and also the symbolic importance of the Holy Places in the daily lives of Muslims, were seen as facilitating a pan-Islamic consciousness. It has been mentioned, even in recent nationalist historiography, that 'the feeling of brotherhood and solidarity (among the Muslims) has been buttressed *over the centuries* by two powerful institutions of Islam – the Haj and the Caliphate.'[5] While in some accounts this has been treated sympathetically and seen as an outcome of genuine and legitimate religious sentiments, others have seen it as a hindrance to the full realization of Indianness among Muslims in the subcontinent.[6] In all these works – no matter what their inflection – little attempt has been made to situate the pilgrimage within a time-frame and to study all its dimensions in detail. This chapter argues that even during the rather brief period in the career of the pilgrimage that we have chosen to focus on, several changes occurred in its organization, nature, significance and meanings. Though limitations of space prevent us from delving into the details of these processes, we shall identify some of them during the course of this chapter. In this context, we shall look at the changing experiences of the pilgrims themselves, the change in the organization of the pilgrimage due to medical necessities, the process of evolution of the colonial position on the Haj, and the change in the meanings of the Haj both for colonial officialdom and for 'Indian Muslims'[7] as it acquired an increasingly political colour. Admittedly, this is a rather wide canvas, but the purpose of the chapter is to illustrate the changeability and dynamisum of the pilgrimage in more ways than one.

Cholera and the Ka'aba

Let us begin by citing a few rather obvious and massive transformations during the period of this study. The opening of the Suez Canal in 1869 represented a huge watershed in the world of marine navigation: it not only 'joined the East and the West' but also dramatically reduced the distance and journey time for travellers to Arabia from South and South-East Asia. What had earlier appeared to be an interminable and hugely expensive journey meant only for the Nawabs and their beneficiaries now seemed within the grasp of even the poor believers. Pauper and indigent pilgrims – to quote an oft-used colonial phrase – now swarmed the ports of Bombay in the hope of setting afloat for Ka'aba in one of the astoundingly huge steamships (as they appeared to the pilgrims) anchored there. Many of them depended on the munificence of fellow pilgrims and many carried a small amount of money doled out by prosperous Muslim merchants and Nawabs seeking to acquire merit indirectly through helping the Hajis.[8]

The opening of the Suez Canal also marked a turning point in European and colonial perceptions of the Haj. This is when we start hearing of the great medical threat presented by the pilgrimage to European nations. The huge outbreak of cholera at Mecca in 1865 and its spread to various European nations had already alerted the latter to this dimension of the pilgrimage.[9] Subsequent outbreaks during the next decade confirmed the linkage between cholera and Mecca.[10] Further, pilgrims from the subcontinent in particular were seen as the most likely carriers of the epidemics. After all, the Ganges delta was the 'natural home of cholera,' and the Indian pilgrims, owing to their 'almost professional filthiness', acted as 'exceptionally dangerous vectors of transmission'.[11]

This perception led to a considerable amount of focus on the Haj and cholera. Several European medical journals, periodicals and international sanitary conferences discussed the issue in great detail. In fact, the Constantinople conference of 1866 was convened with the sole purpose of discussing this question. At all the subsequent conferences a huge amount of attention was also devoted to the subject.[12] Periodicals such as the *British Medical Journal* (*BMJ*) campaigned actively to ameliorate the situation. Ernest Hart, the controversial editor of the journal, made a trip to the subcontinent to persuade Indian Muslims to request the Turkish government to initiate sanitary reforms in Mecca.[13]

Hart's and the *BMJ*'s opinions were, however, somewhat at variance with the stance of most European governments. While the journal held that cholera was caused primarily by insanitary conditions at Mecca, most European governments were staunch in their belief that the disease was carried to Mecca by Indian pilgrims. Thus, while the *BMJ* conducted chemical examinations of water samples from *zemzem* (the holy well), European delegates at international conferences vociferously demanded quarantine for pilgrims from the subcontinent.[14]

In the final instance it was the clamour raised by European nations that proved more effective. In the year 1882, by notification of the Superior Council of Health (Constantinople), all pilgrim vessels from Bombay bound for Jedda were obliged to call at the island of Kamaran in the Red Sea, about 500 miles south of their destination, where they were to observe a quarantine usually lasting around fifteen days, which might be prolonged on detection of any infection.[15] This meant much greater hardships for the pilgrims. Not only did it imply rigorous confinement but it also translated into a substantial financial burden since the quarantines, established to assuage the fears of European nations, had to be paid for by the pilgrims themselves. Speaking of their emotional state during these quarantines, many Urdu travelogues describe the great anxiety, fear and helplessness pilgrims experienced in a situation where the Haj season was fast approaching and they were so near yet so far from their cherished goal.

During the last three decades of the nineteenth century an entire medical apparatus, elaborate and detailed, had been established in and around Mecca. This happened despite the reluctance of both the Sultan of Turkey and the Sherif of Mecca to brook any foreign interference in their sovereign territories. During the Haj season many European countries sent medical representatives to the Hejaz, and medical missions were also dispatched by most of them. Consuls kept a keen watch on the medical situation at Mecca and medical periodicals and journals promptly reported any fresh developments. Quarantines were administered by a Board of Health with representation from all European nations, and they were instituted not just for the Indian pilgrims (Kamaran) but also for the African ones (El Tor). Provisions for medical examination, steam-bath, shower and vaccination were also established at the ports of departure. Each country with a substantial number of pilgrims was to enumerate the medical provisions during the Haj and on board ships in their respective Passenger Shipping Acts. Each ship was to be examined before being granted a Bill of Health. These are a few in the long list of changes demanded from a medical standpoint. The cumulative effect of these regulations was to bring the Haj, an otherwise purely religious phenomenon, into the grid of medical issues. For the faithful it meant that, on the way to the Holy Land, they not only had to live the verses of the Quran but also had to live through quarantine. The extent to which these quarantine stations and other public health institutions were feared and resented is revealed by the Bedouin belief that they were deliberate conspiracies on the part of the British government to infect Arabia with disease.[16]

Though these changes meant greater tribulations for the pilgrims, it might be noted in 'defence' of European medical policies towards the Haj that cholera was instrumental in shaping public health policies wherever it went, and if the regulations for the pilgrims were stringent, they were no less so for disadvantaged citizens within many European nations.[17]

Quarantined! Pilgrims' perceptions of the journey

As a result of these developments, the experience of the ordinary pilgrims undertaking the journey also changed dramatically. For these 'pious passengers',[18] imprisonment at the quarantine station was one of the most powerful experiences of the Haj. While several pages are devoted in their travelogues to describing the magnificence of Mecca, considerable space is also occupied by the exasperating, annoying and tense period of incarceration at the quarantine station. Poems and couplets equalling in number (and perhaps also in the intensity of feeling) those written about the Ka'aba were penned about Kamaran. Quoted below are a few lines by Mirza Irfan Ali Begh, the Deputy Collector of Mainpuri district, though the poem perhaps does not possess adequate literary merit:

> Mid Jeddah and Aden way,
> The quarantine at Kamaran lay.
> The Hajis of the Indian land
> Are first tried on this sand;
> If one can save his life here,
> In going to Haj he has no fear.
> Who does not die in ten days,
> Good luck he has in all his ways.
> . . . O! for the sake of quarantine,
> Thy [god's] prisoners all of us have been.[19]

The ordinary pilgrim had to undergo a dehumanizing process of disinfection. Many complained of the rudeness of quarantine officials and watchmen, and of the 'shameful treatment' accorded to the women in their families. Every passing hour was counted carefully and every new medical incident in the camps observed fretfully. In some cases, due to deaths within the camps, quarantines were extended for as long as two months. Due to the continued aggravation at these stations, there were a few instances of revolt as well. In 1877, when cholera broke out, a quarantine was immediately clamped on the Hajis returning through Egypt. At Gebel Tor, the quarantine for passengers of the *Achilles* went on for twenty-eight days, and threatened to go on for much longer. Driven to desperation, the famished and emaciated pilgrims broke out. One Egyptian soldier was killed and many pilgrims set out for Suez on foot. Later, the captain of the ship was also forced to steer towards Suez. However, on reaching Suez, pilgrims were not allowed to land since they had not completed their quarantine. After many days of this stalemate, the passengers incarcerated the captain and forced open the ship stores. It was only through the presence of a British man-of-war that they could be restrained.[20]

There was a widespread belief among both pilgrims and non-pilgrims that the restrictions had been instituted by the British. Such a sentiment became more powerful as the nineteenth century wore on. In spite of repeated attempts by the colonial authority to inform the Muslim populace that the restrictions had been demanded by the Turkish and European nations, there was continued mistrust of the British.[21] In fact, many periodicals, such as *Azad* published in Lucknow, were openly partisan and supported medical restrictions when they were imposed by the Turkish regime while denouncing them when they had to be instituted by the British.[22] It needs to be emphasized, however, that despite the increasing 'medicalization' of the pilgrimage during our period, for a majority of pilgrims it was primarily an emotional experience. Many undertook the pilgrimage to humble themselves before God, to repent their sins, to seek forgiveness, and to express their love. Indeed, in many of the travelogues the emotions of love and longing appear to be stronger than piety and faith.

The dynamics of inactivity: the stand of the colonial state

At the same time as these changes in the pilgrims' experience of the journey, the Haj also acquired new meanings for the colonial state. In fact, the argument about the dynamism of the Haj is made most forcefully when we focus on this aspect of the pilgrimage. For the British Indian administration, the question of the Haj was involved in an amalgam of medical, commercial and political issues. It is difficult to delineate these influences completely, but what we shall attempt here is to look at the rise and fall of the relative significance of these imperatives in the fashioning of colonial policies at various stages during the period of our study.

Colonial records carry a voluminous correspondence on the subject. What caused this interest? One of the primary reasons, as noted earlier, was the connection between cholera and the Haj emphasized repeatedly by European nations. But this was not the only question of importance. The British Indian administration suspected that the issue of quarantine was being raked up by European powers as a pretext to impose restrictions on the British Indian entrepot trade.[23] Apart from this, a cautious approach towards the Haj was also adopted due to its supposed political significance or the 'strange magnetism' that drew millions of Muslim believers towards it. Simultaneously, the subversive potential of the pilgrimage was also remarked upon in colonial documents, and this fuelled an undercurrent of suspicion against it. What, then, was the colonial state's stand with respect to the pilgrimage, caught as it was between these various imperatives and ideas?

Its policy, throughout our period, continued to be one of non-interference. The Indian answer to the loud European demands for restrictions was a studied silence. No radical and permanent alterations were made either during the plague epidemics of the 1890s, or after the several severe cholera outbreaks at Mecca, or during the early twentieth century when the Haj assumed a more threateningly anti-colonial form and became a symbol of 'political Islam'. In fact, rather than impose any restrictions, the Indian administration tried to facilitate the pilgrimage exactly at the times when the situation demanded the contrary. Special arrangements for the pilgrimage were therefore made during the plague years.[24] Even during the First World War, when there were more pressing demands upon the colonial state, a few ships were still set aside for the Haj.[25]

Underneath this veneer of inactivity, though, furious discussions were taking place on the subject of the Haj. The pilgrimage was also integrally related to transformations within the sanitary and medical administration. In fact, it can be argued that the pilgrimage was, to a large extent, *responsible* for these changes. After all, till the 1880s, it was the linkage between cholera and commerce that engaged the attention of the Indian administration. From the standpoint of trading interests it was important to refute the assertion, rather obvious and beyond requirements of proof to European authorities, that Indian Hajis were the carriers of disease. Several developments within Anglo-Indian medical circles converged to produce the unified stand of the central administration (sanitary or otherwise) that it was impossible for Indian pilgrims to carry seeds of epidemics since cholera, by its very nature, was a non-contagious disease.

The dominance of the theory of non-contagion in South Asia with respect to cholera becomes apparent from the 1870s on, at least at the higher echelons of the sanitary administration. Such a shift took place at least partly due to concerns related to trade and the pilgrimage to Mecca. During this period the sanitary administration, which had become increasingly centralized and hierarchized since the 1860s, used its wherewithal to superimpose the theory of non-contagion over pre-existing and new theories. The 1860s saw several new developments within this administration, all of them producing a more centralized and autonomous sanitary and medical administration.[26] That the impetus for this came from the top can be surmised from a private note sent by John Lawrence, the Viceroy at the time, to the Secretary of State in 1867, stating that 'it will certainly never do to place [civilian sanitary] matters in the hands of the army sanitary commission.'[27] He also noted the urgent need for a central sanitary authority as there was 'practically no central control, and the governments of the minor Presidencies act as they think proper'.[28]

These developments appear in sharp contrast to the rudimentary and inefficient sanitary apparatus which existed till the 1850s and was remarked upon by the Royal Commission on the Sanitary State of the Army in India (1859).[29] As a result of these developments, the ideas of the central government, more in tune with the commercial interests of the Indian empire, managed to displace contradicting ideas and opinions. Any opposition to the theory of contagion was crushed, as is clearly reflected in the following statement made by M.C. Furnell in 1887, when he had retired after thirty years in the sanitary administration, serving in such high posts as the sanitary commissioner and surgeon-general of Madras:

> The theory which has of late found acceptance with the supreme government of India, and which has been more or less authoritatively impressed on the minor presidencies, is, that cholera is not spread by human intercourse or contaminated water, but is due to 'Local Influence'. . . . It is at present in India,

> '*by authority*', the only 'true faith', and woe to the Sanitary Commissioner or medical officer who publishes his belief in any other cause but 'Local Influence'.[30]

The basic cause of this ruthlessness was the commercial interest of the administration, which could be compromised if European theories and concomitant demands for quarantines were accepted. It could be argued, in fact, that during this period the doctrine of free trade was a stronger article of faith than that of non-intervention due to political reasons. In the case of the latter, the colonial government acquiesced, after much protest, to regulatory measures such as quarantines. However, if the suggested measures were in conflict with trading interests, it raised a much stronger reaction. In 1912, for instance, it refused to ratify the International Sanitary Convention since, 'as could be readily seen, the adoption of one or more of the principles would have entailed considerably more onerous restrictions on Indian trade.'[31] Similarly, in 1897, during the plague outbreak, pilgrim traffic to Mecca was suspended, partly because it was feared that otherwise 'European powers would assuredly impose strict quarantine against all India', thus obstructing Indian commerce.[32] The Secretary of State imposed such a measure in spite of warnings by the Viceroy, who cited the decided views of many local governments against a complete suspension for fear of a political backlash. In 1898, when the complete suspension was revoked due to fear of Muslim discontent, and a partial pilgrimage was allowed, this was despite stiff opposition from commercial interests at the ports of embarkation.[33]

Politics and the pilgrimage

The staunch refusal of the Indian state to budge from its non-contagionist position, even after the germ theory had become the watch-word in Europe and Koch's theory had acquired the status of an axiom, can only be explained if we take into account commercial issues. In 1893, when there was great mortality during the Haj, and there was absolutely no controversy in European medical circles regarding the cause of the epidemic, the *Report on the Sanitary Measures in India* still maintained that:

> Anyone who has heard from ship captains and the pilgrims themselves accounts of the filth and the absence of even elementary attempts at sanitation at Camaran, Jeddah and the Holy Cities, cannot but feel that far from India being under the existing circumstances a danger through Europe through the pilgrimage, she is herself in danger from Jeddah and Camaran [*sic.*].[34]

The primacy of commercial imperatives was not, however, to continue for long. Within the space of a few decades, the Haj assumed a stridently political colour in colonial eyes. So strong was this transformation that in 1915, the subject of the Haj pilgrimage itself was transferred from the Sanitary Branch of the Education Department to the Foreign and Political Department. An official noted that:

> The case now properly belongs to the Foreign and Political Department. The Education Department deals with pilgrimages as a part of sanitation. But the sanitary aspect of this case is almost nil and it has resolved itself into a case of general policy.[35]

During this period of what some have chosen to call the 'Islamization' of the Muslims in the subcontinent,[36] a great number of Anjumans or Islamic societies were being formed. Many of them espoused the cause of the Haj and the Hajis. In fact, some organizations such as the Anjuman-I-Khuddam-I-Ka'aba (Society of the Servants of Ka'aba) were formed explicitly with the purpose of facilitating the pilgrimage. Founded by Abdul Bari of the Firanghi Mahal and the Ali brothers, and ostensibly for purposes 'strictly religious, having nothing to do with politics', its potential for creating 'political nuisance' was not hidden from the colonial authorities.[37] In the first year of its existence (1913) the organization had 9,000 members on its rolls and 'through the use of religious symbols, the Ka'aba, the Caliph, the crescent, the green robes and banners, public opinion was aroused, meetings held and funds raised from new sources, from ordinary men and women, both literate and illiterate.'[38] The Anjuman expected to be able to raise substantial funds and it ultimately concentrated on aiding Haj pilgrims, a goal more visible and immediate than the vague 'defence of Ka'aba'. Shaukat Ali went to Bombay and took out a licence as a pilgrim broker. He assured all pilgrims that their tickets, passports and every need would be well looked after with safety and dispatch, all commissions going into the Anjuman's funds for destitute Hajis.[39] Interestingly, Shaukat Ali, when in Bombay as the secretary of the Anjuman, grew a shaggy beard, calling it his 'fiercest protest' against Christendom.[40] Mohamed Ali wrote a letter to Talat Bey, the Turkish Minister of Interior, after the revolution of 1908 with a proposal to establish, in a joint venture, a shipping company that could compete with the powerful British shipping interests, for, said he, 'the Haj traffic must always remain in Muslim hands.' He expected that 'considerable profits could be made by the company if it is properly managed'.[41] He further noted that:

> Every Muslim in India must be reminded of the injunctions of our religion with respect to the Holy Places. More men should visit them than do at present and for this purpose every facility should be provided for the Haj.[42]

It was during and after this period, and particularly during the Khilafat agitations, that the Haj assumed, in the eyes of the colonial authorities, a much greater political significance than ever before. After the ruling authority in Turkey had been deposed and a puppet ruler was established, the feeling of discontent against the British assumed much larger proportions. During these days, it was repeatedly noted in the correspondence between the colonial authorities that a successful completion of the Haj and ensuring 'the excellence of the Hedjaz arrangements' were the only means to pacify the sentiments of the Indian Muslims. The two measures that were advocated, therefore, were: (a) immediate release of all Muslim political detaines whose liberation was not likely to cause any trouble; and (b) arrangements for a cheap and full Haj when the time came.[43]

Talking about the 'political unrest' in India around this time, Denys Bray, the Secretary of the Foreign and Political Department, highlighted rather strongly the political importance and usefulness of the Haj. He noted that:

> Since we last raised the question, the political urgency has been brought into greater prominence. It is now generally recognised that Muslim unrest is not the last among the causes that lie at the bottom of the present internal trouble. At a recent defence committee meeting various devices for allaying this unrest were considered, and it was realized that almost the only course open to us was to exploit the Haj under the new, non-Turkish regime for all it is worth. Despite therefore the palpable objection to any form of subsidy, the department is constrained to force upon the Finance Department the extension (from Rs.5 lakhs to Rs.10 lakhs) advocated.[44]

It was said that Rs10 lakhs 'would be a small price to pay for any measure which could have an appreciable effect on Muhammedan sentiment in this country at the present juncture'. The subsidies had become absolutely essential in 1919 because it was rumoured that the steamship companies planned to raise their fares from Rs125 to Rs200. 'The effect of this', averred an official from Bombay, 'would be positively disastrous.'[45] The Secretary of the Home Department was thus rushed to Bombay to hold talks with representatives of the steamship companies, and after the grant of the subsidy was agreed upon the steamship companies agreed to reduce the fare to Rs125. What is interesting is the panic that seems to have gripped the British administrators on the issue of the rise in fares.[46] While one can only speculate as to whether a successful completion of the Haj could have brought in the enormous benefits that were expected by the British, it is clear that the British Indian administration saw the Haj as an exceedingly important political subject. It had, by the first decade of the twentieth century, been transformed from being a primarily commercial and medical subject to a sensitive political question for the colonial state.

Conclusion

It is beyond the scope of this chapter to discuss several other transformations in the pilgrimage. For instance, the pilgrimage was used during the earlier period (and in fact till late into the nineteenth century) for royal purposes: for displaying the grandeur of kings and Nawabs and to inspire awe in the hearts of subjects. By the turn of the nineteenth century, however, depictions were no longer inextricably connected with royal customs, but became more concerned with eye-catching details and with the unusual.[47] The pilgrimage, especially after the opening of the Suez Canal, became far more 'secular' in nature, though elements of grandeur and display continued to exist.

This chapter has tried to bring out the various changes taking place in the organization, nature and meaning of the Haj from South Asia. Contrary to the assertions of many scholars, we have attempted to highlight the changes not only in the practical organization of the pilgrimage but also in the meanings it had for various sections: for the Indian Muslims (both pilgrims and non-pilgrims), for the colonial state, and for the European nations. In the process, we have also demonstrated the continuous interaction between various aspects of the Haj: its medical, commercial and political facets. We have, in short, tried to reveal the turbulent developments underneath the apparently placid surface of the Haj and tried to break the myth of the 'timelessness' of the pilgrimage.

Notes

1 Ziauddin Sarkar and M.A. Zaki Badawi eds *Haj Studies*, Vol. I, London: Croom Helm, 1979.

2 F.E. Peters, *The Hajj: The Muslim Pilgrimage to Mecca and the Holy Places*, Princeton, NJ: Princeton University Press, 1994.

3 Many of these writings look at them as 'liminal' experiences that could reveal more about the mode of functioning of the society at large. See, for instance, Victor Turner, *Events, Fields and Metaphors: Symbolic Action in Human Society*, Ithaca, NY: Cornell University Press, 1978.

4 They were, in fact, so plentiful that authors of new books on the subject began by apologizing for bringing out another one. The travelogues written during our period of study include Charles M. Doughty, *Arabia Deserta,* Cambridge: Cambridge University Press, 1888; Isabel Burton, *Arabia Egypt India: A Narrative of Travel,* London: William Mullan and Son, 1879; John F. Keane, *Six Months in the Hejaz, Being Keane's Journey to Meccah and Medinah,* London: Ward and Downey, 1887; Hadji Khan and Wilfred Sparroy, *With the Pilgrims to Mecca,* London: John Lane, 1902. The last mentioned travelogue was serialized in the *Morning Post*, London.

5 Bimal Prasad notes this in *Pathway to India's Partition, Vol. I: The Foundations of Muslim Nationalism,* Delhi: Manohar, 1999; emphasis added.

6 The *Vartaman* of 12 October 1947, for instance, noted:

> Flesh and blood of the Hindus though they were, these Hindavi Muslims began to think of themselves as belonging to the Arab and Mughal communities. . . . Rulers like Aurangzeb, and later on the British, never tired of preaching that they [the Muslims] have been the governors of this country, and that their direct links are with Arabia, Persia and Turkey. Their language, appearance, religion and practices are all different from those of the Hindus.

7 This is the category which has been employed in colonial documents to denote interested sections of Muslim opinion within the subcontinent. One of the aims of the larger project, of which this chapter is a part, is to look at the process of formation of this category and to attempt to disaggregate it.

8 A colonial official narrates the story of a woman pilgrim staying at one of the three Musafirkhanas in Bombay who seemed to be in rather dire circumstances. When asked how she expected to defray the expenses of the journey she replied that she intended to beg. Such passengers, the official went on to conclude, were only too common: Bombay Presidency, 1885, General Department, Vol. 125, Maharashtra State Archives, Mumbai.

9 Isabel Burton's account reflects this new perception of Mecca. She noted that:

> Mecca is not only a great centre of religion and commerce; it is also the prime source of political intrigues, the very nest where plans of conquest and schemes of revenge upon the infidel are hatched; and . . . the focus whence cholera is dispersed over the West. Shall a misplaced feeling of tolerating intolerance allow her to work in dark against the humanity? Allah forbids it.
>
> (*Arabia Egypt India: A Narrative of Travel,* London and Belfast: William Mullan and Son, 1879)

10 Between 1865 and 1895 a total of ten outbreaks of cholera occurred at Mecca.

11 This was noted by the Italian delegate at an International Sanitary Conference; quoted in Peter Baldwin, *Contagion and the State in Europe, 1830–1930*, Cambridge: Cambridge University Press, 1999, 139–51.

12 Between 1851 and the end of the century, ten International Sanitary Conferences were convened. Smallpox, yellow fever and plague were the other diseases widely discussed at these conferences. For full details see Norman Howard-Jones, *The Scientific Background of the International Sanitary Conferences 1851–1938*, Geneva: World Health Organization, 1975.

13 Based on his trip and experiences, he subsequently published a pamphlet called *The Nurseries of Cholera: Its Diffusion and its Extinction: An Address Delivered before the Section of Public Medicine of the British Medical Association of Newcastle,* London: Smith, Elder and Co., 1893.

14 C.W. Heaton, a renowned chemist, conducted the examinations and made a comparison between the waters of *zemzem* and the Thames to bring out the 'foulness' of the former. The results he reached regarding the chemical composition of the two samples are reproduced below:

Grains per gallon

	Mecca	*London*
Total solid matter	464.40	8.000
Chlorine	75.50	1.500
Nitrogen as nitrates	13.75	0.180
Nitrogen as nitrites	0.090	–
Ammonia	0.358	0.001
Albuminoid ammonia	–	0.004

Source: Lancet, 5 January 1884, 33–4.

Ernest Hart noted that 'if the water of Zemzem were purified, one of the greatest causes for the mortality at Mecca would be removed.'

15 Dr D. Choudhary, *History of Quarantine and Port Administration in the Port of Bombay*, New Delhi: Government of India Publication, 1955, 75–105.

16 The Secretary of State wrote to the Viceroy in 1899 that, 'There [is] a revolutionary movement of the Bedouins of the hard tribes, who declare that it is the sanitary authorities who have introduced Cholera into their country. They have threatened to attack Jeddah and destroy the new hospital now being built.' The Haj in this year was partly suspended due to this threat: Home Department Proceedings, Sanitary Branch, 31–32, June 1895, National Archives of India (hereafter NAI).

17 For instance, in Britain many of these sanitary reforms were instituted with an emphasis on countering the menace of cholera and in response to the epidemic of 1832. Following the panic generated by the outbreak that year, compilation of statistics on a national scale was started, a General Register Office was established in 1843, and various items of sanitary reform legislation passed, culminating in the Public Health Act of 1848. Further quarantines were also in place till much later in the nineteenth century as a 'First Line of Defence'.

18 This is the title of a wonderful work by on the Haj from South Asia during medieval times: M.N. Pearson, *Pious Passengers: The Haj in Earlier Times*, Dhaka: University Press Limited, 1994.

19 *A Pilgrimage to Mecca*, Benaras: The Chandraprabha Press Company, 1896, 71. Mirza Begh, by virtue of being from a privileged background, could circumvent many of the hardships that ordinary pilgrims had to undergo during quarantine: he had a ready supply of fresh and sweet water, and did not have to undergo the indignity of disinfection.

20 From Dr Potts to Vice-Consul Wylde, Government of India, letter dated 28 February 1878, Foreign Office, file number 195/956, National Archives, United Kingdom.

21 Pamphlets to this effect were distributed in many vernacular languages, and drummers employed to convey the message to the villages, especially in the years when harsher restrictions were in place: Government of Bengal, March 1898, Judicial Department Proceedings (Political Branch), West Bengal State Archives.

22 See for instance a news report published in *Azad*, 17 October 1890.

23 Accepting restrictions on pilgrim traffic through the Suez Canal would also imply subjecting British trading vessels through the canal to disruptions. This was thoroughly unacceptable to the Indian state, especially in a context where the bulk of the traffic through Suez was British. The Secretary to the Chamber of Commerce, Bombay noted that:

> When it is remembered that upwards of 80% of the traffic of the canal belongs to Great Britain, and that a large majority of the delegates forming the International Board represent countries engaged in petty rivalry with, and hostile to, the commercial greatness of England, the Committee respectfully suggests whether, as the only means of removing the vexatious and unnecessary restrictions which are constantly imposed on the trade of India, endeavours might not be made by Her Majesty's Government to procure the abolition of the International sanitary board.
>
> (Government of India, letter dated 22 December 1882, Home Department Proceedings, Sanitary Proceedings volumes, January–July 1883, NAI)

24 In 1902, even though plague was still quite prevalent in the Bombay presidency, the port of Bombay was reopened for the pilgrims. Further, a separate observation camp was opened at Pir Pao in accordance with the Venice Convention at quite considerable cost to the government: Dr D. Choudhary, *History of Quarantine and Port Administration in the Port of Bombay*, New Delhi: Government of India Publication, 1955.

25 Denys Bray, Secretary of the Foreign and Political Department, threatened that,

> if the departments concerned decide that it is not necessary to press for the withdrawal of shipping from more essential services to meet the requirements of the Haj, this department will place the facts of the case before the Secretary of State.
>
> (Government of India, 1918, Foreign and Political Department, Secret-War, File no. 438–490, NAI)

26 To list a few of the developments within the sanitary administration during this period, sanitary commissions were set up in the three presidencies in 1864, a Municipal Health Officer was appointed in presidencies such as Bombay, the policy of registration of births and deaths was put into place, statistical reports began to be maintained, exhaustive reports on diseases such as cholera began to be written, and medical issues came to be somewhat divested of their strong military connections: Deepak Kumar, 'Health and Medicine in British India and Dutch Indies: A Comparative Study', in Joseph Alter ed. *Asian Medicine and Globalization*, Philadelphia: University of Pennsylvania Press, 2005.

27 Letter dated 4 October 1867, John Lawrence Collection, Mss Eur/ F90 32B, Oriental and India Office Collections (hereafter OIOC), London.

28 Letter dated 4 October 1867, John Lawrence Collection.

29 Cited in John Chandler Hume, Jr, 'Colonialism and Sanitary Medicine: The Development of Preventive Health Policy in the Punjab, 1860 to 1900', *Modern Asian Studies*, 28: 1986, 708.

30 *Cholera and Water in India*, London: J. and A. Churchill, 1887, 4, italics in the original. The hierarchical nature of the administration is also reflected in the controversy between

DeRenzy, the Sanitary Commissioner of Punjab, and J.M. Cuningham, the Sanitary Commissioner of India. See Mark Harrison, 'Quarantine, Pilgrimage and Colonial Trade 1866–1900', in *Public Health in British India: Anglo-Indian Preventive Medicine, 1859–1914*, Cambridge: Cambridge University Press, 1994.

31 Records of the Residency of Aden, file number R/20/A/2594, OIOC.

32 From the Secretary of State to the Viceroy, 18 February 1897, *Papers Relating to the Outbreak of Bubonic Plague in India; with Statement Showing the Quarantine and other Restrictions Recently Placed upon Indian Trade*, No. I, Printed for her Majesty's Stationery Office, London: Eyre and Spottiswoode, Printers to the Queen's Most Excellent Majesty, 1897.

33 *Papers Relating to the Outbreak of Bubonic Plague*, No. III, 1898, 113–20; Calcutta was the principal port for the pilgrimage during these years.

34 *Report on the Sanitary Measures in India in 1893–94*, Vol. XXVII, Calcutta: Government of India Press, 137–40.

35 From H. Sharp, Secretary in the Education Department, Government of India, February 1918, Foreign and Political Department Proceedings, Secret-War, Nos 438–490, NAI.

36 Francis Robinson remarks that:

> There [was] an enormous interest in pan-Islamic affairs, which led to an extraordinary increase in the circulation of Muslim newspapers whenever the wider Islamic world suffered crises, like the Russo-Turkish war of 1877–78, the Graeco-Turkish war of 1897, the Balkan wars of 1911–1913, or the last throes of the Ottoman empire and Caliphate from 1918–1924.
>
> (*Muslim Separatism in India*, New Delhi: Oxford University Press, 1993, 61)

37 Gail Minault, *The Khilafat Movement: Religious Symbolism and Political Mobilization in India*, New Delhi: Oxford University Press, 1982, 35. P.C. Ramford, *Histories of Khilafat and Non-Cooperation Movement*, first published 1925, Delhi: Government of India Press, reprinted by K.K. Book Distributors, 1985, the colonial chronicler of the Khilafat movement in India, noted that: 'The activists of the organisation exhibited no desire to be either scrupulous or truthful and some of the members . . . stated that the sacred places of Islam were in danger and that infidels were trying to capture and demolish them.'

38 Minault, *The Khilafat Movement*, 37.

39 Ramford, *Histories of Khilafat*, writes of the episode in these words: 'last year Shaukat Ali, as secretary of the Anjuman, visited Bombay in June and there stimulated an agitation against certain proposed regulations relating to the pilgrims performing the Haj.' The proposed regulations pertained to the compulsory purchase of return tickets by pilgrims and the granting of monopoly of the pilgrim traffic to an English firm which had just then bought up the Arab Steamship Company, 'but it failed in its attempt as we hope it always will' (37).

40 B.R. Nanda, *Gandhi: Pan-Islamism, Imperialism and nationalism*, New Delhi: Oxford University Press, 1989, 134.

41 Mushirul Hasan ed. *Mohamed Ali in Indian politics: Select Writings*, Vol. 1, Delhi: Atlantic Publishers and Distributors, 1982, 66.

42 Hasan, *Mohamed Ali*, 67.

43 Government of India, November 1919, Foreign and Political Department, Sec. E, No. 1/139, NAI. From A.H. Grant.

44 From Denys Bray, Secretary to the Foreign and Political Department, dated 25 April 1919.

45 Letter from the Government of Bombay dated 4 April 1919.

46 The subsidy proposal, however, did meet with some opposition even within government circles. One H.R. Kothawala, special service officer attached to the General Staff, Strait settlements, thought that this was all the handiwork of the pilgrim agents. Due to the

total ban on the pilgrimage, their earnings had fallen drastically and they wanted as many pilgrims this year as possible. They therefore struck upon this strategy of driving into the heads of the British administrators the significance of a large number of pilgrims visiting Mecca: Government of India, November 1919, Foreign and Political Department, Secret E 1/139, NAI.

47 V. Matheson and A.C. Milner, *Perceptions of the Haj: Five Malay Texts*, Singapore: Institute of Southeast Asian Studies, 1984.

4 'Subordinate' negotiations

Indigenous staff, the colonial state and public health

Amna Khalid

The indigenous population of India played a very significant role in the shaping and reshaping of colonial health policy. The response of the general population, and its hostility to certain state interventions such as inoculation and sanitary change during the nineteenth century, are well documented by historians.[1] The response of Indian elites to quarantine imposed in India during outbreaks of cholera and plague has also received the attention of historians.[2]

At a more local level 'native'[3] agency is acknowledged in the importance of the 'native gentlemen' class as it was used to promote measures like inoculation and evacuation of disease-affected areas, which were initially not very popular. Moreover, the growing financial constraints of provincial governments and sanitary administrations made the financial and material assistance provided by leading gentlemen to their communities, such as caste-specific hospitals, absolutely indispensable for effective disease control.[4] Even indigenous healers such as *hakims* and *vaids*, who were actively being displaced by the state's introduction of western medicine, had to be co-opted in the nineteenth century to extend public health measures into rural areas. As early as 1857, *hakims* were used as vaccinators in the Punjab.[5] During the next decade *hakims* in the NWP were also being trained in vaccination techniques and were found to be extremely effective agents for promoting this new public health measure.[6] At the end of the century, when plague broke out at pilgrimage centres, *hakims* and *vaids* were allowed free access to government-built pilgrim camps in order to encourage people to report cases and admit the sick into these institutions.[7]

While the response and significance of elites (national and local), the general public, and even indigenous healers, to public health measures have been the subject of considerable historical inquiry, the role of the subordinate staff actually responsible for implementing measures on the ground remains largely under-studied. Historians of Indian public health have continued to be primarily concerned with the process of policy making in the upper echelons of the sanitary administration.[8] Yet the lower-level staff formed the backbone of the sanitary system, as 'executive officials in India had to deal with vast tracts of country and were generally obliged to communicate with the people through subordinate agents'.[9]

Recently there has been an attempt to shed light on the role of medical subordinates. A recent study by Bhattacharya, Harrison and Worboys offers an analysis of the vaccinators employed for smallpox inoculation programmes in British India.[10] James Mills has addressed the issue of subordinate Indian personnel employed in lunatic asylums in India and how they subverted treatment regimes, at times out of sympathy for the patients and at other times to further their own interests. He highlights how decisions made by these subordinates played a greater part in determining the conditions on the ground than the colonial directives.[11] In other colonial contexts, those of the Belgian Congo and Uganda, Maryinez Lyons has drawn attention to the importance of African medical auxiliaries. She has shown how the actual implementation of medical programmes was in the hands of these African subordinates, whose position in colonial society had an impact on how they discharged their duties.[12]

However, all three of these works focus on *medical* subordinates, either employed directly by the medical service or employed to work inside medical institutions. This chapter makes a significant contribution in that it looks at civilian subordinate staff *outside* the medical circle and their impact on the formulation of sanitary policy. It further seeks to establish where such subordinate personnel, upon whom the successful implementation of policy measures rested, figured in relation to the state.

The term 'subordinate sanitary staff' is a very broad one and needs to be explained at the outset. Countless subordinates were deployed to implement sanitary measures, from the local health officer to 'native' vaccinators and sweepers, from female inspectors to coolies and disinfectors. Before 1896, when plague appeared in India in epidemic form, the deployment of 'native' agency, though sizeable, was not as extensive as it subsequently became. From 1896, however, there was considerable international pressure on the Government of India to contain and control plague. In order to obtain early intimation of cases, prevent concealment and institute the comprehensive anti-plague measures, the government relied extensively on sanitary workers, alongside the staff of other institutions such as revenue departments, famine relief workers, policemen, railway employees and sepoys.[13] During the outbreak of plague, railway inspectors and Indian medical men were deputed to examine train passengers and catch any cases trying to escape detection. Coolies were used to carry out the evacuation and disinfection of plague-infested areas.[14] Hospital assistants and hospital servants became extremely important when epidemic diseases peaked. In Bombay in 1896, the Arthur Road Hospital had to offer significant pecuniary incentives to retain its assistants and servants when people were fleeing the city and replacements were practically impossible to find.[15]

An analysis of the role of all the various groups of subordinate staff is beyond the scope of this chapter, which concentrates on those that formed the bulk of the police force. This group was composed entirely of Indians and for the purposes of this chapter the term 'subordinate police' refers to head constables, constables and local *chaukidars*.[16] The chapter examines the various roles played by subordinate police in implementing sanitary policy at the main pilgrimage sites in the north Western Provinces but evidence is also drawn from other places in northern India to underscore the dependence of the colonial state on subordinate personnel for implementing policy and sustaining the colonial edifice more generally. It studies the difficult and fraught relationship of the police with the pilgrims and the community at large, and examines the general population's view of the police as the coercive arm of the state, embodying the oppressive features of colonial rule. The chapter also sheds light on the tension between those higher up in the colonial administration and the subordinate police. Furthermore, it analyses the manner in which subordinate personnel influenced the making of policy and draws on the events that followed the dispersal of the 1879 *Kumbh mela* and the 1892 *Mahavaruni* fair on account of cholera to study the importance of the police in dispersing crowds.[17] In so doing, it examines the position of the police in relation to the state and the general population. Finally, it shows how towards the end of the nineteenth century opposition to public health measures was also framed in communal terms by those seeking to define a clear 'Hindu identity'.

Subordinate police: the backbone of colonial administration

Before the eighteenth century, the pilgrimage industry was not as extensive as it became in the late eighteenth and nineteenth centuries; pilgrimage was a ritual of the Hindu elite, a signifier of their status and therefore not a very 'popular' practice. During the late 1700s *pandas* (Hindu priests at pilgrimage sites) had patrons, mostly old ruling dynasties and large landowners, and were economically dependent on their patrons, known as *jajmans*. Van der Veer argues that the pilgrimage industry at Ajodhia grew quite rapidly during the late eighteenth and nineteenth centuries, as patronage of elites for this site boomed.[18] This was true not just of Ajodhia but of most pilgrimage sites in north India.[19] Christopher Bayly also notes that while religious centres were established as pilgrimage sites in India before AD 1200, 'it was in a much more recent period that they took on their opulent and elaborate character as ritual complexes.' He observes that most of the bathing *ghats* (platforms or flights of steps leading to a landing on the riverbank used for bathing) and temples at major pilgrimage sites such as Benaras and Gaya were built between 1700 and 1810.[20]

With the advent of colonial rule, older systems of patronage were undermined, creating the need for *pandas* to market pilgrimage more widely and make it accessible to the general population. Socially inferior groups took to this readily, as they understood imitation of elite rituals as a means to better their status,[21] and this made pilgrimage more popular. Moreover, monetization under British control 'created a pilgrim network that was virtually without precedent'. Pilgrimage became a commercial enterprise and 'pilgrim hunters' travelled all over India marketing pilgrimage sites and inducing people to frequent them. Pilgrim tax, one of the factors that attracted the British to these places, further aided the creation of a pilgrimage economy/industry.[22] The development of infrastructure, such as roads and the railway in particular, contributed to the expansion of pilgrimage as a commercial enterprise. Bill Aitken notes that as the railways were extended, the number of pilgrims correspondingly increased, so the construction of railways was not opposed even by orthodox Hindu *pandas*; instead, 'there was a total acceptance of the railroad into the mystical paraphernalia of pilgrimage'.[23]

Thus, the change in social structure accompanied by technological developments encouraged the commercialization of pilgrimage which translated into larger gatherings at these locations. As these congregations grew, the need to monitor and supervise them also increased. Consequently the lower-level police were extremely important for the organization of Hindu pilgrimages, where the risk of epidemics breaking out was palpable as large numbers congregated at these sites. During the eighteenth and nineteenth centuries, dependence on the subordinate police increased exponentially following the increase in the number of pilgrims visiting pilgrimage sites. The *Pioneer Mail*, an Anglo-Indian paper, noted that during these religious fairs, 'the amount of work that is thus thrown upon the . . . police authorities is something enormous.'[24] For *Kumbh melas,* at which extraordinary numbers gathered, policemen from Punjab had to be deployed at the pilgrimage sites to assist the NWP police.[25] During this time, even in the non-pilgrimage context, the duties of the police force went beyond the maintenance of law and order to include the responsibilities of a body that disciplined various aspects of community life. For instance, in Bengal, the responsibilities of the police included revenue work and the serving of writs and summonses, and, in 1871, expanded to incorporate census operations.[26] This was also a time when a new sanitary order was developing in India and the police came to play an increasingly central role in its implementation. The magnitude of lower-level police and their ability to penetrate all areas of public life, not least because they spoke local languages, made them indispensable for colonial rule.

The need to employ locals familiar with the place and people to be policed was recognized early in the nineteenth century when the East India Company replaced the traditional village police with *darogas* who did not belong to the places to which they were deployed. Documenting the failure of this system, the Court of Directors ordered the reinstatement of village police, noting that

> the village police secures the aid and cooperation of the people at large in the support and furtherance of its operations, because it is organised in a mode which adapts itself to their customs. . . . The preservation of social order and tranquillity never can be effected by a few *darogas* . . . wanting in local influence and connection with the people.[27]

The advantage the 'native' police had over European officers in terms of being able to quickly understand local situations through familiarity with the language and people made them very useful for carrying out and monitoring measures on the ground, particularly the organization of large gatherings such as pilgrimages. Commenting on the way in which 'native' police staff were acquainted with their surroundings at the 1867 *mela*, the Magistrate of Saharanpur noted,

> This [familiarity with their surroundings] was of the greatest importance as with so dense a crowd, any accident would have borne its full results before a European Officer, even 50 yards distant, could possibly have come to the spot; and this circumstance alone will indicate how remarkably well the police

must have been instructed in their duties, and the care with which they carried out those instructions.[28]

Their familiarity with the community and the culture made the subordinate police ideal for serving as the eyes of the state to monitor local activities and report the germination of anti-imperial sentiment. The subordinate police provided a means by which the colonial administration could keep a finger on the pulse of political developments on the ground. This was particularly the case after the rebellion of 1857, as the colonial government became keen to establish an institutionalized police force with which to monitor social and political sentiments at the grassroots level.[29] Plans to institute a new police force 'as an agency for the defence of property' were being formulated even earlier. However, the events of 1857 gave new impetus to the creation of a police force for the security of empire, as the Mutiny underlined the danger of relying on armed military troops for internal policing.[30] Pilgrimage sites in particular came to be viewed with considerable suspicion, as meetings to plan several anti-colonial movements had been conducted at these locations.[31] This mistrust was further supported by the discovery that the *pandas* of Allahabad joined the 1857 rebellion and disseminated unrest in the city during that time.[32] The fact that the lower-level police comprised Indians only put it in a better position to observe happenings inconspicuously. To enable a close check on the proceedings of religious fairs, and to ensure general peace and security, it was common for the administration to divide up large areas for administrative purposes and institute a *thana* (police station) in each subdivision. Figure 4.1 shows how such divisions were put into practice at the 1879 fair of *Kumbh mela* at Hardwar.[33] Rora Island, where the majority of the pilgrims camped, was divided into distinctly demarcated sections which were then placed under the control of separate police stations.

The pervasive presence of 'native' police also made them ideal for detecting sickness. These policemen were relied upon to weed out the cases of infectious disease which were being concealed to avoid segregation of the sick from their relatives. Their role as 'sickness detectives' was not confined to fair sites alone. The subordinate police played an active part in the control of venereal disease all over India following the Contagious Diseases Acts by hunting down unregistered prostitutes and forcing them to undergo medical inspection. The hunt for prostitutes was 'generally confided to the police [as] police are the proper agency to employ, being already detectives and available'.[34]

One of the main duties of the police was to ensure the smooth flow of pilgrims visiting the various holy sites and preventing stampedes and bottlenecks. During the 1867 *Kumbh mela*, the first fair that was formally organized by the sanitary department, special bridges were constructed from the pilgrims' camps to the bathing *ghat*. Pilgrims were supposed to use these bridges to return to their camps after bathing. The traffic was to move in one direction only and no one was allowed to turn back. There were separate routes for going to and from the bathing *ghat*. Moreover, unlike in previous fairs, cattle and other animals were not permitted entry into the township. These traffic controls were enforced by the subordinate

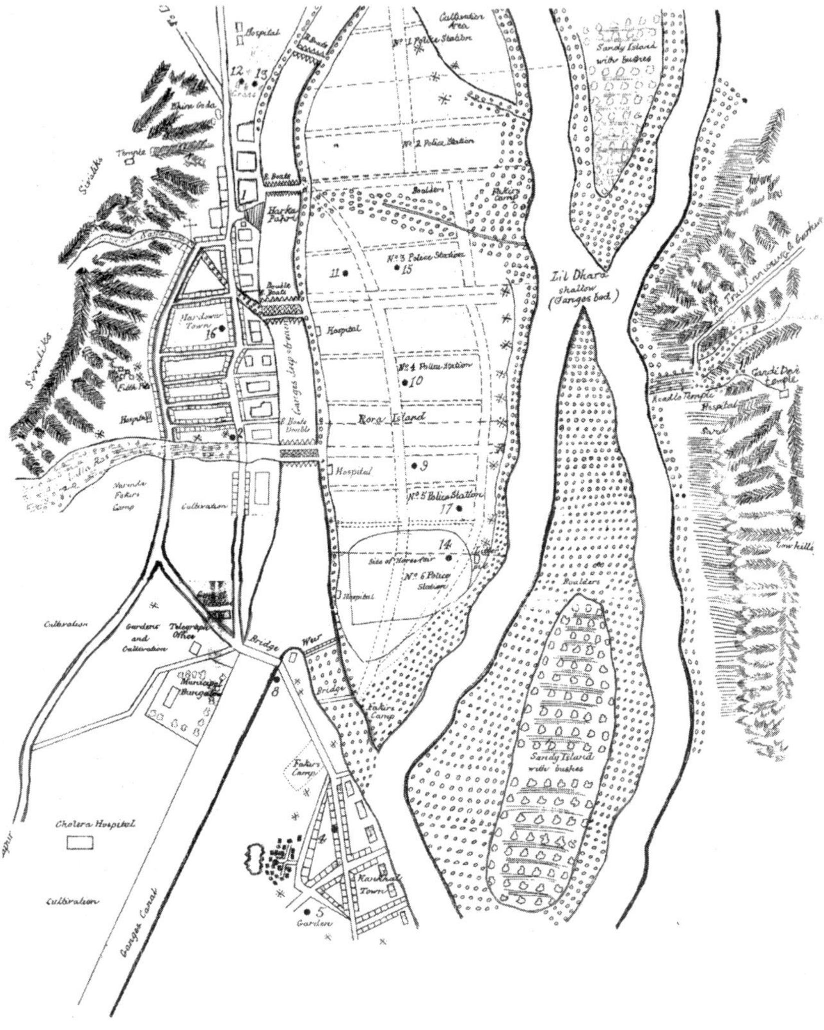

Figure 4.1 Sketch map of the site of Hardwar fair.

police posted along the various paths. While detailing the arrangements made for the Hardwar *mela* of 1879, the Sanitary Commissioner for NWP noted how pilgrims 'were marshalled in orderly lines of encampment in the neighbourhood of the town' by subordinate police.[35] He stated that for the successful management of such an assemblage where everyone converged to the bathing *ghat*, the 'one point of attraction', the continuous flow of pilgrims was crucial. This was the task the police on the ground were entrusted with. During the 1885 *Ardh Kumbh* fair,[36] a system was developed whereby policemen with flags were stationed at certain locations to signal to each other when to open and shut the *ghat* barriers in order to prevent a crowd crush/stampede.[37]

The duties of the police were not limited to enforcing traffic control. The Magistrate of Saharanpur noted that during pilgrimages, all visitors 'wherever encamped were forced to submit to the sanitary rules enforced by the police'.[38] These sanitary rules were comprehensive and included monitoring where people relieved themselves. Latrines and trenches were introduced at Hardwar during the *Kumbh mela* of 1867 but did not prove popular with the general congregation of pilgrims. The Commissioner of Meerut noted, 'I have heard from a "native" gentleman, that rather than go to public latrines, many people, women particularly, abstained from relieving themselves during the two or three days the fair lasted.'[39] What was more problematic was the way pilgrims used open spaces instead of latrines, thereby creating conditions particularly suited to an outbreak of cholera. This issue was one of considerable concern, as the maintenance of surface cleanliness was the first step in implementing sanitary policy. The difficulty of persuading people to use latrines at fairs was also a concern voiced by the Sanitary Commissioner of NWP. He noted how men preferred to go to nearby woods and relieve themselves there.[40] The subordinate police were officially appointed for conservancy duty – that is, herding people to latrines and preventing them from fouling the fair site.[41] Acknowledging the relentless support provided by the police to keep Hardwar clean, the Commissioner of Meerut recorded:

> From the first day to the last, the whole force behaved admirably. Their first duty was a most unpalatable one – the superintendence of the cleaning of places compared with which the Augean stables were pure – . . . much to their praise they made no objection.[42]

A considerable portion of the police deployed at pilgrimages was put on conservancy duty and, in 1869, this conservancy surveillance was formally included in the responsibilities of the police at pilgrimage locations in the North Western Provinces.[43] During the *Kumbh mela* of 1891 most of the subordinate police force were deployed on conservancy duty (see Table 4.1).[44]

The importance of this role of the police was also recognized by railway companies that ran special train services for pilgrims to Hardwar. With the arrival of more passengers than usual, the sanitary state of the railway stations declined rapidly. The Manager of the Oudh and Rohilkund Railway Company observed the sorry state of the Lakhsar Railway Station where pilgrims congregated during bathing fairs. Requesting a larger contingent of government railway police at this station to counter the fouling of the area, he complained, 'The natives prefer to use the open fields, if they can.'[45]

Talwar Oldenburg makes an interesting observation in the context of urban sanitation in the NWP. She notes that the number of sanitary crimes increased sharply between 1869 and 1870. This was not the result of greater vigilance against criminals, but was a consequence of the extension of crimes to include 'urinating along a roadside or creating a sanitary . . . "nuisance"'.[46] This supports the argument

Table 4.1 Duties of the subordinate police at the *Kumbh mela* of 1891 at Hardwar

	Subordinate police staff	
Duties	*Constables*	*Chaukidars*
Treasury and quarter guards	9	–
On duty at railway station	76	4
On toll *chaukis*	50	45
On conservancy duty	126	206
Nine police stations	157	112
At bridges	56	–
At camping grounds in Saharanpur District	36	66
Bathing *ghat*	40	–
Night watches	–	76
Hospital duty	9	–
Escorting prisoners	6	–
Miscellaneous duties	29	17
Detectives	37	–
Reserve	61	74
Total	692	600

Source: NWP General Proceedings January 1892, Proceeding 2, IOL P/4061.

that the police force was increasingly engaged to enforce the sanitary order and further highlights its importance. Indeed, it was intended that the police would set an example to the population at large. In 1870 the Government of NWP decided to construct latrines for the use of police at their stations in the hope that they would lead the way in encouraging new sanitary practices.[47] From this it is evident that while, at one level, the community did perceive the police force as the coercive and enforcing arm of the state, at another level its position in society was respected as it symbolized institutionalized authority. Policemen's higher social status, to which those lower down in the social hierarchy aspired, was used as a means to bring about change in the habits and manners of people.

Sanitary duty at pilgrimage sites also included the enforcement of measures to prevent overcrowding, as congestion was seen as another factor aiding the spread of diseases. Instructions were issued for the posting of a special body of police at railway stations close to fair sites in order to prevent pilgrims from congregating and squatting outside these stations.[48] During the *Kumbh mela* of 1879, the Sanitary Commissioner for NWP paid heed to the issue of pilgrims being crammed into lodging houses which residents of Hardwar rented to them. Due to the extremely high demand during fairs, the rent for one room rose to Rs300. With this kind of money to be made it was not uncommon for the lodging house owners to pack in as many people as possible. In one case, 152 people were crammed into a house intended to accommodate no more than twenty-five. The police authorities who frequented these houses reported that 'the sanitary condition of the rooms generally, from overcrowding and imperfect ventilation . . . was deplorable.'[49] The Sanitary Commissioner decided to tackle this problem head on and had subordinate police visit these establishments in order to have 'their excessive population *thinned* to reasonable limits'.[50] In 1892, the NWP Lodging Houses Act was passed which formalized a licensing fee for lodging houses and institutionalized inspections.

Hence, as the sanitary authorities took decisions to regulate more aspects of these religious fairs, the role and significance of subordinate personnel were further enhanced. For the next *Kumbh mela* of 1891, the pilgrimage site at Hardwar was divided into eight sanitary sections, each monitored by 'sanitary patrols'. The patrols were comprised of the police staff and the vaccination staff as shown in Table 4.2.[51] About 80 per cent of the staff appointed for sanitary patrolling were subordinate police. Their duties had developed to include prevention of overcrowding, ensuring surface cleanliness, reporting and preventing sanitary 'nuisances', reporting other offences, promptly removing the sick to hospitals and making sure that baggage and animals were located properly.[52]

Yet another aspect of the part police played at pilgrimage centres comes to light in years when cholera erupted at the sites and the government called off the fairs, giving orders for pilgrims to return to their homes immediately. Such measures were not welcomed by those who had travelled across the country to perform their religious rites, and the early closure of fairs and dispersal of people was not an easy task. The 1892 *Mahavaruni* fair at Hardwar is a case in point. A few days before the auspicious day of ritual bathing, the pilgrimage was called off on account of an outbreak of cholera. Immediately, orders were issued by the Sanitary Commissioner of NWP to send people back as he believed that all cholera cases were due to the conditions particular to Hardwar. The police were instructed to 'weed' out all the pilgrims from the lodging houses and clear the site. According to the Deputy Superintendent Police Officer (DSP) of Saharanpore, they managed to vacate a considerable part of the site: 'But soon after our backs were turned the Pandas (local priests) gave out that the order to quit had been cancelled; so large numbers of pilgrims returned to Hardwar and we had to go over the same ground again.'[53]

Many pilgrims offered passive resistance; they 'hid in every creek and corner of Siwalik hills, in jungles and in every possible hiding place'. Pilgrims were pushed along, 'some went down by the side street and came back to the same place by another road'. A day before the ritual bathing, 20,000 pilgrims who were about to enter Hardwar were asked to turn back but they adamantly stood their ground. About 50,000 people at Hardwar refused to obey police orders and shouted, '*Nahaenge, nahaenge*' (Will bathe, will bathe) and 'moved down the riverside getting a dip where they could'. Others squatted by the river and shouted, 'You must throw us out, otherwise we will not go'.[54] The task of the police was not an easy one. The DSP stated:

> We often had to form a line of constables behind a crowd of pilgrims who would refuse to move on and push them on. At other times some of them would squat down with their bundles and say, 'It is better to die here; we won't go home (*behtar hai marna yahin; ham nahin jate ghar*).' These had to be forced up naturally and bundles shoved on their heads and pushed on and told to go.[55]

Table 4.2 Composition of the sanitary patrols for each administrative section of the pilgrimage site at the *Kumbh mela* of 1891

	Police staff				*Vaccination Staff*				
Sanitary section	*European inspectors*	*Native inspectors*	*Sub-inspectors*	*Head constables*	*Constables*	*Chaukidars*	*Deputy super-intendents*	*Native super-intendents*	*Vaccinators*
No. 1	2	1	–	1	20	30	1	–	14
No. 2	–	1	–	–	10	16	–	1	8
No. 3	–	1	1	–	15	24	–	–	8
No. 4	–	–	–	1	10	16	–	1	8
No. 5	–	–	1	1	10	8	–	1	8
No. 6	–	1	–	1	10	16	–	1	8
No. 7	–	1	1	–	10	16	–	1	8
No. 8	–	1	1						
–	15	24	–	–	8				

Source: *Report of the NWP Sanitary Commissioner 1891* (Allahabad, 1892), p. 15A.

Without the support of the police any attempts at clearing the site would have been futile; the police were indeed the coercive arm of the colonial state and were relied upon to execute measures which incurred the displeasure of pilgrims.

Lower-level police – particularly *chaukidars* in rural areas – were recognized as 'a valuable component in police machinery . . . and the backbone of police administration'.[56] They were also agents for the collection of birth rates, death rates and statistics related to infectious diseases. In rural Punjab, the village *chaukidar* determined the cause of death and thus, as collector of data used to formulate policy, performed a noteworthy role.[57] After the emergence of plague in India in 1896, this role became even more important. Plague figures, in the first instance, were reported by *thanedars* and *chaukidars* and were then registered at the local police station, which also functioned as a repository of public health data.[58]

The subordinate police thus formed an important pillar of policy implementation. So significant was their role that, in 1909, the Sanitary Commissioner of Mysore State wrote an article stressing the need to expand the official role of the police to include more sanitary duties. He stated that to counter infectious diseases 'the agency must be ubiquitous . . . the policeman is the only ubiquitous agency'.[59]

Pilgrims and the oppressive police *walas*

While the colonial administration was heavily reliant upon subordinate staff to carry out orders on the ground, measures were not executed in a smooth top-down fashion. Significant problems and concerns arose from this dependence on police at local level. A continual concern related to the compilation of health statistics by the police and the village *chaukidar*, 'whose capability of diagnosis is not perhaps equal to his willingness'.[60] The fact that they were not trained medical personnel and were still the main recorders of mortuary statistics had a distinct impact on the quality of data collected. The Sanitary Commissioner of Oudh voiced this concern when he stated, 'the village watchmen who collect the mortuary statistics appear to have got into a bad habit of attributing many deaths to cholera for which it is not responsible.'[61] The problem was particularly acute when the symptoms of various illnesses were similar; the accuracy of the figures was consequently not reliable, particularly in rural areas. As the Sanitary Commissioner of Punjab noted, the cause of death in rural areas was determined by the 'ignorant village *chaukidar* . . . and consequently under Fevers are included almost all disease in which there is a decided rise of temperature'.[62] But there were graver problems generated by the use of these agents. The position of the subordinate police and the powers vested in them created boundless opportunities for them to extort money from people who were at their mercy. The corruption prevalent in the lower ranks of the police was consistently criticized in the vernacular press of the nineteenth century.[63] Table 4.3 shows the salaries offered to the police on duty at the *Kumbh mela* of 1892.[64] The difference between the pay of the subordinate personnel and the inspector level is marked. With these low salaries it is not inconceivable that they needed to supplement their earnings by crooked means.[65] Moreover, part of their already negligible pay was deducted monthly for provision of their uniforms.[66] This

Table 4.3 Statement showing the pay *per mensem* for regular police and *chaukidars* of Saharanpur District employed at the Hardwar *Mahavaruni* fair 1892

Inspectors	*Pay per mensem*
1st grade	Rs225
1st grade	Rs200
2nd grade	Rs150
3rd grade	Rs125
4th grade	Rs100
Sub-inspectors	*Pay per mensem*
1st grade	Rs70
2nd grade	Rs50
3rd grade	Rs30
Head constables	*Pay per mensem*
1st grade	Rs25
2nd grade	Rs20
3rd grade	Rs15
4th grade	Rs10
Constables	*Pay per mensem*
1st grade	Rs8
2nd grade	Rs7
3rd grade	Rs6
Dafadars	*Pay per mensem*
1st grade	Rs16
2nd grade	Rs14
Lance dafadars	*Pay per mensem*
	Rs11
Mounted constables	*Pay per mensem*
1st grade	Rs9
2nd grade	Rs7
Chaukidars	*Pay per mensem*
1st grade	Rs3

Source: NWP Miscellaneous Proceedings,August 1893, Proceeding 30(a), IOL P/4296.

was picked up by the vernacular press which suggested that without an increase in their salaries the level of corruption in the police force could not be checked.[67] Various papers asserted that there was a need for the workings of the police service to be reviewed and reformed as the police force came under increasing criticism.[68] The *Jubilee Paper* noted that:

> The police force was constituted for the protection of the life, property, and honour etc., of the people. But actual experience shows that the police are themselves very often the cause of the destruction of peace and comfort of the people.[69]

The use of policemen for sanitary purposes was viewed with particular scepticism by the general population. *Rahbar*, a vernacular newspaper, expressed this sentiment when it wrote,

> When cholera spreads in any village, the police generally insist on some sanitary reforms which give a world of trouble to the villagers, and which are intended more to afford the police opportunities for practising extortion than for improving public health.[70]

Complaints of police opportunism intensified towards the end of the century when plague inspections were instituted. These inspections were perceived as a means for the police to exploit the population at large, constituting their 'most lucrative source of income'.[71]

The abuse of their power was not confined to extortionate behaviour alone as the accounts of the dispersal of the 1879 and 1892 *melas* revealed. When the 1879 *Kumbh mela* was dispersed on account of cholera, the hill pilgrims, among whom the epidemic initially broke out, were herded back towards their homes. Their normal return route would have been through the Bijnour district from Chandi via Amsot, Najibabad, Nagina and Shekot, their on to Kashipur. However, the police were instructed to divert the pilgrims on to the Garhwal border to Koti Rao and from there to Kashipur so as to protect the population centres in Bijnour district (see Figure 4.2).[72] The manner in which the police forced people to leave was highly questionable and many returning pilgrims died en route. *Almora Akhbar*, one of the major newspapers of NWP, reported:

> The road from Hardwar to Almora was covered with corpses for several days. The conduct of the . . . police, towards . . . hill pilgrims was very objectionable. As soon as cholera appeared at Hardwar, they were compelled to . . . return to their homes, but they were not permitted to pass through towns and villages, and had to travel through forests, where they could get neither food nor water, and died of thirst and hunger.[73]

In a later issue the paper further condemned the behaviour of the police, noting that those on dispersal duty did not allow the pilgrims to cross the river, but

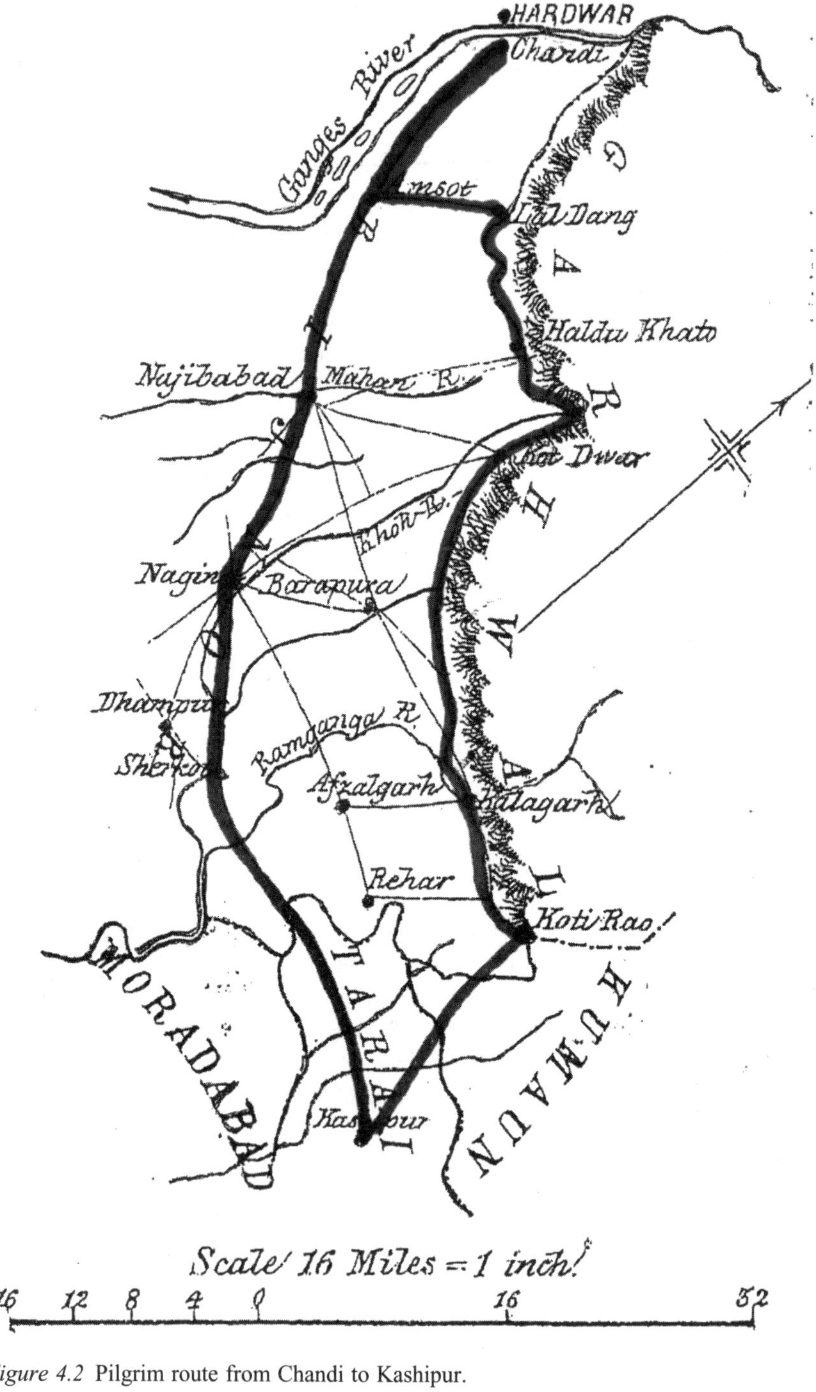

Figure 4.2 Pilgrim route from Chandi to Kashipur.

compelled all of them to remain where they were. The result was that cholera broke out among them owing to the great heat. The police beat them with sticks and even fired guns with blank cartridges to intimidate them. A stampede followed, and the pilgrims fled into unfamiliar desert areas, where many of them perished for want of food and water.[74]

But it was the dispersal of the 1892 *Mahavaruni* fair that opened the floodgates for public criticism of the police force. Local and national 'native' newspapers were awash with accounts of the brutality of police measures to clear Hardwar. The following account published in the *Subodh Sindhu* is representative of the grievances cited by pilgrims:

> The police followed them [i.e. the pilgrims] and compelled them to leave at once, making free use of sticks and setting fire to their huts. Many men put up with kicks and blows, earnestly begging the police officials to allow them to remain till the bathing day, but those hard-hearted officials were inexorable as usual. . . . It is difficult to understand the object of the police in treating people with such undue severity.[75]

Other pilgrim complaints included indecent handling of women by police officers,[76], taking of bribes, and beating a man to death when he refused to sell sweetmeats to the constables. The grievances became more complex when pilgrims asserted that most of the constables were Muslim and that they polluted the sacred bathing pool by entering it wearing their boots.[77] This allegation is an interesting one as it reflects the social dynamics of the period. Whether there was truth in it or not is insignificant; rather the very nature of the accusation is telling. Towards the end of the nineteenth century communal relations were becoming tense and fraught, especially in NWP. Hindu revivalist movements were acquiring momentum and by asserting the difference between Hindus and Muslims, internal differences were being glossed over and a 'unified' Hindu identity was being forged. In 1882 the management of the *Magh mela* at Allahabad was entrusted to a Muslim, City Inspector Saiyid Liaquat Husain. His appointment was objected to on communal grounds.[78] Nonetheless he was kept on as the managing inspector till the end of the 1885 *Magh mela* after which the Joint Magistrate in charge of the fair noted that while Husain carried out his duties very well, it would be better to assign the management of future fairs to a Hindu officer.[79] Thus, in his report of the *Magh mela* of 1886, the Commissioner of Allahabad Division observed that all police officials employed at the fair were Hindus and with this change 'a fruitful source of complaint has been removed'.[80]

During the late nineteenth century, the print media were used to fan the flames of communal tension. The editors of some vernacular papers were staunch Hindu revivalists and used their publications to harness popular emotion to back the 'Hindu' cause. The foremost example is Pandit Gopinath, editor of *Akhbar-i-Am*, a Lahore newspaper. Pandit Gopinath was extremely critical of the government's decision to break up the 1892 fair and condemned the deployment of Muslim constables for the task. He played an important role in compelling the government to hold an inquiry into the conduct of the police during the dispersal of pilgrims in 1892: he organized Hindus all over India to sign a petition laying out the grievances of the pilgrims and demanding an inquiry.[81] Once the inquiry was instituted, editors of other vernacular papers such as *Bangbasi* and *Patrika* also engaged actively in collecting evidence of Muslim constables having entered a temple wearing boots during the fair and having abused worshippers.[82] Another complaint reflecting the kind of communal sentiment being fanned was that Muslim constables not only defiled holy spots by entering holy places with their boots on but also 'discharged urine into the mouths of pilgrims'.[83] The allegation regarding the use of urine to disperse the crowds was not pitched against Muslim constables only. Jagan Nath, a resident of Kankhal, said he witnessed *sipahis* trying to turn back pilgrims who, however, kept saying, 'We will not go without bathing in the Ganges tomorrow.' According to Jagan Nath, the *sipahis* called a sweeper and asked him to fetch urine from a nearby water-closet which he was then made to sprinkle on the pilgrims. It had the desired effect and the pilgrims scattered.[84] Another, Lala Murlidhar, resident of Amritsar, said that he saw the *sipahis* asking an old man sitting by the river to leave. The old man said he could not walk and the *sipahis* summoned a sweeper and asked him to 'make water in this man's mouth'.[85]

Whether these allegations were correct or not is of no concern here. What is interesting is the way they are framed. There are two aspects to these allegations: one, that urine was used; and, two, that sweepers were deployed to discharge/sprinkle the urine on the pilgrims. The first aspect signifies a violation of the idea of physical and ritual purity. Contact with urine is perhaps the worst kind of pollution possible, and there may be no more horrifying way to defile something holy in the popular imagination of Hindus (and probably of any other religious community). Underlying the second aspect of the allegations, the fact that sweepers were asked to do this, is the notion of caste boundaries being violated. Not only was one of a lower caste sprinkling the urine, it was a sweeper, an untouchable. This doubled the humiliation and shows how underlying these allegations were extreme anger and resentment against the idea of existing social hierarchies being disturbed.

The manhandling of Hindu women by Muslim constables was an even more explosive issue and one that was forcefully voiced during the dispersal of the 1892 fair.[86] The president of the meeting of 'the Hindu community' in Lahore alleged that 'the Zenana sanctum was coldly violated' as Muslim constables caught hold of women returning from the *ghats* in 'wet clothes'.[87] Once again, establishing the truth of this allegation is not as significant as the nature of it. It was not just that female pilgrims were pushed around and sexually harassed by the police, but that 'Hindu' women were dishonoured by 'Muslim' constables, which added another layer of complexity to the allegation. While at one level the charge was against government officials misusing their authority, at another there was an expressly communal dimension to it. The issue was being framed in terms of an attack on the 'Hindu' community; women, the symbol of the honour and virtue of the community, were being disgraced by 'licentious' Muslim men. The idea of women's bodies being violated was being used to accentuate the communal divide as it provided a means to forge a unified 'Hindu' identity in opposition to the Muslim community. Charu Gupta argues that by the 1920s the image of the female body was being used as a resource to construct the strong, militant Hindu man needed to protect Hindu women, 'the man who could at once strengthen community identity and undertake a militant nationalist struggle'.[88] She notes that this was happening simultaneously with the construction of Muslim men as lustful and immoral, people from whom Hindu women's honour had to be protected in a forceful manner, thereby provoking the Hindu man to embody the aggression necessary for the preservation of community identity.[89] The events of 1892 suggest that this discourse was already developing well before the 1920s. The *Hindustani*, a vernacular paper published from Lucknow, clearly tried to rouse the passion and anger of Hindu men when the fair was dispersed, by writing:

> The *Hindustani* has received many complaints from pilgrims, but it does not like to give publicity to them, inasmuch as it thinks that men, whom thousands of years of foreign rule have rendered so helpless that they have not the courage to raise a finger to protect their women from ill-treatment, deserve every dishonour.[90]

Public health measures, such as the dispersal of the fair, were being challenged not just in terms of resistance to the state; in fact there was a clear communal agenda that is reflected in the kind of grievances voiced by the vernacular press.

Another complaint was that the police seized pilgrims and pushed them around without any regard for their social status.[91] A complaint of this nature is indicative of some pilgrims' expectations of the police, an institution that for them symbolized state power. The expectation was for all institutions of the state to respect existing social hierarchies. This is confirmed by the *Hindi Pratap*'s cynical characterization of 'the police' when in the dispersal of the 1879 fair they did not show any respect for those of higher status; the paper described 'the police' as 'an easy means of dishonouring respectable people'.[92]

An interesting parallel can be drawn here with Anand Yang's observations regarding police control in rural northern India. He points out that in rural areas the colonial state ruled at arm's length through local elites and used the pre-existing system of *chaukidars* to police the localities.[93] These *chaukidars*, who were recruited from lower castes, were used to taking orders and protecting the interests of the local elites. During the early years of the establishment of the new policing system complaints were common in the rural areas of NWP as well. A Superintendent of Police in the NWP wrote in 1865, 'The *chowkeedar* is often the creature of the *zamindars*, at whose instance he is appointed; he acts only as directed by them.'[94] In the case of rural southern India, David Arnold makes a similar observation, stating:

> The recruitment of constables from locally dominant communities (albeit from their poorer strata) gave them a bias towards the richer peasants, landlords and village heads and against the peasants and labourers of subordinate castes.

> Deference to men of wealth and power was too prevalent a social trait for the subordinate police to be immune, despite their official responsibility.[95]

Furthermore, while the colonial state attempted to control this informal police at the rural level and subordinate it directly, it never quite succeeded because 'they were never completely detached from the networks of estate and village controls.'[96] The prevalence of such a system in the rural areas meant that similar expectations were pinned on the police in the context of pilgrimage management. There were times when the community ties of the police overshadowed the call of duty. For instance, during the dispersal of the 1892 *mela*, when the allegations against the police were overwhelming, there were a few instances when some members of the subordinate force held back from fully executing orders. As noted by Dr Sykes, an officer on site:

> My opinion is that the police were not sufficiently *zabardast*. By *zabardast* I mean coercive. The impression I had was that the police subordinate sympathised with the people and was not overly anxious to carry out the orders about the dispersion. They were not very zealous. I saw with my own eyes that a policeman (constable) who was put on the hospital to prevent people from going into the town, allowed one man to go back.[97]

A similar concern was voiced by Mr S.H. Berkeley, the District Superintendent of Police, Dehra Dun, when he said that

> some Hindu *sipahis* of Sappers and Miners [who were posted at the barriers to prevent people accessing the water] took *lotas* [pitchers] about 14 or 15 from *sadhus* [ascetic priests] at the barriers, filled the *lotas* at Harkipairi and returned them full of Ganges water to the *sadhus*.[98]

Thus subordinates occasionally showed sympathy for the very people they were meant to discipline/restrain and at times this led to a subversion of the directives from their superiors.

The constabulary was recruited from the lower classes and this was often cited as one of the main reasons for the unethical behaviour of its members, complaints against whom were very common. The vernacular press time and again emphasized that 'the defects of the police administration are chiefly due to the circumstance that the force is not recruited from respectable and educated men',[99] but instead from those 'who have been shepherds, bazaar men or poor ryots [peasants]'.[100] But the level of pay offered to constables was far too low to induce those of higher social standing to join the service.[101] Several papers suggested that an increase in remuneration for constables was a prerequisite for attracting those from higher classes.[102] The Indian Police Commission of 1902–3 gave this issue considerable attention and it recommended an increase in the minimum wage of the constabulary to Rs8 per month.[103] Local governments were well aware of the need to increase the minimum wage for the lower ranks. The Government of NWP noted, 'A complete revision of pay is in fact imperatively demanded; in no other way can we secure a police force adequate to the needs of this great province.'[104] However, an increase in the remuneration of the police establishment was not a high enough priority to exact a greater portion of provincial revenue,[105] and the constabulary continued to be drawn predominantly from the most socially depressed classes.

The fact that most of the subordinate police personnel came from the lower classes did not necessarily make them sympathetic to their concerns. Rather, it often meant that others of the same social origins came to be targets of police oppression. Arnold observes that in the rural context,

> it was not uncommon for those who had risen from the peasantry to a position of power over it [such as policemen] . . . to show no solidarity with the peasants, but rather to exploit them, whether for personal gain or in the service of others.[106]

This was the case not only in rural areas, where the colonial presence was 'remote'; the constabulary in urban areas were equally inclined to exploit their official position. While Hardwar was not an urban centre on the scale of Bombay and Calcutta, it was certainly a town of great significance for the colonial state because of its connection with cholera epidemics, and one where the colonial presence/control was by no means 'remote', especially during large fairs. As argued above, even during these pilgrimages the subordinate police served their own interests by misusing their official status of authority in relation to the pilgrims through means such as extortion and bribery or even molestation. The relationship between pilgrims and the police was a strained one, where the latter were viewed as perpetrators of tyranny. This is well illustrated by the definition of city *kotwals* (urban constables) given in a local newspaper: 'descendants of Halaku, Chengis Khan, Nadir Shah, Timur'.[107] Interestingly Halaku, Chengis Khan, Nadir Shah and Timur were all foreign rulers like the British and they epitomized heartless and brutal rule in popular memory. During the plague outbreak the poorer sections of society were often noted to say that 'they do not fear the malady but they dreaded awfully the insult they are subjected to by the police while being carried off to a hospital or inspected on the railway platform'.[108]

This is perhaps why, when those of higher rank were mistreated at the 1892 fair by the police, it made news. Implicit in this grievance voiced by the pilgrims is that the mistreatment of people of lower social standing at the hands of the police was not an extraordinary occurrence but a regular one.[109] Thus the subordinate police were not innocent accomplices in the repression executed by the colonial regime, nor can they be seen as mere subalterns in relation to the superior police. They were active perpetrators of the terror that came to be associated with colonial rule. Their agency is not only visible at moments when they resisted or opposed those higher up in the chain of command; they were thinking agents who often (mis)used their official position to further their own self-interest.

Subordinate police as obstacles to governance

The relationship between those higher up in the colonial administration and the subordinate personnel responsible for implementing their policies was also problematic. While the administration was heavily reliant on the police it was also extremely suspicious of it. This stemmed partly from the discourse of 'natives' being unreliable and inherently corrupt. As Arnold put it:

> The very character of the police organisation . . . institutionalised European distrust of Indians, even when they were servants of the colonial state, and embodied the rulers' conviction that only a rigid system of supervision culminating in European superintendents could check the inherent waywardness of Indian subordinates.[110]

The police used for the purposes of ordering and managing the fairs consisted of 'native' officers who were seen as highly duplicitous, their integrity constantly questioned. As the Secretary to the Government of India stated, 'Subordinate agents . . . may be wanting in discretion, or may have interested motives to serve. Hence instructions issued from purely public motives are apt to be misconstrued.'[111]

In 1868, when the introduction of tickets for pilgrims was being considered, one of the grounds for rejecting it was that the police *walas* who would have to issue them could not be trusted. It was said that 'the ticketing system's adoption will prove a fruitful source of extortion by "native" officials.'[112] A similar reason was given by the United Provinces (UP) Pilgrim Committee early in the twentieth century for instituting a rail tax instead of a poll tax. The aim was to impose a surcharge on rail tickets as it was a more efficient way of collecting revenue than using subordinate police for a poll tax where 'opportunity for petty oppression and peculation are unrivalled'.[113] In 1870 the proposal of the police to remove cholera victims from their homes to hospitals was also rejected on the basis that:

> Any attempt to remove the sick of a large city to a Cholera Hospital must ever end in failure and more than failure: it . . . puts great powers of oppression and bribery in the hands of the 'native' Police through whom such measures are carried out.[114]

Another area where the self-serving behaviour of the police had an impact on government policy was that of land quarantine. The Government of India was reluctant to impose any kind of quarantine as those in office were greatly influenced by the sanitarian school of thought that emphasized the non-contagiousness of cholera and the success of sanitary measures *alone* in curbing its spread.[115] However, another reason for this decision was the room for oppression that such a policy would give to subordinate officials. The Viceroy appointed a special committee to consider the issue of banning people in cholera-infected districts from attending pilgrimages. The committee advised against it on the grounds that perfect quarantine was impossible and 'any arrangements short of perfection must give the police and other petty executive agency, power and opportunity to practise oppression and extortion on a vast number of people.'[116]

The pilgrim complaints detailed in the section 'Pilgrims and the offensive police *walas*' above show that the government's suspicion of the police was not entirely groundless. While the government did not heed the calls for an inquiry into the conduct of the police when the 1879 *mela* was dispersed, the 'native' press put immense pressure on the state to hold an inquiry in the aftermath of the breaking up of the *Mahavaruni* fair of 1892. The British Indian Association, an organization whose members were mainly Bengali *zamindars*, urged the government to institute a commission to look into the manner in which the fair was dispersed.[117] The representation of the British Indian Association bore 500 signatures.[118] This, coupled with Gopinath's petition signed by Hindus from all over north India, finally led the administration to hold a special inquiry into the matter. The reasons for holding this inquiry were twofold: first, as the pilgrims identified the police as an arm of the state, the state felt the need to appear to reprimand and to reform it in order to pacify any potential source of rebellion; second, by directing the focus onto the local police, which was entirely Indian, the sanitary administration absolved itself of blame for a flawed policy.

The inquiry concluded that the force used by the police was reasonable and that many of the complaints were untrue and deliberately constructed to stoke anti-colonial sentiment. The police was cleared of all charges, including beating a man to death, trampling on funeral cakes, kicking an idol, closing temples, killing fish in the sacred pool and paying no regard to social status or gender while dispersing the gathering. The charge of police taking bribes was considered 'not proven'.[119]

While the findings of the Commission appear to show the state's solidarity with the police and its support of its actions, this would be too literal an interpretation. As pilgrims viewed the police as very much part of the colonial state, accepting a weakness in the institution of policing would have been to acknowledge a flaw in the state itself. The authorization of an inquiry was sufficient to establish distance from the subordinate police and to appear to be fair; a further admission of the failings of state policy was perhaps unnecessary. Furthermore, as noted in the *Pioneer Mail*, the report prepared by the Commission was 'rather diffuse' for

> the Commission was practically trying the Commissioner of Meerut and the Magistrate of Saharunpur, two officers of nearly the highest rank in the Provincial service, and no one can have been more conscious than the members of the Commission of the unpleasant responsibility imposed on them of reporting on the conduct of officers senior in rank to themselves.[120]

Thus the very structure and composition of the Commission ensured that the government would be cleared of the charges.

But the events of 1892 most certainly had a strong and lasting impact on the way the police were used in future epidemic outbreaks such as that of plague at the end of the century. Admittedly, the role of subordinate personnel became quite extensive as infected places had to be evacuated and disinfected, and rail travellers detained and examined. Yet, even when the contagious nature of plague was evident and certain provinces requested the Government of India to impose land quarantine on the infected Bombay Presidency to protect the rest of the country, the Government of India declined on the grounds that any such policy would create opportunities for the subordinate police to exploit people.[121] In 1898, the regulation regarding police duties was revised. Referring to and explaining this revision Robert Nathan noted:

> It has not been thought desirable to give the police any power of making domiciliary visits, or of their own motion removing the sick to hospitals, or interfering with them in any way; but when . . . the sanitary or executive authorities in a municipality of cantonment decide on segregation or removal to a public or a private hospital, then the police may be called on to assist.[122]

Time and time again, the government took every opportunity to stress that the flaws in the system of policing were not due to any failing on the part of policy makers and those higher up, but that 'the shortcomings of the Police are in the main incidental to the employment of an indigenous agency.'[123] When the Indian Police Commission of 1902–3 submitted its report underscoring the weaknesses and deficiencies of the police force, the Governor-General felt that publishing the report would not tarnish the image of the colonial state and could be published 'without anxiety' as 'the agency which is exposed and censured is in the main an indigenous agency'. He went on to say that in fact the report would paint the colonial state in a better light for 'the picture itself brings out the difficulty of our task in India, arising out of the nature of the instruments which we are called upon to employ.'[124] Again, in 1905, the Government of India stressed that the corruption in the indigenous agency of the police had social and cultural roots as 'its traditions are "native". . . . The giving and taking of money, whether mere gratuities or something more serious, is still traditional among the Indian people, and quite as much among the givers as among the takers.'[125] The inadequacy of the police system was explained in racial terms; an active effort was made by the government to establish and maintain a distance from the Indian element of the police service whose indigeneity was blamed for the inefficiency and corruption in the policing system.[126]

Conclusion

This chapter has argued that though the resistance offered by pilgrims may account for the failure of some of the measures designed by the state for pilgrimage sites, the subordinate police played a very active role in determining the success of colonial sanitary policy. However, the local police used their official position as the coercive arm of the state to serve their own economic and community-oriented interests.

This, then, brings to the fore the second issue this chapter has aimed to highlight: that of how to categorize a group such as the police in the colonial context. While it is an arm of the state and is perceived as the manifestation of the state by the people, a closer analysis suggests that the lower levels of the police were not entirely subordinated to the concerns of the government. The issue of how the police was viewed is complex. The pilgrims distanced themselves from the police because of their attempts at extortion and because they saw the police as a branch of the colonial state. The colonial state, too, had a difficult relationship with the ground-level police staff: the success of all sanitary measures was contingent upon this group who were simultaneously perceived as corrupt and degenerate by colonial officials. By taking bribes and indulging in similar extortionate behaviour, the police *walas* were not only subverting the agenda of the sanitary administration but were using their official position to serve their own economic and other interests. The question, then, is: where do the police figure in relation to the state and the community? The allegiances of the subordinate police appear to have shifted according to their own interests and they seem to occupy an ambivalent position in relation to the pilgrims and the state. They were not just tools in the hands of the colonial regime, merely executing orders from above; nor can they be seen as 'subalterns' dominated by their superiors, for they were agents actively exploiting those at their mercy to their own advantage.

And, finally, it must be noted that while government policy regarding sanitation was a function of various factors such as the Government of India's relation to Britain, the financial cost of sanitation projects, and the constant fear of indigenous resistance and rebellion, the state's policy regarding pilgrimage management was also shaped by the role of the subordinate police. The support of the police was integral to the success of public health campaigns to control epidemics. As stated earlier in the chapter, there were times when the sanitary administration held back from introducing pilgrimage tickets for fear that it would give far too much power to an already duplicitous police. There were also repercussions for the manner in which local police were recruited for pilgrimage duty. In other words, the state's perception of the nature of the subordinate staff, which was to a great degree based on their behaviour/attitudes, figured significantly in the making of sanitary policy. Subordinate Indian personnel were agents in their own right and their actions impacted the formulation of policy.

By analysing the position and function of the subordinate police, this chapter has argued that the colonizer/colonized binary is often inadequate to understand the operation of public health systems in British India and it is only by studying the role of intermediaries such as the subordinate police that a more nuanced understanding of colonial sanitary policy can be achieved. Such an approach enables a vertical disaggregation of the colonial state and reveals its 'fractured' nature.[127]

Acknowledgements

I would like to thank the Wellcome Trust and the University of Oxford whose support made this research possible. I am also grateful to the editors of this book for their valuable insights and comments.

Notes

1 See for instance David Arnold, *Colonizing the Body: State Medicine and Epidemic Disease in Nineteenth-Century India*, Berkeley: University of California Press, 1993, 141–4; 211–18; 223–32.

2 Mark Harrison, *Public Health in British India: Anglo-Indian Preventive Medicine 1859–1914*, Cambridge: Cambridge University Press, 1994, 117–38.

3 The term 'native' is used to refer to the Indian component of governmental departments. The term 'native' newspapers refers to newspapers published in the vernacular.

4 See North Western Provinces (hereafter NWP) General Proceedings, August 1868, Proceedings 130–137, India Office Library (hereafter IOL), P/438/32; NWP General Proceedings, May 1890, Proceeding 9, IOL P/3597.

5 J.C. Hume, 'Rival Traditions: Western Medicine and *Yunani-Tibb* in the Punjab, 1849–1889', *Bulletin of the History of Medicine*, 51: 2: 1977, 219.

6 The Superintendent General of Vaccination in the NWP noted, 'Several *Hukeems*, etc., have been taught and familiarised with the art of vaccination, and through them doubtless a knowledge of vaccination will have been spread to others, reconciling the apathetic and prejudiced to its adoption' (NWP General Proceedings, August 1869, Proceeding 47, IOL P/484/34).

7 NWP Sanitary Proceedings, December 1897, Proceeding 82, IOL P/5126.

8 A good example of these professional rivalries is Harrison's study of the difference of opinion within the sanitary administration as to how cholera was caused: Harrison, *Public Health*, 102–4.

9 GOI Sanitary Proceedings, August 1881, Proceeding 24, IOL P/1664.

10 Sanjoy Bhattacharya, Mark Harrison and Michael Worboys, *Fractured States: Smallpox, Public Health and Vaccination Policy in British India, 1800–1947*, New Delhi: Orient Longman, 2005.

11 James H. Mills, *Madness, Cannabis and Colonialism: The 'Native-Only' Lunatic Asylums of British India, 1857–1900*, London: Macmillan Press, 2000, 149–63.

12 Maryinez Lyons, 'The Power to Heal: African Auxiliaries in Colonial Belgian Congo and Uganda', in Dagmar Engels and Shula Marks eds *Contesting Colonial Hegemony: State and Society in Africa and India*, London: German Historical Institute, 1994, 202–23.

13 GOI Sanitary Proceedings February 1898, Proceeding 429, IOL P/5421.

14 Evidence given by Lt.-Col. Wilkins, Special Medical Officer in Bombay, *Indian Plague Commission* Vol. 1, London: Eyre and Spottiswoode, 1900.

15 P.C.H. Snow, *Report on the Outbreak of Bubonic Plague in Bombay 1896–1897*, Bombay: Times of India Steam Press, 1897.

16 This understanding of 'subordinate police' is in line with Arnold's definition of the term. See David Arnold, *Police Power and Colonial Rule, Madras 1859–1947*, Oxford: Oxford University Press, 1986, 36.

17 The Kumbh mela is a pilgrimage fair held every twelve years at certain sites. The position of Jupiter determinines the exact time of the *mela*. The *mela* is held in Hardwar when jupiter is in Aquarius, at Allahabad when Jupiter is in Taurus, and at Ujjain and Nasik when Jupiter is in Leo. James Lochtefeld, 'Construction of the Kumbh *mela*', *South Asian Popular Culture*, 2: 2: October 2004, 117. The *Mahavaruni mela* is another large pilgrimage fair which is held at various sites at different intervals.

18 Peter van der Veer, *Gods on Earth: The Management of Religious Experience and Identity in a North Indian Pilgrimage Centre*, London: Athlone Press, 1988.

19 Katherine Prior, 'The British Administration of Hinduism in North India, 1780–1900', University of Cambridge Ph.D. thesis, 1990, 15, 80–7.

20 Christopher Bayly, 'From Ritual to Ceremony: Death Ritual and Society in North India since 1600', in Joachim Whaley ed. *Mirrors of Mortality: Studies in the Social History of Death*, London: Europa, 1981, 162.

21 Van der Veer, *Gods on Earth*, 213. Imitation of the rituals of higher castes was the most common way for lower-caste groups to achieve upward social mobility in the caste hierarchy. Bayly suggests that this process, known as sanskritization, was made possible in the eighteenth and nineteenth centuries by the socio-economic changes taking place in that period: Bayly, 'From Ritual to Ceremony', 162–7.

22 Biswamoy Pati, ' "Ordering" "Disorder" in a Holy City: Colonial Health Interventions in Puri during the Nineteenth Century', in Biswamoy Pati and Mark Harrison eds *Health, Medicine and Empire*, Hyderabad: Orient Longman, 2001, 272–3.

23 Bill Aitken, *Exploring Indian Railways*, New Delhi: Oxford University Press, 1994, 14, 69. For more on this issue see Ian Kerr, 'Reworking a Popular Religious Practice: The Effects of Railways on Pilgrimage in 19th and 20th Century South Asia', in Ian Kerr ed. *Railways in Modern India*, New Delhi: Oxford University Press, 2001, 304–27.

24 'The Hurdwar Fair', *Pioneer Mail*, 19 April 1879.

25 NWP General Proceedings, August 1867, Proceeding 146, IOL P/438/30; NWP Misc(Gen) Proceedings, May 1893, Proceeding 2, IOL P/4296.

26 A. Gupta, *The Police in British India, 1861–1947*, Delhi: Concept, 1979, 64.

27 As noted in *Report of the Indian Police Commission 1902–03*, Simla: Government of India, 1903, 7, IOL L/PJ/6/654/2756. The benefit of employing constables belonging to the districts they worked in was also emphasized by the Indian Police Commission of 1902–3. It stated that while a few particular situations demanded that constables from other districts were more suitable, on the whole 'it is an advantage to have home constables with some local knowledge and more or less under the influence of local opinion' (*Report of the Indian Police Commission*, 38).

28 NWP General Proceedings, August 1867, Proceeding 126, IOL P/438/30.

29 C.A. Bayly, *Empire and Information: Intelligence Gathering and Social Communication in India, 1780–1870*, Cambridge: Cambridge University Press, 1996, 333–4. A couple of decades later, in the 1880s, when anti-cow-killing agitations were rife and communal tensions were on the rise, the Government of India instituted a special intelligence agency within the police department to collect information on and monitor closely political and social movements that were brewing: Arnold, *Police Power*, 186–91. See also Gupta, *The Police in British India*, 77–8.

30 Arnold, *Police Power*, 18. In 1860 the first Indian Police Commission was set up to reorganize and make more uniform the rules and regulations applicable to police in India. For more on the setting up and development of the colonial policing system, see Gupta, *Police in British India*.

31 The *Sonepur mela* in Bihar was the site where plans for the rebellion there were hatched. The fair was also where Hindu and Muslim notables met to plan an anti-imperial movement in 1845: Anand Yang, *The Limited Raj: Agrarian Relations in Colonial India, Saran District, 1793–1920*, Oxford: Oxford University Press, 1989, 18.

32 Kama Maclean, 'Making the Colonial State Work for You: The Modern Beginnings of the Ancient Kumbh Mela in Allahabad', *The Journal of Asian Studies*, 62: 3: 2003, 882–3.

33 *Report of the NWP Sanitary Commissioner 1878*, Allahabad: Government Press, 1879.

34 GOI Sanitary Proceedings, February 1870, Proceeding 17, IOL P/434/45.

35 *Report of the NWP Sanitary Commissioner 1878*, Allahabad: Government Press, 1879.

36 The *Ardh Kumbh mela* is the half-*Kumbh mela* which takes place six years after the *Kumbh mela*. *Ardh* literally means half.

37 'Hurdwar Fair', *Pioneer Mail*, 6 May 1885.

38 *Report on the Cholera Epidemic of 1867 in Northern India*, Calcutta: Office of Superintendent of Government Print, 1868.

39 Quoted in Prior, 'The British Administration of Hinduism', 187.

40 *Report on the Sanitary Arrangements at the Gurhmooktessur Fair of 1868*, Allahabad: Government Press, 1869.

41 NWP General Proceedings, August 1867, Proceeding 127, IOL P/438/30.

42 NWP General Proceedings, August 1867, Proceedings 122–123, IOL P/438/30.
43 Rules to be Observed in the Management of Important Fairs in the NWP, 1869.
44 NWP General Proceedings, January 1892, Proceeding 2, IOL P/4061.
45 GOI Sanitary Proceedings, February 1895, Proceeding 83, IOL P/4753.
46 Veena Talwar Oldenburg, *The Making of Colonial Lucknow, 1856–1877*, Princeton: Princeton University Press, 1984, 71–2.
47 GOI Sanitary Proceedings, February 1870, Proceeding 17, IOL P/434/45.
48 NWP General Proceedings, June 1876, Proceeding 5, IOL P/837.
49 *Report of the NWP Sanitary Commissioner 1878*, Allahabad: Government Press, 1879, 46.
50 *Report of the NWP Sanitary Commissioner 1878*, Allahabad: Government Press, 1879, 46; emphasis added.
51 *Report of the NWP Sanitary Commissioner 1891*, Allahabad: Government Press, 1892, 15A.
52 *Report of the NWP Sanitary Commissioner 1891*, Allahabad: Government Press, 1892. See also *Report of the Pilgrim Committee United Provinces, 1913*, Simla: Government of India, 1916.
53 NWP General Proceedings, December 1892, Proceeding 10, IOL P/4061.
54 NWP General Proceedings, March 1893, Proceeding 77, IOL P/4294.
55 NWP General Proceedings, March 1893, Proceeding 77, IOL P/4294.
56 *UP Police Administration Report 1914*, Allahabad: Government Press, 1915.
57 GOI Sanitary Proceedings, June 1891, Proceeding 103, IOL P/3885.
58 GOI Sanitary Proceedings, October 1905, Proceeding 280 and 281, IOL P/7059.
59 J. Smyth, 'The Policeman as a Sanitarian', *Transactions of the Bombay Medical Congress*, 1909, 472.
60 'Health of the United Provinces', *Pioneer Mail*, 3 November 1892.
61 GOI Sanitary Proceedings, February 1870, Proceeding 17, IOL P/434/45.
62 GOI Sanitary Proceedings, June 1891, Proceeding 103, IOL P/3885.
63 *Rahbar-i-Hind*, 27 October 1879 in *Selections from Vernacular Newspapers in the Punjab, NWP, Oudh and Central India* (hereafter SVN) 1879, IOL L/R/5/56; *Nasim-i-Agra*, 7 May 1893, in SVN 1893, IOL L/R/5/70; *Hindustani*, 11 March 1896, in SVN 1896, IOL L/R/5/80; *Oudh Samachar*, 21 January 1903 in SVN 1903, IOL L/R/5/80.
64 NWP Miscellaneous Proceedings, August 1893, Proceeding 30(a), IOL P/4296.
65 Prior to 1894 there was a tradition of awarding the police force deployed at *mela* sites rewards if their performance was considered worthy. However, while reviewing the expenses of the *Magh mela* of 1893 the Secretary of the NWP noted that the police costs were hefty and found the policy of such rewards 'doubtful'. Within three months he circumscribed considerably the amount to be offered as rewards to police deployed at *melas*, thereby further reducing the earnings of the subordinate police: NWP Miscellaneous Proceedings, May 1893, Proceeding 3 and August 1893, Proceeding 31, IOL P/4296.
66 *Dabir-i-Hind*, 8 November 1879, in SVN 1879, IOL L/R/5/56; *Police News*, 14 January 1896, in SVN 1896, IOL L/R/5/73. The Police Commission of 1902–3 also condemned deductions for uniform from the salary of policemen and urged the government to discontinue them: *Report of the Indian Police Commission*, 40.
67 *Police News*, 24 January 1896, in SVN 1896, IOL L/R/5/73. Some others disagreed and thought that nothing could change the corrupt practices of the police. For example, *Fitnah*, a newspaper from Gorakhpur, stated that an increase in salaries would only lead to more corruption as 'it is as impossible to reform the police as to change the spots of a leopard' (1 June 1892, in SVN 1892, IOL L/R/5/69); *Hindustan* wrote, 'Nothing could be more absurd than to imagine that an increase of one or two rupees in pay will induce the police to forgo their opportunities for amassing wealth quickly, or that this trifling consideration will turn a corrupt policeman into and honest and conscientious

man' (17, 19, 20 and 21 June 1890, in SVN 1890, IOL L/R/5/67). This issue also came up for review during the inquiry of the Indian Police Commission 1902–3 into the state and efficiency of the police force. It was noted that the paltry pay of the constables was one of the factors contributing to their extortionate behaviour. The Commission recommended an increase in their pay, arguing,

> An increase in pay will not turn a dishonest man into an honest official; but where pay is so low . . . its increase will at least remove one very strong temptation for corruption. It is urgently necessary to remove any excuse for dishonesty which Government should never allow to exist, by giving to the constable a living wage and reasonable means of supporting himself and family without resort to dishonest practices.
>
> (*Report of the Indian Police Commission*, 14)

68 *Oudh Akhbar*, 24 June 1891, in SVN 1891, IOL L/R/5/68.
69 *Jubilee Paper*, 16 October 1891, in SVN 1891, IOL L/R/5/68.
70 *Rahbar*, 1 July 1892, in SVN 1892, IOL L/R/69.
71 'The Native View of Plague Regulations', *Pioneer Mail*, 27 April 1900.
72 NWP Sanitary Proceedings, September 1879, Proceeding 6, dated 6 September 1879, IOL P/1280.
73 *Almora Akhbar*, 1 May 1879, in SVN 1879, IOL L/R/5/56.
74 *Almora Akhbar*, 1 June 1879, in SVN 1879, IOL L/R/5/56.
75 *Subodh Sindhu*, 19 April 1892, in SVN 1892, IOL L/R/5/69. See also *Rahbar*, 17 May 1892, *Hindustani*, 4 April 1892 and 18 May 1892, *Bharat Jiwan*, 23 May 1892, *Hindustan*, 14 April 1892, in SVN 1892, IOL L/R/5/69.
76 The manhandling of women by policemen under the pretext of carrying out public health measures was a recurrent theme. The passing of the Epidemic Disease Act in 1897 created considerable panic within both Hindu and Muslim communities in the United Provinces. In 'The Epidemic Disease Act', the *Pioneer Mail* of 25 March 1897 noted:

> Instances of . . . officials of the police or the Sanitary Departments forcing themselves into *zenanas* are . . . being freely mentioned and commented upon in native circles. . . . The *purdah* system is very rigid in these parts and the authorities cannot keep too strict an eye on their subordinates or the police unnecessarily forcing themselves into *zenanas* or removing people therefrom.

77 NWP General Proceedings, March 1893, Proceeding 59, IOL P/4296. Such allegations became quite frequent in the 1890s as communal tensions worsened. There were complaints in the Punjab local press that during the Muslim festival of Id at Rohtak, Hindus were employed as special constables and this interfered with the Muslim tradition of cow slaughter: 'Festival at Rohtak: Alleged Employment of Hindus as Special Constables', 1890, IOL L/PJ/6/291 File 2238.
78 NWP General Proceedings, October 1882, Proceeding 67, IOL P/1812.
79 NWP Misc(Gen) Proceedings, July 1885, Proceeding 8, IOL P/2450.
80 NWP Misc(Gen) Proceedings, July 1886, Proceeding 11, IOL P/2677.
81 NWP General Proceedings, March 1893, Proceedings 30–31, IOL P/4294. Pandit Gopinath was a perpetual thorn in the side of the government and used his influence not only to heighten communal tensions but also to agitate against the state. In October 1897 when plague broke out at Kankhal (a town neighbouring Hardwar) and the Government of India prohibited all railway bookings to stations on the Hardwar line, Pandit Gopinath agitated again and portrayed this measure as an assault on Hinduism. He wrote a letter to the Lieutenant-General of NWP condemning this measure and claiming to be voicing general Hindu sentiment, thereby causing considerable alarm to the administration: NWP Sanitary Proceedings, December 1897, Proceedings 134–142, IOL P/5126.

82 NWP General Proceedings, March 1893, Proceeding 39, IOL P/4294.
83 *Vyapar Hitaishi*, 23 September 1892, in SVN 1892, IOL L/R/5/69.
84 NWP General Proceedings, March 1893, Proceeding 72, IOL P/4294.
85 NWP General Proceedings, March 1893, Proceeding 76, IOL P/4294.
86 NWP General Proceedings, March 1893, Proceeding 59, IOL P/4296; *Bharat Jiwan*, 23 May 1892, in SVN 1892, IOL L/R/5/69.
87 NWP General Proceedings, March 1893, Proceeding 56, IOL P/4296.
88 Charu Gupta, *Sexuality, Obscenity, Community: Women, Muslims, and the Hindu Public in Colonial India*, New Delhi: Permanent Black, 2001, 222–3.
89 Gupta, *Sexuality*, 243–59.
90 *Hindustani*, 18 May 1892, in SVN 1892, IOL L/R/5/69.
91 *Bharat Jiwan*, 23 May 1893, in SVN 1881, IOL L/R/5/70.
92 *Hindi Pratap*, 1 June 1879, in SVN 1879, IOL L/R/5/56.
93 Yang, *The Limited Raj*, 103–10.
94 Captain Dennehy, Superintendent of Police in Humeerpore District, *NWP Police Administration Report 1865*, Allahabad: Government Press, 1866.
95 Arnold, *Police Power*, 64.
96 Yang, *The Limited Raj*, 110. Arnold's research on colonial police in southern India corroborates this and he states, 'The colonial police never served exclusively British interests. Officially or illicitly they also acted in defence of the interests of the Indian propertied classes.' At other times their behaviour was influenced significantly by their community loyalties: Arnold, *Police Power*, 4, 61–3.
97 NWP General Proceedings, March 1893, Proceeding 76, IOL P/4294.
98 NWP General Proceedings, March 1893, Proceeding 76, IOL P/4294.
99 *Tohfa-i-Hind*, 20 June 1890, in SVN 1890, IOL L/R/5/67. See also *Rahbar*, 8 and January 1891 January 1891, in SVN 1891, IOL L/R/5/68.
100 'The Indian Policeman and his Methods', *Pioneer Mail*, 7 January 1898.
101 'The Indian Policeman and his Methods', *Pioneer Mail*, 7 January 1898.
102 *Hindustani*, 15 June 1890, *Azad*, 20 June 1890, in SVN 1890, IOL L/R/5/67.
103 *Report of the Indian Police Commission.*
104 Government Resolution published with the *UP Police Administration Report* 1915, Allahabad: Government Press, 1916.
105 Government Resolution published with the *UP Police Administration Report* 1915.
106 Arnold, *Police Power*, 65.
107 *Hindi Pratap*, 1 June 1879, in SVN 1879, IOL L/R/5/56.
108 'The Native View of Plague Regulations', *Pioneer Mail*, 27 April 1900.
109 This discriminatory attitude of the police has continued well into post-independence Indian society. Recounting the attitude of the police towards pilgrims on a pilgrimage to Orchacha observed on a trip during the 1990s, Mark Tully quotes a senior Indian civil servant who said, 'Our police are only for the poor. They don't touch the rich and the influential' (*India in Slow Motion*, London: Penguin, 2003, xiii).
110 Arnold, *Police Power*, 29.
111 GOI Sanitary Proceedings, August 1881, Proceeding 24, IOL P/1664.
112 *Abstract of Proceedings of the Sanitary Commissioner with the Government of India for 1868*, Calcutta, 1868.
113 *Report of the Pilgrim Committee.*
114 NWP General Proceedings, December 1870, IOL P/438/35.
115 This theory was also a counter argument against the idea of maritime quarantine, which, had it been imposed, would have impacted Britain's position as the leader of global trade. For debates regarding theories of cholera causation and prevention within the sanitary administration of India see Harrison, *Public Health*, 99–111.
116 GOI Sanitary Proceedings, June 1881, Proceeding 49, IOL P/1664.
117 NWP General Proceedings, March 1893, Proceedings 10–14, IOL P/4294.

118 NWP General Proceedings, March 1893, Proceeding 15, IOL P/4294.

119 NWP General Proceedings, March 1893, Proceeding 79, IOL P/4294. *Pioneer*, an English language paper, had predicted that the inquiry would not result in the authorities accepting any blame. Several vernacular papers commented that the inquiry was a farce as the result was a foregone conclusion (*Colonel*, 16 August 1892; *Rahbar*, 9 August 1892). *Hindustani* noted,

> The local officials against whom the complaints were directed supplied both the investigating Magistrates and the witnesses for the defence among themselves: thus the accused were made judges in their own case and allowed to sing their own praises in the official Gazette.
>
> (14 December 1892, IOL L/R/5/69)

120 'The Hardwar Inquiry and its Moral', *Pioneer Mail*, 8 December 1892.

121 GOI Sanitary Proceedings, May 1897, Proceeding 44, IOL, P/5189.

122 R. Nathan, *Plague in India 1896, 1897*, Simla: Government Central Printing Office, 1898.

123 Confidential letter from Secretary of State to the Governor General, 4 March 1904. Papers Relating to the Report of the Indian Police Commission 1902–1903, IOL L/PJ/6/654/2756.

124 Confidential letter from Home Department to the Secretary of State, 19 November 1903. However, the Secretary of State opposed the publication. He realized that withholding the report would lead to attacks on the government by the press but considered this 'a matter of small moment' when compared with the effect the publication would have on the morale of the police; the fact that the government was not in a position to increase salaries by the amount proposed by the Commission and that the report highlighted very prominently the defects of the police system and as yet the government did not have any 'reasonably definite statement of the remedies' (Confidential letter from Sec. of State to the Gov. General, 4 March 1904. Papers Relating to the Report of the Indian Police Commission).

125 Quoted in Arnold, *Police Power*, 65.

126 An interesting parallel can be drawn with a report done by the Metropolitan Police in June 2006. The *Guardian* noted that this secret report was highly controversial as it concluded that Asian officers were more likely to be corrupt because of their cultural backgrounds. It states, 'Asian officers and in particular Pakistani Muslim officers are under great pressure from the family, extended family . . . and their community against that of their white colleagues to engage in activity that might lead to misconduct or criminality' (Sandra Laville and Hugh Muir, 'Secret Report Brands Muslim Police Corrupt', *Guardian*, 10 June 2006). The racial/cultural explanation is eerily similar to the one used during the colonial period.

127 I have borrowed this term from Bhattacharya *et al.*, *Fractured States*.

5 Plague, quarantine and empire

British–Indian sanitary strategies in Central Asia, 1897–1907

Sanchari Dutta

In February 1897, the Indian Foreign Department received intelligence concerning the dispatch of a Russian medical officer to Kashgar. The report further elaborated that the travel restrictions imposed on the Indo-Chinese Turkestan road were designed to safeguard Turkestan and mainland Russia against the plague epidemic raging in India.[1] The regulatory sanctions against Kashmir introduced several important innovations, including the deployment of Cossacks at frontier outposts and attempts to sever existing lines of trade and communication between British India and its neighbours. It is instructive, too, to note that these emerged as the distinctive features of sanitary regulation on the Perso-Afghan frontier and in southern Persia: these areas were commonly held to lie at the heart of the 'Great Game' or Anglo-Russian tensions in Central Asia.[2]

Russia's insistence on establishing a sanitary cordon on the Kashmir frontier appeared dubious to Indian authorities, especially as in February the disease was largely confined to the city of Bombay and had barely taken hold outside the province. Further, the traffic restrictions imposed around the cordon were contrary to the rationale of quarantine as they prevented the Kashgar traffic from crossing over into Kashmir; the restrictions were successful, however, in diverting Kashgar merchants to the markets in Turkestan.[3] A Foreign Department official thus accurately identified the commercial motive of the Russian cordon: 'The opportunity to give a crushing blow to our ever increasing Ladak–Chinese trade', E.H.S. Clark observed, 'had proved too good to be lost'.[4] While Russia's sanitary sanctions against India appeared to be motivated by the desire to divert the Kashgar commerce away from Kashmir into Samarkand, the long-standing Anglo-Russian tensions over Kashmir also contributed towards the general feeling of mistrust.[5] In effect, however, the skirmish over the Ladakh–Yarkand trade was but a microcosm of the larger sanitary conflict over Central Asia that initially involved Russia and British India, but widened with the involvement of other parties with a strategic interest in the region.

The Indian Government's failure to curb the epidemic dimensions of the 1890s plague in the context of the threat posed to Europe was the focal point of deliberation at various international forums.[6] While this offers a starting point into the political implications of the plague pandemic, the magnitude of its international dimensions are yet to be appreciated. Mark Harrison's study of the implications of epidemic

Figure 5.1 British India, the Levant and Central Asia.

cholera and plague on the Haj pilgrimage and on colonial trade is thus important in establishing the connections between sanitary regulation and empire. This connection was, as Harrison demonstrates, revealed and reinforced by the negotiations at the international sanitary conferences at Constantinople and Venice.[7] The purpose of this chapter is rather different from that of Harrison's study, though our concerns overlap at several points. While exploring the interaction between international politics and public health initiatives, this chapter is specifically concerned with the emergence of bubonic plague as a critical factor in the Anglo-Russian competition for influence and control over Central Asia. In fact, it appears that the inherently political nature of international quarantine is consistent with pre-existing public health policies in the region: for instance, until 1897 sanitary cordons were commonly enforced in Baghdad to exclude Shia Muslims from entry into the city.[8]

The relationship between medicine, disease and empire is now an established area of enquiry;[9] yet the implications of disease for diplomacy and regulatory practices have been overlooked until recently.[10] While historians have privileged the role of public memory, social customs and prejudices, fear and panic to explain societal responses to epidemic outbreaks, there is less agreement over the relation between sanitary regulation and politics.[11] Erwin Ackerknecht first established the connection between a nation's political system and its sanitary regulatory policy, positing a binary relation – quarantinist-interventionist and liberal-sanitarian – to account for the prophylactic divergences between nations. In other words, Britain's sanitarian approach proceeded from its liberal tradition that enabled mercantile groups who desired the free passage of maritime traffic and sanitary reformers to effectively lobby against quarantine. Autocratic nations such as Germany and Austria, on the other hand, privileged national interest over the individual to enforce draconian land and maritime quarantines.[12] More recently, Peter Baldwin has fashioned a multi-causal explanation based upon 'geoepidemiological' considerations, to explain and correlate the categories of scientific explanation, regulation and politics. The 'geoepidemiological' approach undermines the importance of political traditions (and thereby, politics) to favour location – geographical, topological and chronological – as the primary variable to dictate prophylactic choices of different European nations.[13] While Baldwin points to the problems of deploying wider categories of 'liberal' and 'despotic', his own emphasis on location falls short of explaining short-term changes in the quarantinist positions of nations. Equally, to disaggregate geography from politics as required by the 'geoepidemiological' approach is neither possible nor desirable in the context of empire, where competing imperial ambitions and strategies reconstituted the political significance of a location, for example the Middle East.

By locating sanitary regulation within the wider context of empire and control, this chapter argues that the sudden concern over the sanitary defence of the Persian Gulf and Anglo-Russian engagement with frontier quarantine reveal the intimate linkages between sanitary regulation and imperial expansion. In both cases, quarantine interacted with, and was shaped by, the dynamics of regional politics. In effect, quarantine was an adjunct of imperialism along the Perso-Afghan frontier, while debates over maritime quarantine at the entrance to the Persian Gulf necessitated imperial engagements in the region. Additionally, imperial sanitary engagement in the region provided the means through which Central Asian diplomacy was increasingly sanitised. In fact, sanitary rivalry both reinforced old tensions and opened up new avenues for competition, while enabling British India to articulate its political aspirations and commercial dominance in Central Asia.

The sanitary defence of the Persian Gulf

The appearance of plague in Bombay in 1896 revived the thorny issue of sanitary surveillance against Indian shipping. It elicited a massive international response as most countries in frequent communication with India introduced quarantine against Indian ports, with varying degrees of severity. In the immediate aftermath of the official declaration of plague, France imposed blanket quarantine against Indian vessels from all ports except two. Similarly, the Egyptian Board of Health demanded a more rigorous treatment of ships than was required by the plague regulations of 1894.[14] The Bombay outbreak also necessitated sanitary precautions in the Middle East, since the region was commonly held to be the point of intersection between Europe and Asia. The cholera epidemic in Mecca of 1893 occasioned debate in the Paris Sanitary Convention of 1894 on the public health hazards associated with the Haj pilgrimage, and especially its role in making Europe vulnerable to the incursions of tropical disease.[15] Although the geographic-epidemiological importance of the Middle East was established by the 1860s, certain developments such as the *Dilwara* scandal further underscored the need for improved sanitary surveillance of the Suez Canal and the Persian Gulf.

In 1897, the *Dilwara*, a passenger steamer sailing from Bombay, docked at the Moses Wells' lazaretto in Suez, with one case of plague reported onboard. The *Dilwara* was subsequently allowed to proceed through the Suez Canal in quarantine, after disembarking the plague-stricken patient and her companion at Moses Wells', since the lazaretto was thoroughly ill-equipped to accommodate all the shipping crew and passengers.[16] Such events engendered the demand for greater sanitary defence against bubonic plague, and for the first time calls were made for the establishment of sentinel stations in the Persian Gulf to bolster the existing provisions for quarantine along the Red Sea. During the same year, the Bombay epidemic and quarantine regulations to prevent its spread were key points of discussion at the Venice Sanitary Convention. The Venice stipulations called for the establishment of sanitary bases in the Persian Gulf as the first bastion against the importation of disease into Europe. On this matter, the British delegate, Thorne Thorne, supported the demand for new sanitary bases at the Persian Gulf;[17] yet his acquiescence at this stage only masked Britain's wider interest in the sanitary politics of the region: the latter were articulated through both constitutional and extra-constitutional involvement in the question of maritime quarantine in the Gulf.

Britain was opposed to the issue of Gulf quarantine due to her long-standing commitment to the free passage of maritime traffic. With the onset of the plague pandemic in the 1890s this was further reinforced by the commercial and political obligations of maintaining an overseas Empire.[18] In the 1890s, Anglo-Indian shipping accounted for over 90 per cent of the total Gulf traffic.[19] Moreover, political expediency further dictated that Britain maintain some semblance of formal presence in the region in order to counter Turkish influence in the Arabian Peninsula.[20] Further, from the geopolitical standpoint of the empire, control over the Gulf was desirable for the defence of British Indian interests. Indeed, the Government of India had for long viewed the Persian Gulf as its own 'sphere of influence'.[21] Britain and British India's shared interest in retaining British control over the Persian Gulf was reflected in British deliberations at Venice, whereby the question of Gulf quarantine was decoupled from the related issue of the Haj pilgrimage: the British delegation to Venice insisted that 'very few pilgrims reach the Hedjaz by way of the Persian Gulf'.[22] Quarantine negotiations on the 'pilgrimage question' had formerly revealed the points of cleavage between the governments of Britain and India, and British India, already crippled by the denial of independent representation at Venice, sought to put forth a unified British position at the convention.[23] This also revealed the tendency among British Indian officials such as Viceroy Curzon to relegate domestic concerns such as the appeasement of Indian Muslims beneath the preservation of empire.

In Venice, the proponents of maritime quarantine, i.e. Russia and, especially, France, were able to achieve minor successes in securing an increase in the incubation period for plague and in the list of commodities officially considered susceptible to the plague microbe.[24] Anglo-Indian interests in the region suffered a more serious setback in the stipulations concerning quarantine in the Persian Gulf. This was formalised through the Ormuz scheme, which made provision for sanitary stations at the entrance to the Persian Gulf.[25] To that effect, the Venice Convention decreed that the proposed posts would be administered by the Constantinople Board of Health, provided that the latter was reconstituted as an international body with greater European representation; the logistics of the sanitary bases would be contingent on an entente between Turkey and Persia.[26] The administration of the sanitary posts was of course closely contested, since it had a direct bearing on regional politics.

The Franco-Russian entente at Venice was strengthened with the involvement of Turkey, which worked to the detriment of Anglo-Indian interests in the region. Although Turkey did not eventually ratify the Convention, it exerted influence over the sanitary proceedings by virtue of its prominence in the Constantinople Board and a more general strategic advantage in the region. The Constantinople Board had discussed the desirability of sentinel bases at the entrance to the Persian Gulf as early as 1897, proposing the establishment of permanent sanitary stations within the Ottoman domain, for example at Basra.[27] Around the same time, the Ottoman authorities sent two investigative 'flying commissions' along the eastern and western shores of the Persian Gulf, to Kuwait and Katif respectively. These gathered intelligence on local conditions and brought the local population into direct contact with the Ottoman administration. The presence of doctors under Ottoman guard in these regions aggravated Britain's apprehensions regarding its tenuous grip on the area, and the Constantinople Board was thus censured for providing the 'skeleton organisation' for Turkish control of the Persian Gulf littoral.[28] Likewise, the Turkish proposal for establishing a quarantine station in Persian territory at Mohammerah was, in many ways, seen as an attempt at a broader plan of extending the political influence of Constantinople over the Shat-el-Arab region.[29]

Britain's opposition to the Constantinople Board, then, was a function both of its strategic interests in the Gulf and of its limited hold over the region. Britain's control over the Persian ports was not ratified by formal arrangement with the Persian government; rather, it derived by default from British Indian governance over the port administration.[30] The Venice proposals concerning quarantine in the Gulf and the subsequent European involvement in the issue collectively threatened to undermine British sanitary control in the region. In fact, the increased costs of port administration at the onset of the quarantine controversy left Britain in sole command of only two Persian ports, Jask and Bushire, as the Persian government bore the expenses of medical personnel and equipment elsewhere.[31] Britain's position was, however, especially weakened by French engagement with Gulf quarantine. From the late 1890s, France steadily emerged as a major player in the Gulf: its involvement varied from a denunciation of British policy in the region with castigatory remarks on Britain's treatment of 'the Gulf as a British lake', to a more visible presence in the form of French cruisers off the coast of Lingah in southern Persia.[32]

At the same time, the constraints imposed by foreign diplomacy upon Britain negated any direct acts of aggression such as annexations; consequently, the British Indian approach to maritime quarantine was cautious and devoid of any initiatives which could be interpreted as diplomatic or territorial encroachment.[33] This primarily acted as a brake on any assertive British actions such as the establishment of sanitary posts in British territory despite the existence of several such bases in the vicinity of the Gulf.[34] Britain's relations with Persia also had a direct bearing on its quarantine policy. At Venice, British delegates supported the demand for establishing the sanitary services on Persian territory at Ormuz or Jask, although it was increasingly apparent to the British delegates that Persia was, at best, an unreliable ally.[35] Concerns over Persia's susceptibility to French and Russian influence, already apparent from the Paris Convention of 1894, were realised beyond doubt by French sanitary engagement in the Gulf and, especially, by its support for Persian autonomy over quarantine administration.[36] Together, these factors fostered a dualism in British sanitary policy, whereby the need to formalise British control over sanitary bases in the Gulf, typically through the Indian Government, had to be balanced with attempts to ensure that the status quo prevailed. The interplay of these two contradictory forces is exemplified, for instance, in the Indian government's engagements with quarantine in the autonomous principalities in the Gulf, especially Maskat and Bahrain.

At the start of the plague outbreak in Maskat, the Indian Government attempted to take sole charge of the administration of port health in both the principalities, through the provision of disinfection apparatus and medical personnel.[37] In each case, earlier assurances guaranteeing British control over port sanitation were withdrawn, allegedly under the influence of the French Resident at Maskat and the Ottoman administration in Bahrein.[38] This committed the British Political Resident in the Gulf, Colonel Meade, to advocate the dispatch of warships into Gulf waters, in an attempt to secure British strength in the region.[39] Although Meade's suggestion failed to elicit sympathy within the Foreign Office, both episodes are indicative of British Indian ambitions in the Persian Gulf. These unsuccessful attempts guided the transition towards a softer position on quarantine in an attempt to secure allies in the region. British India routinely championed the cause of leniency in quarantine against Persia, Bahrain and Maskat, often with greater success than the sanctions against its Indian ports.[40] Sanitary politics also precipitated direct involvement with the internal politics of the region. For instance, India supported Bahrain's claims for autonomy from Ottoman domination with a view to taking control over its port sanitation.[41] More generally, efforts to forestall Russian and French strongholds in the Gulf were carried through in tandem with wider efforts by the governments of Britain and India to build up strong economic interests in southern Persia by supporting local road and railway concessions and subsidising shipping services.[42]

A parallel aspect of British sanitary strategy derived from critical engagement with the stipulations of the Venice Conference. The Venice provisions gave Turkey a free hand in the sanitary arrangements in the Gulf by placing them with the Constantinople Board.[43] British apprehensions regarding the adverse impact of Turkish quarantine control on its trade resulted from the Bahrain fiasco and were reinforced by Russia's influence on Constantinople.[44] Britain therefore launched a campaign thoroughly to discredit Turkish quarantine administration at Basra and Bushire as arbitrary and corrupt.[45] The attacks on the Constantinople Board were also geared to undermine Turkish sanitary authority over the Gulf. Thus, on the one hand, British physicians routinely tried to marginalise the Constantinople Board, referring to it on one occasion as 'a Turkish Department dependent on the real or pretended will of the Sultan',[46] while they insisted, on the other, that the Health Board needed to be reconstituted as an international body, preferably with substantial British representation.[47] Elsewhere, Britain made an abortive attempt to establish the Tehran Sanitary Council as an alternative to the Constantinople Board.[48] This plan was shelved soon after its inception as Anglo-Russian sanitary policies were increasingly criticised by the burgeoning nationalist movement in Persia and by the Belgian Customs Department, both of which collectively intervened to ensure that Persia retained some degree of autonomy in its sanitary administration.[49] Moreover, the Tehran Council became an emerging site for political intrigue by the Russian Legation, which deployed its physicians in the Council to undermine British quarantine administration in southern Persia;[50] German interference in Tehran from 1908 was instrumental in Britain's continued hostility towards the Board.[51]

Britain could consolidate its hold over sanitary arrangements in the Gulf by ensuring cooperation between its medical authorities and the Belgian Customs administration. British sanitary authority was secured on the basis of a bureaucratic protocol under which the British Resident Surgeon at Bushire was both the proper channel for official correspondence regarding quarantine and the sole authority to issue orders to British quarantine doctors in the Gulf ports.[52] Through these means,

Britain was able to successfully forestall rival attempts to end its control over the sanitary arrangements in the region.[53] This policy initiative, albeit lacking the high drama of assertive quarantine propagated by Meade, was nevertheless quite successful. In 1908, as the quarantine controversy was fading on the northern frontier, the British Physician to Constantinople noted on Gulf quarantine that Basra was 'the sole, and very imperfect, quarantine station in the those regions'.[54] In other words, British sanitary diplomacy had triumphed, ensuring that the stipulations of international sanitary conventions concerning Gulf quarantine remained a dead letter.

Forward quarantine on the northern frontier

The establishment of medical checkpoints by Russia and British India along the frontiers of Afghanistan so exacerbated older tensions in the region that from the late 1890s frontier quarantine emerged as a focal point for colonial differences in Central Asia (see Figure 5.2). In April 1897, British intelligence reported the medium-scale movement of troops and 'war-like appliances' across the Russian frontier in the direction of Bokhara and at several points on the Perso-Afghan frontier.[55] Although estimates of the total strength of the Russian force varied widely, there was consensus among frontier officials in Afghanistan and India that the Russian deployment vastly exceeded the requirements of plague duty.[56] In the absence of further details on the scale or purpose of the deployment, British sanitary strategy came to rely extensively on rumours that suggested that the intended purpose of the sanitary cordons in Turkestan was to conceal military activity within the Russian frontier and bolster frontier defences.[57] In any case, the rumours appeared to be authenticated by Russian declarations announcing the intention to annex northern Khorassan if plague broke out in Seistan.[58]

The positioning of Russian soldiers in close proximity of the Indian frontier caused acute anxiety within the Indian administration. Viceroy Elgin observed that a rival military presence on the Afghan frontier had become a matter of 'very real concern', not just for its implications on British India's frontier policy, but equally because it called into question Britain's commitments to Afghanistan.[59] Elgin's concerns drew relevance from the specificities of the political situation in Central Asia. By the 1880s, while few British administrators were genuinely concerned about a Russian military threat to India, the Indian establishment continued to regard a European military deployment across the frontier with great unease as this could encourage local tribal uprisings against the colonial administration.[60] Moreover, in the same period, Britain had renewed its pledge to safeguard Afghanistan against foreign aggression in return for control over Afghan foreign policy;[61] and the militarisation of Russian quarantine systems threatened to test British commitments to Afghanistan's territorial sovereignty, as exemplified, for instance, in the Ishtoi incident of 1897.[62]

That year, Russia established plague pickets in Musabad district on the Perso-Afghan frontier. The Russian sanitary post was interpreted by Afghan guards in Ishtoi as an infringement of Afghanistan's territorial claims to the region, control

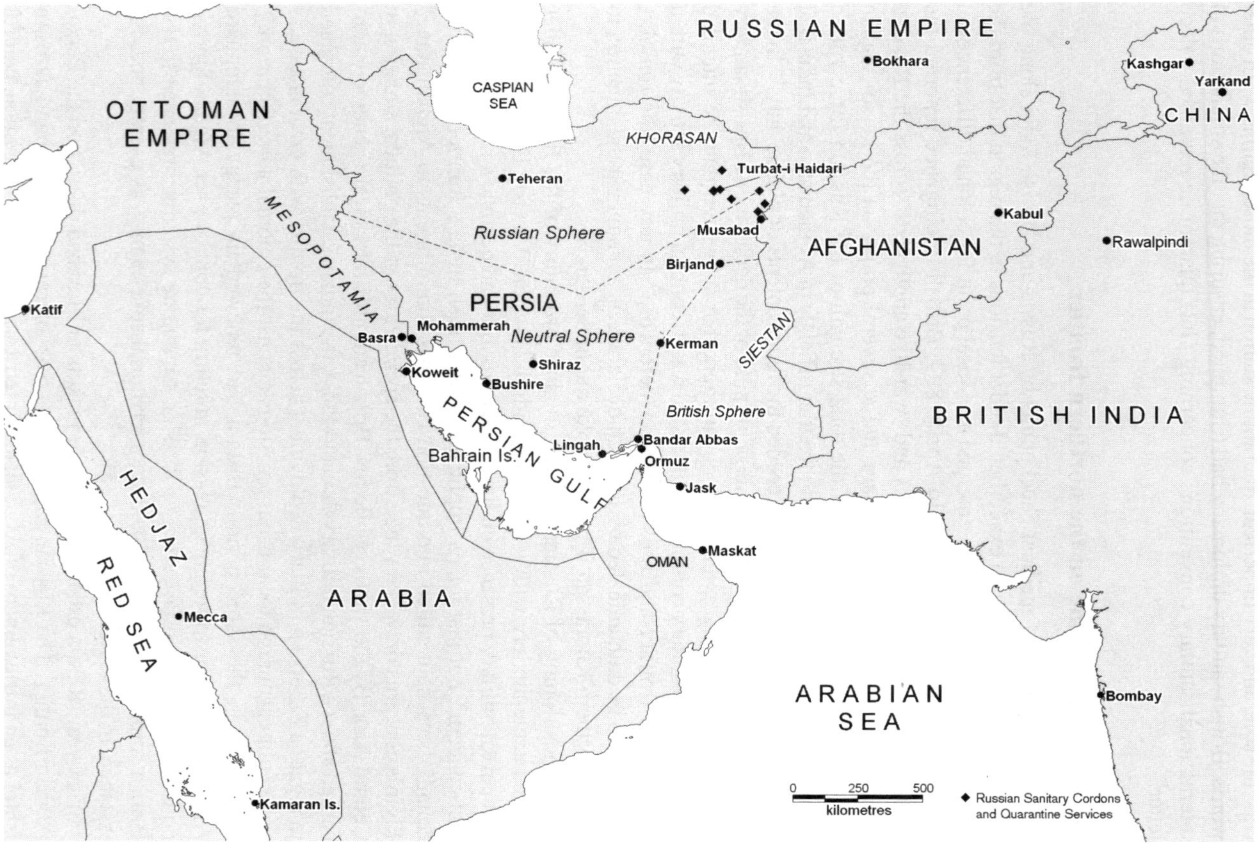

Figure 5.2 Quarantine bases and British sanitary interests in Persia and the Persian Gulf, 1890s.

over Musabad being in dispute by the governments of Persia and Afghanistan. In a minor military skirmish that ensued between the Russian and Afghan guards at Ishtoi, one Afghan and two Russian soldiers perished.[63] Although the Russian soldiers at Ishtoi were soon replaced by Persian guards, Russia's continued military presence along the Afghan frontier contributed to the political instability of the region.[64] More generally, the Ishtoi incident had far-reaching implications on Britain's position in Central Asia. Most immediately, it secured consensus among administrators in India and London that the shift in focus from southern Persia to Afghanistan necessarily undermined Afghanistan's security, and that of Britain which remained pledged to defend it.[65] Britain's position in relation to Afghanistan was further compromised by the realisation that plague had provided St Petersburg with the pretext to open direct correspondence with the Amir under the plea of preventive sanitary measures.[66]

From the 1890s therefore, quarantine and plague prevention emerged as an important variable of Central Asian diplomacy. One facet of this trend was indicated in the incorporation of sanitary directives within the ambit of Anglo-Afghan relations.[67] The Indian Government issued orders to the Amir for the closure of Afghan borders to pilgrims from Central Asia, for instance;[68] the Foreign Office's reiterations of British commitments to Afghanistan as contingent upon the satisfactory implementation of sanitary stipulations from India served to further consolidate this departure.[69] Within India too, quarantine and plague prevention at the frontier provinces – Kashmir, North West Frontier Provinces and Baluchistan – became a central administrative priority.[70] At several towns and villages along the Indian frontier, plague prevention measures included 'special precautions' such as land quarantines, as sanitation received the scrutiny typically reserved for European enclaves, thereby, turning India's border towns into protected environments.[71]

The politicisation of quarantine was clearly visible in the strategic deployment of doctors and medical missions in politically sensitive regions of Central Asia. At the onset of the quarantine controversy, doctors stationed on plague duty in south and eastern Persia performed a distinctly political role. Russia had long expressed concerns that British India's colossal commercial interests in the Gulf would interfere with and impede its efficient sanitary policing of the Persian ports.[72] At the start of the bubonic outbreak in Bushire therefore, the Governor of Transcaspia dispatched doctors to Kerman and Shiraz in order to bolster the sanitary services in the region.[73] Russian sanitary policy elsewhere in Persia appeared to follow a definitive pattern whereby plague or outbreaks of 'plague like diseases' were routinely cited to increase Russia's medical and military presence and undermine British sanitary authority in southern Persia, including at key ports such as Jask and Bander Abbas.[74] In fact, in the course of the plague pandemic, British anxieties over Russian sanitary policing were confirmed by the Shah of Persia, who confided to the Indian Viceroy that sanitary personnel and medical missions were the primary means through which Russia consolidated its position in the south of the country, to the obvious detriment of Anglo-Indian interests in the region.[75] This admission corroborated British intelligence reports which warned that the Cossack cordons on the Khorassan–Siestan route looked fairly permanent and that these routinely interfered with local civil and military arrangements.[76] When pressed on the issue, the Persian government even admitted that the object of the Cossack cordons 'was not so much the exclusion of plague as the placing of every conceivable obstacle in the way of commercial intercourse between India and Khorassan'.[77]

Forward quarantine in southern Persia set an important precedent for Anglo-Russian sanitary policing on the northern frontier, as quarantine cordons and medical missions were established as a mechanism for territorial and diplomatic advance over the heavily contested Perso-Afghan frontier. In the course of the plague pandemic, at least two such missions were proposed: one into Afghanistan and the other for Rawalpindi. In the first case, Russian delegates to the Constantinople Health Board had tabled a motion stating that the recent bubonic outbreak in Samarkand necessitated detailed scientific investigations into the causality of the disease. The medical mission proposed for Afghanistan intended to interrogate and establish the source of disease and specifically confirm the agency of Afghanistan in the importation of the disease into Russian territory.[78] The proposal occasioned much scepticism in both Calcutta and London, not least because the Russian Plague Commission subsequently issued clarifications affirming that the disease in Samarkand was indeed not plague, but 'another virulent form of bubonic disease', though of a 'local nature'.[79] The successive assurances from St Petersburg, which emphatically asserted that the proposed mission to Afghanistan was never an element of Tsarist policy, failed to pacify British anxieties regarding Russian sanitary assertiveness.[80] The British Ambassador to Constantinople, N.R. O'Conor, summed up Russian strategy in Afghanistan thus: 'If we give them an inch in this country they will take an ell'.[81] O'Conor therefore recommended the adoption of 'a determined line' to counter rival ambitions in the region.[82]

In the second case, the proposal originated from Russian Turkestan and concerned the establishment of a plague observation post at Rawalpindi. The post was meant to serve as a base for a medical officer deputed from Kashgar to study the pandemic in Bombay, Punjab and Kashmir, and establish its progress in the direction of the Russian frontier.[83] The proposal was somewhat unclear on the nature and duration of the post, and in India this ambiguity was interpreted to signify that the post would be permanent so long as the epidemic persisted in India, thereby providing the infrastructural base for political intrigue in northern India.[84] In substantiation of the latter, Curzon pointed to the past experience of Russian officials on the northwest frontier who had been expelled from the country on suspicion of espionage.[85] Furthermore, the Russian physician in question, Dr Baumholtz, had often exhibited a definite political dimension, particularly in his tendency to 'discover the plague' where none had appeared to exist.[86] The apprehensions regarding the Russian mission to Rawalpindi were echoed simultaneously in London. The Secretary of State, Mr Brodrick, decreed that 'the existing objections against the recognition of Foreign Consuls at places at the interior of India' would, in this case, 'apply with increased force' against the deployment of a Russian medical officer in the northwest frontier.[87] The Foreign Office called upon the Indian Sanitary Department to furnish statistics to demonstrate the futility of the proposed mission, as it was apparent that a blatant rejection of the Russian proposal could drive it to seek a more sympathetic response from Afghanistan.[88] Eventually, the Indian position rested on the contention that the frontier regions from Attock in Punjab onwards were free of the plague; and the futility of a foreign medical mission to British India was underpinned by the reminder that all foreign medical officers within Indian territory would ultimately remain dependent upon the Indian Sanitary Department for all relevant and reliable medical data.[89]

Although the medical missions – to Rawalpindi and Afghanistan – failed to materialise on either occasion, the incidents nevertheless initiated an important departure in favour of assertive sanitary policy that both informed and challenged Britain's traditional view of quarantine. Thus, in a remarkable divergence from the conventional opposition to quarantine, British administrators along the frontier urged for the imposition of sanitary cordons as a pre-emptive strategy in order to avoid harassment by rival parties. Thus, despite the adverse impact on commerce, the Indian authorities advised their doctor in Persia to impose a cordon as the only means by which to 'avoid the [Russian] quarantine higher up'.[90] Similarly in view of the proliferation of Russian bases in eastern Persia, British administrators in Tehran averred: 'we cannot cavil at Russia establishing a quarantine state at Turbat-i Haidari', as Britain had to pay the price for its traditional laxity on sanitary regulation.[91]

The Russian cordon at Turbat-i Haidari perhaps best exemplifies the Anglo-Russian sanitary antagonism in Persia (see Figure 5.2).[92] Russia instituted the sanitary cordon in February 1897 when the first serious outbreak of plague occurred in Bombay[93] and thereafter it continued to be a source of diplomatic unease between Britain and Russia.[94] Turbat-i Haidari was the centre of the export trade in wool in Afghanistan and in addition to its sanitary purpose, the travel restrictions at the quarantine station diverted the wool trade into markets within the Russian frontier. Moreover, through the development of Afghan-Russian frontier trade, Russian frontier officials hoped to enter into quasi-diplomatic relations with Afghanistan.[95] The Russian quarantine station at Turbat-i Haidari prompted internal debate within the Indian administration on the incorporation of quarantine and sanitary cordons as policy imperatives, as the cordon was of immense military value to Russia. The quarantine station at Turbat-i Haidari afforded Russia a vantage point from which to observe and monitor British military and commercial activity in eastern Persia.[96] British frontier officials in India were keenly aware of the threat posed by Russian sanitary strategies and argued for the adoption of sanitary tactics into British Indian frontier policy. Colonel Yate in Baluchistan was a particularly enthusiastic advocate of this form of expansion; he urged the establishment of a British sanitary cordon near Turbat-i Haidari. Birjand appeared to be particularly well suited for the purpose, as Yate insisted: 'To post our doctors in Seistan would proclaim our abandonment to Russia of everything and everybody to the north of that, so when we are about it for goodness sake let's go for Birjand.'[97]

However, forward quarantine certainly had its share of sceptics, including Viceroy Curzon. Curzon rejected proposals for a British cordon at Birjand in retaliation to the Russian one on the grounds that this would only increase impediments to overland trade while doing very little to undermine Russian influence in the region.[98] Similarly, Curzon pointed out that the Foreign Department's proposals the substitution of Russian cordons by neutral bodies such as the Belgian Customs would only weaken the Indian opposition, which rested on the illegality of Russian quarantine policy within Persia.[99] In any case, despite their political neutrality, Curzon harboured deep suspicion of the integrity of the Belgian Customs, referring to the Belgians on one occasion as 'merely Russians in disguise'.[100] Curzon's cautionary approach towards assertive quarantine contrasts sharply with his forward polices on the northern frontier of British India. His opposition to forward quarantine was, however, not indicative of a lack of faith in the efficacy or viability of quarantine as an arm of diplomacy or as a mode of expansion. For instance, recognising the dictates of political expediency at the Persian ports, Curzon had agreed to defray the costs of sanitary stations from Indian revenue, if it were to be advocated 'on the strongest grounds of Imperial interest'.[101] His opposition to assertive quarantine was more emphatically a function of the practical problems imposed by foreign diplomacy together with Britain's anti-quarantinist tradition, which collectively acted as a brake on expansionist policy initiatives premised on sanitary regulation. Curzon thus vetoed plans for the quarantine base in eastern Persia, on the grounds that an additional British base in Persia would negate India's assertions of the absence of plague in Baluchistan, and in any case Britain was unlikely to counteract Russia's diplomatic and military presence in the region through the deployment of a doctor.[102]

Over time, there was growing realisation within the Indian Foreign Department that very few material gains were to be achieved by way of sanitary expansion, unless Russia contemplated withdrawing its cordons of its own accord. The impasse over the Turbat-i Haidari cordon was a case in point: a British consul had formerly been dispatched to the area, with an escort of twenty *sowars* in defence of British Indian interests in the region.[103] Yet in less than a year, it became increasingly apparent that the decision to establish a British consulate in Turbat-i Haidari with a view to getting the Russians to withdraw their cordon had backfired, for ultimately, as the Foreign Department admitted: 'We are landed with an additional Consulate which gives very little return for our money.'[104]

Conclusion

The negotiations in the Venice Conference revealed the intimate linkages between sanitation and politics, quarantine and empire. Sanitary regulation was essentially a strategic decision guided by commerce and the promise of wider political gains. For the nations concerned, this evolved out of the need to balance the expansionist urges of empire against the constraints imposed by European diplomacy. In the prelude to the First World War, the shifting allegiances of the alliance systems defined the nuances in quarantine policies: this accounted for the varying degrees of severity in the sanitary sanctions against Indian shipping and the shifts in position towards quarantine in the Persian Gulf. For instance, the Anglo-Russian settlement of colonial differences in 1907 occasioned a gradual waning of sanitary antagonism on the Perso-Afghan frontier,[105] while the advent of Anglo-German antagonism as a major force in European and colonial affairs engendered renewed engagement with Gulf quarantine.

Acute colonial competition occasioned the emergence of quarantine – with its various adjuncts – as a viable means of exerting informal imperial control in Central Asia. In fact, quarantine and regulatory sanitation provided the Indian Government with opportunities for pursuing sub-imperialist policies on the northern frontier and in the Persian Gulf. British Indian policies in both cases were guided by a regional conception of Indian defence and heavily influenced by geopolitical conceptions from an Indian standpoint.[106] The dominance of the Persian Gulf was an Indian concern rather than an element of metropolitan policy. At the start of the plague pandemic, the Indian government capitalised on the rhetoric of Russian expansionism to enlist British cooperation at Venice. Britain's arguments about the futility of Gulf quarantine and its separation from the pilgrimage question was the highpoint of Anglo-Indian collaboration. British-Indian strategic interests in the Persian Gulf necessitated the transition to extra-constitutional means of sanitary engagement in the region. Thus, through informal means such as the deployment of medical personnel and apparatus and loans to finance the costs of sentinel bases, the Indian Government was able to secure and safeguard its position in the Gulf. This form of expansion was primarily defensive and guided by perceptions of threat or loss of British Indian influence in Central Asia. Similar conditions were to be found on the northern frontier: in the absence of an antagonistic military strategy, forward quarantine afforded both the means and the pretext for Anglo-Russian expansion in Central Asia. Primarily, however, the scope and limitations of the sanitary intervention were shaped by the dynamics of regional politics. On the northern frontier, sanitary cordons and medical missions were an adjunct of the long-standing Anglo-Russian competition over the region. Likewise, the strategic importance of the Persian Gulf, with its implications for the defence of India and colonial trade, revived imperial engagement in the region.

Finally, the quarantine controversy also highlights the importance of the imperial sanitary engagement as a defining factor in the politics of Central Asia. Contrary to the traditional view of buffer states, some of these were afforded a unique bargaining position by the ability to play off the imperial powers against one another. Additionally, the imperial sanitary intervention was both informed by and a response to the regional political situation. By this means, Oman and Afghanistan were successful in retaining a fair amount of independence;[107] likewise, other states such as Bahrain were able to enlist British Indian support in their struggle for autonomy from the Ottoman Empire. Anglo-Russian sanitary antagonism also provided a focal point for the nationalist movement in Persia from which to successfully lobby for British-Indian investment in the Persian public health system.[108] More crucially, despite the internal debates within the Foreign Department on the viability of assertive sanitation, the quarantine controversy both reinforced old tensions and opened up new avenues for competition, while enabling British India to put forth an independent political agenda in Central Asia. Plague truly embodied the 'tensions of empire':[109] British Indian engagements with plague prevention outside its frontiers were framed in the rhetoric of the 'Great Game' of empire and expansion, thereby enabling quarantine to emerge as the critical factor in the 'Central Asian question' and its relation to British India.

Acknowledgements

This is a slightly revised version of a paper that received the Curzon Memorial Essay Prize, University of Oxford, 2005. I am grateful to Mark Harrison for his comments on an earlier draft. Nigel James graciously helped with the maps; spellings of the names of places have been retained as they appear in the original records.

Notes

1 Government of India (hereafter GOI) Foreign Frontier A, May 1897, 60–83 (68) National Archives of India, Delhi (hereafter NAI).
2 On Britain and Russia's competing political claims over Central Asia, see for instance Briton Cooper Busch, *Britain and the Persian Gulf, 1894–1914*, Berkeley: California University Press, 1967. The following accounts provide the British-Indian perspective on the larger conflict over Central Asia: S. Gopal, *British Policy in India, 1858–1905*, Cambridge: Cambridge University Press, 1965; G.J. Alder, *British India's Northern Frontier, 1865–1895: A Study in Imperial Policy*, London: Longmans, 1963. For a brief mention of the sanitary aspects of the imperial rivalry, see Firuz Kazemzadeh, *Russia and Britain in Persia, 1864–1914: A Study in Imperialism*, New Haven, Conn.: Yale University Press, 1968, 409–12.
3 GOI Foreign Frontier A, May 1897, 60–83 NAI.
4 E.H.S. Clarke, 16 April 1897, in Notes, KW 2 to GOI Foreign Frontier A, May 1897, 60–83 (70–6) NAI.
5 For a lively discussion of the importance of Kashmir in the context of Anglo-Russian tensions over Central Asia, see Peter Hopkirk, *The Great Game: On Secret Service in High Asia*, London: John Murray, 1990, 321–9.
6 Raj Chandavarkar, 'Plague Panic and Epidemic Politics in India, 1896–1914', in Paul Slack and Terence Ranger eds *Epidemics and Ideas: Essays on the Historical Perception of Pestilence*, Cambridge: Cambridge University Press, 1992, 203–40, Ian J. Catanach, 'Plague and the Tensions of Empire: India, 1896–1918', in David Arnold ed. *Imperial Medicine and Indigenous Societies*, Manchester: Manchester University Press, 1988, 214–43.
7 Mark Harrison, 'Quarantine, Pilgrimage and Colonial Trade: India 1866–1900', *Indian Economic and Social History Review*, 29: 2, 1992, 117–44; more recently, idem., 'Disease, Diplomacy and International Commerce: The Origins of International Sanitary Regulation in the Nineteenth century,' *Journal of Global History*, 1, (2006), 197–217. See also Norman Howard-Jones, *The Scientific Background to International Sanitary Conferences, 1851–1938,* Geneva: WHO Chronicle 28/10, 1975.
8 GOI Foreign Internal A, December 1897, 34–63 (34) NAI.
9 For British India see: David Arnold, *Colonising the Body: State Medicine and Epidemic Disease in Nineteenth Century India*, London and Berkeley: California University Press, 1993; Mark Harrison, *Public Health in British India: Anglo-Indian Preventive Medicine, 1859–1914*, Cambridge: Cambridge University Press, 1994; *Climates and Constitutions. Health, Race, Environment and British Imperialism in India 1600–1850,* Delhi: Oxford University Press, 1999; Anil Kumar, *Medicine and the Raj: British Medical Policy in India, 1835–1911*, Delhi: Sage Publications, 1998; Biswamoy Pati

and Mark Harrison eds *Health, Medicine and Empire: Perspectives on Colonial India*, Delhi: Orient Longman, 2001.

10 Amir Afkhami has recently placed the sanitary antagonism between Russia and Britain in the wider context of the competing political claims over Iran and as a focal point of nationalist sentiment in Iran. Amir Afkhami, 'Iran in the Age of Epidemics: Nationalism and the Struggle for Public Health, 1889–1926', Ph.D. thesis Yale University, 2003, chs 4 and 5.

11 See for instance: Chandavarkar, 'Plague Panic and Epidemic Politics in India'; Claude Quetel, *The History of Syphilis*, translated by Judith Bradmore and Brian Pike, Oxford: Polity Press, 1990, 7; Charles Rosenberg, *Explaining Epidemics and Other Studies in the History of Medicine*, Cambridge: Cambridge University Press, 1992, ch. 13; Paul Slack, 'Introduction', in Slack and Ranger, *Epidemics and Ideas*, 3,5,8,10.

12 Erwin H. Ackerknecht, 'Anticontagionism between 1821 and 1867', *Bulletin of the History of Medicine*, 23:5, 1948, 562–93.

13 Peter Baldwin, *Contagion and the State in Europe, 1830–1930*, Cambridge: Cambridge University Press, 1999.

14 R. Nathan, *The Plague in India, 1897, 1898*, Vol. 1, Simla: Government Press, 1898, 415–16.

15 Howard-Jones, *Scientific Background to International Sanitary Conferences*, 71.

16 Nathan, *Plague in India*, 408–9.

17 Sub-enclosure of Enclosure 1, in GOI Foreign External A, July 1905, 89–92 (89) NAI.

18 Harrison, 'Quarantine, Pilgrimage and Colonial Trade'.

19 In 1897, this figure stood at 98 per cent: F.G. Clemow, 20 October 1903, in Sub-enclosure to Enclosure 1, to GOI Foreign External A, July 1905, 89–92 (89), 3 NAI.

20 F.G. Clemow, 20 October 1903, Sub-enclosure to Enclosure 1, in GOI Foreign External A, July 1905, 89–92 (89), 8 NAI.

21 For the strategic importance of the Persian Gulf prior to the discovery of petroleum, see, for instance, Bernard Porter, *The Lion's Share: A Short History of Imperialism, 1850–1970*, London: Longman, 1975, 84–8.

22 Sub-enclosure to Enclosure 1, in GOI Foreign External A, July 1905, 89–92 (89), 3 NAI.

23 Harrison, 'Quarantine, Pilgrimage and Colonial Trade'; Howard-Jones, *Scientific Background to International Sanitary Conferences*, 71–2, 78–9.

24 *The Venice Sanitary Convention, 1897* (English transl.), Simla: Government Central Press, 1897, ch. XIV.

25 *Venice Sanitary Convention, 1897*, ch. XIV.

26 GOI Foreign Internal A, June 1897, 357–60 NAI.

27 GOI Foreign Secret External, August 1908, 297–348 (328), 37, NAI.

28 Sub-enclosure to Enclosure 1, in GOI Foreign External A, July 1905, 89–92 (89), 5 NAI.

29 Enclosure 1, to GOI Foreign, External, August 1899, 432 NAI.

30 Sub-enclosure to Enclosure 1, of GOI Foreign External A, July 1905, 89–2 (89) NAI.

31 Sub-enclosure to Enclosure 1, of GOI Foreign External A, July 1905, 89–2 (89) NAI.

32 GOI Foreign Secret External, June 1902, 45–8 NAI.

33 Minute by Sir R. Thorne Thorne, Enclosure to Pro No. 70, in GOI Foreign Secret External, March 1899, 66–74 NAI.

34 GOI Foreign Secret External, March 1899, 67 NAI.

35 GOI Foreign Internal A, December 1897, 34–63 (36) NAI.

36 Minute by Sir R. Thorne Thorne, Enclosure to GOI Foreign Secret External, March 1899, 66–74 (60) NAI.

37 H. Harvey, 1 March 1900, in R. Nathan, 2.3.1900 in Notes to GOI Foreign External A, May 1900, 36–78 (38) NAI; GOI Foreign Secret External, November 1899, 46–68 NAI; GOI Foreign Secret External, August 1899, 120–71 NAI.

38 GOI Foreign Secret External, November 1899, 46–68 (61–2) NAI; GOI Foreign Secret External, August 1899, 120–71 (124) NAI.

39 GOI Foreign Secret External, August 1899, 120–71 (124) NAI.
40 GOI Foreign Internal A, December 1897, 34–63 (56) NAI.
41 F.G. Clemow, 20 October 1903, Sub-enclosure of Enclosure 1, P. No. 89 in GOI Foreign External A, July 1905, 89–92, 6 NAI.
42 Glen Balfour-Paul, 'Britain's Informal Empire in the Middle East', in *Oxford History of the British Empire: The Twentieth Century*, Judith M. Brown and Wm. Roger Louis eds Oxford: Oxford University Press, 1999, 490–514.
43 GOI Foreign Internal A, December 1897, 34–63 (36) NAI.
44 GOI Foreign Secret External, July 1899, 158–159 NAI.
45 GOI Foreign Internal A, December 1897, 34–63 (36) NAI; GOI Foreign Internal A, April 1897, 15–33 NAI; GOI Foreign Secret External, August 1899, 120–71 (140) NAI; F.G. Clemow, 20 October 1903, Sub-enclosure of Enclosure 1, Pro No. 89 in GOI Foreign External A, July 1905, 89–92, 6 NAI.
46 GOI Foreign Secret External, August 1908, 297–348 (328), 37 NAI.
47 W.S. Morris, 3 October 2004, in FD Notes to GOI Foreign External A, July 1905, 89–92 NAI.
48 GOI Foreign Internal A, December 1897, 34–63 (56) NAI.
49 GOI Foreign Secret External, January 1905, 158–217 NAI; Afkhami, 'Iran in the Age of Epidemics', ch. 5.
50 FD Notes to GOI Foreign Secret External, August 1908, 297–348 (332) NAI.
51 B. Williams, in FD Notes to GOI Foreign Secret External, August 1908, 297–348 (301) NAI.
52 FD Notes to P. No. 172 in GOI Foreign Secret External, January 1905, 158–217 NAI.
53 GOI Foreign Secret External, January 1904, 4–24 (6) NAI.
54 F.G. Clemow, 20 October 1903, Sub-enclosure of Enclosure 1 of P. No. 89, to GOI Foreign External A, July 1905, 89–92, 6 NAI.
55 GOI Foreign Secret Frontier, April 1897, 214–361 (282) NAI.
56 The Governor of Rushtak estimated that 2,000 Russian troops were deployed on the Afghan frontier. Tehran and Meshed reports make a conservative estimate of a 500-member Cossack force. EHS Clarke, 4 March 1897, in K W No. I, Part I, to GOI Foreign Secret Frontier, April 1897, 214–361 (283) NAI.
57 W.J. Cunningham, 15 February 1897, in KW No. I, Part I, in GOI Foreign Secret Frontier, April 1897, 214–361 (224) NAI. See also GOI Foreign Secret Frontier, April 1897, 214–361 (283, 288), NAI.
58 W.J. Cunningham, 5 March 1897, in KW No. I, Part I, in GOI Foreign Secret Frontier, April 1897, 214–361 (286–7) NAI.
59 GOI Foreign Secret Frontier, July 1897, 97–163 (112) NAI.
60 M. Yapp, 'British Perceptions of the Russian Threat to India', *Modern Asian Studies*, 21:4, 1987, 647–65.
61 Sneh Mahajan, 'The Problem of the Defence of India and the Formation of the Anglo-Russian Entente 1900–1907', *Journal of Indian History*, 58:1–3, 1980, 175–92; Ian Nish, 'Politics, Trade and Communications in East Asia: Thoughts on Anglo-Russian Relations, 1861–1907', *Modern Asian Studies*, 21:4, 1987, 667–78.
62 GOI Foreign Secret Frontier, June 1897, 1–77 (72) NAI.
63 GOI Foreign Secret Frontier, July 1897, 97–163 (98) NAI.
64 GOI Foreign Secret Frontier, July 1897, 97–163 (112) NAI.
65 N.G.S., 11 October 1899, in Notes to GOI Foreign Frontier A, February 1899, 130–5 (130–1) NAI.
66 GOI Foreign Secret Frontier, July 1897, 373–9 (378) NAI.
67 GOI Foreign Secret Frontier, June 1897, 1–77 (Notes to 17–20) NAI.
68 N.G.S., 11 October 1899, in Notes to GOI Foreign Frontier A, February 1899, 130–5 (132) NAI.
69 E.H.S. Clarke, 12 March 1897, in FD Notes to GOI Foreign Secret Frontier, April 1897, 214–361 (313), NAI.

70 B.K.B, 11 January 1905, in Notes to GOI Foreign Internal B, February 1905, 216, NAI; GOI Foreign Internal B, July 1899, 87–90, NAI; GOI Foreign Internal B, June 1902, 110–1, NAI; GOI Foreign Internal B, November 1902, 1–2, NAI.
71 GOI Foreign Secret Frontier, May 1897, 253–370 (328) NAI; N.G.S., 11 October 1899, in Notes to GOI Foreign Frontier A, February 1899, 130–5 (130–1) NAI.
72 See also Afkhami, 'Iran in the Age of Epidemics', 201–22.
73 GOI Foreign Secret External, August 1899, 210–29 (216) NAI.
74 GOI Foreign Secret Frontier, June 1897, 87–150 NAI; Enclosure 1 to GOI Foreign, Secret External, September 1988, 203–13, (208) NAI.
75 GOI Foreign Secret External, July 1900, 14 NAI.
76 Kazemzadeh, *Russia and Britain in Persia*, 409, 410.
77 'GOI to Hamilton, July 3 1902', cited in Kazemzadeh, *Russia and Britain in Persia*, 411 (note 57).
78 GOI Foreign Secret Frontier, February 1899, 121–34 (121) NAI.
79 GOI Foreign Secret Frontier, February 1899, 121–34 (133 A) NAI.
80 GOI Foreign Secret Frontier, April 1899, 112–18 (113) NAI; GOI Foreign Secret Frontier, July 1899, 52–8 (58) NAI; GOI Foreign Secret Frontier, July 1899, 52–8 (58) NAI.
81 Ell is a historical unit of measurement, equalling approximately 12 inches.
82 GOI Foreign Secret Frontier, February 1899, 121–34 (124) NAI.
83 GOI Foreign Secret Frontier, December 1905, 151–5 (151) NAI.
84 E.H.S. Clarke, 19 August 1905, in Notes to GOI Foreign Secret Frontier, September 1905, 34–6 (34) NAI.
85 Curzon to Secretary of State, 25 August 1905, in GOI Foreign Secret Frontier, September 1905, 34–6 (35) NAI.
86 GOI Foreign, Secret Frontier, September 1905, 34–6 (35) NAI.
87 GOI Foreign Secret Frontier, December 1905, 151–5 (152) NAI.
88 GOI Foreign Secret Frontier, December 1905, 151–5 (152) NAI.
89 S.M. Fraser, 19 August 1905; J.T.W Leslie, 22 August 1905, in Notes to GOI Foreign Secret Frontier, September 1905, 34–6 (34) NAI.
90 R. Nathan, 14 September 1897, in Notes to GOI Foreign Secret Frontier, 260–92 (291) NAI.
91 E.H.S. Clarke, 8 July 1897, in GOI Foreign Secret Frontier, 260–92 (289) NAI.
92 For a discussion of the strategic importance of Turbat-i Haidari on the Russian quarantine line in eastern Persia, see Afkhami, 'Iran in the Age of Epidemics', ch. 5.
93 GOI Foreign Secret Frontier, October 1897, 260–92 (286, 289) NAI; GOI Foreign Secret Frontier, January 1904, 257–8 (257) NAI.
94 GOI Foreign Secret Frontier, January 1904, 257–8 (257) NAI.
95 GOI Foreign Secret Frontier, January 1904, 257–8 (257) NAI.
96 Afkhami, 'Iran in the Age of Epidemics', 254–6.
97 Col. C.E. Yate, 14 October 1902, in Notes to GOI Foreign Secret Frontier, January 1904, 88–223 NAI.
98 C[urzon], 30 April 1904, in Notes to GOI Foreign Secret Frontier, January 1904, 88–223 (109, 124) NAI.
99 FD Notes to Curzon (124); GOI Foreign Secret Frontier, October 1902, 63–72 (67) NAI.
100 C[urzon], 22 August 1902, in FD Notes to GOI Foreign Secret Frontier, October 1902, 63–76 (68) NAI.
101 GOI Foreign Secret External, August 1899, 210–29 (213) NAI.
102 C[urzon], 30 April 03, in Notes to GOI Foreign Secret Frontier, January 1904, 88–223 (98) NAI.
103 FD Notes to P. No. 169 in GOI Foreign Secret External, January 1905, 158–217 NAI.
104 EHS Clarke, 9.5.1905 in Notes to GOI Foreign Secret Frontier, July 1905, 188–94 (188) NAI.

105 On the Anglo-Russian informal treaty over accession in Persia and for mutual accommodation, see: Kazemzadeh, *Britain and Russia in Persia*, 28–32, 292; M.E. Yapp, 'British Policy in the Persian Gulf', in Alvin J. Cottrell ed. *The Persian Gulf States: A General Survey*, Baltimore, Md.: Johns Hopkins University Press, 1980, 73–4.

106 Philip Derby, *Three Faces of Imperialism: British and American Approaches to Asia and Africa, 1870–1970*, New Haven, Conn.: Yale University Press, 1987; Gopal, *British Policy in India*; Alder, *British India's Northern Frontier.*

107 For a discussion of the external relations of Afghanistan in the context of Anglo-Russian tensions, see especially Nish, 'Politics, Trade and Communications in East Asia'.

108 Afkhami, 'Iran in the Age of Epidemics', 253.

109 This phrase derives from a paper title by Ian Catanach; see Catanach, 'Plague and the Tensions of Empire'.

6 Medical research and control of disease

Kala-azar in British India

Achintya Kumar Dutta

The process of colonization made the colonial administration face terrible diseases in India. These threatened the army, white civilians and the economy of the colony, and generated a lot of insecurities and anxieties. To tackle the diseases and protect the 'crown jewel' of the British empire, western medicine and medical men were brought to India. At the same time, the introduction of western medicine into India by the British generated a host of complexities that have significance for the history of medicine in colonial India. This chapter focuses on the growth of medical research related to black fever or *kala-azar* and the way the government responded to it. At the same time, it delineates the extent to which the work of the researchers was utilized by the colonial government in order to control the disease.

Medical research and the government

Let us begin with a brief look at the state of medical research in India in general and the government attitude to it. It may be observed from the available literature that despite the prevalence of major endemic and epidemic diseases, medical research in India was not organized until the close of the nineteenth century.[1] The government had no systematic medical research policy in the nineteenth century. Though from the 1860s on it adopted and followed the practice of deputing medical officers for field inquiries on the causation and prevention of some diseases, institutional research was almost non-existent.[2] Any medical research carried out during this time was the product of medical officers' personal enterprise. Institutional medical research in India only began to emerge from the beginning of the twentieth century when some institutions with laboratory research facilities were founded in north and south India, culminating in the Calcutta School of Tropical Medicine (1920) and the All India Institute of Public Health and Hygiene (1932). A central body for coordinating and monitoring the medical research of these institutions was also established with the creation of the Indian Research Fund Association (IRFA, 1911). But these institutions worked under certain limitations and the progress of medical research was frequently hampered. The need for amenities for research and the dearth of scientific workers was still acutely felt.[3]

There has been much criticism of the medical research that developed in India during colonial rule. It is argued that India, 'the largest disease laboratory in the

British empire', provided ample opportunities for scientific and medical explorations; yet the British Indian Government seems to have done little to encourage medical research. Indian Medical Service (IMS) officials and eminent researchers such as Sir Leonard Rogers, Lt.-Col. Megaw and Sir S. S. Sokhey in the 1920s and 1930s lamented the utter neglect of medical research in India and criticized the government for its lack of concern.[4] Recent studies, likewise critical, argue that the research structure that eventually evolved was the result of a piece-meal and ad hoc response to sudden epidemic emergencies, and that there existed no enduring foundation for the growth of medical science in the country.[5] But this argument is not accepted by some contemporary western scholars. Mark Harrison is of the view that much of the government's plan for a more extensive network of laboratories remained on paper, but it would be unfair to claim that research laboratories provided no enduring foundation for the growth of medical science in India.[6] It is hard to deny the contributions of colonial medical research institutions to the growth of scientific knowledge even in post-independence India. But the development of medical science and the public health system in British India was not an organic one.

Both scientific education and research were underdeveloped in the colonies.[7] Research and education were not intimately connected here: medical colleges were meant for medical education only, and any research carried out in them in the nineteenth century was not remarkable. The colonial government is said to have been less interested in medical research and did not approve any large outlay on it. The relative neglect of medical science is in sharp contrast to larger investments in botanical, geological and geographical surveys from which the British hoped to gain substantial economic and military advantage, while medical science did not hold any such promise.[8] The government's parsimonious attitude towards medical knowledge becomes apparent time and again. Ross, the famous medical scientist who discovered the malaria vector, was given a lower salary because of continuing with research and Rogers decided to pursue his investigations into *kala-azar* on minimum pay.[9] It was military affairs, not medical research, that received priority. This point is illustrated by the fact that Ross was not relieved from military duty even when the Maharaja of Patiala offered to finance his malaria investigations on a full-time basis (1895).[10] Ross became very critical of the government's lackadaisical attitude to medical research. He perceived it as unwilling to promote medical research in India and to make use of the hundreds of potential investigators (in the military hospitals) whom it could have set to work for almost nothing.[11]

The Medical Department, perhaps more than any other, had felt the effect of financial stringency.[12] Medical research seemed to have been considered an expensive undertaking, involving large amounts of money. In spite of repeated recommendations for the development of research made by medical experts, the British Indian Government paid little attention to it. Financial considerations prevented the implementation of Prof. E.H. Starling's recommendation in the early 1920s to the creation of a Central Research Institute at Delhi.[13] Funding for medical research was curtailed and cut back. On the recommendation of the Retrenchment Committee, the Government of India drastically reduced the number of research personnel and the funds allocated to medical research. When it discontinued its annual contribution of Rs5 lakh to the IRFA, research then was reduced.[14] Primarily dependent on funds provided by the Government of India, the IRFA had struggled on through hardships and impediments. Any change for the better was followed by a war, a retrenchment, an economic depression or some other setback.[15] The Bhore Committee, appointed to review health conditions in India in 1943, also pointed out that a grant of Rs4 lakh was miserably inadequate for medical research needs in such a vast country.[16]

Similarly, the parsimonious attitude of the government was fully exposed in the health care services, which received lower priority than military and political affairs. The organization of public health was understaffed and the condition of village dispensaries was deplorable. The government did not of course remain completely idle, and the measures to control fatal diseases had some effect but were inadequate. The government spent a very small amount on public health. In 1943 expenditure per head on medical relief and public health for India was between 3 and 4 *annas* per annum. Of this only one-third went to preventive medicine, very little compared to the UK where Rs54 per head per year were spent on medical relief alone.[17] Though the government made some attempt to tackle health problems by setting up research institutions like the Calcutta School of Tropical Medicine, the Bombay Bacteriological Laboratory, the King Institute, Guindy, the Pasteur Institute, Coonoor and so on, the existing public health structure was not satisfactory.[18] A sound organization and ample allocation of funds were necessary.

Research on *kala-azar*

It is against this background that we must attempt to understand medical research on *kala-azar* and its control in India. It has already been pointed out that medical research in nineteenth-century India was mainly the result of individual enterprise by IMS officers, who even without adequate government support carried on with their work and made some contribution to the growth of medical knowledge. Even Ross's world-famous discovery of the transmission of malaria by mosquitoes and Donovan's discovery of the *kala-azar* parasite were made without encouragement or support from the government. By the later decades of the nineteenth century, the discoveries of parasitology shed new light on the environmentalist explanation, making the environment an indirect, rather than a direct, cause of disease. Apart from the notice of 'difference' between Indians and Europeans, tropical climate was held responsible for the diseases, even after the discovery of the 'germ theory'. India's disease and dirt became markers of its difference in imperial literature.[19] India had to be as distinct epidemiologically as it was racially and culturally. Nevertheless, by the late nineteenth and early twentieth centuries, researchers in the IMS had convincingly formulated a 'germ theory' for India's deadly ailments – malaria, plague, cholera and *kala-azar*. Although, as Douglas Haynes has shown, much of this research was driven by narrowly professional motives, as medical officers in the colonial world sought to advance their careers at home by contributing to the progress of a universal medical science, still the new bacteriological explanation of the disease inevitably challenged the whole ideology of 'difference'.[20] There is much criticism of IMS officers for fostering divisions, competition and rivalry among themselves and for being bureaucratic and suspicious of others' work in the new sciences of bacteriology and parasitology.[21] Yet their researches stimulated specialized research in India and convinced the government of its utility. At the same time they protested against the financial constraints holding back material improvements in public health and demanded better sanitation and health care facilities.[22]

As in the case of other infective diseases, they struggled hard when a *kala-azar* epidemic caused havoc and became a serious public health problem in late nineteenth-century India. The most celebrated of those who worked on *kala-azar* and its cure were Rogers, Mackie, Hume, Castellani, James, Christophers, Shortt, Napier, Knowles and Brahmachari. The subject of *kala-azar* was an important one from a practical as well as a scientific point of view, as the disease was the cause of a vast amount of suffering and death in India. The prevention of this disease was a function of exact knowledge as to its causation. Therefore, the government should have promoted and actively assisted research on the subject by every means in its power. But it did not.

Kala-azar (visceral leishmaniasis) is an infective disease caused by the protozoan parasite Leishman Donovan body which is transmitted to the human body by certain species of sandflies. It is characterized by a fever of long duration sometimes acute or sub-acute, enlargement of the spleen and frequently also of the liver, anaemia and progressive emaciation. *Kala-azar* was a fatal disease and occurred both epidemically and endemically in India during the colonial period. It had an adverse impact on the population due to its high mortality rate of more than 98 per cent. *Kala-azar* was prevalent in a large part of eastern India, the worst-affected areas being Assam, Bengal and Bihar. It also occurred in Madras and certain parts of Orissa and the United Provinces. In India *kala-azar* broke out in epidemic form in Assam, Bengal and Bihar at intervals of 15–20 years, each episode lasting three to four years.[23] But it was not a specifically Indian or tropical disease, also being prevalent in China, the Mediterranean basin, European countries such as Italy, Spain and Greece, and also South America. It thus became a global phenomenon in the twentieth century.

It took a heavy toll of human lives and caused serious depopulation in Assam, Bengal and Bihar. Mortality from *kala-azar* was extremely serious and it is difficult to gain any exact idea of the absolute number of deaths it caused. For instance, *kala-azar* caused the death of 123,245 persons in Assam in the last decade of the nineteenth century.[24]

But it caused many more deaths indirectly. The labour force was depleted by death and desertion and the efficiency of the remaining labourers was impaired. Consequently, cultivation ceased on extensive areas in the affected districts, and the land lost its value.[25] *Kala-azar* took such a deadly form in Assam that many areas became veritable 'valleys of death', and the province became known as a notorious centre of virulent *kala-azar*. The Garos called it *sarkari bemari* (British

Government disease) or 'saheb's disease' (British disease), not because the Europeans suffered from it, but because, they said, the disease was unknown among them before the sahebs took over their country.[26]

Prior to 1903, the aetiology of *kala-azar* was unknown in the medical world and confusion prevailed over the true nature of this epidemic disease. *Kala-azar* was then generally misdiagnosed by medical practitioners as a 'bad form of malaria'. But none could explain its fatal outcome and how it spread. After the discovery by Pasteur that many diseases are caused by the growth of certain minute organisms in the body, several attempts were made to identify the *kala-azar* parasite, but it remained elusive for a long time. Until 1903 medical men in England and India had no definite ideas about the true nature of this disease, which was known by different names such as Dum Dum fever, malarial cachexia, *kala-dukh* and *jwar-vikar*.[27]

It is difficult to identify the date when *kala-azar* first appeared in India. It has been pointed out by a number of scholars that before the 1820s few accurate records of visceral leishmaniasis (*kala-azar*) can be found since there were very many fevers in the tropics, malaria had not yet been identified, and 'died of a fever' was a widely used phrase.[28] Thus the fever that erupted in Jessore (1824–5), known as *jwar-vikar* and the outbreak of the dreaded Burdwan fever in 1863–74 were thought to be the same as *kala-azar*. Leonard Rogers maintained that *kala-azar* had spread to Assam from Rangpur in Bengal. He was also of the opinion that the Burdwan fever which caused havoc in Burdwan district in the 1860s and 1870s was a *kala-azar* epidemic.[29] But in neither case was he able to trace a direct connection between the diseases. U.N. Brahmachari of Bengal Medical Service concluded from both clinical and statistical evidence that Burdwan fever was of malarial origin.[30] Interestingly, most of the health officials (for instance, Dr James Elliot, Dr J.G. French, Dr David Wilkies and so on) who served in Burdwan in the 1870s observed both remittent and intermittent fever during the epidemic there.[31] Some of them found that in some places Burdwan fever was amenable to quinine, whereas others observed that quinine had only a temporary effect on the disease. Most of the officials used the term 'epidemic fever' or 'malarial fever' instead of malaria.

There is no denying the fact that *kala-azar* occurred in Bengal in the nineteenth century. But Rogers's assertion that the *kala-azar* epidemic in Assam was an extension of the epidemic fever of North Bengal cannot go unchallenged; nor is it tenable to maintain that the outbreak of Burdwan fever in 1863–74 was a *kala-azar* epidemic. This will probably remain a matter of controversy until a direct connection between the two is established. However, it appears that in some of the epidemics malaria and *kala-azar* coexisted and that in others one of the diseases was more prevalent. Perhaps in Assam, *kala-azar* was more common and in Burdwan epidemic malaria was more common.[32]

Kala-azar became a matter of concern for the government from the early 1880s when it began to be a serious menace in certain parts of Assam. The rapid progress of the disease towards the areas close to tea gardens alarmed the government. British investments in tea plantations might be at stake if the garden workers and areas surrounding the gardens were infected by this disease. It was also causing heavy depopulation in the tea-growing districts of Assam.[33] Therefore, the government, in order to arrest the diffusion of the disease immediately organized special medical relief measures, establishing dispensaries at various suitable centres and employing a number of medical subordinates to travel about and visit people in their homes. However, these measures proved ineffective. Because the medical men and subordinates had little idea about the aetiology of the disease until the parasite was identified in 1903, in most cases they treated it as malarial fever and were unsuccessful.

Attempts were made by medical practitioners of all shades to counter the terrible scourge but to no avail. Allopathic doctors in Bengal and Assam plied their patients with large doses of quinine, thymol, arsenic and fluorides, homoeopaths with their own preventives,[34] *kavirajs* and *hakims* delved deep into the ancient wisdom of India and Greece, but to no avail. Preventive measures like the segregation and evacuation of the healthy population and disinfecting operations, such as fumigation of houses with burning sulphur, washing of beds with strong boiling carbolic lotion, could not reduce the infection.[35]

In a deteriorating situation the health officials felt the need of more medical knowledge. On their recommendation, the government initiated scientific investigations into *kala-azar* from the 1880s. The first IMS officer employed on a *kala-azar* investigation in Assam was D.D. Cunningham who had done some work on a disease called Delhi boil in 1885.[36] However, he was unable to distinguish *kala-azar* from malaria. In 1889 G.M.J. Giles, sent to Assam on special duty to investigate *kala-azar*, believed that all those afflicted were suffering from malaria, and hence spleen enlargement had no importance in the causation of *kala-azar*. He later concluded that *kala-azar* was ankylostomiasis or hookworm disease. He did not think that climate or the small amount of forestation created by man or the proximity of swamps had any influence on the disease, though most health officials in India still believed in the miasma theory of disease.[37] The civil surgeons and other health officials in Assam who had the opportunity to study this disease did not, however, accept Giles's conclusion since hookworm disease was found in apparently healthy people in many areas where there was no *kala-azar*. Foremost among them was E. Dobson who maintained that the Assam epidemic was only a pernicious form of malarial cachexia.[38] Doubt over the nature of the disease was expressed by medical officers and civil surgeons of Assam from 1891–5 and they finally determined to reinvestigate the question. As the disease progressed further, the government ordered further investigations. In 1896 Leonard Rogers was sent in and Ronald Ross followed him in 1898. Both Rogers and Ross concluded that *kala-azar* was a virulent form of malaria,[39] despite the fact that malarial parasites could not be found in the patients. In spite of the availability of microscopes and slides this view was maintained, though well-known investigators such as Stephens and Christophers, in a Report to the Royal Society (1901), stated that they had seen over eighty cases of 'malarial cachexia and enlarged spleen' which did not show any malarial parasites.[40] C.E. Bentley also investigated *kala-azar* in Assam and suggested that *kala-azar* was due to an unpigmented malarial parasite. But later he suggested that *kala-azar* was a Malta fever.[41]

Thus all these investigations proved to be of little value in the sense that they could not achieve anything substantial and only confounded the confusion. Their observations and conclusions revolved around the question of whether the Assam epidemic was malaria or ankylostomiasis or a combination of both, or a new distinct disease. In other words, prior to the discovery of *Leishmania donovani*, there were two main opinions regarding the nature of this epidemic. One was that *kala-azar* was a kind of malaria and the other was that it could not be malarial. Sir Patrick Manson pointed out in 1903 that *kala-azar* might be caused by a micro-organism similar to the sleeping sickness parasite (trypanosoma), given certain points of similarities between the two diseases. But he believed that the disease was not malaria or ankylostomiasis.[42]

Kala-azar had been in existence in Madras for, at least thirty years before the arrival of Charles Donovan, who discovered the *kala-azar* parasite in India. The disease, known as the 'Blacktown Fever',[43] was limited in its occurrence in Madras Presidency, being confined to Madras town and particularly to the old city called Blacktown, later known as Georgetown. That it was a peculiar fatal malarial fever had been a matter of medical and sanitary discussion for several years since the early 1890s. It had long been perceived that the cases recognized as malarial fever and accompanied by enlargement of the spleen did not respond readily to quinine treatment.[44] The government's failure to investigate the disease was perhaps due to the fact that it had not reached alarming proportions and there was no tea industry in Madras to be affected by it.

However, in the year 1903 the causative agent of the disease was discovered as a result of systematic efforts by William Boog Leishman and Charles Donovan. Leishman carried out his research in Victoria Hospital, Netley, in Great Britain and Donovan in Madras Medical College in India. They discovered the *kala-azar* parasite almost simultaneously but independently in two different corners of the world. Henceforth, the parasite has been known as Leishman Donovan body (L.D. body) and the disease as *Leishmania donovani*. By 1904 it was established that L.D. body was the causative agent of *kala-azar*, the disease that had already caused havoc in the northeastern parts of the country. Thus the confusion and controversy so far prevalent among the medical experts of the world came to an end.

Donovan carried out research on this sui generis disease on his own initiative for quite some time and after careful examination he identified the killer under the microscope. He sent his slides to Ross and Charles Laveran (the French army surgeon who discovered the malarial parasite in 1880) and received their favourable comments. He also suggested after careful examination of the smears of spleenic and peripheral blood from endemic areas of *kala-azar* in Bengal and Assam that Assam *kala-azar* was similar in nature. Thus he established for the first time that the so-called malarial cases in Madras were identical with those of *kala-azar* in Assam.[45]

Ross showed interest in Donovan's work on *kala-azar* and urged him to conduct further research. He recognized the significance of Donovan's work and called the attention of the Secretary of State for India to it.[46] In a letter to Donovan dated 21 November 1903 he wrote, 'The matter appears to be of such importance that government ought to give you assistance in prosecuting the study of it, and not leave you without help as it left me.'[47] Although Donovan continued his research on *kala-azar* and its transmission long after 1903, he received little support from the government. In fact academic as well as administrative support to scientific research was crucial in nineteenth-century India, but neither Donovan nor Ross was lucky enough to receive this support. The subject of Donovan's research was an important one as the disease was then causing havoc in India. But if he had submitted a scheme or asked for any financial assistance, he would have been laughed at, censured or transferred.[48] His work and his discovery of the causative organism of *kala-azar* were wholly the result of his individual enterprise.

There was much discussion in the medical press regarding the new parasite. Subsequently the government initiated investigations into it and sent Lt. Christophers and Captain James to Madras to confirm of the new discovery of the parasite and do further research into the aetiology of the disease.[49] The Tropical Disease Committee of the Royal Society agreed with Major Ross that it was highly desirable for a complete study of this new parasite to be undertaken and carried out without delay. They requested the Government of India to support this project, and work on this parasite was thus quickly taken up in India.[50] During the next decade, Christophers provided his classic description of the pathology of *kala-azar*; Rogers demonstrated by culture that the parasite was a flagellate; Patton gave a clear account of the development of the various forms of the parasite in an insect host; while Mackie suggested, for the first time, the probable role of the sandfly as the transmitting agent.

Medical technology, prophylaxis and control of *kala-azar*

However, after the causation was confirmed, the question of cure and transmission of the disease arose. There was still no known remedy. The role of modern medicine was still limited. Drugs such as quinine, thymol, alkalis and some others were given to the *kala-azar* patients in the hope that they might do some good. Most of the village dispensaries were of a rude and uninviting nature and could not give any relief to *kala-azar* patients. Patients were disappointed at the doctors' failures and reluctant to undergo treatment. As has already been stated, preventive measures, including the regulations provided by the Imperial Epidemic Diseases Act of 1897 (Act III of 1897),[51] could not check the progress of *kala-azar*. The prevalent prophylaxis was found to be a fruitless exercise and *kala-azar* continued to kill the people of India.

It was not until 1915 that modern medical technology could be used successfully against the disease in India. Among those responsible for this success were Leonard Rogers of IMS and U.N. Brahmachari of the Bengal Medical Service. Leonard Rogers first introduced the antimony treatment to India in 1915 in the form of tartar emetic. It is, however, known that Drs Di-Christina and Caronia of Sicily obtained remarkable results from the use of this drug to treat *kala-azar* in the Mediterranean basin before Rogers introduced it into India.[52] The success of the antimony treatment seems to have been reported even earlier, as the Brazilian Doctor Gaspar Vianna used tartar emetic in the treatment of *dermal leishmaniasis* in South America in 1913.[53] But Rogers claimed to have discovered the remedy without previous knowledge of the work of the Brazilian and Italian doctors. In any case, use of this drug was also beginning in India at the same time, and Rogers, Mackie, Hume, Castellani and Brahmachari were the pioneers in the treatment of Indian *kala-azar*.

The introduction of the antimony treatment was a great advance in *kala-azar* research in India. About 70 per cent of cases could be cured with this drug.[54] But certain defects soon became apparent. Tartar emetic had some serious toxic effects which were observed by Rogers himself and also by Napier of the Calcutta School of Tropical Medicine (CSTM). It was then replaced by the better-tolerated analogue, sodium antimony tartrate, which was the first in a succession of antimony derivatives to be tested for the treatment of *kala-azar* by the young Brahmachari, who first used it in 1915.[55] But it was not a very safe drug either. In fact, the antimony treatment for *kala-azar* cases was not satisfactory and had certain disadvantages. It was long and tedious, the treatment with tartrates extending over a period of two to three months during which an average of thirty injections had to be given for a complete cure.[56] Patients grew tired of it and consequently a very large number failed to complete the full course of treatment. Certain very disagreeable symptoms were associated with the administration of the tartrates, such as coughing, vomiting and aching joints, and these provided a further incentive to patients to discontinue their treatment too early.[57] And, finally, a certain percentage of cases showed no improvement when treated by these drugs. N.C. Kapur, Resident Physician of the Medical College Hospital, Calcutta, observed in 1925 that a certain percentage of *kala-azar* cases proved resistant to both tartar emetic, and sodium antimony tartrate.[58]

Thus the antimony treatment was not very successful in the fight against *kala-azar*. Treatment was difficult to enforce in a state like Assam, then a hotbed of *kala-azar*, as patients discontinued it altogether or continued it only very irregularly after a few injections, making a complete cure very unlikely. In 1924, out of 48,770 cases treated in Assam, 16,733, or about 33 per cent, stopped treatment before the completion of their course.[59] So the uncured patients could become danger to others.

Though many practitioners were satisfied with this treatment, Upendranath Brahmachari was not content with these drugs and mode of treatment. He felt that to overcome the problem a more efficacious drug was necessary, one able to effect a complete cure in a much shorter time. With this end in view, Brahmachari continued his research on the chemotherapy of antimonial compounds. Between 1915 and 1921 he carried out many experiments in a small laboratory attached to the Campbell Medical School in Calcutta. He first synthesized several new inorganic antimonials and achieved some success in treatment with colloidal metallic antimony.[60] But, dissatisfied with these results, he turned his attention to organic aromatic antimonials. From 1920, receiving financial assistance from the Indian Research Fund Association for further research into the treatment of *kala-azar*, Brahmachari carried out experiments with various salts and compounds that he prepared, and tested them on animals (guinea pigs, rats) and in selected instances on humans. Finally, in early 1921, Brahmachari produced his brainchild, urea stibamine.

Upendranath Brahmachari (1875–1946) was born in Jamalpur (Bihar) and gained a B.A. with honours in Mathematics and an M.Sc. in Chemistry. As a student in the Calcutta Medical College, he obtained the degree of Doctor of Medicine and a Ph.D. in Physiology. He was very interested in tropical medicine and his knowledge of chemistry and mathematics perhaps stood him in great stead in his research into the preparation of urea stibamine. He served in different medical institutions in Calcutta, but spent the longest period at the Campbell Medical School (now Sir Nilratan Sirkar Medical College and Hospital), where he discovered urea stibamine, the most efficacious drug for *kala-azar*.[61]

His discovery of urea stibamine was not accidental nor was it easy. It occupied many years of research, a self-imposed task which he carried out with single-minded devotion and dogged tenacity. Though funded by the IRFA, Brahmachari had to work under great difficulty. No proper laboratory facilities were available to him at the time and he had to carry on his research in a small room without a water tap or gas point and lit by a kerosene lamp at night, and often beset by troubles and difficulties from many quarters.[62]

On the basis of experience and results gained from a series of cases in Shillong, H.E. Shortt and R.T. Sen concluded in 1924 that urea stibamine was superior to any of the other antimony preparations in general use and thus the most efficient drug for the treatment of Indian *kala-azar*.[63] Shortt recommended its trial in certain approved centres in endemic areas. Intensive treatment with urea stibamine throughout Assam after 1927 resulted in remarkable cures and fewer relapses.[64] Major Shortt, then Director of the *Kala-azar* Commission, described urea stibamine as a 'dramatic medical breakthrough'. It could effectively cure the disease within a short period making it less likely that patients would discontinue treatment before a complete cure. 'This was a dramatic curative success in tropical medicine and urea stibamine became the routine treatment in India with its many thousands of cases.'[65] The Public Health Report of 1933 claimed that approximately 3.25 lakhs of valuable lives had been saved in Assam as a result of this cure.

It also proved very effective in resistant cases of *kala-azar* which were non-responsive to other drugs. Urea stibamine thus became an established drug, which successfully combated the disease and saved the lives of innumerable victims. In 1933 the Director of Public Health of Assam noted that '*urea stibamine* was our mainstay in the treatment of *kala-azar*'.[66]

In fact, for most of the period of British rule, investigations into *kala-azar* were undertaken by individual workers on their own initiative and it was not until 1924 that a team of specialists was assembled to make a concerted effort to resolve outstanding problems with regard to this ailment.[67] In this context, the government and health officials played a very positive role. Government support undoubtedly contributed to the success of treatment by the new drugs found by researchers. Civil and health officials focused on the gravity of the situation caused by *kala-azar* and were looking for new remedies for the disease. In 1924, a special *Kala-azar* Commission was appointed by the Government of India, with S.R. Christophers as its director, to study the disease. With its headquarters at the Pasteur Institute in Shillong, the Commission was the outcome of a discussion in October 1923 at a conference of scientific workers in Calcutta where the members strongly stressed the need for organized work on *kala-azar*. The Commission was sponsored by the Government of India and the IRFA, and by grants-in-aid from the governments of Assam, Bengal, Madras, Bihar, Orissa and the United Provinces.[68] The Commission worked for six years and produced a flood of information on almost every aspect of the *kala-azar* problem.

In addition to the Commission, an Ancillary *Kala-azar* Enquiry was established at the Calcutta School of Tropical Medicine under the direction of R. Knowles with L.E. Napier and R.O.A. Smith as his assistants. Special *kala-azar* research wards were created in the Pasteur Institute and the Medical Research Institute at Shillong. The resulting recommendations led the government to initiate mass treatment with organic compound of antimony. *Kala-azar* research was also facilitated by the funding of the Indian Tea Association, Assam Branch, and the IRFA. Research into the disease continued under the auspices of the IRFA at the Pasteur Institute, Shillong, and at the CSTM, till the end of the British rule. Experiments conducted in these institutions on the vector's behaviour, early diagnosis of *kala-azar* by an easy pathological test, new drugs like SAG (sodium antimony gluconate) and so obviously added to knowledge about this fatal disease. But it was not until 1942, nearly forty years after the discovery of the parasite, that the sandfly was conclusively proved to be the vector of *kala-azar*. The *Kala-azar* Commission has been disbanded in 1931, and there was a lull lasting some years in research activities on this subject. But investigation on transmission was pursued under the auspices of the IRFA and finally the problem was resolved in 1942.[69] It was undoubtedly a great achievement of medical research in India and was the outcome of years of devoted work by the researchers of the CSTM, the *Kala-azar* Commission and other *kala-azar* research units of the IRFA.

Thus members of the IMS and Subordinate Medical Service pursued research on *kala-azar* for over fifty years and collectively contributed to a thorough understanding of the disease. *Kala-azar* also became the subject of enquiry by western scientists. Sir Patrick Manson and Dr Low studied *kala-azar* cases in the Seamen's Hospital in London. Captain Statham of the Royal Army Medical Corps also worked on it.[70] But India is believed to have played a more important part in *kala-azar* research than any other country in the world.[71]

Control measures: a critique

It may be observed from the above account that all probable methods of defeating *kala-azar* were known. Work was also carried out to establish the hypothesis that treatment of all cases in an area where it was endemic could help to control, if not eradicate the disease there. The fact that modern insecticides such as DDT, pyrethrum, etc. were effective against the sandfly was also known. But little was done by the state to utilize this knowledge, and the disease was far from under control.

In Bengal, recorded incidence of *kala-azar* (which is probably a fraction of the actual incidence of the disease) had been more or less steady for the twenty years from 1924 to 1943. Though the disease was showing signs of regression in certain districts in West Bengal, a study of the figures relating to its incidence carried out by P.C. Sengupta showed that the trend was towards an increase in a number of districts in East Bengal, particularly in Chittagong, Dacca and Faridpur districts in 1944.[72] In fact there had been a widespread increase of *kala-azar* incidence in different areas of Bengal. Even in Calcutta, where a clear focus of infection was discovered in about 1920–1, the disease had not only become more prevalent by 1947 but had also spread to other areas of the town.[73]

In Assam there had been outbreaks of *kala-azar* in epidemic form on several occasions. In Bihar an epidemic of *kala-azar* lasted from 1939 to 1941. Surprisingly, despite all the knowledge of the disease, its cause, diagnosis, treatment and prevention, *kala-azar* persisted in many parts of east and northeast India (viz. Bengal, Bihar and Assam) and it was increasing towards the end of the British rule. Mortality due to *kala-azar* continued to rise. The number of deaths caused by it in Bengal rose from 16,766 in 1925 to 21,642 in 1938.[74] The government actually failed to provide *kala-azar* treatment to the affected villagers. Most of them were left to their fate and died untreated. The weak public health policy of the government was responsible for this shameful picture.

In fact, the measures adopted by the government to tackle this disease in India were too limited. After 1920 in Bengal, responsibility for the situation was left to the local authorities – district boards and union boards – but the financial grants allocated to them were far from adequate. The number of *kala-azar* centres was very small. The district boards failed to cope with the situation, given their limited infrastructure and resources. The *Sanjivani* of 22 June 1895 points out that there was not a single charitable dispensary within 16 or 17 miles of the places stricken by *kala-azar* in Assam. People were dying like cats and dogs without medical treatment or attendance.[75] The number of *kala-azar* patients became so great that available CSTM staff were unable to deal with them.[76]

Carrying out a large-scale survey into the incidence of the disease and treating the sick could have constituted a successful campaign against *kala-azar*. But that did not happen as the government did not spend enough on it. Even Rogers had noted that with sufficient funds and medical staff a very great deal could have been done to eradicate this terrible disease.[77] The people of Assam, Bengal and Bihar were not opposed to western medicine. They quickly realized the benefits of successful medication and came to dispensaries to obtain it. But the government could not make treatment available to all the rural masses.

Government expenditure on the treatment of *kala-azar* was very small. The government sanctioned a very small sum to the district boards in Bengal.[78] Its grants to tackle a widespread outbreak of the disease in Bihar in the 1920s and 1930s were not adequate, amounting for example to Rs10,150 in 1926, Rs5,000 in 1927, Rs7,500 in 1932 and Rs10,000 in 1933.[79] In 1938 there were a large number of cases of *kala-azar* in Bihar, particularly in the north of the province, but the authorities believed the area to be only slightly infected, and failed to pay adequate attention to it.[80]

A resolution was proposed in the Bengal Legislative Council in 1930 to increase the annual grant to Carmichael Medical College and Hospital from Rs5,000 to Rs10,000. But Mr C.W. Gurner, Secretary to the Government of Bengal (Medical Department), replied that the financial resources of the Medical Department were not sufficient to cover the increase. He promised to consider the matter again when the budget had been increased.[81] Government measures to combat *kala-azar* were not satisfactory in Bengal, although the disease became such a serious problem that it received attention from politicians. The issue of *kala-azar* was raised on several occasions in sessions of the Bengal Legislative Council from 1918 onwards. Councillors such as Brojendra Kishore Ray Chaudhuri, Jatindranath Chakraburtty, Maulavi Kasiruddin Ahmad and A.F.M. Abdur Rahaman asked questions repeatedly on research into *kala-azar*, arrangements for its treatment in the village dispensaries, the allocation of funds, steps taken by the government to control the disease and so on.[82]

The state of public health was certainly bad in Bengal. The villages in Dinajpore district had inadequate numbers of dispensaries. The union boards demanded the creation of enough properly stocked dispensaries for there to be one within six miles of anywhere in the district. They emphasized the need for immediate and adequate medical attention because many people were dying from malaria and *kala-azar* in the 1930s.[83] John Anderson, the Governor of Bengal in the 1930s, has also noted the deficiency of public health services in Bengal, observing that formerly healthy districts had become hotbeds of malaria.[84] A similarly dismal picture was also noted by Arthur Dash, Secretary to the Government of Bengal in 1927. He pointed out the wretched condition of a *kala-azar* dispensary in Bengal, which was staffed by an untrained medical practitioner.[85]

On the other hand, the government seems to have been reluctant to accent the courageous new proposals made by research scientists for further investigation into *kala-azar*. When the Director of the *Kala-azar* Commission, H.E. Shortt, applied for financial assistance to enable him to undertake experiments into transmission on human volunteers, his request was refused and he was forbidden to undertake the experiments.[86] The authorities may have been frightened by the possibility of accidents in such experiments. But the volunteers, who were being highly paid, were unlikely to die as treatment was at hand. Shortt was not the man to be deterred by what he regarded as 'spineless higher authority'. He continued the experiments for several months and ultimately met with success. Members of his scientific staff, knowing the background, were of the opinion that it was unjustifiable to put full responsibility for these experiments upon Shortt, and refused to participate in the proposed experiments unless ordered to do so by the Director. Shortt gave the order and his courageous decision led to proof of the mode of transmission of *kala-azar*.[87] This incident provides an excellent illustration of the way in which IMS members sometimes had to act on their own initiative and bear the full responsibility for the consequences of their actions. The apathetic attitude of the Government of India to medical research has been criticized by researchers like Ross and Haffkine and also by the Bhore Committee (1943). It has been argued by scholars that medical research in India did not receive priority but came second to political and economic imperialism.[88] They also mention that medical research was almost non-existent outside a few big institutions in Calcutta, Delhi, Madras and Kasauli. The paucity of equipment and funds, the lack of full-time professors and assistants, and the development of the Medical College in isolation from the university and other science departments would seem to be responsible for this failure. The post-war Health Survey Committee was of the opinion that the central government had little influence on the handling of epidemics, medical educational standards and research in the provinces.[89]

The IRFA's medical research was hampered by the First World War. Research into *kala-azar* in Assam and Madras was closed down. Efforts were made to find a Bacteriological Department officer to take charge of the whole enquiry into *kala-azar* in Assam, but the shortage of officers available for civil duty made it impossible.[90] Moreover, the government was not liberal in spending money on *kala-azar* research in India. Grants recommended for *kala-azar* research at the CSTM, the Medical School in Darbhanga (Bihar) and the Pasteur Institute in Shillong (Assam) were not sufficient.[91] Funds were extracted from India for research in England on 'tropical diseases', although the same arrangement was denied to the colony. An Advisory Committee for Tropical Diseases Research Fund was constituted by Mr Chamberlain, the Colonial Secretary in 1904. In 1910 the Government of India contributed £500, while the Imperial Government provided £100. From this fund grants were made to the Schools of Tropical Medicine in London and Liverpool.[92]

In fact government reluctance to finance medical research was apparent not only in the case of *kala-azar* but also in that of malaria and some other diseases. In 1904 Col. W.G. King, Sanitary Commissioner of Madras, proposed undertaking an investigation into the difference between various types of fever and their aetiology, a topic, which could be of much scientific interest. But the Madras Government ignored the proposal because of its financial implications.[93] In fact the government paid little attention to research on the prevention, cure and eradication of disease, and only took palliative measures when forced by necessity.

Moreover, no effective means of prevention, based on accurate epidemiology of the disease, had been devised. Ongoing research had already added to the existing knowledge and provided important clues pointing to the sandfly as the vector of this disease. But measures for vector control had not been found even after 1942 when the mystery of how *kala-azar* was transmitted was finally solved and the Director of Public Health of Assam advocated further preventive measures mainly for controlling the vectors. Moreover, surveys could not be carried out thoroughly during the Second World War years due to paucity of doctors. *Kala-azar* caused a great deal of morbidity and mortality as late as the 1940s. Work continued on early detection and treatment of patients, but nothing was 'done to prevent the spread of disease by a direct attack on the transmitting agent'. No short-term or long-term projects for vector control, either by spraying insecticides (pyrethrum or DDT) or by providing better sanitation, were undertaken even after the war.[94]

Sanitary improvements and public health measures had long ago been suggested by Ross and Rogers to control diseases like malaria and *kala-azar*. But the government paid little attention. In his 1944 report the Director of Public Health of Assam mentioned that apart from insecticide spraying, improvements to sanitation in rural areas and liberal use of limewash in village houses could be effective for making conditions unfavourable for the sandfly. It could be argued that improvements in rural sanitation in India were constrained by the vastness of the subcontinent, geographical barriers and lack of personnel.[95] But lack of funds and the unwillingness of the government to initiate sanitary reforms seem to have been the primary obstacles. The government could have done more to tackle the incidence of *kala-azar*, at least in the infected areas in eastern India. The conservative and superstitious beliefs of the Indians might possibly have impeded sanitary reforms but this cannot be a defence for inadequate sanitary improvement. It was a government failure. The people would certainly have cooperated when they saw the benefits of better sanitation, just as they cooperated when the government imposed compulsory treatment for *kala-azar* and other regulations under the Epidemic Diseases Act.

Surprisingly, the question of village sanitation remained almost untouched, and even conditions in almost all the towns of Assam, Bengal, Bihar and other parts of India remained thoroughly unsatisfactory till the close of British rule. The recommendations of the Royal Commission (1857) on sanitation were initially accepted by the Government of British India and subsequently a Sanitary Act was passed (1864). But the vast majority of the villages in India received no sanitation.[96] In 1890 a Sanitary Board was formed for Assam to provide sanitation in some villages near the district or sub-divisional headquarters, but its recommendations were not implemented satisfactorily in most districts.[97] The post of sanitary inspector did not even exist in Assam before 1914. In the 1890s, the Sanitary Commissioners of Assam reiterated that sanitary works had not been realized satisfactorily in every municipal area owing to shortage of funds. Nor were the district boards and other local bodies in a position to do much in this respect. In the rural areas there was no system for the conservation and protection of the water supply. It is true that pollution of the water supply did not seem to be directly connected with the prevalence of *kala-azar*. Thus, planters in Assam and the Duars in general were reluctant to invest in sanitary improvements. Consequently, apart from *kala-azar*, diseases like dysentery and hookworm remained perennial health problems on the plantations. Mortality from infective diseases like dysentery and cholera were associated with the insanitary conditions in the tea gardens. Yet the planters were not convinced that expenditure on sanitation would be advantageous.[98] The living conditions of workers in most of the tea gardens were not good, consisting of small unventilated and damp rooms where the *kala-azar* vector could find easy shelter and bite the victims.

Conclusion

It may be concluded from the above that despite the availability of methods likely to eradicate it, including prophylaxis, *kala-azar* could not be prevented. The existing medical knowledge and the benefits of research on the disease could not be properly utilized by the government to deal with this fatal enemy of the people. Lack of funds and lack of positive will on the part of the government undermined the complete conquest of the disease.

Acknowledgement

The research for this chapter was made possible by generous funding received from the Commonwealth Scholarship Commission and the Wellcome Trust, UK.

Notes

1 Deepak Kumar, *Science and the Raj*, New Delhi: Oxford University Press, 1997, 165.
2 For details, see *Report of the Committee on the Organisation of Medical Research under the Government of India*, Calcutta: Department of Education, Health and Lands, 1929, 6 (hereafter *Report on OMR*); E.W.C. Bradfield, *An Indian Medical Review*, Delhi: Government of India Press, 1938, 192; Mark Harrison, *Public Health in British India: Anglo-Indian Preventive Medicine 1859–1914*, New Delhi: Foundation Books, 1994, 113.
3 For details, see *Report on OMR*, 11; C.G. Pandit and K. Someswara Rao, *Indian Research Fund Association and Indian Council of Medical Research 1911–1961, Fifty Years of Progress*, New Delhi: Indian Council of Medical Research, 1961, 3.
4 Shirish Kavadi, 'State Policy, Philanthropy and Medical Research in Western India, 1898–1962', *Wellcome History*, 27, 2004, 5–6.
5 Kumar, *Science and the Raj*, 170.
6 Harrison, *Public Health in British India*, 157.'
7 Michael Worboys, 'Science and the Colonial Empire, 1895–1940', in Deepak Kumar ed. *Science and Empire: Essays in Indian Context*, Delhi: Anamika Prakashan, 1991, 13–27.
8 Kumar, *Science and the Raj*, 178; Zaheer Baber, *The Science of Empire: Scientific Knowledge, Civilization and Colonial Rule in India*, New Delhi: Oxford University Press, 1998, 140–52.
9 Kumar, *Science and the Raj*, 178.
10 Kumar, *Science and the Raj*, 169.
11 Anil Kumar, *Medicine and the Raj: British Medical Policy in India 1835–1911*, New Delhi: Sage Publications, 1998, 205.
12 *Annual Report on the Working of Hospitals and Dispensaries under the Government of Bengal for the Year 1933*, Calcutta: Bengal Government Press, 1934, 11.
13 Government of India, Education and Health, Medical Branch, Proceedings No.1, August 1922, National Archives of India, New Delhi (hereafter NAI).
14 Government of India, Education, Health and Land, Sanitary Branch, June 1923, Proceedings No. 21; Government of India, Education, Health and Land, Health Branch, May 1925, Proceedings Nos 20–21, NAI.
15 Pandit and Rao, *Indian Research Fund Association*, 23.
16 Pandit and Rao, *Indian Research Fund Association*, 23
17 Dr Janet Vaughan, 'Papers on Health Survey Committee, India', Memorandum, Part I, 7, Wellcome Trust Archives (WTA), London.
18 Andrew Balfour and H.H. Scott, *Health Problems of the Empire: Past, Present and Future*, London: W. Collins, 1924, 136.
19 Thomas R. Metcalf, *Ideologies of the Raj*, New Delhi: Foundation Books, 1998, 173.
20 Metcalf, *Ideologies of the Raj*, 175.
21 Harrison, *Public Health in British India*, 150–1: Ira Klein, 'Medicine and Culture in British India', in Abhijit Dutta, Keka Dutta Roy and Sandeep Sinha eds *Explorations*

in History: Essays in Honour of Prof. Chittabrata Palit, Kolkata: Corpus Research Institute, 2003, 77–105.

22 Klein, 'Medicine and Culture', 102.

23 T.H. Davey and W.P.H. Lightbody, *The Control of Disease in the Tropics*, London: H.K. Lewis, 1956, 141.

24 *Annual Sanitary Report of the Province of Assam for the Year 1891*, Shillong: Assam Government Press, 1892, 17 (hereafter *ASR, Assam*); *ASR, Assam for the Year 1894*, Shillong: Assam Government Press, 1895, 23–4; *ASR, Assam for the Year 1895*, Shillong: Assam Government Press, 1896, 29; *ASR, Assam for the Year 1896*, Shillong: Assam Government Press, 1897, 30; *ASR, Assam for the Year 1897*, Shillong: Assam Government Press, 1898, 28; *ASR, Assam for the Year 1899*, Shillong: Assam Government Press 1900, 29; *ASR, Assam for the Year 1900*, Shillong: Assam Government Press, 1901, 5.

25 Leonard Rogers, *Report of an Investigation of the Epidemic of Malarial Fever in Assam or Kala-azar*, Shillong: Assam Secretariat Printing Office, 1897, 132 (hereafter *Report of Epidemic in Assam*).

26 Rogers, *Report of Epidemic in Assam*, 166.

27 Upendranath Brahmachari, *A Treatise on Kala-azar*, London: John Bale Sons and Danielson, 1928, 1.

28 For details, see Mary E. Gibson, 'The Identification of Kala-azar and the Discovery of Leishmania Donovani', *Medical History*, 27, 1983, 203–13.

29 Leonard Rogers, *Fevers in the Tropics*, London: Henry Frowde: Hodder and Stoughton, 1908, 33.

30 Brahmachari, *A Treatise on Kala-azar*, 3–7.

31 For details, see Brahmachari, *A Treatise on Kala-azar*, 2; Mary E. Gibson, 'The Identification of Kala-azar', 203–13; Arabinda Samanta, *Malarial Fever in Colonial Bengal 1820–1939: Social History of an Epidemic*, Kolkata: Firma K.L.M., 2002, chs 3 and 4; Dr John Elliot, *Report on Epidemic Remittent and Intermittent Fever Occurring in Parts of Burdwan and Nuddea Divisions*, Calcutta: Bengal Secretariat Office, 1863, 21–9.

32 Brahmachari, *A Treatise on Kala-azar*, 8; Acharya Prafulla Chandra Roy and Prabodh Chandra Bandopadhyay, 'Kala-azar O Tar Pratikarer Itihas' (in Bengali) [Kala-azar and the History of its Remedy], *Bharatvarsa*, Bhadra, 1348 Bengali Year (August–September 1941), 305–7.

33 *The Lancet*, 5 July 1913, 33.

34 Homoeopath doctors, such as Dr M Nandi, Dr Nripendra Chandra Ray and Dr Abhaypada Ghosh, claimed that *kala-azar* could be cured by homoeopathic medicines – arsenic, antim tart, apis mel, etc. For details, see Dr M. Nandi, *Homiopathik Mate Kalajwar Chikitsa* (in Bengali) [Treatment of Kala-azar in Homoeopathy], Calcutta, 1926, 26, 36–7; Nripendra Chandra Ray, *Kalajwar O Uhar Homiopathik Chikitsa* (in Bengali) [Kala-azar and Its Homoeopathic Treatment], Dacca, 1332 Bengali Year (1925), 9–28.

35 Upendranath Brahmachari, *Gleanings from My Research: Kala-azar, Its Chemotherapy*, vol. I, Calcutta: University of Calcutta, 1940, 186.

36 PP/ROG C 1/1–88 Rogers Papers, WTA, London.

37 G.M.J. Giles, *A Report of an Investigation into the Causes of the Disease Known in Assam as Kala-azar and Beri-Beri*, Shillong: Assam Government Press, 1890, 1–2, 40, 63–6.

38 D. Basu, 'Clinical Features of Beri-Beri', *Transactions of the First Indian Medical Congress held at St. Xavier's College, Calcutta, 24th to 29th December, 1894*, Calcutta: Caledonian Steam Printing Works, 1895, 71–6.

39 P.E.C. Manson-Bahr, 'Old World Leishmaniasis', in F.E.G. Cox ed., *The Wellcome Trust Illustrated History of Tropical Diseases*, London: The Wellcome Trust, 1996, 206–17; Ronald Ross, *Report on the Nature of Kala-azar*, Calcutta: Office of the Superintendent of Government Printing, 1899, 68.

40 H.H. Scott, *A History of Tropical Medicine*, vol. 1, Baltimore: The Williams and Wilkins Company, 1942, 551.
41 PP/ROG – C. 1/1–88 Rogers Papers, WTA, London.
42 Sleeping sickness is a long-known disease of the African jungles, endemic in Equatorial Africa and America. See B.I. Williams, 'African Trypanosomiasis', in Cox ed. *The Wellcome History of Tropical Diseases*, 178–91.
43 C. Donovan, 'Kala-azar in Madras', in *Transactions of the Bombay Medical Congress*, 1909, 159–66 (Wellcome Trust Library).
44 *Fortieth Annual Report of the Sanitary Commissioner with the Government of Madras 1903*, Madras: Superintendent Government Press, 1904, 18 (hereafter *Report of Sanitary Commissioner, Madras*); *Report of Sanitary Commissioner, Madras 1899*, Madras: Superintendent Government Press, 1900, 49; Government of Madras, Local (Municipal) G.O. No. 1598M, 29 October 1903, British Library, London.
45 Donovan, 'Kala-azar in Madras', 166.
46 WTI/DON/A2/6 Donovan Papers, WTA, London.
47 WTI/DONA1/2 Donovan Papers, WTA, London.
48 'Reminiscences of Donovan's Colleagues and Assistants', in D.V. Subha Reddy ed. *Special Supplement for the Golden Jubilee of the Discovery of Kala-azar in 1903 by Major C. Donovan*, Madras: Secretary, Indian Association of History of Medicine, no date, vii.
49 Government of India, Home Department, May 1904, Proceedings No. 109 Oriental and India Office Collection (hereafter OIOC), British Library, London; *Annual Report of the Sanitary Commissioner with the Government of India for 1902, and 1903*, Calcutta: Superintendent Government Printing, India, 1903 and 1904, 112–13, 97, 124–5; *Report of Sanitary Commissioner, Madras 1903*, 18.
50 Government of India, Home Department, May 1904, Proceedings No. 111, OIOC.
51 For details, see *ASR, Assam for the Year 1916*, Shillong: Assam Government Press, 1917, 11.
52 Brahmachari, *Gleanings from My Research*, 442.
53 *Tropical Diseases Bulletin*, 5, 5, 15 January 1915 – 15 June 1915, London, 269. Following the publication by Gaspar Vianna of cases of dermal leishmaniasis in South America successfully treated by intravenous injections of *tartar emetic*, Di-Christina and Caronia experimented with this treatment in cases of infantile *kala-azar*. The results they obtained were so encouraging that they were led to publish a note in the *Tropical Diseases Bulletin* in the hope that others would give the method a trial.
54 P.C. Sengupta, 'History of *Kala-azar* in India', *The Indian Medical Gazette* (hereafter *IMG*), LXXXII, 1947, 283.
55 Wallace Peters, 'The Treatment of *Kala-azar* : New Approaches to an Old Problem', *Indian Journal of Medical Research*, 73 (supplementary), January 1981, 1–18.
56 'The Treatment of *Kala-azar*', *IMG*, December 1928 (editorial), 707; *Annual Public Health Report of the Province of Assam for the Year 1923*, Shillong: Assam Government Press, 1924, 11 (hereafter *APHR, Assam*).
57 *IMG*, December 1928 (editorial), 707.
58 N.C. Kapur, 'Observation on the Treatment of *Kala-azar* with Urea Stibamine in the Medical Outpatient Department of the Medical College Hospitals, Calcutta', *IMG*, LX, May 1925, 206–10.
59 *APHR, Assam for the Year 1923*, Shillong: Assam Government Press, 1924, 11 and *APHR, Assam for the Year 1924*, Shillong: Assam Government Press, 1925, 15.
60 Philip D. Marsden, 'The Discovery of Urea Stibamine', *Revista da Sociedade Brasileira de Medicina Tropical*, 19, 1996, 115.
61 For biographical/research details related to Upendranath Brahmachari, see Achintya Kumar Dutta, 'Upendranath Brahmachari in Pursuit of Kala-azar', in Chittabrata Palit and Achintya Kumar Dutta eds *History of Medicine in India: The Medical Encounter*, Delhi: Kalpaz Publications, 2005, 139–55.

62 'Conquest of *Kala-azar*', *Science and Culture*, 6: 9, 1941, 529.

63 H.E. Shortt and Ram Taran Sen, 'Urea Stibamine in the Treatment of *Kala-azar*', *Indian Journal of Medical Research*, 11:2, 1923, 653–9; and 'Final Report on the Use of Urea Stibamine', *Indian Journal of Tropical Medicine*, 12:2, 1924, 335–6.

64 Treatment with urea stibamine along with existing drugs began in the Pasteur Institute, Shillong, in 1922 and gradually increased afterwards; *see The Seventh Annual Report of the King Edward VII Memorial Pasteur Institute, Shillong for the Year ending December 1923*, Shillong: Assam Government Press, 1924, 3.

65 *Triennial Report on the Working of the Dispensaries in Assam for the Years 1926, 1927 and 1928*, Shillong: Assam Government Press, 1928, 5; MSS/EUR, '*In the Days of the Raj and After, Doctor, Soldier, Scientist, Sikari*' by H.E. Shortt, 73, OIOC (hereafter MSS/EUR, *Shortt's Papers*.).

66 Brahmachari, *Gleanings from My Research*, 458.

67 Papers of H.W. Mulligan; for details, see the manuscript entitled 'The Indian Medical Service: A History of Its Medical Research 1600–1982', Ch. 4, 88, contained in Papers of H.W. Mulligan, WTA, London (hereafter Mulligan Papers). Mulligan's MSS was not published.

68 Government of Assam, Local Self-Government Department, Medical Branch, September 1924, Proceedings No. 17; Medical Department, Medical Branch, June 1931, Proceedings No. 52, OIOC.

69 Mulligan Papers, 89; P.C. Sengupta, 'History of Kala-azar in India', *IMG*, May 1947, 281–6.

70 W.S. Patton, 'Preliminary Report on the Development of the Leishman-Donovan Body in the Bed-Bug', in *Scientific Memoirs No. 27*, Calcutta: Superintendent Government Printing, 1907, 3.

71 L.E. Napier, 'India's Contribution Towards the Solution of Kala-azar Problem', *Indian Medical Record*, February 1930, 18.

72 'History of Kala-azar in India', *IMG*, May 1947, 281–6.

73 'History of Kala-azar', *IMG*, May 1947, 281–6.

74 *Bengal Public Health Report for the Year 1926*, Calcutta: Bengal Secretariat Book, 1927, 52 (hereafter *BPHR*); *BPHR for the Year 1939*, 74.

75 *Confidential Reports on Native Papers for the Week Ending the 29 June 1895*, West Bengal State Archives, Calcutta.

76 *Annual Report of the Calcutta School of Tropical Medicine Institute of Hygiene and the Carmichael Hospital for Tropical Diseases for the Year 1924*, Calcutta: Bengal Government Press, 1925, 9.

77 Leonard Rogers, *Recent Advances in Tropical Medicine*, London: J. and A. Churchill, 1928, 33–4.

78 For details see Kabita Roy, *History of Public Health: Colonial Bengal 1921–1947*, Calcutta: K.P. Bagchi, 1998, 71–2.

79 *Triennial Report on the Working of the Hospitals and Dispensaries in Bihar and Orissa for the Years 1932, 1933 and 1934*, Patna: Bihar Government Press, 1935, 11, 11 and 14, respectively; *Annual Returns of Hospitals and Dispensaries in Bihar and Orissa for 1926*, Patna: Bihar Government Press, 1927, 3 (hereafter *ARHD in Bihar and Orissa); ARHD in Bihar and Orissa for 1927*, 3; *ARHD in Bihar and Orissa for 1932*, 2.

80 *Reports of the Kala-azar Commission, India, Report No. 1 (1924–1925)*, Calcutta: Thacker Spink, 1926, 277; *Annual Public Health Report of the Province of Bihar for the year 1938*, Patna: Bihar Government Press, 1940, 18.

81 *Annual Report of the Working of Carmichael Medical College, Belgachia, Calcutta for 1930–31*, Calcutta: Bengal Government Press, 1931, 6–7.

82 Proceedings of the Bengal Legislative Council 1918–1928, relevant pages (School of Oriental and African Studies Archives, London).

83 MSS/EUR, Papers of Frank Owen Bell, Part 2, Tour to Dinajpore in 1938–39, 33–34, OIOC.

84 MSS/EUR: Papers of Sir John Anderson Governor of Bengal, 1932–39, Part 14A, 11–14, OIOC.

85 MSS/EUR, The Memoirs of Sir Arthur Dash, Part 2, 43, OIOC.

86 Mulligan Papers, 100.

87 MMS/EUR, *Shortt's Papers*, 112–13.

88 Kumar, *Medicine and the Raj*, 207.

89 Vaughan, 'Papers on Health Survey Committee, India', 1944, Part I, 11, WTA, London.

90 *Annual Report of the Board of Scientific Advice for India for the year 1915–16*, Calcutta, 1917, 181 (hereafter *Report of the BSA*); and *Report of the BSA for 1919–20*, Calcutta, 1921, 55.

91 *Report of the Scientific Advisory Board of the Indian Research Fund Association for the Year 1938*, New Delhi: Indian Research Fund Association, 1940, 195 (hereafter *IRFA Report*); *IRFA Report* for the year *1939*, New Delhi: Indian Research Fund Association, 124; *IRFA Report for the Year 1940*, New Delhi: Indian Research Fund Association, 154; *IRFA Report for the Year 1943*, New Delhi: Indian Research Fund Association, 145.

92 *Annual Report of the Working of Carmichael Medical College, Belgachia, Calcutta for 1930–31*, Calcutta: Bengal Government Press, 1931, 6–7.

93 V.R. Muraleedharan, 'Malady in Madras: The Colonial Government's Response to Malaria in the Early 20th Century', in Kumar ed. *Science and Empire*, 101–14.

94 *APHR*, *Assam for the Year 1944*, 11; Extract from the File No. MPH 4/42, dated 5 February, 1942 of the Government of Assam, Medical Department (Public Health) Proceedings in the *APHR, Assam for the year 1940*; H. E. Shortt, 'Recent Research on Kala-azar in India', *Transactions of the Royal Society of Tropical Medicine and Hygiene*, 39:1, 1945, 13–29.

95 Harrison, *Public Health in British India*, 191.

96 Balfour and Scott, *Health Problems of the Empire*, 128, 136; *APHR, Assam for the Year 1944*, 14.

97 *ASR, Assam for the Year 1890*, Shillong: Assam Government Press, 1891 (Appendix B), 41.

98 Ralph Shlomowitz and Lance Brenan, 'Mortality and Migrant Labour in Assam, 1865–1921', *Indian Economic and Social History Review*, 27:1, 1990, 85–110.

7 The leprosy patient and society

Colonial Orissa, 1870s–1940s

Biswamoy Pati and Chandi P. Nanda

Contemporary scholarship on leprosy in colonial India has seen social historians of medicine focusing on several aspects of the disease. These range from where leprosy developed and the health concerns it posed to the asylums and the patients in them.[1] After all, leprosy did have serious meanings in colonial India. The speculative discourses on its causes included racist assumptions that linked it to the diet and eating habits of the colonized race. In fact, fear of the disease in the 'home' country created a mindset that seems to have gripped the colonial administration, including its medical wing, even after Hansen's discovery of the bacillus in the mid-1870s. The contribution of missionaries has some significance, especially in the period when the causes of leprosy were not known, as well as in the post-Hansen phase, though missionary interventions related to leprosy began in the early years of the twentieth century in Orissa.[2] Subsequently, Gandhian political discourse created new possibilities for the people affected by the disease through his attempt to create a new environment for negotiating it.

This chapter attempts to explore the social history of leprosy in colonial Orissa. It begins by touching upon the popular, *adibasi* (viz. tribal) perceptions of the disease and indigenous healing methods, including the initiatives undertaken by the ruling chiefs of Keonjhar, a princely state. It then proceeds to focus on the way leprosy was located by the colonial health establishment. Viewed from within the framework of its concern for public health, the chapter then delineates the ambiguities and inner conflicts related to leprosy interventions in Orissa. Finally, it examines the life of the people inside the leprosy asylum at Cuttack and unravels some of the complexities involved in the way they negotiated it.

Traditional healing methods

We begin by exploring what can perhaps be called traditional methods of treating leprosy; focusing on the former princely state of Keonjhar. Our discussion is based on the palm-leaf manuscripts preserved by the descendants of the erstwhile ruling family of Keonjhar and on popular oral traditions.[3] Although these palm-leaf manuscripts describe several aspects related to treating leprosy in Keonjhar from the seventeenth century, it is highly possible that – given the search for 'ancientness' of most of the princely states in colonial Orissa – they might actually have been produced only in the nineteenth century.[4]

The palm-leaf manuscripts and the popular oral tradition suggest that one of the kings who ruled before the seventeenth century had learnt in a dream about the usefulness of the Bhramaramari plant as a cure for leprosy, and was 'advised' to popularize the plant for the welfare of the people. The raja (king) regarded this dream as a divine intervention – a theme that is stressed in the popular oral tradition. In the dream, the king was ordered to find the plant in a specific site in a dense forest. He was given detailed instructions on how to use it for the treatment of leprosy. This dream became the basis for a process associated with the virtual deification of the plant and its subsequent ascendancy to the position of a local goddess in the region. Subsequently, the royal order of Keonjhar state employed a priestly class called *dehuri* for the worship of the Bhramaramari plant in the woods. The *dehuri* enjoyed certain privileges and were also entrusted with responsibility for collecting parts of the Bhramaramari plant, which were handed over to the raja of Keonjhar.[5]

The small branches of the Bhramaramari plant, received from the *dehuri*, were preserved in the royal store-house known as the Bhramaramari Bhandara (store-house), under the supervision of a royal officer called Gantayita. Leprosy patients from different parts of the state and beyond thronged the gate of the palace in the hope of receiving the Bhramaramari medicine. They openly assembled at the palace without any fear of the stigma attached to leprosy. The medicine was given to leprosy patients with detailed instructions on how to use it. However, with the growth of print culture, an instruction leaflet entitled *Byabastha Patra* ('Information regarding the use of medicine') was supplied to each patient with the medicine. As the principal devotee of the goddess, the king distributed the medicine personally, free of cost, to the patients at his doorstep. From the point of view of his people this enabled him to demonstrate his charitable inclination, through which he could assert his position as their chief.

The palm-leaf manuscripts provide details explaining the use of the Bhramaramari medicine to patients. They list the various spices, leaves and portions of the plant, which were to be dried and ground. These ingredients had to be converted into paste, and the prescribed quantity applied (twice daily) by leprosy patients, who were also instructed 'not to see the face of women', avoid non-vegetarian food, milk, and anything sour or sweet. They were advised to avoid massages while bathing. The instructions also stressed that patients should stay isolated indoors. The prescribed diet included hot rice, dried salt and *kalara* (bitter gourd leaves) and emphasized the use of warm and boiled water. After remaining isolated for a period of one to three weeks, the patients were expected to come out and offer *bhog* and *puja* to Shiva and Balabhadra, the state deities of Keonjhar both of whom had to be approached for their blessings for a cure.

The dietary prescriptions, with their stress on vegetarianism, demonstrate a significant level of Hinduization. The stress on warm and boiled water seems particularly striking and perhaps reflects interaction with the colonial medical system. The idea that 'male' patients should not see the 'face of women' illustrates the priority given to the treatment male patients. It also suggests that sexual restraint seems to have been prescribed. Although the importance attached to segregation and enforced sexual restraint can be read as a pointer to the process of Hinduization itself, it is worth speculating on whether it had anything to do with an awareness that human contact could spread leprosy. Interestingly, segregation was also emphasized in the colonial mode of treatment of leprosy.

Leprosy and the colonial interventions

Over the nineteenth century the colonial administration traced the source of the disease to centres of pilgrimage like Puri. Leprosy seems to have received serious attention from the colonial authorities as early as 1874. The presence of those affected by the disease at Puri, which was identified as a major centre for leprosy – where they begged for alms and received charity during the annual congregation (viz. *ratha jatra*) – posed serious concerns for the colonial administration. In fact, the Magistrate of Puri and the President of Puri Leprosy House proposed a law to empower the magistrate 'to get any person of Pooree examined by the Civil Surgeon to ascertain whether he was suffering from the disease of leprosy'. Those found to have leprosy were to be confined in a suitable asylum.[6] In fact, the Leper's Act III of 1898 – an all-India Act, introduced in 1901 to replace the Bengal Leper Act of 1895 – provided for the establishment of asylums to which 'lepers may be sent from specified areas, for the arrest of pauper lepers found wandering in such areas, and for their detention in an asylum'. It also empowered the local government to prohibit lepers from engaging in certain trades or occupations that were likely to endanger public health.[7] Thus, people affected with leprosy were treated not as patients suffering from a disease but as prisoners. This logic became associated with a class offensive directed against the poor affected by leprosy and seems to have been the basis of colonial policy vis-à-vis leprosy.

The colonial administration had to grapple with the problem of having to deal with people affected by leprosy wandering about in Puri. As articulated, this was primarily because of the presence of a large number of charitable pilgrims, *mathas* and *dharmasalas*. In fact, as felt by the Civil Surgeon, with the constantly available charity of pilgrims and *mathas* open to them, those affected by leprosy were not likely to come to the hospital. In a typically colonial/racist comment, which had distinct class overtones, he attributed the disease to the fact that 'the lower classes [of] Uriyas are a dirty race and have no ideas of cleanliness and sanitation'. He discarded the 'putrid fish theory' as a cause for the spread of leprosy in the district and in fact suggested that leprosy was very uncommon among people who ate badly cured and rotten fish.[8] The Civil Surgeon's Report recorded that 259 males and 36 females were treated for leprosy in various dispensaries during 1902 and 1903. It saw no reason to identify the characteristics of the leprosy patients in Puri town.[9] The colonial administration was after all not concerned about the poor and basically wanted to isolate and 'invisibilize' them so that they did not pose any problem to the urban population of Puri.

It was against this backdrop that the idea of establishing a 'leprosy system' at Puri gained momentum. In fact, the Magistrate and Chairman of the Puri municipality, J.R. Blackwood, strongly advocated the creation of a leper asylum in Puri and sought to raise the necessary resources for it as early as 1904. He mentioned that he had collected about Rs3,000 in the form of donations from members of the colonial bureaucracy and some of the local elites.[10]

He hoped that the government would make a liberal contribution since Puri was 'a noted place of pilgrimage for the Hindus'. When forwarding the proposal to the Secretary, Government of Bengal (Municipal Department), for approval, the Commissioner not only endorsed the Magistrate's idea of raising public subscriptions for an asylum at Puri, but also stressed that a 'leper asylum has long been regarded as a real want in Puri'. He hoped that the chiefs of Orissa and elsewhere would view this as a positive development and would 'be glad to give money to assist its establishment'.[11]

The proposal to build the leprosy asylum financed by the collection of public donations was finally accorded approval by the government in January 1905. However, while approving the proposal, the Government of Bengal sought information regarding how much the institution would cost, where the resources would come from, and how it would be managed. The government suggested the possibility of collaboration with the Leprosy Mission in India and the East for the establishment of the asylum. Given the level of responsibility involved, it also warned that 'the scheme [for the asylum] must receive the full approval of Government in respect of all the features of its management' before it could be started.[12]

The debates on the setting up of the leprosy asylum reveal that the middle-level officials of the colonial bureaucracy felt strongly that such an institution was needed. However, the high-ranking bureaucratic order regarded the proposal with a certain amount of apprehension. It seems to have been overwhelmed by the financial implications.

Responding to some of the clarifications sought by the government in March 1905, the District Magistrate of Puri came up with a full-fledged scheme for the leprosy asylum.[13] He was the chairman of the Puri Leper Asylum Committee, which also included Babu Sarat Chandra Rai as secretary and Babu Jagabandhu Patnaik and Rajkishore Das as members. The detailed report by the Magistrate highlights the thinking of the middle-level bureaucracy. It estimates the initial expenditure on building the asylum at Rs2,000–3,000, with recurrent expenditure of approximately Rs1,000 per annum. It advocated the idea of public subscriptions. The report specified that the management of the leprosy asylum would be vested in a committee consisting of the District Magistrate of Puri, who would act as the President. As suggested, he would be assisted by the Munsif as the Secretary, with the Temple Manager and the special Sub-Registrar as the other members of the committee. It also envisaged appointing a conservancy inspector as the executive officer, who would remain under the direct supervision of the Magistrate. Emphasizing the fact that the central object of the scheme was to provide accommodation for indigent, homeless leprosy patients, the Report made it clear that 'an important but not essential object of the scheme is also to provide food and clothing'. Whereas the first objective was regarded as fundamental, the second was not. The Report detailed the statistics of those affected with leprosy in Puri town and identified thirty-eight people who were homeless and were located in different places (seven in Singhadwar, five in Marcona Road, five in Gundicha Mandir, three in Bada Danda, twelve in Lokenath Ghat, and six others who lived under the trees on the bank of Narendra tank). It referred to a census taken three to four months previously, which had identified sixty-six. It attributed the decrease to the deaths of these people during the 'recently experienced cold weather'. The mitigation of such suffering was declared to be 'the main object of the present scheme'.

The Leper Asylum Committee also recommended separate huts for the leprosy patients, instead of one large *pucca* building. It also sought to discard the Gobra asylum model of Calcutta which was described 'as a jail system', since its primary objective 'appears to be the protection of the community against lepers'. It mentioned the 'frequent attempts . . . made by the lepers to escape' and deserved that a *pucca* building would fail to secure the main objective since the 'lepers don't want it. They have never lived in a *pucca* building in their lives and prefer privacy to stone walls and *pucca* floors.' At the first available opportunity, the District Magistrate showed the Commissioner of the Division the kind of houses which 'the lepers made for themselves when not interfered with by a public authority'. Besides appreciating this pre-existing site, the report observed: 'A *pucca* building is not within our resources and must therefore be discarded whatever may be the arguments in its favour.' As felt, 'if one kept in mind the expenditure, this would hardly offer anything better'.

It found that the pre-existing site had some advantages. Thus, as explained there

> is a small tank which is not interfered with by others. Secondly, there is a flower garden, the flowers of which do much to brighten the . . . place. It is therefore now proposed to follow on the lines which nature has already laid down for our guidance.

Arguing strongly for the construction of the asylum near the site of temple of Loknath, the tutelary god of those affected by the disease, the committee opined that:

> It is his shrine to which they repair for worship and it is when sleeping alongside the walls of his temple that they hope to receive a heavenly sign, which will indicate to them how they can be cured of the fell disease. It is therefore alongside of this temple that the site has been selected. The site has other advantages. It is well outside of the town. It is situated in a stretch of barren sand close to the sea, and the place is therefore fresh and healthy. Above all, we have a practically unlimited tract of land belonging to the municipality lying on our hands, which at present produces no revenue and affords innumerable sites for tiled huts. We get the land for nothing. Whether therefore, the question be looked at from the side of religion, sanitation or economy, a better site cannot be obtained.

The Committee examined the financial implications of the project in detail. The idea was not to have any medical attendants and, if possible, have the Civil Surgeon occasionally visit the patients as a matter of 'charity'. The only expenditure envisaged was the amount needed to construct thirty-eight huts, which were estimated to cost Rs50 each. It was hoped that the patients would be fed *mahaprasad* regularly, 'once daily and also be given uncooked rice, dal and vegetable'. The Committee stated that Babu Radha Charan Das, a 'zamindar of Balasore', had already provided Rs207–5–4 per annum for this purpose and some Mahantas of Puri had consented to feed up to forty-eight people. The Committee also mentioned the possibility of raising charitable donations from pilgrims visiting Puri, stating that Rs2,412 had already been collected. It was felt that a maximum of two people would have to be employed (with a salary of Rs6 a month each) to carry *mahaprasad* from the *muthas* to those affected by leprosy. There was no provision for clothing and small comforts. Consequently, all that was expected from the government was a grant to build 'a few huts'. In fact, if 'the drain of private charity' dried up, things could 'revert to their former state'.

It seems that the basic purpose was to provide a hut and a regular supply of food and prevent those affected by leprosy from begging on the streets. This, it was hoped, would protect the community 'automatically . . . from the lepers without inconvenience to the lepers themselves'.[14] In fact, when forwarding the Puri Leprosy Committee's proposal for the approval of the government, the Commissioner of Orissa Division expressed this object.[15] E.A. Gait, the Secretary of the Government of Bengal, had no hesitation in approving this scheme involving free accommodation and food supplied with the aid of organized private charity.[16]

The success of the initiatives to establish a leprosy settlement at Puri in 1905 was further reinforced by a scheme to house 'all the straying lepers of the district by erecting a suitable building' in 1907, a proposal for which was submitted to the Government of Bengal.[17] Among larger public initiatives, a meeting of the 'leading gentlemen' of Orissa Division was held at Cuttack (in 1907) 'to consider the best means for the improvement of the condition of lepers in Orissa'. A consensus was reached whereby a building suitable for the asylum should be erected at Puri to house nearly 300 wandering lepers, including males and females, Hindus and Mohammedans, to ensure segregation of all those affected by leprosy under the Leper's Act III of 1898. It was also resolved to set up local committees at Cuttack, Puri and Balasore, headed by a Central Committee at Cuttack, to monitor the collection of subscriptions for the asylum.

While supporting the above scheme, the Commissioner of Orissa pleaded to the government for funds to erect a suitable building for a leper asylum at Puri and meet its annual expenses. However, the Government of Bengal, while taking note of this proposal, reminded the Commissioner of the Orissa Division that the scheme for the asylum at Puri (mooted in 1905) was based on the understanding that government support was not needed. It also pointed out that the original intention of the scheme was to build not a *pucca* house but 'a range of huts to provide shelter for the lepers'. Remaining non-committal, it observed that until concrete proposals were submitted showing the financial overheads and details related to its management, no assistance could be promised.[18]

In 1908, the Commissioner of the Orissa Division also appealed to the Government of Bengal for the extension of the Leper Act to the district of Sambalpur, given the view of the district administration of Sambalpur that 'lepers are a menace to the people amongst whom they live and it is impossible to ensure that they will do nothing to endanger the health of others'.[19] He referred to the Barapali Sanitation Committee, which had sent him a list in March 1908 of twenty-seven leprosy-affected people who, they hoped, would be sent to an asylum. Mr Moberly, the Deputy Commissioner, repeated the request and urged the extension of the Act to Sambalpur district. He quoted the Civil Surgeon's view that this was absolutely necessary as there were a large number of leprosy-affected people on the Raipur-Sambalpur road from whom the general population needed protection.[20]

The Government of Bengal wanted to know if there was an asylum to house these people and if the expenses of transport and maintenance of the 'paupers' and others affected by the disease could be met. The Deputy Commissioner pointed out that the number of leprosy patients in the district was small and that they could be accommodated in one of the existing asylums. He stated that the cost of transport could be met from 'contract contingencies' and the District Council could be asked for a small grant. In his view, not all the leprosy-affected people reported in Barapali would fall within the definition of the term 'pauper lepers', but the power given by Sec. 9.11 of the Act would be most useful in controlling them.[21]

The Commissioner, on the other hand, agreed that the Act should be extended to Sambalpur district. However, he felt that since there were very few leprosy-affected people in the district (viz. forty-nine males and eighteen females) it was necessary to send them to the Purulia asylum, which had already been declared a 'leper asylum' under the Act.[22] This provided the Government of Bengal with the necessary argument against the extension of the Act to Sambalpur district. In the circumstances, the Lieutenant Governor did not consider it necessary to extend the Act to the district.[23]

How do we locate the issues and debates associated with the establishment of the leprosy asylum? In an overall sense, it was premised on the question of colonial investment and public charity. Moreover, there was a distinct class angle in the way the disease seems to have been associated with the poor. In fact, the idea of removing those affected by leprosy from public view was designed to keep them confined and isolated, as well as invisible to society. This implied segregating leprosy patients in centres of pilgrimage like Puri in order to protect the population. As seen, the urban elites of Orissa seem to have unquestioningly accepted this position for fear of contracting the disease. They thus legitimized the drive of the colonial establishment against the leprosy-affected poor.

The colonial administration was clearly reluctant to spend any resources and its efforts seem to have been dependent on charity. Thus, sensitivity to the wants of leprosy patients, cited as a reason for creating a space for them on the basis of what already existed near the Loknath temple, and for ensuring a regular supply of *mahaprasad*, needs to be seen within this framework. Ironically, in many ways both these matched and perhaps reinforced the idea of divine wrath/punishment. Sections of the colonial bureaucracy and the local elites made the initial donations for setting up the asylum. The latter included some zamindars who put in financial resources under the Provisions of Charitable Endowment Act of 1890[24] and some *mohunts* (priests) of Puri who agreed to feed some of the leprosy-affected or sections from among the emerging Oriya middle class. This offered the local elites an opportunity to engage in charitable activities and get incorporated into the colonial power structure.

Life inside the Cuttack Leprosy Asylum

The colonial perception of leprosy and leprosy patients underwent some changes by the 1920s when leprosy became curable. This was the context that saw the establishment of the Cuttack Leprosy Asylum in 1919. It was located 5 miles east of Cuttack, on an area of 30 acres, on the banks of the river Mahanadi. It could accommodate 240 inmates. The complex included a hospital with twenty beds, a laboratory, a dispensary, an operating theatre, a weaving shed and a meeting hall. The Mission to Lepers, which worked through the local Baptist Mission, provided an Honorary Superintendent to manage the asylum. This government-aided institution also received contributions from local bodies and some of the feudatory chiefs. The basis of the treatment was 'rubbing Hydnocarpus oil on the body of those affected by the disease'. 'Satisfactory results' were said to have been achieved, and in 1930-1 thirty-five patients were discharged 'symptom free' and 'none reported a recurrence of the disease'. Leprosy clinics were also opened at the dispensaries of Pattamundai, Mahanga and Jagatsingpur.[25]

Changes in leprosy patients' place in society are apparent in the 1920s. Not only had leprosy become a curable disease, but Gandhi's ideas and writings on working with leprosy sufferers undoubtedly played a part. The formation of the province of Orissa (1936) and the popular ministry (in 1937) seem to have led to the evolution of a policy to eradicate leprosy. Thus, a three-pronged strategy, including isolation, treatment and propaganda,[26] was articulated to combat leprosy. The propaganda component was taken very seriously: 20,000 leaflets were printed in 1938 in different languages and circulated in the province.[27] In a campaign to reach women, six female leprosy assistants were recruited for each of the six districts (in addition to the twenty-four doctors dealing with leprosy in Orissa).[28] As part of a plan to extend the Cuttack Asylum to accommodate more patients, a ward for children was created. Further resources had to be invested in such improvements to the asylum.[29] Although some scholars have studied how leprosy patients interacted with the asylum and the efforts to confine them in colonial India, further and more detailed research is still needed.[30] With this in mind, the sources available to us from the Cuttack Leprosy Asylum are examined next.

A few general points need to be made on the basis of information related to the asylum for the 1926–47. Some patients were cured and discharged. The initiatives for their rehabilitation imply that some were sent to training centres to learn a craft that would enable them to earn their livelihood. However, many inmates died in the asylum. For those who stayed alive, their confinement meant immense unhappiness and pain. Many tried to escape. Besides expressing their unwillingness to stay, many did not return after going out on leave. Some others were dismissed for 'bad conduct': this demonstrates not only their irritation and anger, but also perhaps a strategy for getting away from the asylum. The registers also refer to many inmates who 'absconded' from the asylum, and, although the details are not systematically recorded, this seems to have peaked in 1937 when the popular Congress ministry assumed power in Orissa.

In 1920, very soon after the establishment of the Cuttack Asylum, some of the inmates complained that 'they could not cook their food themselves and had no one of accepted caste to cook for them'. They also refused 'to move on to the ward for advanced cases where cooks were provided'.[31] Discipline was also seen as a problem. These features need to be located alongside a general aversion to the hospital. A report states: 'The fact that advanced cases who usually will die, have to go at present into the general ward, no doubt, frightens many inmates suitable for hospital treatment.'[32] Thus, Purusottam, whose right leg was 'useless', was sent to the hospital for treatment but left 'on his own accord'. Consequently, the very fear of death – largely associated with the general ward of the asylum – needs to be emphasized in explanations of why some inmates chose to run away from the asylum.[33]

On occasion, inmates had no choice but to leave without permission. Thus, Bhikari Behera – a male inmate – left without permission to attend to his ailing daughter. It was felt that he should be readmitted and his four-year-old daughter, who was 'very thin and emaciated', should be sent to the 'untainted ward' in the asylum for treatment. Such problems seem to have led to an official consensus to grant leave to inmates of the asylum to enable them to attend to urgent family matters such as the death or serious illness of a relative.

There was often confusion in identifying the disease, and patients wrongly suspected of having leprosy also found their way into the asylum. In 1920 the health inspector of Cuttack referred to a few 'doubtful' cases. Thus Nidhi Dehuri, who 'appeared to be suffering from syphilis', and Banchhanidhi Biswal, who suffered from 'malnutrition', were inmates of the leprosy asylum. Likewise, Ananta Senapati (male), Labanyabati Swain, Lachna, Chudhuri Bewa and Bhana (females) did not have leprosy.[34] The Civil Surgeon also noticed 'a blind female non-leper sitting in one of the cook rooms in the male part of the Asylum'.[35] All these people were discharged.

The intermingling between those who had leprosy and those who did not, and between those who had acute symptoms and those not severely affected by the disease, seems to have been a problem for the inmates, the authorities of the health establishment and visitors to the asylum. In fact, in 1924 a visitor to the asylum seems to have been particularly upset by this feature. While suggesting measures to remedy the problem, he urged that those who were showing 'signs of recovery' should be kept 'apart from those who [are] badly affected by the disease'.[36]

Some patients showed signs of improvement during treatment. However, they stayed in the asylum, perhaps because they did not have any where else to go. This led to a deterioration in their condition. Thus, when both Sundari Das and Kuntia were reported to have vastly improved, they were moved to the observation ward for three months. Subsequently, although they were 'declared cured' as early as 1921 they stayed in the asylum.[37] Later on, in 1926, Sundari Das was found to have been 'infected' with the disease.[38] We are also told about Bedi (a woman) who was sent from Phulbani by the Sub-Divisional Officer. Even after it was found that she did not suffer from leprosy, she continued living in the asylum because of her 'bad condition'[39] – which in essence means her poor social origins.

However, other patients attempted to escape from the asylum in numbers that seem to have gathered momentum during the 1920s. In June 1922, eleven male patients from the Bargarh Sub-Division who had been inmates for more than two years attempted 'to leave the institution despite persuasion and remonstrance' from those in charge of the asylum.[40] The District Magistrate labelled them 'unreasonable grumblers' who pretended to be dissatisfied since even after two years at the asylum their condition had not improved and they regarded the rice and cloth supplied to them as 'insufficient and not good'. Subsequently, the health establishment identified the 'real motive', which was that 'they [had] become tired of staying at one place and they [wanted] to go about begging and enjoying freedom'. The Leprosy Committee went on to warn them of 'the risk and danger' involved in the 'foolish act' of leaving the institution. In this connection, it also emphasized the need to construct a compound wall round the male blocks, the inmates of which found it very easy to leave the asylum without permission and wander around and beg in the neighbouring villages. We also find references to inmates escaping the asylum after indulging in petty thefts. Thus, Babuli Behera (of Bamapada village, Balasore) escaped from the asylum in February 1925, taking property worth about Rs7–8–0 with him. A similar allegation was made against another inmate after he had escaped.[41]

There are also examples of people helping those affected by the disease, by admitting them into the asylum. Moreover, after being cured they seem to have been accepted by society. Bhikari Prusty was sent to Cuttack Asylum by a government pleader, Durga Prasanna Dasgupta. After he was cured he left the asylum with another person (a government pleader of Cuttack, Babu Kedarnath Roy) to be employed as a domestic servant.[42] Similarly, when a student of the Ravenshaw Girls' School, Cuttack, got the disease she was sent to the asylum through the initiative of Sashibhusan Ray, one of the pioneers of *Utkal Sammilani* and a nationalist activist.[43]

Many women, if discharged, did not have a home to go to and would as a result 'wander' round as beggars. This problem led some in the colonial health establishment to foreground the 'crying need' for a 'colony' to house men and women, where they could be given light work. The concern for children in the asylum was premised on the hope of a 'safer future' since they were expected to be more responsive to treatment. It was hoped that they would return to their homes after being cured.[44]

On 5 April 1940 what may be called the first strike among the inmates of the

Cuttack Asylum was reported.[45] Under the leadership of Daitari Das, the inmates met the Honorary Superintendent of the asylum and protested against the method of treatment followed by the medical department and about the poor quality of the rice that was distributed. As a mark of protest, a number of patients refused to come for their routine injections the next day. They further resolved that they all would leave the asylum in the event of any one of them being dismissed.

This development prompted the formation of a committee headed by Dr Ansurddin, the District Leprosy Officer, to look into the grievances of the inmates. It found that the patients were dissatisfied with the treatment given and the attitude of the doctor, but after allowing the patients to present their 'grievances' individually, it realized that most of these were 'frivolous'. Two of the patients, Sudarshan Satpati and Madan Mangi, complained that they had made no progress since they had joined the asylum. Madan also complained about the injection given to him. After listening to their grievances, the committee ordered them to leave the asylum since 'they were not satisfied with the treatment extended to them'.

Once this order was announced, the other patients 'threatened to leave in a body' and 'some started marching off towards the gate'. This crisis prompted the authorities to seek the help of the police to maintain 'order' in the asylum. The police who rushed to the asylum immediately 'controlled the situation and did not allow any of the patients to go away'. The Inspector of Police arrived to 'mediate'. The patients demanded that the doctor be transferred. They also opposed the decision to dismiss the two patients. When they were told that they would be forgiven if they apologized and withdrew their statements, both Sudarshan and Madan complied and were allowed to continue residing in the asylum.

In another incident in 1947, a patient – Narsingha Naik, an ex-Indian National Army activist – assaulted the Medical Officer and overseer of the asylum with a *lathi*. The police who enquired into the incident made no arrests. Narsingha was a member of the asylum's Boy Scouts Organization, and the Superintendent of the asylum suspected the scout master of engineering the whole incident, and recommended the suspension of the Scouts Organization.[46] Although there is no proof, the timing of this particular event seems to be significant and it may have had some connection with the coming of *swaraj* and independence.

The poverty of many or most of the inmates is self-evident. This partly explains the confusion regarding whether many of them had leprosy or not. In many cases, people who did not have leprosy or had been cured continued to live in the asylum because they had nowhere else to go. The problem appears to have been particularly acute for women. Entering the asylum seems to have meant that they had lost their homes for ever. The case of the blind woman unaffected by leprosy who apparently found shelter in the asylum could be mentioned here. In this sense at least many of the poor inmates of the asylum seem to have turned the logic of confinement upside down in accordance with their survival strategies.

When considering those who tried to escape, we should bear in mind the very bad living conditions in the Cuttack Leprosy Asylum. In 1939 this was attributed primarily to overcrowding (which implied that even unused kitchens, the observation ward and 'untainted' ward were converted into general wards to accommodate 114 patients over and above the sanctioned strength of 270 – instead of new rooms being built). There were other problems like corruption. A petition submitted by a senior compounder (doctor's non-medical assistant, employed by the colonial administration) of the Cuttack Asylum, Dhirendra Kumar Das, to the Superintendent describes some of the problems. In his petition Dhirendra appealed for forgiveness and admitted that he had not maintained proper accounts of the donations received by him and that he was prepared to return the money he had misappropriated.[47] This implies that resources meant for inmates were siphoned off. All this material offers clues about the functioning of the Cuttack Leprosy Asylum and how it was perceived by the inmates.

Conclusion

This chapter has explored features related to leprosy. It began by outlining what can perhaps be described as indigenous *adibasi* attitudes to the disease and its treatment. However, these attitudes had associations with both the brahminical/Kshatriya order and the colonial health system. The traditional method of treating the disease had significant characteristics that are visible in the way the *adibasi* world and the durbar at Keonjhar negotiated it. As shown, there were deeper and more complex implications that sustained this drive from the point of view of the durbar. At the same time, a social historian of health and medicine has to see this as a process related to the feudal order's search for legitimacy in the crisis-ridden period of the nineteenth century. This made the Keonjhar durbar not only accept leprosy as a disease but also provide space for its treatment through what was to become a formal process.

We also examined specific aspects of the colonial interventions and the inner conflicts, contradictions and tensions in the colonial establishment vis-à-vis leprosy, as well as the low priority given to what was clearly perceived as a disease of the poor. This factor perhaps motivated the colonial interventions, which had the support of the Oriya middle class. In fact, class perceptions vis-à-vis the poor – coupled with the insecurities created by the disease – resulted in a virtual class offensive directed against those affected by leprosy. Consequently, these people were seen as prisoners who had to be removed from society and confined to the asylum – which was in effect a jail – or the 'colony'.

Denied of any 'private space' to hide their disease, the homeless poor wandered through the streets, unlike the affluent classes who could conceal it in their personal, private space. This factor does not seem to have been understood. Consequently, it was only the leprosy-affected poor who posed a serious problem not only to the colonial administration but also to a section of the Oriya middle class. As seen, middle-class opinion legitimized this colonial class offensive, demonstrating that the anxiety was shared. The charitable initiatives of some members of the middle and landed classes need to be interpreted as part of their attempt to be incorporated into the colonial order.

It is impossible to say anything substantial about the perception of leprosy by society beyond certain generalized points. The disease was stigmatized and seen as 'God's curse' or part of a person's destiny. Nevertheless, a class component of the colonial official discourse affected the census operations that itemized the 'number of lepers' in different parts of Orissa. It united the medical, administrative and judicial establishments in a path-breaking decision to arrest or remove those affected by leprosy so as to 'invisibilize' them.[48] In this context the traditional feudal order at Keonjhar appears to be strikingly tolerant vis-à-vis the leprosy patient, compared with the colonial establishment or its middle-class legitimizers.

This chapter has also discussed how inmates interacted with the Cuttack Asylum and the world outside. This was marked by serious complexities as well as by the shifts and changes linked to the discovery of a cure for leprosy in the 1920s, which was reinforced by Gandhi's efforts for the welfare of those affected by the disease. While these developments opened up new possibilities, a remarkable degree of continuity characterized the idea of 'confinement', in many ways reinforced by the social origins of those affected by leprosy.[49] This 'past' survives today; after all, beyond the world of politics, the murder of Graham Staines in 1999 also demonstrates the location of the disease and those affected by it, as also the people who work with them.[50]

Acknowledgements

The support and encouragement of the Wellcome Unit for the History of Medicine, University of Oxford, for the collection of sources, and especially Dr Jo Robertson, is gratefully acknowledged. We would also like to thank Dr Jane Buckingham for her comments and suggestions. Needless to say, the normal disclaimers apply.

Notes

1 The pioneers in this field have been Sanjiv Kakkar, *The Patient, the Person: Empowering the Leprosy Patient*, New Delhi: Danlep, 1992; idem, 'Leprosy in British India, 1860–1940; Colonial Politics and Missionary Medicine', *Medical History*, 40: 2, 1996, 215–30; idem, 'Leprosy in India; The Intervention of Oral History', *Oral History*, 23: 1, 1995, 37–45; and idem, 'Medical Developments and Patient Unrest in the Leprosy Asylum', in Biswamoy Pati and Mark Harrison eds *Health, Medicine and Empire: Perspectives on Colonial India*, Delhi: Orient Longman, 2001, 188–216; and Jane Buckingham, *Leprosy in Colonial South India: Medicine and Confinement*, Basingstoke: Palgrave, 2002. Shubhada Pandya, ' "Regularly Brought up Medical Men": Nineteenth-century Grant Medical College Graduates, Medical Rationalism and Leprosy', *Indian Economic and Social History* Review, 41: 3, 2004, 293–314, discusses Indian medical students and the way they perceived leprosy. See also James Staples, *Peculiar People, Amazing Lives: Leprosy, Social Exclusion and Community Making in South India*, Delhi: Orient Longman, 2007, which provides valuable contemporary insights.

2 This is clear from the Mission to Lepers in India and the Far East (founded in 1874), *Twentieth Annual Report for the Year 1894*, London: John F. Shaw, 10–11, which lists areas where it was active in India.

3 M.M. Mishra, 'A Note on Leprosy: Sources Based on the Palm-leaf Manuscripts of the Rajasabha of the Erstwhile Keonjhar State', Oriya, unpublished. These manuscripts represent what can perhaps be seen as a shift from an oral to a written tradition.

4 This was associated with the very process of securing legitimacy from the colonial power and saw a virtual competition among the different princely states of Orissa, which sought

to prove their 'ancientness'; for details see 'The Brief Histories of Each of the 24 States (1909)', R/2 (285/1), Crown Representative Papers, India Office Library, London.

5 According to oral tradition, the Bhramaramari plant was originally found around a forest-ridden village called Kuntala in Keonjhar. It was believed that its medicinal qualities developed with the ripening of the trunk. Its name (Bhramaramari) was derived from the wandering beetles which met their death when they came into contact with the plant. Hence the name Bhramaramari came to mean the killing of beetles (*bhramara* = beetles; *mari* = to kill). Perhaps the death of a large number of beetles that happened to fly over the plant spurred the imagination of the *adibasi* folk to give it this name. In their perception, the plant itself emerged as a centre of divinity – a goddess possessing healing qualities.

6 Joseph Armstrong, Acting Magistrate and President, Pooree Leprosy House Committee, in his proposal to the Commissioner of Orissa, Accession Number 39792, Board of Revenue, Secretariat Records (loose), Orissa State Archives (hereafter OSA).

7 L.S.S. O'Malley, *Census of India, 1911, Volume V, Bengal, Bihar and Orissa and Sikkim, Part I, Report*, Calcutta: Bengal Secretariat Book Depot, 1913, 425.

8 The Report of Captain E.E. Waters, Civil Surgeon, Puri, to the Inspector General of Civil Hospitals, Bengal, 30 March 1904, in 'Leprosy in Bengal', Municipal Department, Medical Branch, 1904, Government of Bengal, B. Document, Acc. No. 12655, OSA. Interestingly, O'Malley, *Census of India, 1911, Volume V, Bengal, Bihar and Orissa and Sikkim, Part I, Report*, refers to the Conference of Leprologists held at Berlin in 1897, which had concluded that the disease was communicated by the bacillus, although its conditions of life and methods of penetrating the human organism were unknown. The conference had speculated that it probably entered the human body through the mouth or the mucous membrane. It delineated with a degree of certainty that humans alone were liable to be affected by the bacillus. It maintained that leprosy was contagious, but not hereditary, though it had resisted all efforts at cure. It discussed the theory of Mr Jonathan Hutchinson, FRS, that the bacillus entered the body through the stomach and not through breath or by the skin; in most adult cases it was caused by the bacillus entering the stomach due to consumption of 'badly cured fish' in a state of 'partial decomposition' or because of insufficient cooking. As suggested, the bacteria were not present in any other kind of edible fish and were found especially in fish 'imported from a distance'; a small quantity of 'tainted fish' was enough to introduce the disease. Nevertheless, it added: 'Mr. Hutchinson's theory is not confirmed by the result of the census over the areas where leprosy is most prevalent' (426). It should be mentioned here that *sukhua* or dried sea fish is still part of the ordinary people's diet in different parts of Orissa.

9 Report of Captain E.E. Waters, Acc. No. 12655.

10 Report of the Magistrate, Puri, J.R. Blackwood, 24 December 1904, Government of Bengal, Municipal/Medical, B.Doc., Acc. No. 12686, OSA.

11 Semi-official note from E.F. Growse, Commissioner of Orissa Division, to the Secretary to the Government of Bengal, Municipal Dept, undated, 1904, Acc. No. 12686.

12 Letter from L.P. Shirees, Secretary to the Government of Bengal, Municipal Dept, to the Commissioner of the Orissa Division, 25 January 1905, Acc. No. 12686.

13 'Leper Asylum in Puri', Government of Bengal, Municipal/Medical, 1905, B. Doc., Acc. No. 12700, OSA.

14 Leper Asylum in Puri, Acc. No. 12700, OSA.

15 Memorandum sent by E.F. Growse, Commissioner of the Orissa Division, 24 March 1905, to the Secretary, Government of Bengal, Acc. No. 12700, OSA.

16 Letter of E.A. Gait, Secretary to the Government of Bengal, Municipal Department, 19 April 1905, Acc. No. 12700, OSA.

17 Government of Bengal Municipal/Medical, B. Doc., Acc. No. 12940, OSA.

18 Letters from Chief Secretary, Government of Bengal to Commissioner, Orissa Division, 27 May and 11 June 1907, Municipal/Medical, Acc. No. 12940.

19 'Proposal to Extend the Leper Act to the District of Sambalpur', B.Doc., Acc. No. 12962.
20 Letter of the Commissioner, Orissa Division, 22 May 1908, Acc. No. 12962.
21 Letter from the Deputy Commissioner, A.N. Moberly, 4 May 1908, to Commissioner of the Orissa Division, Acc. No. 12962.
22 Letter of the Commissioner, Orissa Division, 25 May 1908 Acc. No. 12962.
23 Proposal to extend to Leper Act to the District of Sambalpur, Acc. No. 12962.
24 Letter from the Commissioner of the Orissa Division, F.W. Duke, to the Secretary to the Government of Bengal, 1 November 1905, Municipal/Medical, B.Doc., Acc. No. 12760, OSA. An 'endowment' was created by certain zamindars of Balasore for the maintenance of a Leprosy Settlement at Puri. In fact, this was officially designated as the Samanta Raj Narayan Das (named after Babu Raja Narayan Das, a zamindar of Balasore) Endowment for feeding the people in the asylum; see also *Bihar and Orissa District Gazetteers*: *Puri*, Patna: Superintendent of Government Printing, 1929, 151, for details.
25 L.S.S. O'Malley, *Bihar and Orissa District Gazetteers: Cuttack*, Patna: Superintendent Government Printing, 1933, 76.
26 G. Verghese, *Annual Public Health Report of the Province of Orissa for the Year 1937 and the Vaccination Report for the Year 1937–38*, Cuttack: Orissa Government Press, 1939, 24.
27 G. Verghese, *Annual Public Health Report of the Province of Orissa for the Year 1938 and the Vaccination Report for the Year 1938–39*, Cuttack: Government Press, 1940, 40.
28 G. Verghese, *Annual Public Health and Vaccination Report of the Province of Orissa for the Year 1940*, Cuttack: Government Press, 1942, 30.
29 G. Verghese, *Annual Public Health Report of 1937 and the Vaccination Report, 1937–38*, Cuttack: Orissa Government Press, 1939, 24, and Verghese, *Annual Public Health Report of the Province of Orissa for the Year 1938 and the Vaccination Report for the Year 1938–39*, 31, refer to the plan to extend the Cuttack Asylum by constructing a children's ward for which Rs15,000 were to be obtained from the King George V Memorial Fund, and the sanction of Rs36,000 for anti-leprosy work by the government, respectively.
30 Sanjiv Kakkar, 'Medical Developments and Patient Unrest in the Leprosy Asylum, 1860–1940', in Biswamoy Pati and Mark Harrison eds *Health, Medicine and Empire: Perspectives on Colonial India*, Delhi: Orient Longman, 2001, 188–216.
31 Report of the Health Inspector, Visitor's Book of Hind Kustha Nibarana Sangha (hereafter HKNS), 14 July 1920.
32 Report of Civil Surgeon, HKNS, 11 November 1920.
33 Report of Inspector General of Civil Hospital, Bihar and Orissa, HKNS, 25 April 920.
34 Report of the Health Inspector, Cuttack, HKNS, 4 July 1920.
35 Report of the Civil Surgeon, HKNS, 11 November 1920.
36 Report of a Visitor to the Asylum, HKNS, 22 March 1924.
37 Report of the Collector and Civil Surgeon, HKNS, 19 March 1921.
38 A Report of the District Magistrate, HKNS, 7 June 1922, visitor's comment on the asylum, HKNS, 31 March 1926.
39 Report of Quarterly Meeting of Leprosy Board, 1 December 1927 and 19 March 1928, HKNS.
40 Report of the District Magistrate, HKNS, 7 June 1922. In fact, this is clear from the day-to-day activities of the inmates in the Hind Kustha Nivarana Sangha of Cuttack: Report of the District Magistrate, HKNS, 7 June 1922.
41 Inspection Report of the District Magistrate and the Retired Civil Surgeon, HKNS, 28 April 1925.
42 Inspection Report, HKNS, 2 February 1925.
43 Report of the District Magistrate, Cuttack, HKNS, 10 March 1922. This girl was eighteen years old and was from Parlakhemundi, then in the Madras Presidency. While admitting

such patients, the Leprosy Board realized that 'on the successful treatment of the case, depends greatly the spread of the reputation of the institute outside of Orissa.' *Utkal Sammilani*, also known as the Utkal Union Conference; was a body comprising feudal chiefs, landed elements and the Oriya middle class that was established in 1903. Its aim was to unite the province of Orissa, parts of which were in the Bengal Presidency, the Central provinces and the Madras Presidency.

44 Speech delivered by Mr Lazarus, Honorary Superintendent of the asylum, HKNS, 24 March 1939; in fact, the problem of overcrowding can be judged from the fact that about seventy patients were being refused admission every year by the 1930s.

45 Report of a strike among the inmates, 5–6 April 1940, HKNS.

46 Report of Leper Asylum Board Meeting, HKNS, 15 November 1947. The idea of organizing a Boy Scouts group in the asylum originated in 1930, as seems to be suggested in the Quarterly Report of the Meetings of the Cuttack Leprosy Asylum Board, HKNS, 26 April 1930. The Indian National Army was set up by the famous Indian Nationalist Subhas Chandra Bose in 1943 to fight British colonialism.

47 Petition sent by D.K. Das, Senior Compounder, Cuttack Leper Asylum, HKNS, 1 March 1948.

48 The point regarding the loss of space of the leprosy patient in colonial India seems to have connections with the other complexities as well; for details, see Jane Buckingham, 'The "Morbid Mark": The Place of the Leprosy Sufferer in Nineteenth Century Hindu Law', *South Asia*, 20: 1, 1997, 57–80. Her argument is that the judicial authorities placed more emphasis on leprosy as a legal impediment to inheritance than the *dharmashastras* and by the end of the nineteenth century had shifted the basis of legal judgement on eligibility for inheritance from the 'religious', as emphasized in the *shastra*, to the medical. In this sense – largely inadvertently – the effort which was to 'know' Hindu law transformed it. She refers to the dual process of Anglicization and brahmanization of the *dharmashastra* which altered the legal status of the leprosy sufferer (80).

49 It is difficult to say anything about the way the people affected by the disease located themselves in the context of these changes. At the same time, the report of an inmate's suicide in 1953 outlined in the Visitor's Register of the HKNS for the 1926–53 phase perhaps demonstrates the agonized existence and alienation suffered by the inmates of the Cuttack Asylum.

50 An Australian missionary, Graham Staines and his wife worked in a home for the leprosy affected in Manoharpur, in the Mayurbhanj district of Orissa. Staines and his two children were murdered on 22 January 1999 by right-wing 'Hindu' fascists for his alleged role in 'converting' tribals to Christianity.

8 Institutions, people and power

Lunatic asylums in Bengal, *c.* 1800–1900

Waltraud Ernst

This chapter focuses on the institutional history of psychiatric institutions established by the British in Bengal during the nineteenth century. It looks at patient numbers and segregative admission policies, the mixed economy of mental health care and the plurality of approaches pursued by different practitioners and asylum staff, and evidence of abuse and kindly treatment. It also engages with the question whether the 'subjugation of unreason' and panopticon-style warehousing of the insane were key features in colonial institutions in Bengal. It finally argues that actual medical regimes, management structures and patient-doctor relationships were diverse and not always fuelled by the preoccupations of colonial and medical hegemonic power alone.

Asylums for 'natives' and Europeans

The history of British specialist institutions for the mentally ill in Bengal began during the second half of the eighteenth century, concomitant with the invasion of Indian territories by the English East India Company. The procedures involving 'mad' Indians and Europeans at that period closely echoed practices in Britain, where private individuals engaged in the 'madbusiness' offered rooms in their homes to local authorities and the fee-paying relatives of mentally ill people. In Calcutta, likewise, people considered 'mad' were sent to a Mr G. Kenderine's private lunatic asylum, which catered mainly for the colonial community.[1] The number of patients at this period was very small. The majority of the mentally ill among the Indian population remained, as before, under the care of relatives in their communities, while lower-class Europeans, who belonged mainly to the military, were more commonly confined within regimental jails and hospitals. In 1787, Assistant Surgeon W. Dick, who was later to become the East India Company's Examining Physician in London (1809–18), offered his medical services and the lease of his private lunatic asylum to the Government of Bengal. From then onwards, the practice of sending mentally ill company employees of both civil and military background to Dick's establishment became routine, although a great number of military people were still dealt with within their regiment.[2] On Dick's return to England in 1802, the colonial authorities decided to establish a 'government asylum', and the housing and provision of victuals and clothing were entrusted to an assistant surgeon or surgeon, who was also responsible for the patients' medical treatment at fixed rates.

Despite its name, the 'government asylum' still resembled too closely institutions involved in the much criticised private 'trade in lunacy', which was then widespread in England. Just as in England, the system in Bengal was open to abuses and corruption. The 'madbusiness' was soon to be restricted in the wake of lunacy reformers' campaigns for the establishment of non-profit-making government institutions during the first two decades of the nineteenth century.[3] In 1817, in line with lunacy reform legislation in England, the parliamentary board of control and the court of directors of the East India Company followed social trends in England closely and therefore objected to a company employee acting as the private contractor for the provision of victuals.[4] The company had been sensitised to potential allegations of corruption, not least by the famous trial of Warren Hastings. What is more, colonial authorities in India were subject to thorough scrutiny of every aspect of their administration during the regular parliamentary investigations into the state of the company's affairs, prior to the renewal of its royal charter (in 1813, 1833 and 1853). The regulations drawn up in 1817 therefore stipulated that the commissariat rather than the asylum superintendent was to provide for the approximately thirty to forty patients then confined at Calcutta and that both the province's medical board and the chief magistrate had to examine the institution monthly and write a report on its management and the condition of every patient.[5]

There was scope for corruption, and its prevention, also in the various 'native lunatic asylums' that had been established during the first decades of the nineteenth century in the different districts of Bengal province, at Rasapagla, Patna, Murshidabad, Bareilly, Benares and Dakha. These institutions confined about 750 Indian 'lunatics' between them by 1820.[6] As in the asylum in Calcutta, medical officers and subordinate staff in institutions for 'natives' engaged in the art of economising on food provision. High catering bills were drawn up that matched equally sophisticated – though not blatantly exaggerated – diet plans, while low-quality food in small quantities was distributed to the patients. The medical board disapprovingly confirmed the existence of such practices when it noted in 1816 that in many cases the surgeon in charge provided food 'too meagre as adapted to persons in good bodily health',[7] putting this down to

> an arrangement by which the interest of the surgeon was put in opposition to his duty, and by which there was too much reason to believe that, on some occasions at least, the health and life [of the patients] was sacrificed to the avarice of the Surgeon.[8]

Conditions in the native lunatic asylums left something to be desired not only in regard to food supply. By the 1820s, the buildings themselves, in Calcutta as well as in the provincial urban centres, had become 'utterly inadequate',[9] 'defective' and 'highly objectionable'.[10] The Rasapagla Asylum near Calcutta, for example, was the main institution providing for irritating, mischievous and violent Indians taken off the capital's streets; it contained on average 150 lunatics. Following an inspection and thorough checks of the institutional statistics, the medical board pointed out breathlessly in 1818: 'In short . . . a worse situation could not be found'.[11] In a similar vein, the asylum at Murshidabad, which served a large catchment area, was regarded as 'wholly unfit', the building being 'altogether a wretched place even in its best state . . . and now falling to ruins'.[12] At Patna, the asylum just one year after its inauguration was said to 'labour under disadvantages greater even than those pointed out' as existing in Murshidabad,[13] while the premises at Benares bore the 'appearance more of a prison than of an Asylum for Lunatics'.[14] The Bareilly Asylum, described by the superintending surgeon as being 'in excellent repair, airy, clean and . . . well constructed for its purpose',[15] was considered objectionable by the medical board on account of four inmates having to share cells no bigger than 10 by 8 feet (approx. 3.1 by 2.8 metres).[16]

The medical authorities concluded in their overall assessment of Bengal's institutions for Indian lunatics: 'without wholly building them anew, it is not easy to propose any effectual remedies'.[17] However, no major changes were implemented at the time and the extensive defects were seen to sporadically and only 'when practicable'.[18] Reformed asylum management and improved institutional conditions clearly found their way more promptly into the place designed for the reception of Europeans.

The situation was not to improve much during the second half of the nineteenth century, even when new asylums were established at Cuttack, Dullunda and Berhampore, and the wretched establishments at Murshidabad and Rasapagla eventually closed down. In fact, in the Cuttack Asylum, only opened in 1864, deficient drainage and 'disgusting' sanitary arrangements were already the subjects of complaint in the very first report, just one year after its inauguration.[19] Similarly, at Dakka, where another ward had been added on to the existing premises in 1866,[20] the superintendent recommended that the place 'should be pulled down' on account of 'insufficient accommodation' and the 'defective state of all the cells'.[21] The old Murshidabad Asylum at Moydapore was eventually demolished in 1866 and additions were made to the asylum in Dullunda (succeeding Rasapagla) to allow for the transfer of inmates from Murshidabad.[22] However, accommodation at Dullunda itself was 'without doubt very insufficient',[23] in spite of a new ward being built to accommodate the additional patients.

Overcrowding in 'native lunatic asylums' remained a problem throughout the nineteenth century. It was clearly perceived as such by the medical authorities, but never rectified by the colonial government. By 1872, the situation was considered even more serious in Bengal 'than in any other' of the provinces under British rule.[24] The population then confined in the asylums of Dullunda, Moydapore, Berhampore, Dakha, Patna and Cuttack was 52 per cent in excess of the buildings' envisaged capacity.[25] In order to ease the pressure on the institutions, the superintendent at the Dakka Asylum, who had been 'highly praised by the . . . Inspector-General and numerous intelligent visitors' for his style of management,[26] experimented with the boarding out of harmless lunatics to the 'more respectable classes of Natives'[27] – a practice that had in Europe become known as the 'Gheel system'. However, the trial proved difficult to supervise and unsuccessful in alleviating overcrowding to any great extent. It was therefore not implemented on a wider scale.[28]

The European lunatic asylum at Bhowanipur, Calcutta

It is perhaps not surprising, given the colonial context, that the Bengal Government showed greater willingness to fund measures that alleviated the conditions of inmates at the Calcutta Asylum, which was dedicated to the reception of Europeans and Eurasians of 'all but the lowest classes'. The erection of a purpose-built government facility, about two miles from Calcutta, to replace the existing ramshackle premises, had been suggested in 1817.[29] However, this plan was abandoned when an assistant surgeon came up with a more cost-saving and convenient proposal. Mentally ill people of European origin were to be sent to Britain once a year, during the favourable shipping season, and a 'house of reception' was to be kept on a small scale only to take care of patients awaiting a passage.[30] To this temporary facility, a privately owned house later also known as 'Beardsmore's Bedlam', the East India Company sent its lunatics from 1821 onwards. Mr I. Beardsmore, former soldier and subsequently a keeper in the earlier asylum, ran this institution as his main business or 'sole means of livelihood'. He reserved thirteen rooms for government employees who had gone mad and charged a lower rate than the one levied in the previous, government-run institution.[31] However, his rates were said to have still been on a similar level as those charged at 'Spence's', one of Calcutta's exclusive hotels – although it was thought that 'there it's to be feared the comparison ends'.[32]

In spite of the authorities' intention of keeping the institution and thus the expenses small scale, the number of patients was to grow steadily. This was due to long-term or 'incurable' lunatics accumulating. These were patients of 'European habits' but not pure European parentage, who were not entitled to be sent to Britain: mainly Eurasians and Armenians. When an official inquiry into Beardsmore's asylum in 1852 found it objectionable on account of its private ownership and obsolete in terms of the techniques of moral management and curative efficiency then favoured in Britain, the erection of a new government asylum was mooted. An expert from England 'conversant with the admirable systems of management and care which have been for some time practised there for the benefit of these unfortunates' was to be put in charge.[33] Government clearly had one eye on how the hitherto prevalent system might have appeared to officials scrutinising reports from Bengal during the investigation of the East India Company's administration that was due the following year, in 1853. The asylum building was therefore purchased from Beardsmore's widow and the inmates were to be looked after by a new surgeon, with the proprietress in attendance on the female ward.[34] In the end, the new superintendent was not recruited from Britain. A candidate who had been on the service list for many years was hired instead. He had acquired experience in the management of the insane during his superintendence of the lunatic asylum in Penang during the 1840s and was said to be 'familiar with' the treatment regime pursued at the Bicêtre in France.[35]

The change in management structure and medical supervision was considered acceptable to the Board of Control back in Britain and things remained for a couple of decades 'almost exactly . . . in essentials, both of construction and management' as they were in the 1850s,[36] apart from some improvements that had to be made following building damage sustained during the cyclone of 1867.[37] The place's 'pleasing feature of rural quiet' commented on by Dr T. Cantor in 1857 was 'still there' in the 1870s, when the gardens were described as 'still more like "a gentleman's carefully tended pleasureground" '.[38] No revelations about shockingly miserable conditions were reported during this period as had been the case in regard to the asylums for Indians. On the contrary, facilities were described in altogether approving tones, highlighting preferences that were particularly close to the heart of the Victorians: pleasant surroundings and sanitary improvements that guaranteed cleanliness. The O'Kinealy Committee, reporting on medical expenditure in Bengal in 1879, thus pointed out appreciatively that apart from a new 'fine day room of iron work covered with creepers and resembling a conservatory' for the female patients, a walk, 'covered in with trellis work, affording a shady lounge' and an orchid house, some important sanitary improvements had been made. New latrines had been provided, the dry-earth system of conservancy introduced, shower-baths substituted for the old bathing tubs, and 'the cages – for they were little better – in the upper storey of the female ward [. . .] abandoned'.[39]

A few other measures were taken in the second half of the nineteenth century that had an impact on costs and the composition of the asylum population. In the early 1860s, European inmates who had been confined in Calcutta for many years because their relatives and home parishes could not be identified were shipped off to Britain after all. Expenses in pauper asylums there were considerably lower than the rates incurred in institutions in Bengal. This measure led to a temporary decrease in numbers, from fifty-three to twenty-six, which suited colonial authorities keen on restricting indoor relief of any kind in India. But figures rose again just a few years later. During the late 1860s, the average number of inmates confined at Bhowanipore was again relatively high, with about twenty Europeans and thirty or so Eurasians.[40] This was to change drastically, however, with the introduction in 1869 of new procedures, which took full effect from 1873.[41] It was decided to remove directly to Bombay (Mumbai) for embarkation back to Britain all those military lunatics who were not on the Bengal military contingent. Similarly, in 1872, twenty-six insane seamen, and many more in the years to follow, were swiftly sent back to Europe through the shipping office, leading not only to reductions in inmate numbers, but also to great savings for the government of Bengal.[42]

It is clear that many of these measures were taken with an eye on cost reduction. However, they also chimed well with the colonial authorities' ambition to restrict the number of down-and-out and 'undesirable Europeans' in the East. Insane Europeans, along with prostitutes and vagrants, were an uncomfortable sight for those keen on presenting themselves as discreet, cultured and distinguished rulers. Institutions meant to contain and keep them out of sight, such as lunatic asylums and workhouses, were not only disproportionately costly on account of the better conditions demanded within a colonial setting for even lower-class Europeans, but also too enduring a measure for a colony that favoured a temporary European presence rather than the permanent fixtures of a European settler colony.

Given the Bengal Government's ambition to reduce the number of inmates in the European asylum, the establishment continued to survive in relatively good shape and order without the pressures of overcrowding so characteristic of the sorry state in native lunatic asylums. It seems though that the reputation of the European asylum began to suffer towards the end of the nineteenth century. Ever fewer Europeans of the 'better classes' were admitted, an indication that it had come to be seen more and more as a 'public institution', with all the negative connotations of similar establishments in Britain during the period of the expansion of the county asylum sector, which catered mainly for the poor. However, despite the deterioration of 'public image', conditions in this relatively small-scale institution, 'primarily intended for Europeans and Eurasians', but also admitting 'races similar to them in birth or habits, such as Americans, Jews and Armenians', were still at any one period far superior to those prevalent in the native lunatic asylums throughout the province.[43]

The mixed economy of mental health care provision and segregative admission policies

As had been the case in the earlier part of the nineteenth century, in the latter decades, too, a variety of different amenities was available for the disposal and care of the insane in the plural medical market in Bengal. Apart from the Calcutta asylum and the various 'native lunatic asylums', private establishments existed which received well-to-do patients of Eurasian and Indian background and European patients unconnected with the East India Company or unwilling to be confined alongside lower-class soldiers and sailors. In fact, Beardsmore, the owner of the asylum in Calcutta from 1821 to 1840, had started his business venture with private patients of a 'respectable class' prior to his contract with government.[44] However, the majority of mentally ill people stayed with their friends and relations. As the medical board explained, 'from natural affection and also from disinclination to lodge their relatives in a public Mad House, however well conducted, the patients are retained by their families'.[45] Dr J. Macpherson, in medical charge of the Calcutta Lunatic Asylum in 1854, estimated that among Eurasians and Armenians, twice as many were taken care of by their friends as were admitted to the asylum.[46] Corresponding estimates for the proportion of mentally ill Indians being looked after in their communities would have been at least as high, not least because under the Asylums Act of 1858 admission to the 'native lunatic asylums' was restricted to the violent and those who committed crimes, effectively excluding all those who were in contemporary parlance described as 'harmless idiots'. The restrictions imposed on admission authorities by the 1858 Act were not enforced to any great extent. However, the government duly issued an order a couple of years later, in 1862. As envisaged by the Act, indoor relief was to be restricted to cases of violence, thereby preventing the overcrowding of institutions with people who were sent by relatives and the civil authorities merely on account of exhibiting strange but non-violent behaviour. The order was adhered to with much zeal, occasioning a steep decline in admissions, which was aided further by the requirement that henceforth relatives ought to pay for the maintenance of asylum inmates.[47] In response to the changed circumstances, some medical officers, like the Deputy Inspector-General of Hospitals, Dr John Balfour, pointed out that 70–75 per cent of lunatics deprived of early admission to the asylum 'could have been cured had [they] been sent in at an earlier date'.[48] Others, like Dr A. Payne, who was soon to gain a reputation for his hard-nosed attitudes towards the Indian insane, considered the decreased admission figures 'to have been productive of beneficial rather than of injurious consequences', stressing the cost savings and alleviation of overcrowding.[49]

There clearly prevailed different views among the representatives of the medical establishment in regard to the relative weight accorded to financial and strictly medical matters. Medical officials in Bengal were expected by the colonial government to reduce expenses and to rely on the indigenous communities to pay for medical services. Yet not all practitioners were easily swayed by arguments in favour of economy and families' responsibilities towards their mentally ill relatives, if the implication was that medical treatment suffered or, as it was put, 'persons really of unsound mind' were prevented from 'being placed under treatment'.[50] The colonial authorities in contrast tended to reassert their restrictive, cost-saving admission policies when quizzed by the medical board. At times, they resorted to strangely ambiguous resolutions that lacked clear guidelines and were open to varied interpretations, for example: 'the objects of these Asylums are insufficiently understood, and their resources too rarely made available to the wants of the country'.[51] This kind of statement was quite characteristic of official attitudes towards the asylum sector during the second half of the nineteenth century: in principle, wider access to treatment in asylums and the extension of institutional services for the benefit of the wider population were considered a good thing. However, this principle was not to be encouraged too enthusiastically for fear that major new investments in the asylum sector on a scale comparable to and lamented by so many in England and Wales would become necessary.

In regard to the case of drastically reduced admissions following the government orders circulated in 1862, a compromise was eventually found, which resulted in the eventual recovery of the admission rates to their former levels. Government relented, advising magistrates that the object of the new regulations had been 'solely to enforce care and circumspection on the part of the Local Officers'.[52] More specific guidelines about what exactly the envisaged 'care and circumspection' was to involve were specified in 'Dr Mouat's Rules', which laid down, among other things, that lunatics were to arrive at asylums fully clothed, fed and in a healthy condition.[53]

Madness at large and the 'subjugation of unreason'

Despite annual fluctuations occasioned by changes in admissions and discharge policies, the number of inmates confined in Bengal around 1900 still added up to not quite 1,000.[54] At that period, one asylum for 'Europeans and Eurasians only' and five 'native lunatic asylums', located at Dullunda, Berhampore, Dakha, Patna and Cuttack, were administered by the Government of Bengal.

This meant that during the second half of the nineteenth century, overall numbers remained more or less stagnant, as two of the native asylums available in the 1850s were no longer under the control of the Bengal Government on account of the redrawing of provincial boundaries. Institutional provisions for the Indian insane in Bengal were not extended during the very period when British colonial rule in India is regarded as having reached its first pinnacle and when colonial power was supposed to have been all-pervasive, with British medicine and education being mainstays of the package of the 'civilising mission' and the major sources of redress for the restrictions imposed by alien government. This raises important questions, which have not been answered convincingly in the existing literature on the development of colonial medicine.

It seems that fledgling colonial psychiatry in Bengal was not accompanied by the kind of institutional warehousing of the insane observed in the large-scale asylums in England and Wales in the late nineteenth century. This phenomenon has been so evocatively enshrined in the ringing Foucauldian phrase of 'the great confinement of the insane', echoing the earlier Benthamite paradigm of the panopticon. We need to explain why we do not see similar phenomena within a political context that could well be expected to put as much emphasis on the surveillance, incarceration and control of the mad as is it did in regard to colonial subject peoples generally. It well may be the case that the colonial government had become aware of the sheer scale of the medical and public health problems they faced on the Indian subcontinent, an area at least ten times larger than Britain. The strong preference among influential government officials for outdoor rather than indoor relief and reliance on *laissez-faire* policies and private philanthropy, in Britain as much as in Bengal, may have been yet other factors. This still leaves us to explain why the institutional confinement of the mentally ill was considered less important than clamping down on *thugees*, for example, or the establishment of medical schools, leper colonies or dispensaries, especially as attitudes and control measures towards the mad became much more severe in Britain itself during this period.

Rather than pursuing a Foucauldian agenda of the 'subjugation of unreason', it seems that the colonial state relied, on a practical level, on the very same indigenous institutions and practices that it so forcefully condemned and vowed to substitute with what it considered more enlightened and truly scientific procedures. The colonial government was able to conveniently exploit the fact that great parts of the indigenous population preferred their own traditional ways of dealing with the mad, as these were culturally and socially familiar and acceptable, while at the same time it condemned these choices as unenlightened and backward. The colonial government thus gained in two ways. First, it was able to legitimate colonial rule on the ideological level through the ubiquitous medical rhetoric of 'the greatest benefit to humankind' being imbued on subject peoples. Second, it relied on and exploited at the same time indigenous provisions for what would otherwise have involved immensely costly health and welfare measures.

Given the limited extent to which institutionalisation was practised in British India even during the second half of the nineteenth century, it is difficult to determine the incidence of various forms of mental illness among Europeans and Indians in Bengal. Even the number of European and Indian insane soldiers and officers under treatment or confined within the regiments is difficult to calculate as regimental health statistics were neither detailed nor precise; not all of them included 'insanity' as a separate diagnostic category; and there was no uniform pattern of diagnostic assessment.[55] There were only rough estimates, as noted by an asylum superintendent in 1854 in regard to Europeans:

> about one European soldier has annually passed through the Asylum, and probably nine more may have gone home with the invalids, not being considered bad enough cases to be sent to the Asylum or may have been sent with invalids, via Bombay, or may have died in the acute stage.[56]

What is more, there is evidence that in many cases the lower ranks in particular were dealt with by punitive measures such as incarceration and whipping when they behaved in odd ways that jeopardised military discipline and duty. In the case of the European and civilian population, numbers on the extent of mental problems are even more difficult to ascertain, as we need to rely on census statistics, which were notoriously unreliable in regard to social demographic indicators such as health and morbidity data.

However, we do know from contemporary newspaper accounts and complaints to town magistrates that an unknown number of European and Indian lunatics were roaming the streets, annoying and scaring members of the European public. These were usually picked up by police and sent either to jail or to hospital. Only occasionally did they end up in the lunatic asylum and only if they had been involved in violent threats to the European community or acts perceived as potentially dangerous, 'indecent' or constituting a nuisance (such as fakirs wandering around naked, causing sensitive British ladies great embarrassment and the inconvenience of having to resort to their smelling salts). 'Tractable' patients, in contrast, were routinely sent back to their relatives or village of origin, as was reported by the superintendent at Rasapagla.[57] The situation changed somewhat in the later decades of the century when emphasis began to be placed on the importance of early admission, cure efficiency and the entitlement to medical treatment of 'harmless' lunatics. Although it is difficult to ascertain exact figures for the mentally ill in the various communities, whether violent or harmless, it is clear that those confined in colonial institutions constituted but a small fraction of overall numbers.

Despite the small number of people institutionalised, medical practitioners in Bengal perceived insanity to be on the increase, especially from the middle of the century onwards. This was of course the period when military expansion in India had reached a new height and parts of Bengal had been under British control and subject to the influence of British 'civilisation' for a considerable period. In 1852, when the number of inmates at the Calcutta asylum had reached about sixty (in contrast to an average of thirty-five in the 1820s),[58] the increase was considered to be 'one of the natural consequences of the changes that have . . . taken place in the population of the city, its participation in the universal progress of improvement and enterprise, and the increase during the long interval of almost every social evil'.[59]

The view that social change and progress breed social evil had been a central theme of some social critics, religious reformers and cynics alike, in Britain as much as in India. The incidence of madness among 'natives' in 'less civilised countries' was thought to be lower and to account for the relatively small number of Indians confined in 'native lunatic asylums'.[60] By the 1850s, the total number of inmates in the seven asylums in Bengal had reached around 1,000 – a very small number indeed, if overall population numbers in this province are considered.[61] As discussed above, such small numbers were of course due to restrictive admission procedures, a well-established tradition of care in the community and families being expected to cope with mentally ill relatives. Yet the 'civilisation' paradigm lent itself to explain low institutionalisation rates, even if the chosen rhetoric became more 'medicalised' as the century progressed.

The superintendent at Patna, for example, pondered in 1866 on the 'great difference in temperament between the Native and Englishman'. He explained it in terms of the former being 'less *sthenic* than the latter' and therefore making 'the Native [. . .] less liable to bodily or mental derangement'.[62] The differentiation of 'asthenia' (increased excitement or irritability) from 'sthenia' (diminished excitement or irritability) was based on theories put forward by John Brown (1735–88) a whole century earlier and popular even in the late nineteenth century. Its explanatory rationale fitted in well with European doctors in India who considered the Bengalis a 'feeble' and 'effeminate' race, and thus less prone to violent outbursts and mental derangement.[63]

Other theories and suggestions of appropriate nomenclature were also put forward. After all, the field of medicine was not streamlined but characterised by pluralism, despite attempts at standardisation and uniformity made by the Medical Act of 1858. Some, like the inspector-general of hospitals, for example, thought that Brownian terms, but not necessarily the phenomena and propensities they were meant to describe, were obsolete. He explained in 1871 that the term 'debility' was preferable and expressed the 'same truth which in former returns appeared under the terms asthenia, cachexia, anemia, exhaustion, etc., namely the dissolution caused in brain disease by simple impairment of the vital energies and wasting of the organism'.[64] He further reiterated the importance of uniformly applied diagnostic categories rather than reliance on doctors' observations of patients' specific symptoms. This preference became a mandatory requirement from the 1870s onwards when forms were sent out to doctors, with pre-determined disease categories, a clearly circumscribed nomenclature for symptom descriptions and a note that reports should be kept short. From then onwards asylum reports and patients' case histories focused on more narrowly medical issues. As a consequence, background details on individual patients, such as their social and cultural circumstances, and their antics and opinions on a variety of non-medical matters, were no longer considered relevant information that should guide doctors' treatment plans. This also implied the near disappearance, as the century progressed, of seemingly humane, yet patronising and derogatory, comments like the one of 1868 by Surgeon R.F. Hutchinson of the Patna asylum: 'We must give the native credit for having feelings like ourselves. We must allow him a conscience which, though it be frequently dormant, is still open to the chidings of remorse'.[65] The patient-doctor relationship became more uniformly medicalised and separated from moral judgements and racial prejudice – at least on paper and in official reports.

Doctors and the asylum staff

It had been clearly established from the end of the eighteenth century that any lunatic asylum, whether intended for Europeans or Indians, ought to be supervised by a European surgeon or assistant surgeon. However, European asylum superintendents did not always spend much of their working time at the asylums.[66] Indeed, apart from some particularly committed doctors, they could not really do so as a rule, as they had other public duties and were permitted to attend to at times large private practices. Up to 1905, when specialist doctors were eventually appointed as full-time asylum superintendents,[67] almost every asylum was an 'additional charge' on the area's civil surgeon. The suggestion that they were mere 'figureheads' and decorative symbols of colonial power may therefore seem justified. In fact, the day-to-day management of asylums and the implementation of superintendents' regulations were left almost entirely to the Indian sub-assistants.

In terms of numbers, the European staff employed in the asylum at Calcutta during the first half of the nineteenth century seems to have been consistently lower than that of private asylums in England – where the average was one attendant per three patients. It was, however, on a par with public asylums, for which one attendant per twelve or seventeen, patients was common.[68] However, institutions in India, those for Europeans as well as those for Indians, were staffed generally with a considerably larger number of servants than was usual in private and public establishments in Europe. These servants, exclusively Indians, performed a wide range of menial as well as service tasks and contributed considerably to the comfort of asylum inmates. How these men and the occasional matron for female patients related to inmates and what sort of treatment and care they imparted is rarely specified in the voluminous asylum reports, although complaints about their assumed ignorance and unreliability were legion, mitigated by evidence of occasional praise bestowed on them by some of their superiors.[69]

However, even if it was correct to suggest that superintendents' role was to act as water-carriers of colonial power structures, they were still subject to scrutiny by the medical board in medical matters and constituted the major agents of change (or stasis) for the specific institutions under their charge. They determined the extent of comfort and care provided for inmates. Crucially, even if part of the patients' food was at times diverted to provide additional income for Indian staff, the European superintendent was responsible for the diet schemes for different classes of inmates.[70] He therefore literally sealed the fate of inmates, as evidenced by fluctuating death rates dependent on changing dietary regimes. The situation at the Benares Asylum is a good case in point.

On the occasion of his appointment as superintendent of the asylum, Civil Surgeon J. Leckie reported in 1853 that during the 1840s an average death rate of 36 per cent had prevailed. He explained that the deaths had been occasioned by the sort of bodily diseases to which not only the insane but all inmates of public institutions were prone in India, mainly dysentery and diarrhoea.[71] However, he had also found that in 1844 the rate increased sharply to 8 per cent in excess of figures reported in preceding years when the daily allowance of *atta*, the main staple food, had been reduced to nearly half the former amount. The surgeon who had introduced this drastic cut in provisions had considered the provision 'quite sufficient' and had kept it at the decreased level for five years.[72]

Leckie concluded that

> the greater mortality in the Asylum was more than to other causes owing to the difference of Dietary [regime] between [Benares] and the Asylums at Delhi and Bareilly. . . . The Patients in the Benares Asylum were in consequence predisposed to the access of Disease and too weak when it comes to resist its force.[73]

When the new superintendent brought the dietary regime into line with the ones in the other asylums, his point was proved, as the change had indeed a 'salutary effect upon the condition of the inmates generally, and . . . led to the marked reduction in the number of deaths'.[74] However, despite these findings, the medical board did not consider it appropriate to make a minimum quantity of food supplies compulsory in the various native lunatic asylums. It could therefore happen that a few years later Surgeon G. Paton, newly appointed superintendent of the asylum in Delhi, again introduced a diminished diet, again with drastic consequences for inmates there.[75]

Although inmates at the asylum in Calcutta did not suffer from diminished food rations as badly as those in 'native asylums', conditions even there still depended very much on the superintendent's style of management. In 1856, for example, when Surgeon T. Cantor became superintendent of the institution, one of his first recommendations was to reduce expenditure by curtailing second-class patients' food provision – while remarking haughtily that the scale of diet 'for the First class /Ladies and Gentlemen/ was unexceptionable'.[76] As the greater part of asylum inmates' daily routine was orientated around feeding and exercise times, the manipulation of victuals must have had a considerable impact. Even Cantor himself acknowledged this fact when he stated that the 'importance of habitual physical comfort to mental recovery renders the diet in Lunatic Asylums more expensive than in a Hospital'.[77] In a more sinister way, Surgeon G. Paton of Delhi had been similarly aware of the importance of food to the patients, as he used withdrawal of food as a form of punishment, pointing out that he considered it 'an easy and unobjectionable means by which to enforce Discipline amongst the patients'.[78] A certain measure of contempt and cruelty towards people of lower-class and non-European racial origin seems to have been shared by Cantor and Paton – both no doubt backed up by the prevailing social ideology during the Victorian era, which led to the atrocious and punitive approach in Britain itself towards the poor and colonised peoples such as the Irish.

As far as control and safety in asylums were concerned, keepers and servants were seen as 'essential', in fact, 'no less [so] than cells'.[79] Yet there were many occasions when both were compromised by lack of staff. During the time of the old Government Asylum (before 1821), invalid European soldiers had been employed as stewards and keepers alongside Indian servants and cleaners. The intensity of care shown by the European staff had not always been satisfactory, as is evidenced by complaints by the medical board. In 1821, for example, it wished that 'the person holding the situation [of assistant steward and apothecary] were older, steadier and more disposed to remain among the patients'.[80] In 1836, the acute shortage of European staff was criticised on the ground that 'without the Agency of this class of attendants [namely Europeans] the moral treatment so effectively resorted to in improved practice, cannot even be attempted'.[81]

Apart from a large contingent of Indian sweepers, gardeners, water-carriers, cooks, servants and the like, the staff in the asylum at Calcutta typically consisted of four employees for an average of thirty-five patients: three Europeans (one apothecary, two keepers), one East Indian (prior to 1836 being described as a 'lad and female superintendent [*sic*]'). [82] Complaints about the number and expertise of Indian subordinate staff were throughout the nineteenth century as numerous as those advanced in regard to Europeans. The central argument was in both cases that

> a sufficiency of Male and Female keepers, not hired by the day or week like common labourers, but permanently engaged and taught by experience and appropriate instruction to manage persons suffering under various forms of mental derangement, is in our opinion indispensable to an Institution worthy of the patronage of Government.[83]

It seems that both European personnel, from superintendent down to keepers, and Indian staff were subject to frequent allegations of corruption, incompetence, negligence and, at times, cruelty. There is evidence for this, particularly up to the 1870s, when asylum reports were still less standardised and consequently suspicions of abuse could be expressed more easily. Indian subject people were clearly no less prone to act with their own self-interest in mind than Europeans were. However, we do not find only evidence of corrupt and abusive behaviour and racial and social class prejudice in the institutional records. On many occasions the devotion and professionalism of European as well as Indian subordinate staff were commented on and, on occasion, highly praised and rewarded financially. For example, Dr A. Fleming, the superintendent at Murshidabad, remarked in his asylum report of 1866 on the 'good conduct of Sergeant Trawley, the European Overseer', describing him as a 'steady, sober, efficient officer, and admirably adapted from his temper and knowledge of Native Character for his present position'.[84] He even suggested that, in the event of the planned abolition of the asylum at Murshidabad, Trawley 'may be suitably provided for'.[85] A few years earlier the superintendent had reported that

> the Native Doctor, though an unpassed man [i.e. no medical certificate] and deficient in many of the qualifications of a good Native doctor, has been so long at the Asylum and gained so much experience in the management of Insanes [*sic*], to whom he is invariably kind, that he is most useful.[86]

Fleming recommended that his 'pay be increased by Rupees 20 in consideration of his long service (1846), and the almost prison life he leads at the Asylum'.[87]

There are also traces of contrasting judgements among European doctors of the qualities of their native staff. Dr Payne, for example, was in charge of both the European Lunatic Asylum in Calcutta and the 'Native Lunatic Asylum' at Dullunda. He had proved on many other occasions to be one of the most prejudiced medical officers in Bengal, treating lower-class Europeans and Eurasians as well as Indian inmates harshly and with considerable contempt. In his report of 1865, he complained about his dissatisfaction 'with the conduct of the native doctor, Shaik Bahadoor'.[88] The inspector-general of hospitals, who had already commented very critically on the 'signs of mal-nutrition in the form of scorbutic gums' at Dullunda and the insufficiency of the food rations provided by Payne, disagreed in no uncertain terms with the superintendent's judgement of his native assistant: 'he is an excellent man, and was selected by me quite on account of his exceptionally good conduct and *character*'.[89] He even added in defence of the experienced but newly appointed Indian doctor an implicit criticism of the superintendent's skill at personnel management: 'The duty is a new one, and it is difficult to meet with any native subordinate who will do all that Dr Payne points out as the native doctor's duty, uninstructed. For such instruction time is required'.[90]

Uniform regulations and varied practices

From 1856, when the Government Asylum was established in Calcutta under the superintendence of Surgeon T. Cantor, clear sets of rules were drawn up by him for the guidance of both the subordinate medical and the 'Native Establishment', namely for the five subordinate European or Eurasian officers and the Indian employees respectively.[91] The first and foremost rule for the guidance of matron, apothecary, steward and the two overseers related to the tension inherent in the application of therapeutic measures in the best interest, but against the will, of the patients, namely the boundaries between aggressive-punitive and supportive-curative aspects of medical treatment: 'Unwearied kindness is under all circumstances to prevail in the treatment of the patients, and care is to be taken that no curative measure ever is suffered to acquire the appearance of vindictive Spirit or Punishment.'[92] This principle was translated for the Indian staff into more specific, down-to-earth guidelines. It was simply impressed on them that they ought to 'abstain from harsh language, threats, abuse, blows and all other acts of oppression or violence'.[93]

In a similar vein, subordinate European officers had to show 'discretion' and 'not to divulge to idle curiosity the extravagances which it may be their painful duty to witness',[94] that is, to preserve patient confidentiality. Indian subordinate staff were simply prohibited from playing an active role in patients' attempts at communicating with the outside world, like carrying 'letters, Messages or articles to or from the patients'.[95] In fact, the duty of Indian servants was restricted to mainly menial and security tasks. The eighteen keepers were to patrol the wards and premises,[96] the servants were expected to get on with cleaning, cooking and gardening 'quietly' and 'without talking loudly',[97] and both keepers and servants had to report any unusual occurrences or emergencies to the superior staff.[98]

The superior staff had to pass any reports of emergencies on to the superintendent and ensure that the Indian employees did their duty diligently.[99] In contrast to the duties of the 'Native Establishment', Cantor considered it 'impracticable concisely to define' the tasks of his subordinate medical employees.[100] It seems to have been assumed by him that superiors knew how to implement the spirit of his regulations, while only the 'natives' required precise instructions. However, despite their wordiness, the sets of rules and regulations drawn up by Cantor in the 1850s were no more transparent or clearly defined in regard to exactly how patients ought to be treated (rather than what ought *not* to be done to them). Cantor's rules, which were commended by the medical board, remained therefore just as vague and open to individual interpretation as the wide range of ad hoc practices prevalent during previous decades.

During the latter half of the nineteenth century, job descriptions for staff and asylum rules seem to have been no more transparent to outside observers than in previous decades. In addition, it is reasonable to assume that the way rules and duties were implemented varied considerably from asylum to asylum. There is much evidence for this. Dr Payne, for example, bore a name that may have been commensurate with how subordinate staff, patients and his medical peers must have experienced him. The extremely high death rates during his term of office at Dullunda gave rise to much criticism among other medical officers of the very restricted dietary provisions and the overly hard work regime he maintained, incidentally sparking off a lengthy debate on the relationship between diet, scurvy and death rates.[101]

In sharp contrast to Payne's attitude and management strategies, which were fatal for so many of the inmates under his charge, there is also evidence of others pursuing more kindly regimes. The superintendent at Patna, Dr J. Sutherland, for example, noted in his report of 1863 that work such as 'pounding bricks, for which a considerable profit is derived in other Asylums, has always appeared to me to be unsuited to Insane patients, and to have too much of the character of a punitory occupation'.[102] The diet in his institution was 'liberal and varied, and no trace of scorbutus (showing a defective dietary) is ever seen in the Asylum'.[103] Even if some concession has to be made to the overly confident and flamboyant style of Victorian narrative, Sutherland's following statement, documented in an official asylum report, suggests a less severe and prejudiced, if not kindly and warm, attitude towards 'native lunatics' than Payne's:

> Visitors are always pleased with the happy and contented appearance of the inmates; personally I feel a degree of affection for the unfortunate beings under my charge; I know most of them by name, and am familiar with all their whims, oddities and delusions. Some of them are very interesting from their humour and other peculiarities. One of these, well known to every visitor of the Asylum, Hyder, always addresses them in the most absurd jargon of broken English that can be imagined, his countenance lighting up by degrees to a broad grin. Looking the person he is addressing full in the face, he generally ends a long rigmarole of incoherent talk with 'go to hell you black fellow', and then bursts into a loud laugh.[104]

The superintendent at Dakha shared Sutherland's views, especially those on compulsory work. He pointed out:

> Lunatics with the delusion of greatness strongly impressed on the mind, are most difficult to induce to work. Compulsion in some form is necessary, and as the delusion remains, notwithstanding the work, the effect on the mind cannot be beneficial. I have therefore not done so much to get work from this class.[105]

Sutherland's successor at Patna, Dr R.F. Hutchinson, seemed even more concerned about the general wellbeing of his inmates. Soon after taking charge, he introduced a practice that was 'attended with the happiest consequences'.[106] He had

> all the insane taken out for a long *walk*, morning and evening, in alternate parties. After the first walk it was touching to hear the mother of the Asylum, who had not been beyond the Walls since 1845, dilate upon the strange and beautiful 'wilayut' she had seen; the green fields and umbrageous trees she had passed; the multitudes of men and women she had come across; and, stranger than all, the wonderful thari she had seen with a mem and babas inside. Morning and evening the paguls are to be met walking along in quiet order, the males leading, and the females following; should it fall to his turn, an old insane leads the way singing at the top of his voice, and clapping his hands in tune.[107]

Not every medical officer was inclined to appreciate Hutchinson's sentiments. His other innovation, the introduction of 'nautches' (Indian dancing and music performances), was in fact described in the strongest of terms by the deputy inspector-general of hospitals, Dr Dunbar, as 'injurious'. Hutchinson depicted these entertainments as bi-monthly events that gave 'great delight' to the insane:

> I always make a point of being present to insure order (which is quite unnecessary), and watch the physiognomies of the patients during the performance. The latter is a most interesting study; for you see the restless eye of the maniac fixed in steady gaze, and the vacant expression of the imbecile lit up with evident delight; the crying and drivelling of the idiot are now still; and hands ever ready for mischief now beat time to the song and drum.

He also narrated the case of 'an old patient, *the* character of the place', who was quietly listening, his body swaying to and fro to the cadence of the music; the native air 'hillee millee punnee ao' was commenced, and its well-known notes seemed to call up memories of the past, for the quiet listener started to his feet with active agility, and commenced dancing vigorously to the great astonishment of the professional. The infection spread, and a second insane sprang on to the dhurree, and joined in the dance and song.[108]

Quite clearly, Hutchinson did not hold the same derogatory views some of his compatriots had of popular Indian entertainment, or the punitive ideas advanced by some of his colleagues such as Payne. Hutchinson's approach was shared by Dr Stewart (at Cuttack) and Dr J. Wise (at Dakha). They, too, permitted these entertainments for the inmates and agreed 'that they are attended with benefit to the patients'.[109]

This sort of evidence, which can be found alongside prejudiced statements and repressive actions, should induce us to develop more sophisticated statements than the all too sweeping assumption that medical doctors in colonial situations were always, and merely, water-carriers of colonialism and disciplining agents of unmitigated and unkindly medical power. Unlike the rhetoric of medical and colonial discourse, actual medical practices and practitioners' attitudes and behaviours are much more 'messy' and diverse, and are perhaps not always intrinsically hegemonic and exploitative simply because they were applied within a colonial context. To conceive of them exclusively as manifestations of hegemonic power runs the danger of wrongly reifying colonial and medical power as all-pervasive forces.

Conclusion

During the early part of the nineteenth century, emphasis was on the adequate transfer of the main characteristics of colonial society's social stratification and racial segregation into the lunatic asylum. The inmates remained what they had been in society outside – members of a certain race, class and gender, with the corresponding status, to which particular consideration, amenities and comfort were due. They were then seen as lunatics merely in the sense that they had a temporary affliction in *addition* to what they *were* as members of civilian and military society.

However, from the 1850s onwards, new medical paradigms and psychiatric procedures came to influence the treatment of the mentally ill, and with them a sharpened focus on medical professionalism, expertise and training came to the fore. The specific nature of inmates' condition, too, and not merely whether they were 'violent' or 'tractable', 'incurable' or 'curable', 'physically diseased' or 'feeble-minded', became an ever more important criterion for the classification of patients. Emphasis came to be placed on issues of a more narrowly medical nature, on diagnosis and aetiology rather than mainly a description of symptoms.[110] From this stage, the records of lunatic asylums make more difficult reading for historians as the available sources tend to focus more narrowly on institutional statistics on the one hand, and on case reports imbued with medical jargon, on the other.

If we look at medicine and psychiatry not only as systems of knowledge and colonial power, but also as interactive practices and processes, phenomena such as the emergence of 'the patient role', increased professionalisation and medicalisation become additional important trajectories that at times cut across and interact in a complex way with those of colonial power issues. All these dimensions require our attention. We may need to consider the possibility of a shift in power relations within colonial medical institutions in the later decades of the nineteenth century when the management and treatment of the insane became gradually subjected to the more narrow dictates of medical expertise and new scientific paradigms. This is not to suggest that issues of colonial power, race and social class discrimination were no longer relevant. Nor would it be right to assume that all asylum superintendents during that period turned into heartless and power-obsessed psychiatric technocrats as issues of medical power increasingly came to the fore. Rather, historians of colonial medicine may need to reassess the relationship between medical and colonial power. More emphasis may need to be on the power of *medical* discourse as well as on people's embrace of (rather than always and only resistance to) colonial institutions as one of a plurality of options available to them within the mixed economy of private and public health care provision. Finally, we may want to ask to what extent colonial health provision witnesses from the late nineteenth century onwards not so much the colonisation of the 'native' body and mind as the medicalisation of colonial power.

Acknowledgement

I would like to express my thanks to the Wellcome Trust for funding the research from 1986 to 1988 on which this chapter is based. An earlier version appeared in *Journal of Asian History*, 40: 1, 2006, 57–72.

Notes

1 D.G. Crawford, *A History of the Indian Medical Service, 1600–1913*, London: Thacker, 1914, vol. 2, 400.

2 Even by the middle of the nineteenth century, when more uniform procedures for the disposal of mentally ill Europeans were in place, only a small number of the military insane were dispatched with invalids from military camps in the interior, 'up-country', to the Asylum in the provincial capital: J. Macpherson, 'Report on Insanity among Europeans in Bengal, Founded on the Experience of the Calcutta Lunatic Asylum', *Calcutta Review*, 26, 1856, 592–608; *Royal Commission on the Sanitary State of the Army in India*, London: Eyre and Spottiswoode for HMSO, 1863, vol. 1.

3 W.L. Parry-Jones, *The Trade in Lunacy. A Study of Private Madhouses in England in the Eighteenth and Nineteenth Centuries*, London: Routledge and Kegan Paul, 1972.

4 Oriental and India Office Collections, London (hereafter IOR): Bg Mil D, 8 April 1817, 6.

5 IOR: Bg Pub L, 28 October 1817, 9, 28.

6 W. Ernst, 'The Establishment of "Native Lunatic Asylums" in Early Nineteenth-century British India', in G. Jan Meulenbeld and Dominik Wujastyk eds *Studies on Indian Medical History*, Delhi: Motilal Banarsidass, 2001 [1987], 182, Table 1. In the province of Madras one asylum in the capital itself, as well as in Chittoor, Tiruchchirappalli and Masulipatnam, had been constructed: W. Ernst, 'Colonial Lunacy Policies and the Madras Lunatic Asylum in the Early Nineteenth Century', in Biswamoy Pati and Mark Harrison eds *Health, Medicine and Empire. Perspectives on Colonial India*, Hyderabad: Longman Orient, 2001. Bombay province secured lunatics of both Indian and European background in one small institution in Kolaba, a small peninsula of what has now become Mumbai (Bombay), and provided for Indian lunatics in remoter areas at Pune, Surat, Ahmadabad, Lahore and Karachi. On asylums in Bombay, see W. Ernst, 'Racial, Social and Cultural Factors in the Development of a Colonial Institution: The Bombay

Lunatic Asylum, 1670–1858', *International Quarterly for Asian Studies*, 22: 3–4, 1992, 61–80.
7 IOR: Bg Mil D, 8 April 1816, 3f.
8 IOR: Bg Mil D, 8 April 1816, 2, 12.
9 IOR: Bg Pub L, 28 October 1817, 9, 28.
10 IOR: Med B to Govt, 22 July 1818; Bg Jud Proc, 28 August 1818, 53, 48f.
11 IOR: IOR: Med B to Govt, 21 February 1818; B Coll, 1820/1, 617, 15.373, 20.
12 IOR: Med B to Govt, 22 July 1818; Bg Jud Proc, 28 August 1818, 53, 48f.
13 IOR: Med B to Govt, 22 July 1818; Bg Jud Proc, 28 August 1818, 53, 48f.
14 IOR: Med B to Govt, 22 July 1818; Bg Jud Proc, 28 August 1818, 71f.
15 IOR: Med B to Govt, 22 July 1818; Bg Jud Proc, 28 August 1818, 81.
16 IOR: Med B to Govt, 22 July 1818; Bg Jud Proc, 28 August 1818, 81.
17 IOR: Med B to Govt, 22 July 1818; Bg Jud Proc, 28 August 1818, 19.
18 IOR: Med B to Govt, 22 July 1818; Bg Jud Proc, 28 August 1818, 6. Even at Dacca and Murshidabad, where the erection of new premises had been already under way since 1818, the design of these buildings was declared to raise strong doubts about whether they would guarantee adequate facilities. IOR: Med B to Govt, 22 July 1818; Bg Jud Proc, 28 August 1818, 53, 47, 54.
19 *Annual Report of the Insane Asylums in Bengal for the Year 1865*, Calcutta: Bengal Secretariat Office, 1866.
20 *Annual Report of the Insane Asylums in Bengal for the Year 1865.*
21 *Annual Report of the Insane Asylums in Bengal for the Year 1866*, Calcutta: Bengal Secretariat Office, 1867.
22 *Annual Report of the Insane Asylums in Bengal for the Year 1865.*
23 Asy Sup to Principal Insp Gen, Med Dep, 8 February 1866, 14; *Annual Report of the Insane Asylums in Bengal for the Year 1865.*
24 *General Report, No 6, on the Lunatic Asylums, Vaccination, and Dispensaries in the Bengal Presidency*, Calcutta: Office of Superintendent of Government Printing, 1876, 2.
25 Surg-Gen to Sec to Govt India, Mil Dep, 24 November 1875, 2; *General Report, No. 6, on the Lunatic Asylums, Vaccination, and Dispensaries in the Bengal Presidency.*
26 *Annual Report of the Insane Asylums in Bengal for the Year 1869*, Calcutta: Bengal Secretariat Office, 1870.
27 *General Report, No 6, on the Lunatic Asylums, Vaccination, and Dispensaries in the Bengal Presidency*, 17.
28 *General Report, No 6, on the Lunatic Asylums, Vaccination, And Dispensaries in the Bengal Presidency.*
29 IOR: Bg Pub L, 28 October 1817, 9, 28.
30 IOR: Minute by Governor-General, 6 November 1818; Bg Pub Proc, 27 November 1818, 6. Committee for reporting on the proposed measure of sending Insane Patients to Europe, 12 January 1819; Bg Pub Proc, 22 January 1819, 31.
31 IOR: Bg Pub D, 28 June 1820, 91ff. Mr I. Beardsmore to Med B, 16 February 1821; Bg Pub Proc, 20 February 1821, 33. Med B to Govt, 5 March 1821; Bg Pub Proc, 1 June 1821, 39. Med B to Govt, 16 February 1821; Bg Pub Proc, 22 June 1821, 42. Bg Pub L, 2 July 1821, 58f.
32 IOR: Accountant Gen to Govt, 21 March 1850; Bg Pub Proc, 28 August 1850, 13, 1.
33 IOR: Minute by Governor-General (Lord Dalhousie), 14 June 1852; Bg Pub Proc, 24 June 1852, 10, 7. Bg Pub L, 9 July 1852, no para.
34 IOR: India Pub Works D, 20 August 1856, 16 f.
35 IOR: Asylum Report, 14 June 1856; Bg Pub Proc, 24 June 1856, 52, no para.
36 *Report on the Lunatic Asylums in Bengal by the Committee Appointed to Inquire into Medical Expenditure in Bengal*, Calcutta: Bengal Secretariat Press, 1879, 20.
37 *General Report on the Lunatic Asylums, Vaccination, and Dispensaries in the Bengal Presidency*, Calcutta: Office of Superintendent of Government Printing, 1870, 1.

38 *Report on the Lunatic Asylums in Bengal. Bengal Medical Expenditure (O'Kinealy) Committee*, Calcutta: Bengal Secretariat Press, 1879, 36.
39 *Report on the Lunatic Asylums in Bengal. Bengal Medical Expenditure (O'Kinealy) Committee*, 36.
40 *General Report, No 6, on the Lunatic Asylums, Vaccination, and Dispensaries in the Bengal Presidency.*
41 Memorandum, 17 December 1877; *Report on the Lunatic Asylums in Bengal. Bengal Medical Expenditure (O'Kinealy) Committee.*
42 Memorandum, 17 December 1877; *Report on the Lunatic Asylums in Bengal. Bengal Medical Expenditure (O'Kinealy) Committee.*
43 *Annual Report of the Insane Asylums in Bengal for the Year 1865*, 18.
44 IOR: Med B to Govt, 5 March 1821; Bg Pub Proc, 1 June 1821, 39.
45 IOR: Med B to Govt, 27 March 1851; Bg Pub Proc, 24 June 1852, 8, 4.
46 Macpherson, 'Report on Insanity among Europeans in Bengal'.
47 The fall in numbers admitted to the asylums was considerable (comparing numbers in 1861 and 1862): Dullunda (142 vs. 78), Moydapore (61 vs. 18), Dacca (95 vs. 87), Patna (52 vs. 40). Resolution, Govt of Bg, 15 June 1863; *Annual Report of the Insane Asylums in Bengal for the Year 1862*, Calcutta: Bengal Secretariat Office, 1863.
48 Resolution, Govt of Bg, 15 June 1863; *Annual Report of the Insane Asylums in Bengal for the Year 1862.*
49 Resolution, Govt of Bg, 15 June 1863; *Annual Report of the Insane Asylums in Bengal for the Year 1862.*
50 Inspector Gen, Med Dep to Sec to Govt Bg, 30 April 1863, 3; *Annual Report of the Insane Asylums in Bengal for the Year 1862.*
51 Resolution, Govt of Bg, Med, 15 June 1863, 6; *Annual Report of the Insane Asylums in Bengal for the Year 1862.*
52 Resolution, Govt of Bg, Med, 15 June 1863, 6; *Annual Report of the Insane Asylums in Bengal for the Year 1862.*
53 *Annual Report of the Insane Asylums in Bengal for the Year 1862.*
54 At this stage on average about thirty-five people were confined in the European asylum in Calcutta and about 900 in the five native lunatic asylums (namely Dullunda, Berhampore, Dakha, Patna and Cuttack). By the beginning of the twentieth century, the one asylum for 'Europeans and Eurasians only' and the five native lunatic asylums were administered by the Government of Bengal. Provincial boundaries were redrawn during the course of the nineteenth century. At the turn of the century, the asylums at Benares and Bareilly were administered by the Government of the North-Western Provinces and Oudh, alongside those of Lucknow and Agra. Asylums at Jubbulpore and Nagpore were then part of the Central Provinces, and the asylums at Delhi and Lahore were assigned to the Government of Panjab.
55 See for example the varied accounts from regimental hospitals on occasion of the investigation into the state of health of the army in India: *Royal Commission on the Sanitary State of the Army in India*. See also: IOR: Proceedings of Special Committee: Measures for the Better Preservation of Health of European Soldiery, 10 October 1827. Bg Mil L, 26 April 1828, 53–71.
56 J. Macpherson, 'Report on Insanity among Europeans in Bengal', 603. On the basis of his own calculations he arrived at a 'number absolutely sent away from their Regiments for insanity' of 8.5 per thousand (in the period 1848–51), estimating that the number admitted to hospital, rather than a lunatic asylum, had been 2.7 per thousand.
57 IOR: Summary of Correspondence, 30 October 1847; B Coll, 1852, 2,494, 141,296, 51. See for detailed numbers for the period 1820–40, Table 2 in W. Ernst, 'Colonial Lunacy Policies and the Madras Lunatic Asylum in the Early Nineteenth Century', 189.
58 IOR: Table Shewing the Number of Public Patients Treated in the Lunatic Asylum at Bhowanipore, and the Results from 1 January 1824 to 30 December 1850, 10 February 1851; Bg Pub Proc, 24 June 1852, 7.

59 IOR: Med B to Govt, 10 March 1851; Bg Pub Proc, 24 June 1852, 6, 5.
60 IOR: Med B to Lieut Gov, 10 October 1854; NWP Pub Proc, 12 December 1854, 87.
61 IOR: Med B to Lieut Gov, 10 October 1854; NWP Pub Proc, 12 December 1854, 1.
62 Robert F. Hutchinson, Sup Patna, 20 January 1866; *Annual Report of the Insane Asylums in Bengal for the Year 1865*.
63 See for similar arguments being advanced in regard to malaria: D. Arnold, ' "An Ancient Race Outworn": Malaria and Race in Colonial India, 1860–1930', in W. Ernst and B.J. Harris eds *Race, Science and Medicine, 1700–1960*, London and New York: Routledge, 1999, 123–43.
64 J. Campbell Brown, 13 July 171; *Annual Report of the Insane Asylums in Bengal for the Year 1870*, Calcutta: Bengal Secretariat Office, 1871.
65 Surgeon R.F. Hutchinson, MD, Patna, 1 January 1868; *Annual Report of the Insane Asylums in Bengal for the Year 1867*, Calcutta: Bengal Secretariat Office, 1868.
66 Asylum inspection reports frequently commented on this, as in the case of Moydapore Asylum, where 'the personal appearance of the inmates exhibited indications of anything but interest and care', causing the inspector to 'urgently press for the appointment of a resident medical officer'. This suggestion was, however, not taken up – presumably, as usual in similar cases, on financial grounds: *Annual Report of the Insane Asylums in Bengal for the Year 1869*.
67 W.S. Shaw, 'The Alienist Department of India', *Journal of Mental Science*, 78, 1932, 331–41.
68 Parry-Jones, *The Trade in Lunacy*, 154, 186.
69 See: W. Ernst, 'Out of Sight and Out of Mind: Insanity in Early Nineteenth-century British India', in Joseph Melling and Bill Forsythe eds *Insanity, Institutions and Society, 1800–1914*, London and New York: Routledge, 1999, 245–67.
70 See: J. Mills, *Madness, Cannabis and Colonialism*, Houndsmill: Macmillan, 2000, 158–9.
71 IOR: Civil Surgeon to Med Board, 16 April 1853; NWP Pub Proc, 15 June 1853, 149, 3. See also Table 3, 192, in Ernst, 'The Establishment of "Native Lunatic Asylums" '.
72 IOR: Civil Surgeon to Med Board, 16 April 1853; NWP Pub Proc, 15 June 1853, 149, 3.
73 IOR: Civil Surgeon to Med Board, 16 April 1853; NWP Pub Proc, 15 June 1853, 149, 4.
74 IOR: Civil Surgeon to Med Board, 16 April 1853; NWP Pub Proc, 15 June 1853, 149, 4.
75 IOR: India Pub L, 6 November 1850, 10ff. India Pub P, 25 August 1852, 44. Civil Surgeon to Med B, 11 February 1853; NWP Gen Proc, 15 June 1853, 150, 6.
76 IOR: Asy Report, 14 June 1856; Bg Pub Proc, 24 June 1856, 52, no para.
77 IOR: Summary of Correspondence, 30 October 1847; B Coll, 1852, 2, 494, 141, 296, 40.
78 IOR: Civil Surgeon to Med Board, 16 April 1853; NWP Pub Proc, 15 June 1853, 149, 10f.
79 IOR: Med B to Govt, 31 May 1836; Bg Pub Proc, 13 July 1836, 19.
80 IOR: Bg Pub L, 4 January 1821, 245.
81 IOR: Med B to Govt, 31 May 1836; Bg Pub Proc, 13 July 1836, 19, no para.
82 IOR: Chief Mag, Med B to Govt, 4 May 1836; Bg Pub Proc, 18 May 1836, 12.
83 IOR: Chief Mag, Med B to Govt, 4 May 1836; Bg Pub Proc, 18 May 1836, 12. Med B to Govt, 7 May 1836; Bg Pub Proc, 18 May 1836, 15 No para.
84 A. Fleming, 20 January 1866; *Annual Report of the Insane Asylums in Bengal for the Year 1865*.
85 A. Fleming, 20 January 1866; *Annual Report of the Insane Asylums in Bengal for the Year 1865*.
86 *Annual Report of the Insane Asylums in Bengal for the Year 1862*.

87 *Annual Report of the Insane Asylums in Bengal for the Year 1862*. The native doctor was described as 'a Christian' who 'was educated at the Native Hospital here by the late Civil Surgeon, Dr. Keane'.
88 *Annual Report of the Insane Asylums in Bengal for the Year 1865*.
89 Emphasis in original. *Annual Report of the Insane Asylums in Bengal for the Year 1865*.
90 *Annual Report of the Insane Asylums in Bengal for the Year 1865*.
91 IOR: Asy Report, 14 June 1856; Bg Pub Proc, 24 June 1856, 52, no para.
92 IOR: Asy Report, 14 June 1856; Bg Pub Proc, 24 June 1856, 52, no para. Rule 1 (Subordinate Officers).
93 IOR: Asy Report, 14 June 1856; Bg Pub Proc, 24 June 1856, 52, no para. Rule 1 (Native Establishment).
94 IOR: Asy Report, 14 June 1856; Bg Pub Proc, 24 June 1856, 52, no para. Rule 11 (Subordinate Officers).
95 IOR: Asy Report, 14 June 1856; Bg Pub Proc, 24 June 1856, 52, no para. Rule 6 (Native Establishment).
96 IOR: Asy Report, 14 June 1856; Bg Pub Proc, 24 June 1856, 52, no para. Rule 4 (Native Establishment).
97 IOR: Asy Report, 14 June 1856; Bg Pub Proc, 24 June 1856, 52, no para. Rule 3 (Native Establishement).
98 IOR: Asy Report, 14 June 1856; Bg Pub Proc, 24 June 1856, 52, no para. Rule 5 (Native Establishment).
99 IOR: Asy Report, 14 June 1856; Bg Pub Proc, 24 June 1856, 52, no para. Rule 2 (Subordinate Officers).
100 IOR: Asy Report, 14 June 1856; Bg Pub proc, 24 June 1856, 52, no para. Rule 2 (Native Establishment), Rule 4 (Subordinate Officers).
101 *Annual Report of the Insane Asylums in Bengal for the Year 1865*.
102 *Annual Report of the Insane Asylums in Bengal for the Year 1862*.
103 *Annual Report of the Insane Asylums in Bengal for the Year 1863*.
104 *Annual Report of the Insane Asylums in Bengal for the Year 1863*. This same passage has been interpreted quite differently in Mills, *Madness, Cannabis and Colonialism*.
105 *Annual Report of the Insane Asylums in Bengal for the Year 1862*.
106 *Annual Report of the Insane Asylums in Bengal for the Year 1865*.
107 *Annual Report of the Insane Asylums in Bengal for the Year 1865*.
108 *Annual Report of the Insane Asylums in Bengal for the Year 1865*.
109 *Annual Report of the Insane Asylums in Bengal for the Year 1867*.
110 See *Asylum Reports*, from about 1863 onwards.

9 'Prejudices clung to by the natives'

Ethnicity in the Indian army and hospitals for sepoys, *c.* 1870s–1890s

Samiksha Sehrawat

Between 1916 and 1918, mounting pressure from the Parliament, the British press and the Mesopotamia Commission placed the introduction of station hospitals for Indian troops very high on the agenda of the Indian Government. The new station hospital system was adopted in 1918–19, over forty years after it was first proposed, leading the government to claim:

> So far as the Indian soldier is concerned, the Indian station hospital is a new amenity of life in the army, introduced during the great war of 1914–18. Before the war the Indian soldier was treated in his regimental hospital. . . . The equipment of a regimental hospital consisted, at the best, of beds, mattresses, and pillows, a small stock of blankets, a pair of medical panniers, and a somewhat scanty supply of medical and surgical necessities. . . . [T]he introduction of the Indian station hospital, based upon the analogy of the British station hospital, was a departure of supreme importance . . . the medical attention which the sick Indian soldier now receives is *incomparably* superior to what he received before the war.[1]

This eulogy to the station system begs the question why station hospitals were not introduced by the government earlier. Proposals to abandon the regimental hospital system and introduce general/station hospitals in India had been made from 1876. After much deliberation, the station hospital system was introduced for British but not for Indian troops in 1882. Yet proposals to extend the system to Indian troops recurred in 1883, 1886 and 1892. In the last two instances, the system was apparently abandoned because of the belief that Indian soldiers had a strong aversion to station hospitals as these institutions violated their ethnic customs. This link between sepoys'[2] ethnicity and military hospital arrangements for them had been made as early as 1876:

> His Excellency [the commander-in-chief] is no doubt aware of the repugnance which natives have to these general [station] or field hospitals, where they are more or less subject to certain discomfort in the way of food, cooking, bedding,

> and personal attendance, which they are spared by their comrades when in the hospital of their regiment. Moreover, the native soldier dreads isolation from his officers and brethren, and is apt to fancy that, when away from their influence and personal knowledge of their particular feelings and prejudices, the sick may be subjected to operation and the dead to needless autopsy.[3]

This link between Indian troops' ethnicity and military hospital arrangements for them became part of the administrative wisdom of the military department and continued to shape curative care for Indians in the army in the twentieth century. The Lukis Committee, appointed in 1910 to consider the adoption of the station hospital system, reproduced these beliefs about Indian soldiers' attitudes to hospital care even though it marked a departure from earlier decisions by strongly recommending the station system:

> [I]t must be remembered that the native soldier usually dislikes going to hospital, even to a regimental one; he is in constant communication, on matters affecting his personal or family interests, with his friends in the ranks. . . . It is of utmost importance that the Indian Army should not acquire a belief that a man will be neglected or lost sight of in the proposed station hospitals; any such idea may have a serious effect on recruiting; and everything possible must be done not to withdraw any of his existing privileges when he happens to be a patient.[4]

The persistence of nineteenth-century essentializations of Indian soldiers in twentieth-century administrative discourse, and often into contemporary accounts of the Indian army, calls for an examination of the initial moment of the formation of these ideas within the army, the circumstances of their articulation and the form they took.

The interest in this history of the 'martial races' encompasses a wide range of historiography, from accounts of the relationship between the colonial state and the Indian soldier[5] to sociological analyses of particular ethnic groups that were considered martial.[6] Recent years have also produced analyses of the impact of this discourse on the Punjab, the home of most 'martial' groups and the main recruiting base of the colonial Indian army.[7] This historiography, due to its preoccupation with the constructions of 'martial race', and the regional shifts this brought about in recruitment, has failed to engage with the crucial role of ethnicity in sustaining the army in colonial India from its inception.[8] The historiography of martial ethnicity in the French and British African empires[9] has pointed to the importance of exploring the sociological context of recruitment[10] and to the importance of tracing the anthropological roots of ideas of martiality.[11] Reconstructing the administrative decisions that shaped military discourse regarding sepoys and locating the military needs for these decisions within the larger socio-economic context of the Indian army would be essential for introducing a chronological perspective and inflecting current conceptions of 'martial races' as a static construction.

Despite the close relationship between the army and medicine in colonial contexts, which has been acknowledged by the historiography of medicine in India, neither the medical history nor the military history of South Asia has explored the issue of military healthcare provision for Indian troops.[12] Radhika Ramasubban has argued that colonial medicine in British India was 'enclavist' and prioritized healthcare for Europeans within enclaves such as the army while neglecting the health of Indians.[13] David Arnold and Mark Harrison's pioneering work qualifies this argument, contending that although the army was a special medical arena that was subject to closer and greater medical attention than civil society in colonial India, it also mirrored the broader ambitions of Western medicine and colonial rule in India.[14] Arnold's overview of the colonial state's attitude to Indian soldiers points out that the hospital and medical care provided them in the nineteenth century was inferior to that provided to British troops, but does not investigate the issue any further.[15]

This chapter seeks to address this historiographical lacuna by analysing the history of military attitudes and decisions regarding hospitals for Indian troops. It will examine the formation of military essentializations regarding Indian troops by officers who realized the close relationship between the troops' ethnicity and military service. By tracing the history of administrative decisions regarding hospitals for Indian troops, the chapter will explore how economic and military compulsions shaped army policy.

Hospitals and the regimental system: essentializing sepoy ethnicity, *c.* 1874–80

Medical treatment within the army was regimental in the 1870s – that is, each regiment had its own medical officer and its own regimental hospital, which was expected to possess all the equipment and staff required to cater to the medical needs of the regiment's men. With the substitution of the regimental system by the general/station system in the British army in 1874, the adoption of the new system for both British and Indian troops was considered for the army in India. The plans for medical arrangements during the Second Anglo-Afghan War (1878–80), made by Surgeon-General J.H. Ker Innes, Principal Medical Officer for the British Forces in India, used general or base hospitals that combined the medical resources of all regiments of one division, but these plans were implemented for British troops only. The Indian forces could not be informed of the new plans till a few days before mobilization. This resulted in a mixed system, with the British forces of the campaign adopting the general hospital and Indian regiments continuing in the early part of the campaign with regimental field hospitals. The new system encountered considerable resistance from military officers, although the trial seems to have generated support for general field hospitals among medical officers executing the policy.[16] The support for regimental medical organization was considerable during the period from 1876 to 1880, both from the Commander-in-Chief, Sir Frederick Haines, and from within the Indian Government.[17]

The regiment was the basic unit of army administration in India as in Britain and regiments were considered essential to both military discipline and troop morale. Military and regimental authorities believed that it was essential for the colonial army in India to maintain the 'wholesome principle' that 'regiments should be self-contained and capable of instant detachment from an army, wholly or in part, and with or without other troops, and be capable of remaining apart for considerable periods'.[18] Regarding the hospital system to be adopted in the army, military authorities were clear that '[a]ny new system which weakens or destroys this principle should . . . be very carefully considered before adoption in India'.[19] The replacement of the regimental hospital system, which was considered especially compatible with the regimental basis of the British army, by general field hospitals during war or army maneouevres, and general station hospitals when the army was stationed in military stations, was resisted by regimental and higher military officers.

Proponents of the regimental hospital system, such as Surgeon-General C.A. Gordon, Principal Medical Officer of the British Forces in Madras, advocated it on the grounds of its congruence with the regimental military organization. He argued that being mobile establishments embedded in regiments, regimental hospitals were ideal for sudden and unexpected mobilization of forces and for long marches, which had characterized military deployment in India.[20] According to Gordon, the 'ambulant' regimental hospitals were also best suited for Indian military operations which encompassed 'an extensive tract of country'.[21] Others pointed out the desirability of the regiment being 'complete' with its own hospital and medical officer who was familiar with the troops and their medical histories.[22] For peacetime, the regimental hospital was regarded as ideal because functioning as a *regimental* officer, the medical officer was intimately known to the regimental commanding officer and facilitated the imposition of military discipline over men: 'Commanding officers, as a rule, get on much better with officers belonging to their corps than with outsiders, and vice versa. . . . Medical officers who have not done duty in regiments are deficient in their ideas of discipline.'[23]

Yet Innes pointed out that the conditions of warfare had been altered – railway transport obviated the necessity of long marches and since more than one regiment was located at most stations, the old regimental medical organization was no longer required.[24] Further, he argued that 'In a campaign the regimental hospital with its own staff, transport and stores, is but an encumbrance, repeated in its every detail as many times as there are separate regiments and other marching units.'[25] The general hospital was advocated because it was believed to facilitate more efficient evacuation of the sick and wounded from the front to the base.[26] The new system was favoured also because it allowed provision for sick soldiers 'according to large averages instead of being subject to the fluctuations of smaller [regimental] ones'.[27] Despite the support that the 1878 trial of the general hospital system received, it was not adopted for British troops in peacetime till 1882 and for both British and Indian troops for the army deployed in the field till 1884.[28] The residual opposition to a modification to the regimental medical system was even more emphatic in the case of Indian regiments.

Although the same problems of disrupting the regiment as a self-contained unit for administration and discipline were seen as disincentives for the adoption of the station system for sepoys, it was believed that in the case of Indian troops special difficulties would be encountered. Chief among these was the belief that sepoys were 'naturally averse' to hospitals, although regimental hospitals were 'more in accordance with [their] habits, peculiarities, and prejudices'.[29] This view was shared widely by the central government, military authorities and medical officers of Indian troops. Haines, writing in 1877 against recommendations for the station hospital for Indians, elaborated:

> [N]o measure could be devised more calculated to engender serious misunderstanding or be more disliked by the soldiers of the Native Army [than the introduction of station hospitals].There are certain prejudices clung to by the natives of this country which are common to no other races; and experience has shown that to ignore them is dangerous, and that [Indian] patients in hospitals must be treated by medical men who know their language and are conversant with their manners, customs and diets.[30]

The Army Organization Commission of 1879, which solicited views regarding the relative merits of the two systems, also emphasized the 'special objections which apply to Native troops' with regard to the station hospital system.[31] Such views essentialized sepoys as irrationally bound to their customs and 'prejudices'. These essentializations ignored the commonalities in Indian attitudes towards non-regimental hospitals shared with British troops. For instance, some of the objections made to the adoption of station hospitals for Indian troops were not very dissimilar to the objections made in the name of British troops. For example, Surgeon-General G. Smith's contention that '[a] sepoy has strong objections to strange hospitals and strange doctors, and to association when sick with strangers'[32] was almost identical with the following statement made regarding British soldiers: 'Soldiers *hate* to be treated by strange doctors.'[33]

An explanation for the foregrounding of the 'prejudices' of Indian troops is indicated by the following elaboration of the consequences of the new system feared by colonial authorities:

> [These] feelings . . . however strange they may be to our minds, have at times past not only created uneasiness and discontent, but have given rise to insubordination and mutiny, and in this respect field and general hospitals may be jeopardising the contentment and confidence of the men, and the popularity of active service or camps of exercise causing evils which more than counterbalance the advantages which in other respects they undoubtedly possess.[34]

For colonial military authorities, the prevention of any severance of the close relationship between ethnicity and colonial military service was vital as it was believed that such disruption would cause both military insubordination (echoing anxieties created by the 1857 Mutiny) as well as a decline in the popularity of military service and recruitment. Recruitment in the Indian army was conducted through sepoy officers who returned to their native villages with recruiting parties and used their ethnic networks to persuade potential recruits to join the army.[35] These patterns of military recruitment replicated earlier traditions of military service or *naukari* familiar to the men who were recruited.[36] This form of recruitment created companies or regiments that were composed of men from the same ethnic group, resulting in an overlap between ethnic and regimental identities.[37] Military authorities found this interconnectedness of ethnicity and regiment useful as it facilitated regimental cohesion, allowed the exercise of military discipline through ethnic hierarchies and bolstered the morale of troops by identifying the regiment's honour with communal pride.[38] These links between Indian troops' ethnicity and military service in the colonial army were therefore of vital importance to military administrators. Measures that interfered with the ethnicity of Indian troops tended to be unpopular with both regimental commanding officers and with the military high command. However, the sense of finality with which the 'natural aversion' of sepoys to non-regimental hospitals was declared disregarded the troops' ability to adapt to innovations.[39]

Medical reorganization and the drive for military economy

The prominence given to the alleged aversion of Indian troops to the station system by military authorities in the 1870s obscured the two other factors which were central to nineteenth-century debates regarding hospital arrangements for Indian troops: the desire to reduce military expenditure and the reorganization of medical services in India.

The reduction of military expenditure – an issue of concern for the Indian Government from the early nineteenth century – continued to be important in the late nineteenth century.[40] The sharp increase in total military expenditure due to the Second Anglo-Afghan War[41] created pressures to economize, and the Army Organization Commission (1879)[42] was appointed to consider the retrenchments possible in the army in India. Military budgets were closely monitored in this period and after the 1880s the 'excessive' military expenditure of the Government of India was criticized by Indians.[43]

The reorganization of medical services in India took place against this search for avenues of military retrenchment. There existed two military medical services in nineteenth-century India – medical officers responsible for the health of British troops stationed in India who were part of the British Army Medical Department; and the medical officers of the Indian Medical Department who were responsible for the health of Indian troops. By 1877, the maintenance of this dual system was perceived by the Indian Government as inconvenient, extravagant and 'unserviceable', and schemes were proposed to reorganize the medical services.[44] The Army Organization Commission of 1879 also made suggestions for medical reorganization with the aim of rationalizing the cumbrous medical establishment. The streamlining of the medical services required the amalgamation of the two services and various ways of accomplishing this were proposed during this period. Although the administrative posts of the two services were amalgamated (1880), the executive duties continued to be distinct, with the result that officers of the British service could not be appointed to the medical charge of Indian troops nor could officers of the Indian service treat British soldiers. The result was that officers of one service could not relieve or assist officers of the other service, necessitating the maintenance of larger establishments than would have been required under a single medical service or under a system where interchangeability was permitted. This ensured that schemes and proposals which envisaged the reduction of medical officers would be favourably entertained by the Indian Government.

The proposals to introduce station hospitals for both British and Indian troops were considered as a part of these discussions and were recommended because the station system was expected to require fewer medical officers than the regimental one. The Eden Commission drew attention to the savings possible from the reduction of medical officers in executive charge of military hospitals through the adoption of the station system.[45] The analysis of military expenditure between 1872–3 and 1883–4 concluded that a net decrease in military medical expenditure had indeed occurred as a result of the introduction of British station hospitals in 1882.[46] Indeed, Lord Ripon (Viceroy, 1880–4) had been optimistic about similar reductions through 'the possible introduction of the station hospital system, or a modified form of it' in Indian regiments.[47] Though its schemes for medical reorganization aimed at reducing military expenditure were not accepted by the India Office, the Indian Government was still considering ways of reducing the number of executive officers in the Indian Medical Department in November 1883:

> [E]conomy demands that steps should be speedily taken to reduce the present excessive expenditure on the medical services. The Government of India are inclined to believe that the number of medical officers now attached to the army in India, both European and native, is considerably in excess of what is required.[48]

The Principal Medical Officer of the British Forces in India, Sir A.D. Home, was familiar with the economies that had been made possible by the reduction of executive medical officers in the British Army Medical Department and suggested the adoption of the same measures for the Indian Medical Department:

> [T]he Government of India pays for a needlessly expensive medical service for its Native troops . . . a similar excess existed until lately with regard to the medical service for British troops in India, but in 1880–81, Government recognising this, replaced regimental with station hospitals, and consequent on the replacement, it has been able to reduce . . . the executive officers of the Army Medical Department. . . . [A saving could be effected by] adopting an analogous system for the Native Army.[49]

However, on investigation, it was discovered that this measure could lead to *additional* expenditure on new buildings for the proposed station hospitals. It was also believed that recruitment in the Indian Medical Service (IMS) could be further affected by the withdrawal of monetary privileges associated with the charge of

Indian regimental hospitals by IMS officers. Ruling out the system, Commander-in-Chief D.M. Stewart elaborated:

> Taking everything into consideration and looking to the fact that there is at the present moment much dissatisfaction in the Indian Medical Service, His Excellency [Stewart] thinks it would be unwise to do anything which would increase that dissatisfaction, as it would doubtless prevent good men from entering the service, and the Commander-in-Chief therefore recommends that nothing should be done towards introducing the station hospital system into the Native Army, for the present at all events.[50]

These developments hint at a persistent problem that the Indian Government encountered in maintaining two medical services recruited from the same pool of medical graduates in Britain. The main source of medical officers for both the British Army Medical Department and the Indian Medical Department were the British medical graduates who were interested in a military career.[51] One of the consequences of the competition between the two services for these graduates was that the one that offered better terms tended to attract the best recruits, creating problems for recruitment in the other. The IMS had been the more popular of the two services till the Royal Warrant promulgated in 1879 for the British medical service improved its terms of employment, leading to a gradual reduction in the popularity of the IMS.[52] The British War Office, preoccupied with maintaining high recruitment levels in the British medical service, rejected the Indian Government's medical reorganization schemes as these could affect the attractiveness of the British Army Medical Department, either through economies within India or by improving terms offered to IMS officers. A note by Lieutenant-General Wilson on the subject in 1881 summed up the situation thus created:

> [Enormous expenditure results] from the competition of three medical services – the Royal navy, the Army Medical Department, and the Indian Medical Service. For no sooner does one of these services gain some small advantage in the way of pay, pensions or allowances, than one of the other at once puts forward claims for still further advantages. Committees are organized, the press is worked, circulars are distributed, the medical schools are visited, and by one means or another effective measures are taken for cutting off the supply of candidates for vacancies [in the medical service]. A brief period of embarrassment follows, and the Government attacked is obliged to yield to the influence of the agitation and well-organized clamour.[53]

Such a situation placed great emphasis on protecting the existing terms of employment in the IMS and gave considerable authority to the opinions of IMS officers who could be considered knowledgeable about what made the IMS attractive to recruits. So significant was this context that proposals to adopt the station hospital system were only ever considered within India because it was hoped that the system would facilitate the rationalization of medical services through the reduction of executive military medical officers.[54] Indeed, the improvement of medical treatment for soldiers seems to have been marginal at best to decisions regarding which hospital system to maintain.

The station hospital question in the Roberts era, 1886–93

The suggestion by Ripon that reductions in the IMS might be possible through the introduction of Indian station hospitals was taken up in 1886 by the Secretary of State, Lord Kimberley, in an atmosphere of rising concern regarding the possibility of 'candidates of inferior ability' being recruited to the IMS:

> [T]he objections to the introduction of the station hospital system arise not so much from doubts as to the desirability of any reduction of establishment which it might entail, as from the practical difficulties in the way of working it. While fully recognizing the force of these objections, I shall be glad to hear of the adoption of any modifications of the present system which may tend to economise labour.[55]

The reports submitted to the Indian Government on the adoption of the station system by the representative of the British Army Medical Department, Surgeon-General C.D. Madden, and that of the IMS, Surgeon-General B. Simpson, differed. Madden favoured the adoption of the system, arguing that it would result in the replication of the reduction in expenditure and improved efficiency achieved in the British case. However, Simpson disagreed with the proposals, arguing that Madden's proposed reductions in the IMS would

> deprive a large number of officers of the allowances they now draw as in charge of regiments – a measure which, while amounting to a breach of faith on the part of the Government towards the medical officers who entered the service under the conditions of the last warrants, would indubitably interfere to a serious extent with recruitment for the service in the future.[56]

It is clear that since medical reorganization was such an integral part of the proposals regarding station hospitals, factors linked with the terms of medical service but unrelated to the suitability of a hospital system for the troops shaped opinions as well as decisions regarding the system.[57]

Referring to earlier deliberations in 1876–7, which had underlined 'native repugnance' to station hospitals, Simpson suggested that the views of regimental commanding officers of Indian regiments be ascertained regarding the popularity of the system before introducing it. Though regimental officers were instructed to ascertain 'as quietly as possible . . . the real feeling of the Native ranks' regarding station hospitals, the responses of the regimental officers ought to be read cautiously as there were limits to the transparency of exchange between sepoys and the officers, given that the latter were told to be careful not to 'give rise to alarm or unfounded rumours' regarding hospitals. Further, claims that officers could represent the wishes of the Indian troops cannot be taken at face value, as the troops were unlikely to contradict their superiors' opinions.[58]

As mentioned above, regimental officers preferred the regimental hospital system and had objected to earlier attempts to modify it on the grounds that it facilitated organization within the regiment. Medical officers, when attached to the regiment, provided additional surveillance of the troops and thus facilitated more effective control. For instance, Brigadier-General McQueen 'Deprecate[d] severing any of the ties which bind the men to their medical officers whose influence has often . . . worked beneficially for the maintenance of a good and loyal spirit, and the men learn both to trust, love and respect him'.[59] It was believed that the regimental hospital system was more likely to detect malingering, of which Indian troops were widely suspected.[60]

It is hardly surprising that some of the responses were emphatically against abandoning the regimental system. Yet, despite the resistance of regimental officers to earlier attempts to adopt the non-regimental hospital system, it is remarkable that the most common point of agreement for the officers was not so much an emphatic rejection of the new system as a concern to prevent the violation of ethnic or caste taboos, whatever the form of hospital adopted.[61] Of special concern were the commensality taboos that reflected status relations between different ethnic groups through rules regarding sharing food. Members of an ethnic group would not like their food to be touched by or shared with men from ethnic groups believed to be inferior to them in status. In the regimental hospitals (where hospital cooked food was not provided), such taboos were preserved as a patient's food was cooked by comrades who belonged to the same ethnic group.[62] However, it was believed that such taboos would be difficult to observe in a centralized hospital where all ethnic groups were expected to be housed and 'dieted' communally, irrespective of the ethnicity of the patient or the cook.[63] Officers pointed out that such a violation might affect the popularity of military service adversely, discouraging recruitment, though no possibility of a mutiny was contemplated by any of the officers consulted.[64]

The intimate relationship between ethnicity and military service in colonial India was well known to regimental officers, but this did not lead to the rejection of station hospitals in every instance. Some officers suggested that station or modified station hospitals that accommodated ethnic practices could be acceptable. According to Capt. A.W.T. Radcliffe, Commanding Officer (CO) 14th Sikhs,

> The native officers and men of the Regiment raise no objections to the establishment of the station hospital, provided arrangements could be made for the men of different castes being kept separate, and their cooking and watering be carried out without offending their religious customs.[65]

These instances suggest that sepoys were more concerned with preventing the violation of ethnic taboos than with the continuation of the regimental system, and were willing to negotiate a resolution that could allow the introduction of a novel medical system if it did not compromise their ethnic identity or status. Indeed,

Indian opinions indirectly represented in the government record show that the sepoys expressed a desire for medical care not merely for themselves but also for their families.[66]

Significantly, Col. H. Chapman, CO 8th Bengal Cavalry, implied that Indians were not so different from British troops as to be totally antagonistic to the station hospital: 'Col. Chapman states that if the station hospital has been found to work well with British troops, he can urge no substantial reason against its introduction into the Native Army'.[67] This undermined the essentialization of sepoys. Some, like Major H. Will, CO 1–2nd Goorkhas, whose men were accustomed to the station hospital system on service and at Dehra Dun, considered 'that the introduction would be a most distinct advantage'; while others made suggestions to adapt the proposed hospital system.[68] In fact several officers claimed that the troops would *accept* the measure if the government was in earnest. For instance, Col. A.G. Handcock, CO 6th Bengal Infantry, 'Does not recommend any change, but thinks that if Government are determined to alter the system, the men of the regiments would raise no objections'.[69]

Of all the officers whose opinion was taken into account, only nine commanding officers rejected the proposed station hospital outright. Three officers ruled it out less equivocally, pointing out the factors (such as the violation of ethnic taboos) which rendered the station system unsuitable, whereas the other nine officers saw the station hospital as a distinct, in the view of some even a desirable, possibility. Despite this mixed opinion, the government claimed that

> the majority of commanding officers consulted, as well as His Excellency the Commander-in-Chief [Lord Roberts] and the Surgeon-General with the Government of India [Surgeon-General B. Simpson], are of the opinion that the introduction of station hospitals for the Native army would be so distasteful to the native soldier as to tend to a directly calamitous result in destroying the popularity of military service.[70]

The Indian Government's decision – expressed 'forcibly'[71] – was accepted by the India Office, even though it was not entirely persuaded. Indeed, one member of the council referred to the Indian Government's objections to the system as 'of a very frivolous and inconclusive description'.[72]

Despite the Indian Government's emphatic conclusion of 1886 that 'all idea of introducing the station hospital system in the Native army should now be definitely abandoned', another trial of the system was sanctioned in 1892 by the government with the approval of the Commander-in-Chief, Lord Roberts. Indeed, the adoption of station hospitals had been considered for the Madras Presidency in 1887, less than a year after the declaration. In both cases, the exigencies of medical reorganization and the desire for military economy proved attractive enough to cause the government to ignore its own declaration that the station hospital scheme be definitely abandoned. The trial of the system in Madras was proposed because it was believed that medical officers could be reduced in the Madras establishment. Enquiries revealed, however, that 'instead of effecting an economy, the introduction of the station hospital system . . . [in Madras] would lead to a large initial outlay and a permanent increase of expenditure under establishment'.[73] This possibility led to the abandoning of the scheme.

Meanwhile, the reorganization of the medical services in India was engaging the attention of the Indian Government, which sought to reduce its expenditure by unifying the two medical services and thereby reducing the number of executive medical officers required. It was during these deliberations that Roberts agreed to a trial of the station system for Indian troops at two stations – Rawalpindi and Calcutta. Reports were submitted by medical officers who supervised the trial of the station hospital – Surgeon-Major W.A. Mawson in Rawalpindi; Deputy Surgeon-General J.C. Morice and Surgeon-Major A.B. Seaman in Calcutta. Although the report from Calcutta strongly recommended the system, the reports from Rawalpindi were more mixed. Supporting the adoption of the new system, the medical officers at Calcutta wrote: 'A station hospital for Native troops is clearly a necessity for Calcutta, the regimental hospital cannot satisfactorily deal with and adequately dispose of all the exigencies that arise here'.[74] In Rawalpindi, the regimental officers believed the new system to be unsuitable for Indians, all officers being 'averse to the change'.[75] The commanding officers stressed the importance of the close interpersonal relationship between Indian troops and the regimental medical officer and rejected the new system, arguing that sepoys had abstained from hospitals during illness rather than go to the unfamiliar medical professionals at the trial station hospital.[76] One of the officers argued that the new system would 'not [be] conducive to the efficiency of regiments from a military point of view'.[77] These views were not very dissimilar to those of regimental officers who had objected to the adoption of a non-regimental system in 1886.[78] Mawson had himself noted the resistance to non-regimental organization on the part of commanding officers:

> Among British [regimental] officers . . . I have had no definite complaint from any one; but they naturally prefer, as an almost invariable rule, to be attended by their regimental medical officer (with whom they are usually well acquainted and probably on terms of intimate friendship) to being under the charge of a doctor whom they scarcely know.[79]

The essentialization of 'native' troops intrinsic to the contention that non-regimental hospitals were unsuited to the 'native' army ignored the common preference of both Indian troops and their British officers for medical attendance by a professional with whom they were familiar. Regarding the attitude of Indian troops themselves to the station hospital system, Mawson felt that no conclusive ideas could be formed: 'As regards the popularity of the station hospital amongst the men, I am not in a position to speak positively. I can only say that I have not heard any complaints.'[80] Mawson himself gave a qualified but firm vote in favour of the new system:

> If it would be possible to devise a system by which these advantages can be obtained without sacrificing the equally valuable ones of the regimental system,

> it appears to me the interests of the State and all parties concerned would be best served by adopting it.[81]

His report indicates that Indian troops availed themselves of the hospital frequently during the trial: 'In addition to men admitted into the hospital and those detained for the day, there is every morning a considerable number of men suffering from trivial complaints, who . . . [are] examined and prescribed for before sending them back to duty.'[82] Mawson believed that the station system, if properly adopted, would provide better medical treatment for sepoys and professional advantages to military medical officers.[83]

As in 1886, the commander-in-chief's conclusion in 1892 that 'the station hospital system is not suited to the Native Army' seemed to accept the regimental bias of military officers, and to amplify military beliefs that essentialized Indian troops.[84] Yet this begs the question why Roberts did not let his earlier decision – which had also concluded that the compulsions of ethnic customs and regimental requirements did not permit the introduction of station hospitals for Indian troops – stand. The answer lies in a note by Roberts dated 6 July 1889:

> It has been decided not to apply the system of station hospitals to Native troops; but as it has worked so well for British troops and as it would be an economy in point of numbers, and would certainly give more elasticity, I would not object to its being tried tentatively at one or two selected stations.[85]

Roberts's hopes of reducing medical officers through the station system and economizing thereby were not fulfilled by the trial. The Rawalpindi report showed that new buildings would be needed which would add to expenditure rather than reduce it.[86] A reduction in expenditure by decreasing the number of medical officers was also found unfeasible:

> In introducing the station hospital system, it may have been anticipated that a reduction in the number of medical officers could be made, but I fear that this is not practicable consistent with efficiency and true economy. When the change was effected in the British Army, each regiment had more than one medical officer attached to it; but such is not the case in the Native Army. . . . If the medical officer is unable to [fulfil his multifarious duties] . . . the interests of his patients and consequently of the state must suffer.[87]

Indeed, the record indicates that medical officers had pointed to this problem from the very outset.[88] Comparing the medical establishment for British and Indian forces in 1886, Simpson had shown that reduction of medical officers for Indian forces was not possible because the number allocated was at the minimum acceptable scale:

> The daily average sick per mille of strength of British troops of India, as a whole, is about twice that of the native army. If, then, 5 officers be required

> to every 1000 of British troops . . . 2 per mille for Indian troops would not be too high a proportion . . .. [T]he proportion is very nearly 1.5 only to 1,000 men [in 1886]. I cannot think that this low figure can with safety be diminished.[89]

Nevertheless, Roberts and the government had decided to attempt the 1892 trial in the hope that reductions in medical officers would be possible.[90] The interest in the India Office for a similar economy is evident from their enquiries regarding its success.[91] When the expectations could not be fulfilled by the trial, there was very little incentive to continue with it; this is clear from the final word on the 1892 experiment written in the India Office after it was informed of the decision to abandon the station system: 'The one argument in its [the station hospital system's] favour was its economy, but if that would not be effected, the regimental system should undoubtedly be maintained.'[92]

Conclusion

This chapter has explored the link between Indian troops' ethnicity and colonial military establishments' attitudes towards it. The historiography on 'martial races' has located the 1880s–90s as a period of the shift of recruitment to 'martial races' in the Punjab. However, a sharp focus on this shift obscures the continuities in colonial military recruitment, which relied on recruitment through ethnic networks throughout the nineteenth and early twentieth centuries before the stresses of the First World War. Scholarly focus on the 'constructed' nature of 'martial race discourse' fails to appreciate the conceptual significance of ethnicity in providing the discursive basis for the colonial state's military policy.[93] The transposing of the regiment – which functioned as the basis of British military administration – with ethnicity allowed the colonial state to harness ethnic identities, hierarchies and allegiances for military recruitment, organization and deployment. Analysis of the colonial army's policy towards Indian military hospitals reveals that the essentialization of Indian troops as irrationally attached to customs predated the 'martial race discourse'. Further, Roberts's 1892 reversal of the 1886 decision which was based on such essentialization indicates that the ascendancy of the 'martial race discourse' was neither as unilinear nor as powerful as existing historiography suggests. Although the preservation of the basis of military service by Indian troops – the link between ethnicity and regimental organization – carried considerable weight in decisions regarding hospital arrangements for Indian troops, equally important was the state's desire to secure medical experts for its administration without sacrificing the drive for military economy that dominated this period. The extent to which the IMS and the interests of its members played a role in shaping decisions is also significant and reveals the power of British medical professionals in a colonial context. As medical experts who could not be easily replaced and for whose recruitment the colonial state had to compete, IMS officers enjoyed considerable power in shaping the Indian government's medical policy.

The importance of reducing military expenditure dominated discussions regarding medical reorganization and the station hospital system to such an extent that it left a lasting legacy of association between economizing and medical arrangements for Indian troops. This contributed to the widening of the gap between hospital facilities for British and Indian troops – which was evident even in the nineteenth century – to such an extent over the twentieth century that it was believed to have been a major contributing cause to the scandalous breakdown of medical arrangements during the Mesopotamia Campaign. Witness reports to the Mesopotamia Commission (1917) reveal the appalling levels to which this policy reduced Indian military hospitals: ' "I doubt," one IMS witness says to us, "whether you gentlemen would consider that the Sepoys' hospitals in peace time in India are hospitals at all." Sir Havelock Charles described them as "a disgrace to the Government of India".'[94]
The Commission also criticized the Indian military authorities for a policy of strict economy, which led to the severe medical breakdown during the Mesopotamia Campaign:

> in no branch of military expenditure was the pressure [to economize] so much felt as in connection with the medical establishments. According to high medical authorities the whole standard of medical establishments, of hospital equipment, and of field ambulances in India [had] been . . . much below that in vogue in the British Army. In consequence of the financial pressure alluded to, little or nothing was done to raise this standard, whilst reserves, both of personnel and materiel, had been reduced to a very low ebb.[95]

The late nineteenth-century debates regarding hospital arrangements for Indian troops that have been examined here played a significant part in intensifying this tendency. The continuation of these tendencies till their trenchant criticism in 1917 was predicated on the prominence given to the alleged aversion of Indian troops to the station system by twentieth-century deliberations regarding Indian military hospital arrangements, which elided the role of other factors such as medical rationalization. Despite the continuing durability of the link between the reduction of medical officers and the adoption of station hospitals, this association was far less visible in twentieth-century decisions than the link between Indian ethnicity with the question of station hospitals.[96]

Acknowledgements

I am grateful to the Felix Scholarship, the Wellcome Trust, the Beit Fund, and the Arnold Fund, University of Oxford, for support provided for the research for this chapter. I also want to thank Prof. Mark Harrison and Manu Sehgal who both helped me formulate my ideas through their discussions, advice and support.

Notes

1 *The Army in India and its Evolution: Including an Account of the Establishment of the Royal Air Force in India*, Calcutta: Superintendent Government Printing, India, 1924, 120–1.

2 The term 'sepoy' was a corruption of the word 'sipahi', and referred to an Indian soldier in British employ.

3 From H.K. Burne, Military Secretary, Government of India (hereafter GoI), to Adjutant General, India, 14 December 1876, Military Department Proceedings, GoI, January 1877, Proceeding no. 96, IOR/P/951, British Library (hereafter BL).

4 *Report of the Committee appointed to Consider the Introduction of Station Hospitals for Indian Troops in Place of Regimental Hospitals*, Simla: Government Central British Press, 1910, 24.

5 Much of the work on Indian soldiers' relationship with the colonial army falls into the trap of accepting the claims of Indian military authorities regarding the sepoys, despite claims of objectivity. See, for example, Philip Mason, *A Matter of Honour: An Account of the Indian Army, its Officers and Men*, London: Cape, 1974. This perspective sometimes seeps into David Omissi's pioneering work, *The Sepoy and the Raj: The Indian Army, 1860–1940*, Basingstoke: Macmillan in association with King's College, London, 1994.

6 See, for instance, Lionel Caplan, *Warrior Gentlemen: 'Gurkhas' in the Western Imagination*, Providence, RI, and Oxford: Berghahn, 1995.

7 Tan Tai Yong, *The Garrison State: The Military, Government and Society in Colonial Punjab, 1849–1947*, New Delhi; London: Sage, 2005, looks at recruitment in the Punjab and its role as a 'home front' in the First World War. Rajit K. Mazumder, *The Indian Army and the Making of Punjab*, Delhi: Permanent Black, 2003, considers the socio-economic impact of recruitment on society and politics in Punjab.

8 An excellent exception is Dirk H.A. Kolff, *Naukar, Rajput, and Sepoy: The Ethnohistory of the Military Labour Market in Hindustan, 1450–1850*, Cambridge: Cambridge University Press, 1990. There are no such accounts for later periods. Also see Seema Alavi, *The Sepoys and the Company: Tradition and Transition in Northern India, 1770–1830*, Delhi; Oxford: Oxford University Press, 1995.

9 See, for instance, Timothy Parsons, ' "Wakamba Warriors Are Soldiers of the Queen": The Evolution of the Kamba as a Martial Race, 1890–1970', *Ethnohistory*, 46: 4, 1999, 671–701; and Joe Lunn, ' "Les Races Guerrieres": Racial Preconceptions in the French Military about West African Soldiers during the First World War', *Journal of Contemporary History*, 34: 4, 1999, 517–36. Heather Streets's *Martial Races: The Military, Race and Masculinity in British Imperial Culture, 1857–1914*, Manchester: Manchester University Press, 2004, which seeks to locate the 'martial race discourse' in an imperial context, fails to take into account the inter-colonial connections of the discourse.

10 Mustafa K. Pasha's *Colonial Political Economy: Recruitment and Underdevelopment in the Punjab, Pakistan*, Oxford: Oxford University Press, 1998, considers the case of Pind Dadan Khan in Punjab to explore the economic conditions which rendered military service an alternative source of income for peasants of the region. Prem Chowdhry, *The Veiled Women: Shifting Gender Equations in Rural Haryana, 1880–1990*, New Delhi: Oxford University Press, 1994, makes a similar argument for recruitment in Rohtak district, Haryana.

11 Gloria Goodwin Raheja's analysis of the entextualization of proverbial speech in colonial administrative records provides some interesting insights but does not probe military documents in any detail: Raheja, 'Caste, Colonialism, and the Speech of the Colonized: Entextualization and Disciplinary Control in India', *American Ethnologist*, 23: 3, 1996, 494–513. Cynthia Enloe's insightful study of the relationship of ethnicity with state security provides a very useful framework for such analysis of the colonial Indian

military labour market: Enloe, *Ethnic Soldiers: State Security in Divided Societies*, Harmondsworth: Penguin, 1980.

12 Historians such as Douglas M. Peers and Philippa Levine have touched upon some aspects of army medicine in colonial India, but their focus has remained on white British troops: Peers, 'Soldiers, Surgeons and the Campaigns to Combat Sexually Transmitted Diseases in Colonial India, 1805–1860', *Medical History*, 42: 2, 1998, 137–60; Levine, 'Venereal Disease, Prostitution and the Politics of Empire: The Case of British India', *Journal of the History of Sexuality*, 4: 4, 1994, 579–602. The only work on Indian troops' healthcare is Mark Harrison's analysis of the issues of discipline and dissent related to the military medical care provided to Indian troops during the First World War in his 'Disease, Discipline and Dissent: The Indian Army in France and England, 1914–15', in Roger Cooter, Mark Harrison and Steve Sturdy, eds, *Medicine and Modern Warfare*, Amsterdam: Rodopi, 1999, 185–203.

13 Radhika Ramasubban, 'Imperial Health in British India, 1857–1900', in Roy MacLeod and Milton Lewis, eds, *Disease, Medicine and Empire: Perspectives on Western Medicine and the Experience of European Expansion*, London: Routledge, 1988.

14 David Arnold, *Colonizing the Body: State Medicine and Epidemic Disease in Nineteenth-Century India*, Berkeley, Los Angeles and London: University of California Press, 1993; Mark Harrison, *Public Health in British India: Anglo-Indian Preventive Medicine 1859–1914*, Cambridge: Cambridge University Press, 1994.

15 Arnold argues that healthcare for soldiers reflected the 'ruling bias and racial prioritizing that was evident in colonial society as a whole . . . colonial indifference toward, or neglect of, Indian health was strengthened and rationalized by indigenous resistance, or at least by the expectation of Indian resistance' (Arnold, *Colonizing the Body*, 94).

16 Response to questions of the Army Organization Commission regarding the medical arrangements during the Second Anglo-Afghan War, *Report of the Army Organization Commission of 1879*, Simla: GoI, 1879 (henceforth *AOC Report*), vol. 4, IOR/L/MIL/17/5/1687/1, BL, 859–62.

17 Haines was commander-in-chief from April 1876 to April 1881, and Lord Lytton was the viceroy 1876–1880.

18 H.K. Burne, Military Secretary, GoI, to Adjutant General, India (henceforth AGI), 14 December 1876, Prog. no. 96, Military Department Proceedings (henceforth, Mil.), GoI, January 1877, IOR/P/951, BL.

19 14 December 1876, Prog. no. 96, Mil., GoI, January 1877, IOR/P/951, BL.

20 Summing up the arguments, Surgeon-General Innes stated that regimental hospitals were believed to complement military regimental organization because it was

> considered necessary to regard all corps as capable of acting as independent units, complete in themselves, ready at any moment to take to the field or to undertake marches of long duration, and partly because a single corps may be quartered in a detached post.
>
> (*AOC Report*, vol. 4, 853).

21 Surgeon-General C.A. Gordon, Principal Medical Officer (PMO), Madras, to Quarter-Master-General, Madras, 24 July 1879, included in *AOC Report*, vol. 4, 840–1.

22 See evidence by Surgeon-General G. Smith, Indian Medical Department (IMD), *AOC Report*, vol. 4, 852; and by the PMO, Hyderabad Circle, quoted by Gordon: 'the [regimental] surgeon well known to, and well knowing the constitution and previous history of, every member of the regiment' (840).

23 PMO, Hyderabad Circle, quoted by C.A. Gordon.

24 Innes in *AOC Report*, vol. 4, 853.

25 Innes, *AOC Report*, vol. 4, 859.

26 Innes, *AOC Report*, vol. 4, 860.

27 Innes, *AOC Report*, vol. 4, 855.

28 General field hospitals were authorized as the medical component of the army in the field in the India Army Circulars, 1884. The first trial of this new organization during the Camps of Exercise of 1885–6 indicates that military officers were still opposing the system: Prog. no. 714–17, Mil., GoI, November 1886, IOR/P/2765, BL.

29 Smith, *AOC Report*, vol. 4, 852.

30 Letter from AGI to Military Secretary, GoI, 4 May 1877, Prog. no. 607, Mil., GoI, May–June 1880, IOR/P/1529, BL.

31 *AOC Report*, 113.

32 Smith, *AOC Report*, vol. 4, 851.

33 PMO, Hyderabad Circle, quoted by Gordon, *AOC Report*, vol. 4, 840.

34 Prog no. 96, Jan 1877, Mil., BL, IOR, P/951.

35 Alavi, *Sepoys and the Company*. Also see Yong, *The Garrison State*, esp. chs 1–2.

36 Kolff, *Naukar, Rajput, and Sepoy*.

37 The period between 1870 and 1890 was marked by debates regarding military organization and the best way of organizing Indian troops of different ethnic backgrounds within regiments. Initially, different 'class' companies (recruited from the same ethnic group or 'class') were organized into regiments (called mixed regiments as they mixed companies of different ethnic groups in one regiment). Later in the period, entire regiments would be recruited from the same ethnic group ('class regiments'). In both cases, sepoys of the same ethnic background were grouped together at the level of a basic military unit – whether the company or the regiment.

38 My analysis of the significance of the overlap of ethnic and military unit identities is based on the seminal work by Cynthia Enloe on the use of ethnicity by states for military recruitment and deployment: Enloe, *Ethnic Soldiers*.

39 The possibility of such adaptation is hinted at by medical officers such as Surgeon-General Beatson, who, while admitting that general hospitals had been unpopular with sepoys during the Second Anglo-Afghan War, argued that this had been due to the hospitals' imperfect organization, and such distaste could be overcome in peacetime station hospitals: *AOC Report*, vol. 4, 861.

40 For Bentinck's efforts at reduction of military expenditure through reorganization in the 1820s–30s, see D.M. Peers, *Between Mars and Mammon: Colonial Armies and the Garrison State in India, 1819–1835*, London: I.B. Tauris, 1995. Despite the politico-economic importance of the pressures to reduce military expenditure in India in the second half of the nineteenth century, these themes have not attracted the critical scrutiny of economic and military historians of South Asia.

41 The changes in the pound–rupee exchange rate during the Second Anglo-Afghan War were another contributory factor in increasing the Indian government's expenditure.

42 This commission was also known as the Eden Commission after its chairman, Sir Ashley Eden. See V. Longer, *Red Coats to Olive Green: A History of the Indian Army 1600–1974*, Bombay: Allied Publishers, 1974, 117–24.

43 Longer points out that at the very first session of the Indian National Congress in 1885, a resolution was passed criticizing 'the proposed increase in the military expenditure' (*Red Coats to Olive Green*, 124). For a sympathetic representation of early nationalists' views on the need of curtailing Indian military expenditure in the late nineteenth century, see Bipan Chandra, *Essays in Colonialism*, Hyderabad, Orient Longman, 2000, 144–5, 188, 194–6, 203 and 293.

44 H.J.E. Ford, *The Medical Services in India: A Note on their History and Organization*, Simla: Government of India, 1889, IOR/L/MIL/ 17/5/2007, BL.

45 See *AOC Report*, 114–17; H.W. Norman, 'Memorandum on Financial Result of Proposed Changes in Army Organization in India', 24 May 1883, IOR/L/MIL/17/5/1709, BL.

46 The net reduction in military medical expenditure was Rs1,61,007, to which the amalgamation of the administrative posts of the medical services and the use of locally manufactured cinchona also contributed: Newmarch, 'Note on the Military Expenditure

for the Army in India from 1872–3 to 1883–4', Prog. no. 1215A, Mil., GoI, January 1886, IOR/P/2755, BL.

47 Military Despatch no. 222, from the GoI to the Secretary of State for India (SoS), 17 June 1881, Military Collection 2/9, 'Proposed Introduction of Station Hospitals for Indian Troops, 1881–1893' (henceforth, 'Military Collection Indian Station Hospitals, 1881–93'), IOR/L/MIL/7/163, BL.

48 From Military Secretary, GoI, to AGI, 16 November 1883, Prog. no. 1402, Mil., GoI, October 1884, IOR/P/2308, BL.

49 From Surgeon-General, His Majesty's Forces, Bengal, to AGI, 4 December 1883, Prog. no. 1403, Mil., GoI, October 1884, IOR/P/2308, BL.

50 From AGI to G. Chesney, Military Secretary, GoI, 20 September 1884, Prog. no. 1406, Mil., GoI, October 1884, IOR/P/2308, BL.

51 Recruitment from Indian medical graduates remained minuscule in this period. Indeed, the Eden Commission suggested further ways of reducing the number of Indian-educated medical men in the IMS, paras 361–2, 120–1. For a discussion of the relative professional, social and educational status of IMS officers, see Harrison, *Public Health in British India*, 19–35.

52 The maintenance of officers of the British Service on higher emoluments offered by the Royal Warrant of 1879 placed an additional financial burden on the Indian Government, further increasing the pressure to economize.

53 Quoted in H.J.E. Ford, *The Medical Services in India: A Note on their History and Organization*, Simla: Government of India, 1889, IOR/L/MIL/ 17/5/2007, BL, 18.

54 It is remarkable that from 1876 till 1910, in each of the nine instances where the introduction of the station hospital system was considered, the main motivation was the potential reduction of IMS officers in charge of Indian troops.

55 Military Despatch no. 53, SoS to GoI, 11 March 1886, Prog. no. 731, Mil., GoI, November 1886, IOR/P/2765, BL.

56 B. Simpson, 'Report on the Station Hospital System for the Native Army' (henceforth, 'Report'), Prog. no. 734, Mil., GoI, November 1886, IOR/P/2765, BL.

57 It is significant that professional advantages to IMS officers were marshalled as an argument in favour of the adoption of the station system:

> The officers of the IMS would also benefit considerably by the introduction of station hospitals. The value of their professional work will be gauged by their brethren of their service, and the system would train them in the duties which would be required of them on active service, namely the working of field and general hospitals, which in principle are analogous to station hospitals. Moreover, by reducing the establishment of the executive, the opportunities for attaining administrative provision would be greater.
>
> ('Memorandum on the Station Hospital System for the Native Army' (henceforth, 'Memorandum'), Prog. no. 734, Mil., GoI, November 1886, IOR/P/2765, BL.)

58 Confidential Circular Letter from the AGI to Officers Commanding, 10 August 1886, Prog. no. 736, Mil., GoI, November 1886, IOR/P/2765, BL.

59 'Abstract of Replies to Adjutant Generals' Circular "Confidential" No. 3398-B of 10th August 1886, respecting the Introduction of the Station Hospital System for Native Troops' (henceforth, 'Abstract of Replies'), Prog no. 736, November 1886, Mil., GoI, IOR/P/2765, BL. 'Under the regimental system a medical officer, being a part of the regiment, usually gains a great deal of information, and acquires a knowledge of the men which is of use to him in the performance of his duties.' (Surgeon-Major W.A. Mawson, 'Report on the Working of the Experimental Station Hospital for Native Troops at Rawal Pindi, from 1 August 1891 to 31 January 1892' (henceforth, 'Report on Rawal Pindi'), Prog. no. 2697, Mil., GoI, December 1892, IOR/P/4165, BL, 548).

60 Brig-Gen. Norman, 'Abstract of Replies'. For a medical officer's concurrence in this belief, see 'Col. G.J. Kellie's Memoirs', typescript, No. 7507–56, National Army Museum (NAM), 50, 225.
61 Officers who rejected the system cited the dangers of the violation of ethnic customs and those accepting modifications emphasized that the new system could accommodate these customs. The views of Col. G.R. Hennessy, CO 15th Sikhs, are representative of this fear: 'Away from their own hospitals complaints of harsh treatment are frequent, the native subordinates being always ready to inflict petty annoyances and wound their caste susceptibilities' ('Abstract of Replies').
62 See Smith's description of the regimental arrangements for feeding patients in *AOC Report*, vol. 4, 851. In contrast, patients in station hospitals would be expected to eat food prepared in the hospital that was expected to aid their recovery.
63 Col. Barrow, CO 10th Bengal Lancers, pointed out that in the new system 'soldiers' feeding becomes a difficulty; men would be suspicious and unhappy about their food not knowing where it came from and who cooked it' ('Abstract of Replies').
64 Col. A.R. Chapman, CO 1st Bengal Cavalry, wrote: 'Men of the higher castes would object to take medicine from the hands of low-caste medical subordinates . . . [If this were] made known abroad, it may affect the stamp of recruits to be got in future' ('Abstract of Replies'). Col. H.W. Gordon, CO 20th Punjab Infantry, and Capt. W. Faithful, 21st Infantry, also believed that the popularity of military service would be affected adversely: 'Abstract of Replies'
65 See also similar views expressed to Lt.-Col. G. Young, CO 1–1st Goorkhas, by the two Gurkha officers consulted: 'Abstract of Replies'.
66 Lt.-Col. G.S. Hills, CO 28th Punjab Infantry: 'In the regimental system the men get to know their medical officer and attendants, their wives and children are treated. . .. Under the station hospital system . . . the treatment of a *purdahnasheen* (wife of a soldier) would be a difficulty.' Col. A.R. Chapman, CO 1st Bengal Cavalry, pointed out that, 'The medical officer of the regiment has always willingly attended the native officers when sick in their own houses and this indulgence which is now gratefully appreciated would be lost' ('Abstract of Replies').
67 'Abstract of Replies'.
68 For instance, Capt. A.W.T. Radcliffe, CO 14th Sikhs, held that,

> The native officers and men of the Regiment raise no objections to the establishment of the station hospital, provided arrangements could be made for the men of different castes being kept separate, and their cooking and watering be carried out without offending their religious customs.
>
> ('Abstract of Replies')

69 According to Col. C.R. Pennington, CO 14th Bengal Lancers,

> 'the native ranks certainly would prefer the regimental hospital but if it is deemed desirable to establish station hospitals, [Col. Pennington] can anticipate no difficulty to its introduction provided each corps has its separate ward and as little change as possible in medical officers . . . . if the medical officer has experience in the treatment of natives and a knowledge of their prejudices, *the system after a little while will work very well.*'
>
> ('Abstract of Replies'; emphasis added)

70 Despatch no. 180 of 1886, GoI to SoS, 1 November 1886, Prog no. 731, November 1886, Mil., GoI, IOR/P/2765, BL.
71 Military Despatch no. 377, SoS to GoI, 23 December 1886, 'Military Collection Indian Station Hospitals, 1881–93'.
72 Note on the Minute by the India Office Council, 20 December 1886, 'Military Collection Indian Station Hospitals, 1881–93'.

73 From Military Secretary, Government of Madras to Military Secretary, GoI, 18 November 1887, Prog. no. 1953, Mil., GoI, February 1888, IOR/P/3245, BL.

74 From Surgeon-Major A.B. Seaman, Medical Officer in Charge, Station Hospital, Native Troops, to the Administrative Medical Officer, Presidency District, dated 12 February 1892, Alipore, Prog. no. 2697, Mil., GoI, December 1892, IOR/P/4165, BL, p. 554. Morice was equally approving, even recommending that 'young medical officers of the IMS be sent to Calcutta for a tour of duty at this station hospital' (Deputy Surgeon-General J.C. Morice, to Adjutant-General, Presidency District, 15 February 1892, ibid.)

75 From Major-Gen. Gluck, Commanding Rawalpindi District, to PMO, Her Majesty's Forces in India, 19 April 1892, ibid.

76 See opinions expressed by Major C. Hogge, CO 33rd Punjab Infantry; Col. H.W. Webster, CO 30th Punjab Infantry; and W.H. Scott, CO 11th Bengal Lancers, Prog. no. 2697, Mil., GoI, December 1892, IOR/P/4165, BL.

77 See letter from Col. Webster, Prog. no. 2697, Mil., GoI, December 1892, IOR/P/4165, BL.

78 In contrast to Rawalpindi, the overwhelming opinion of the regimental officers associated with the experimental trial of the Calcutta station hospital was very positive. Of the three commanding officers consulted, only one thought that the regimental hospital was preferable: ibid.

79 Mawson, 'Report on Rawal Pindi', Prog. no. 2697, Military Department Proceedings, India, December 1892, IOR/P/4165, BL.

80 'Report on Rawal Pindi', 547–8.

81 'Report on Rawal Pindi', 548.

82 'Report on Rawal Pindi', 545–6.

83 'Report on Rawal Pindi', 548.

84 From PMO, Her Majesty's Forces in India, to Military Secretary, GoI, 26 October 1892, Prog. no. 2697, December 1892, Mil., GoI, IOR/P/4165, BL, 544.

85 Roberts, 'Can Any Further Reduction Be Made in the Indian or Army Medical Staff', *Minutes, Notes and Co. by Gen. Sir F. Roberts, Commander-in-Chief in India* (henceforth, *Minutes and Notes*), vol. 6, part 1, 1877–December 1889, Roberts Papers, No. 7101–23–96, NAM, 412.

86 'The small detached dispensaries and offices of the old regimental hospital are quite unsuited to the present system. If the station hospital system is to continue, I would suggest that to meet present wants another block of buildings be erected.' ('Report on Rawal Pindi', 547).

87 'Report on Rawal Pindi', 546.

88 *AOC Report*, vol. 4, 862. The Army Organization Commission had also admitted that due to the 'very economical scale on which Indian hospitals were organized, the only savings possible were from the reduction of medical officers' (*AOC Report*, 344).

89 Prog. no. 734, Mil., GoI, November 1886, IOR/P/2765, BL.

90 Military Despatch no. 32 of 1891, GoI to Lord Cross, SoS, 25 February 1891, 'Military Collection Indian Station Hospitals, 1881–93'. Ironically, Roberts, who has been associated with Indian troops in both popular and scholarly literature in the Indian Army saw the improvement in hospital and nursing arrangements for British troops in India as an important achievement of his years in office. For Indian troops, his record reflects a concern for reducing medical expenditure rather than improving medical facilities: Roberts, 'Note on the Principles on which the Administration of the Army in India should be Based', 1 April 1893, *Minutes and Notes*, vol. 6, part 2, January 1890-April 1893, 1305–6.

91 Military Despatch no. 14 of 1892, SoS to GoI, 28 January 1892, 'Military Collection Indian Station Hospitals, 1881–93'.

92 Note on the Minute by the India Office Council, 7 February 1893, 'Military Collection Indian Station Hospitals, 1881–93'.

93 See, for instance, Streets, *Martial Races: The Military, Race and Masculinity in British Imperial Culture 1857–1914*, especially, 121–42.

94 'Medical Findings and Recommendations', Report of the Mesopotamia Commission, Parliamentary Papers (Commons), 1917–18, vol. 16, 95.

95 Report of the Mesopotamia Commission, Parliamentary Papers (Commons), 1917–18, vol. 16, p. 6.

96 The reduction of medical officers through the adoption of station hospitals was a constant concern from the 1870s till 1914.

10 Racial pathologies

Morbid anatomy in British India, 1770–1850

Mark Harrison

This chapter takes morbid anatomy as a case study through which to examine the relationship between colonial expansion and the production of medical knowledge. Relatively little attention has been paid to this aspect of the colonial medical encounter in comparison with the role played by medicine in the colonization of indigenous societies. Nevertheless, the significance of colonial expansion for the development of British medicine was profound. Medical practitioners working in India not only modified European medical knowledge but also made important and independent contributions to the development of medicine at home. Morbid anatomy was one branch of European medicine in which colonial expansion made a great deal of difference. As is well known, the development of morbid anatomy in Britain was constrained by the difficulty of obtaining bodies for dissection, at least until the passage of the Anatomy Act in 1832.[1] For this reason, the British tradition in morbid anatomy is normally considered only as a precursor to more important developments that took place in revolutionary Paris, associated with the work of Xavier Bichat and others.[2] British morbid anatomy has thus received little attention as a phenomenon in its own right and the received wisdom is that it did not become an important part of British medicine until after 1815, when British students flocked to the Paris hospitals after the conclusion of hostilities with France.[3]

In reality, however, morbid anatomy played an important part in British medicine long before 1815; it had also developed independently in ways that one would normally associate with Parisian pathological anatomy: i.e. an increasing interest in the pathology of tissues as opposed to organs, and the correlation of post-mortem findings with bedside observation. These important developments have been obscured because no historian of morbid anatomy has hitherto looked at medical practices in Britain's colonies, where morbid anatomy was *central* to both disease theory and therapeutics long before 1815. This was especially true of British India, where hundreds of British surgeons were stationed by the end of the eighteenth century, employed by both the East India Company and the armed services of the Crown. By 1785 there were 234 surgeons in the Company's armies alone,[4] their numbers fostering a spirit of independence and self-confidence that impressed many contemporaries.[5] Post-mortem dissections were carried out routinely in Indian military and naval hospitals from the middle of the eighteenth century, contrasting sharply with the situation in Britain itself. Although dissection in British charitable hospitals was becoming more common by the end of the century, it was still far from routine, because many families were not easily persuaded of the importance of autopsies to the advancement of medical knowledge.[6]

The second purpose of this chapter is to examine the significance of pathological anatomy in the elaboration of racial ideas. The term 'race' must be used with caution because this was a time of transition from rather fluid notions of physical difference, characteristic of the eighteenth century, to biologically essentialist and hereditarian notions, typified by the writings of Robert Knox and others in the mid-nineteenth century. Although I have discussed this shift and its broader political significance in previous work,[7] I have not, until now, examined in detail how these ideas were worked out in the anatomico-pathological writings of the period. For ease of exposition, I shall concentrate on two of the most widely read and cited British medical authors of the period: James Johnson and William Twining, although I shall sketch out developments prior to and after their active professional lives, especially the attempt to produce a pathological 'map' of India, which enlisted the help of Indian students of Calcutta's new medical college. In this endeavour, as in most of the writing on pathological anatomy, the human body was viewed as a microcosm of its environment, social and environmental dissolution being reflected in bodily decay. But the pattern of decay appeared to manifest itself differently in the bodies of Indians and Europeans, according to their habits, customs and constitutional traits. It is this complex relationship between heredity and environment that I attempt to unravel below.

Morbid anatomy and British medicine 1810

Before examining the pathological works of British medical practitioners in India, it is worth reminding ourselves of what was distinctive and important about pathological anatomy. Eighteenth-century medicine had been based very largely on the close observation of symptoms, on the *outward* signs of disease. On this basis, Carl Linné (Linnaeus), William Cullen and others had constructed elaborate classificatory systems, known as nosologies, akin to the former's classification of plants. Comparatively few medical practitioners looked inside the body to aid their understanding of disease, even though it was acknowledged that some forms of disease left distinctive marks on the viscera, which could be revealed through post-mortem examinations. Even where dissection was practised as an adjunct to medical education, as in Edinburgh, post-mortem dissections were usually cursory and sporadic.[8] The main reason was the very limited supply of bodies, which, until the Anatomy Act of 1832, was insufficient to meet demand, even when resort was had to resurrectionists and body snatchers.[9]

Despite these limitations, a small minority of medical practitioners did make post-mortem examinations the basis of their pathological theories. One of the best known of these was Giovanni Battista Morgagni (1682–1771), whose *On the Seats and Causes of Disease* was published in Latin in 1761, and translated into English in 1769. It has been suggested that Morgagni's volumes, though admired by some medical practitioners, were too unwieldy and long-winded to make much of an impact.[10] This may be understating Morgagni's importance but comparatively few prominent practitioners took a similar route to the elucidation of disease or, more importantly, made use of pathological observations to improve their clinical practice. The two most prominent exceptions to this rule were John Hunter (1728–93) and his nephew, the physician Mathew Baillie (1761–1823). Hunter, who was famed for uniting medical theory with surgical practice, linked morbid appearances in particular parts of the body (particularly inflammation) to more general pathological changes. Baillie trained at the Great Windmill Street Anatomy School – owned by John Hunter's brother, William – and at St George's Hospital, where John Hunter was Surgeon. After the death of William Hunter, Baillie became proprietor of Windmill Street, which was an unusual position for an elite physician. Baillie described the structural changes caused by disease and hoped to popularize post-mortem examinations as a way of identifying different ailments.[11]

What all of these, and other eighteenth-century works, on morbid anatomy had in common was that they concentrated on particular organs. This 'solidist' pathology was quite different from the fluid and essentially humoral systems of pathology that had preceded it, and later provided the intellectual basis of the 'pathological anatomy' that emerged in France around 1800. Bichat and subsequent French pathological anatomists, however, began to look at tissues rather than whole organs.[12] Although John Hunter was interested in the inflammation of particular membranes, he is not generally considered the originator of systematic tissue pathology because his central concerns remained the local treatment of abscesses and gunshot wounds, and the comparative anatomy of normal and diseased organs. Moreover, because of the limited availability of cadavers in Britain, pathological anatomy did not, as Russell Maulitz has observed, serve as a vehicle for uniting the professions of medicine and surgery as it did in France, where revolutionary laws permitted the dissection of corpses at public hospitals. Pathological anatomy thus appears to have been of interest only to a relatively small minority of medical practitioners, most of whom were concentrated in Edinburgh and London.[13]

But, if we look further afield to Britain's colonies, we see a very different picture, in which post-mortem dissections were common and in which pathology and treatment were firmly grounded on morbid appearances, well before 1815 and even before 1800. There is one obvious explanation for this difference: the abundance of cadavers for dissection and the absence of any legal or ethical restrictions upon their use. Military and naval surgeons, including those of the Company's armies and Marine, found it far easier to obtain corpses for dissection than their civilian counterparts, and this was especially true of the East and West Indies where death rates were far higher than at home. As in the case of the indigent sick who expired in the Paris infirmaries, there were no families to claim the bodies of European soldiers in India and few cared about the fate of 'the scum and refuse of England', as Robert Clive described them.[14] By the 1790s, the post-mortem dissection of cases appears to have been the rule rather than the exception.

The Company had founded small hospitals in its factories as early as the 1670s and by the end of the century there were modest, though more or less permanent, establishments in Calcutta, Bombay and Madras.[15] These provided a context in which patients could be closely monitored and in which clinical observations could be correlated with evidence from post-mortem dissections. The Company surgeon James Annesley believed that

> there is no class of practitioners who have more ample means of advancing our knowledge of diseases [than military surgeons in India] . . . they have complete control over their patients; and new remedies and means of treatment may be employed, and *post-mortem* examinations may always be made by them without restriction.[16]

Other British-Indian practitioners also celebrated the opportunities afforded for the post-mortem observation of disease.[17] Working in a hot climate necessarily meant that dissections had to be conducted almost immediately after death but, as Annesley pointed out, this could be an advantage since it generally provided more accurate information.[18]

The great opportunities presented by medical work in India were not lost on the Company's surgeons and those of the British armed forces, who were noted during the eighteenth and early nineteenth centuries for their innovative and empirical approach to medicine.[19] The medical institutions typically attended by those entering the services – Edinburgh University and the London anatomy schools – were among the most innovative in Europe. Like the armed services themselves, they attracted men who were excluded from Oxford and Cambridge – and hence from the metropolitan physician elite – by virtue of their humble backgrounds or dissenting views. Untrammelled by doctrine, they prided themselves on their independence and professed a self-consciously experimental approach to medical practice.[20] Lastly, the nature of their practice meant that military and naval surgeons were predisposed towards the medicine of populations rather than individuals,[21] a tendency that was both reflected and compounded by the increasing use of statistical analysis and the trial of mass remedies in military and naval hospitals. These developments implied and contributed to the objectification of diseases and patients, which is significant in view of the development of abstract ideas such as 'race'. Medical practice in the armed forces in British India thus exhibited all the features normally associated with 'hospital medicine', to use Norman Jewson's terminology: i.e., the state as patron, a professional career structure, an emphasis on cases rather than persons, on diagnosis and classification, and a focus on organic lesions rather than total psychosomatic disturbance.[22]

The lack of constraints upon post-mortem dissections in India meant that they played a far larger part in the investigation of disease and its treatment than in Britain. If published works are a reliable guide to practices in India, then the importance of morbid anatomy seems to have grown rapidly from the middle years of the eighteenth century – when it was still subordinate to symptomatology – to the 1790s, by which time it had become equally, if not more, important.

The status of morbid anatomy in the middle of the century is illustrated by John Clark's *Observations on the Diseases in Long Voyages*, which was first published in 1773, and which was one of the most widely consulted medical texts in India over the next three decades. Clark went out to India as a surgeon on the Indiaman *Talbot* and served in the Company's hospitals in Madras and Calcutta from 1768 to 1771. During this time, he appears to have carried out quite a few post-mortem dissections of Europeans who had died from such diseases as remittent fever and hepatitis. The dissections are described in some detail but he saw them as less significant than the close observation and recording of symptoms. Unlike some later writers, Clark maintained that 'Dissections throw no light into the proximate cause of . . . disease, as they only shew its effects.'[23] Nor did Clark draw lessons from post-mortem dissections for his treatment of disease: he learned solely from bedside observation.

Yet dissection did lead Clark to pronounce with some certainty on the tendency of diseases to affect particular organs of the body and to speak of the 'seat' of diseases such as remittent fever. The latter, for example, was said to be in the stomach and duodenum. Dissection also led him to associate this and other fevers with a copious secretion of acrid bile, although, unlike later writers, he was uncertain as to whether this was a cause or a consequence of disease.[24] Post-mortem examinations, according to Clark, were also useful in determining whether a patient had died from a disease of the liver, for the symptoms of such complaints were not always visible while the patient was alive. 'Although there are common characteristic symptoms of the disease,' he explained, 'yet so insensible is the liver, that suppurations have been found on dissection, when there have been no reasons to suspect inflammation or any other disease of this organ.'[25]

During the 1780s post-mortem findings carried greater weight than they did in Clark's day and contributed to a growing emphasis upon the liver as the seat of most Indian diseases. This is clear from John Peter Wade's *Paper on the Prevention and Treatment of the Disorders of Seamen and Soldiers in Bengal* (1793), which was based on several years' practice in Bengal during the 1780s. Although Wade admitted that dissections could provide 'fallacious information', he insisted that post-mortem evidence pointed clearly and unanimously to the role of the liver in the production of fevers and dysentery.[26] This connection was deemed to be a causal one and all manner of fevers were attributed to one single cause: vitiated bile.[27] Wade explained that 'There is no one form of fever in Bengal, but what has occasionally been found connected with the liver, the most violent and continued kind would seem to accompany the acute affections of the liver, and the slow and intermittent fevers, chiefly the chronic diseases of that part.'[28] It was the same with dysentery, according to Wade, who followed the renowned Madras physician, Dr Paisly, in attributing fluxes (dysentery) to liver disorders caused by heat rather than the effects of miasma.[29] Wade's therapeutic practices were also based firmly on the evidence of post-mortem dissections, although he himself appears to have conducted few. In cases of fever and dysentery, he placed great reliance on mercury, which had already acquired a reputation in India as a treatment for liver complaints. Mercury was thought to relieve liver obstructions and to act as a purgative, removing vitiated bile from the intestines.[30] The use of mercury in the cure of fluxes and fevers became very popular in India over the next two or three decades, and spread via military and naval surgeons to the West Indies, and even to Britain itself.

Another morbid anatomist working in India during the 1780s was the naval surgeon Charles Curtis, who published *An Account of the Diseases in India* in 1807, some years after his return to Britain. This is a particularly interesting work as it provides further evidence of the importance of post-mortem dissections for disease theory and therapeutics in India, and because it demonstrates many of the features that one would normally associate with Bichat and the Parisian pathologists. Curtis, who worked at the Naval Hospital, Madras, from 1781 to 1782, conducted many post-mortem dissections by himself and in conjunction with other surgeons at the hospital. These dissections convinced him that both fluxes and fevers in India were produced by a 'superabundant and vitiated bile'.[31] His approach was to correlate post-mortem findings with the symptoms of these diseases, and to relate the symptoms exhibited at different points in the disease to affections of different parts of the intestines.[32]

Curtis also conducted post-mortem dissections of patients who died from hepatitis and from a comparatively rare disease known as *mort-de-chien*, whose symptoms closely resemble those of cholera. This disease normally occurred sporadically at various locations around the coast of India, having probably arrived from deltaic Bengal, where the disease was endemic. *Mort-de-chien* normally affected Indians but occasionally claimed European victims, as in the case of the crew of the *Medea*, who contracted the disease after landing on the Coromandel coast. Curtis's observations of the sailors admitted to the naval hospital at Madras, and his dissection of some of the fatal cases, convinced him that *mort-de-chien* was yet another disease of disordered bile, having its origin in derangement of the liver.[33]

Whereas Clark had described simply the state of various organs, Curtis was concerned with the inflammation of membranes or tissues. Elsewhere, for example, he refers to the thickening of the 'covering membrane' of the liver and the turgid quality of the mesenteric vessels of the ileum.[34] This is reminiscent of the tissue pathology of Bichat, although there is no mention in Curtis's work of the Parisian pathologists and his book was based on notes made nearly two decades before the publication of Bichat's first treatise on pathological anatomy. The most striking similarity is with the work of his contemporary John Hunter, whose treatise on gunshot wounds also described the inflammation of various membranes. It is presently unclear where Curtis undertook his surgical training, and whether there is any connection between him and the Hunters or Mathew Baillie, but it would seem that Hunter and Baillie were not alone in refining the organ-based pathology of the earlier eighteenth century, and that the British tradition in morbid anatomy which they typified was far more widespread than has hitherto been acknowledged.

Curtis's work is also significant in another respect: in that it articulates the common belief that liver disorder was the almost inevitable result of prolonged exposure to the Indian climate. 'It is a matter well established from extensive observation,' he wrote, 'that in all hot climates, and in India more than any, a superabundant and vitiated condition of the bilious secretion, is in a manner a constitutional temperament.'[35] It was now commonly believed that Europeans in India would invariably fall ill with some generalized complaint, known variously as 'the bile' or 'the liver'. Mr E. Hay, a Company servant in Calcutta, wrote to a friend in England in 1784 that a mutual acquaintance, Mr Wheler, had 'lately recovered from a severe Attack of the Liver', which had troubled him for some weeks. The recovery was short-lived, however, for within a few months Mr Wheler's 'liver' had returned, with fatal consequences.[36] By the 1790s, such notions were also commonplace among eminent medical authorities in Britain, not least Dr William Saunders, a fellow of both the Royal College of Physicians of London and the Royal Society, and a senior physician at Guy's Hospital. Saunders was Britain's greatest authority on diseases of the liver and he become convinced, on the basis of Indian post-mortem findings, that a disordered liver was the cause of many of the ills of tropical climates. '[I]n India,' he wrote, 'the fever and dysentery, which are considered as the endemiae of the country, have been found, on dissection, to be accompanied with diseases of the liver.'[37]

Saunders was in complete agreement that the liver was the organ most affected by heat, and that its chief effect was an increased secretion of bile. An excess of bile in the body, according to Saunders, produced nausea, loss of appetite, indigestion, diarrhoea and 'general languor of the body'.[38] Some contemporaries found in these ideas an explanation for what they reckoned to be the 'indolence' and 'fatalism' of India's natives. William Falconer, another fellow of the Royal College of Physicians and the Royal Society, claimed that 'the bilious disposition of the inhabitants of these countries, has some share in causing their indolence.' He explained that bile,

> although intended by nature to be an active stimulus to the intestines, exerts an effect totally different when absorbed into the circulatory system. It there produces an *aversion to motion* . . . from which effect it may reasonably be supposed to contribute towards forming this part of their character.[39]

Both Falconer and Saunders claimed to notice similar features among some of their patients – Saunders's in London, Falconer's in Bath – who had returned to England after long residence in the tropics.[40] These unfortunate creatures had, in effect, become 'tropicalized', their constitutions irreparably damaged by prolonged exposure to heat.[41] But Saunders differed in one fundamental respect from Falconer, in that he credited Indians with some degree of immunity from the worst effects of heat upon the liver.[42] This constitutional adaptation appeared to be deeply ingrained: the product of generations of exposure to a tropical climate.

James Johnson

The idea that different races had evolved slowly to fit their environment was an important theme in the writings of the naval surgeon James Johnson, who became one of the foremost authorities on the diseases of tropical climates. Johnson's career provides us with a classic illustration of a surgeon-apothecary who rose from humble origins to the pinnacle of the medical profession. Like many of his contemporaries, Johnson looked to the armed forces as a vehicle for professional advancement, punctuating periods of naval service with periods of intensive study, and making use of all the medical opportunities the service presented. A sketch of his early career is instructive because it shows the prominence of dissection in his surgical training at the London anatomy schools, training that would encourage him to seek the signs of disease within the body and not only in its symptoms. Fortunately, Johnson's early career is well documented, owing to a long and detailed obituary written by his son in 1846 in the *Medico-Chirurgical Review*, a journal that Johnson founded and edited until shortly before his death.[43]

James Johnson was born in February 1777 in County Derry, the son of a poor farmer. At the age of fifteen, he became apprenticed to a surgeon-apothecary in County Antrim and remained there for two years until transferring to another surgeon-apothecary in Belfast. Johnson then set off for London to further his medical career, securing a position as an apothecary's assistant. After regular attendance at lectures in surgery and anatomy, he passed a creditable examination at Surgeon's Hall in 1798, and was appointed surgeon's mate in the Navy later that year. In his first year in the Navy, Johnson travelled to Newfoundland and Nova Scotia, availing himself of every opportunity to study cases in naval hospitals. On returning to London in 1799, he again threw himself into his studies, passing a second examination at Surgeon's Hall in 1800, which enabled him to find employment as a full surgeon on board another naval vessel sailing to Gibraltar.

On his return, Johnson attended the Great Windmill Street Anatomy School and placed himself under two surgeon-anatomists, Mr Wilson and Mr Thomas. He soon acquired great skill as a dissector and was allowed to prepare the subjects for his teachers' lectures. Within a few months, Johnson was giving daily demonstrations in anatomy. In 1801 he applied again to the Naval Medical Board for a ship, with a strong recommendation from Mr Wilson to the effect that Johnson had 'actually lived in the dissecting-room of Great Windmill Street during the last six weeks'. He was accepted and gained employment on a sloop serving in the North Sea, but found himself without employment following the peace of 1802. Having already impressed the eminent naval physician Sir Gilbert Blane with his knowledge and enthusiasm, Johnson was soon appointed to the *Caroline*, the ship in which he was to travel to the East Indies. En route, the *Caroline* anchored off Madeira and the coast of Brazil, where Johnson had the opportunity of studying a range of diseases. From South America, the vessel rounded the Cape and steered to Ceylon, and thence to Madras and Bengal, anchoring in the Hughly at the end of September 1803. From here, the *Caroline* set sail for Rangoon, returning to Bengal in November. It was then that Johnson had his first encounter with the deadly remittent fever of the Ganges Delta, which claimed the lives of many seamen in the Company's Indiamen and British naval vessels.

With Bengal as its base, the *Caroline* was sent on various missions in the East Indies: to the Andaman Islands, to the Malay coast and the Spice Islands, to Coromandel and to China. In November 1805, suffering from persistent dysentery, Johnson left Bengal for England, where he arrived in January 1806. Soon after his arrival, Johnson wrote an entertaining account of his travels in the East – the *Oriental Voyager* (1807) – and, despite his shattered constitution, returned to the dissecting and the lecture rooms. The prize money that he had obtained during his three years' service enabled him to enter as a student at Guy's and St Thomas's, where he formed the acquaintance of the eminent surgeon Sir Astley Cooper. In the autumn of 1806 Johnson returned to Northern Ireland to get married, and shortly afterwards obtained a post attending prisoners of war at the naval depots at Plymouth and Portsmouth, making close observations of the diseases among them. In 1808 he was appointed to the *Valiant* in which he saw a great deal of active service in the Channel before being sent on the disastrous expedition to Walcheren, infamous for the loss of many soldiers to fever. After quitting the *Valiant*, he turned his notes on disease into what became his principal work – *The Influence of Tropical Climates on European Constitutions*, which was first published in 1813. The book went through six editions, the last in 1841, revised with the help of another old India hand, James Ranald Martin. One of the distinguishing features of the work was its grounding in pathological anatomy and its use of recent experimental work in physiology. The first two editions show more than a nodding acquaintance with the literature of French pathological anatomists but the emphasis on pathological anatomy more than likely grew out of his London training and his experiences in India, where he had the opportunity to conduct post-mortem examinations on a regular basis.

Like many of his predecessors in India, Johnson placed great emphasis on excessive (or sometimes deficient) biliary secretion as a cause of many diseases including hepatitis, dysentery, cholera and certain types of fevers. He found evidence of vitiated bile wherever these disorders occurred, appearing in post-mortem dissections as a mass of black or dark-green fluid.[44] Other sure indicators of bilious fever were inflammation of the small intestine, turgesence in the venous system, and engorgement of the viscera with blood. From the appearance of the organs after death, Johnson also hoped to find some means of treating the potentially fatal remittent fever of Bengal. Describing one of the first fatal cases he experienced while moored in the Hughly, Johnson recalled that he

> had the body conveyed to a convenient place, in hopes dissection might afford some clue to my future efforts. On laying open the abdomen, I was surprised to find the liver so gorged . . . with blood, that it actually fell to pieces handling it.[45]

The dissection impressed upon his mind the importance of venesection as a means of reducing inflammation and engorgement – notwithstanding the strictures of Clark and most previous writers on the diseases of tropical climates.[46] Johnson persisted in this course of action throughout his time in India and was later credited with reintroducing the practice of blood-letting in fevers to India, although he continued to use bleeding in conjunction with, and as precursor to, calomel.[47]

Johnson believed that biliary disorders were endemic to Europeans in India because their bodies were poorly equipped to cope with extreme heat. Bodies that were not accustomed to such a climate, he claimed, suffered from increased secretion of bile, which became vitiated when it was too copious to be used up in digestion. However, unlike previous writers, Johnson differentiated between the regions of India in which climate contributed more or less to hepatic derangement. Hepatic diseases, he insisted, were more common in Madras than Bengal because the latter had some remission from heat during its 'tropical winter'.[48] Unlike Dr Saunders, he argued that hepatic derangements occurred solely because of exposure to heat and not from an 'indigenous and local poison', i.e. a particular kind of miasma.[49] They were to be found to a greater or lesser extent across the tropical world, including the West Indies, from which Saunders claimed they were absent.[50]

According to Johnson, heat alone was sufficient to cause hepatic derangement because a 'sympathy' existed between the skin and the liver, i.e. between perspiration and biliary secretion. Thus, when a European arrived in India and began to sweat profusely his biliary secretion also increased. This notion is similar to that expounded by Bichat some years before, but Johnson criticized Bichat for misunderstanding the relationship between climate and internal secretions. Whereas Bichat had insisted that a cold, damp atmosphere made internal secretions more abundant, Johnson maintained that the reverse was true.[51] Unfortunately for Europeans, there was little that could be done to counteract this tendency, for, while they might become acclimatized to a certain extent, complete adaptation was impossible. As I have pointed out elsewhere, Johnson warned repeatedly that European constitutions were fundamentally unsuited to tropical climates and that Europeans would 'degenerate' if they remained in India too long.[52] Indians, by contrast, rarely appeared to suffer from hepatic disorders: the reason, according to Johnson, being the gradual adaptation, over many generations, of their cutaneo-hepatic systems. Johnson went so far as to suggest that Indians owed their colour to an active, though no longer pathological, biliary secretion.[53]

This notion was similar to that of one Dr Smith, who attributed the colour of Indians to the superabundant secretion of bile and its secretion on the surface of the body.[54] But Johnson's explanation differs in that it emphasizes instead the 'sympathy' between perspiration and biliary secretion. Also notable is Johnson's insistence that certain races were uniquely adapted to certain climates. These ideas appear to anticipate the racial doctrines of mid-nineteenth-century writers such as Robert Knox, who embraced Cuvier's opinion that no alteration or change had taken place in any animal – including man – since the earliest time. But, unlike the Cuverians, Johnson was prepared to admit that very gradual changes had occurred in the structure of plants and animals in response to climatic conditions.[55] He believed that it was possible for man to adapt to a new climate but only after *many* generations: a view which may have owed something to his reading of Erasmus Darwin's *Zoonomia* (1794–6). Johnson was therefore less optimistic about the prospects for acclimatization than many of his predecessors, including the naval surgeon James Lind (1716–94) and the army surgeon John Hunter of Jamaica (d. 1809), who both believed that the human body could become fully acclimatized to a new climate within a single lifetime.[56] Just as pathology had moved from humours to solids, and as medicine had come to be based on the internal as well as external manifestations of disease, differences between human beings were seen increasingly as fixed and innate. Johnson may have been predisposed by his intensive training in anatomy to look for such differences, in much the same way as he was disposed to search within the body for knowledge about disease.

William Twining

It is impossible to say exactly how far Johnson attributed different pathological signs to racial characteristics, although his generalizations about race and environmental adaptation suggest strongly that he believed certain characteristics were unvarying across generations. This was also the opinion of the civil surgeon William Twining, who attributed the apparent differences in disease in European and Indian bodies to both lifestyles and constitutional peculiarities. William Twining (1790–1835) was Assistant-Surgeon at the Calcutta General Hospital and during his time there he conducted numerous post-mortem examinations which formed the basis of his two books: *Clinical Illustrations of the More Important Diseases of Bengal* (published in Calcutta in 1832 and again in 1835) and *A Practical Account of the Epidemic Cholera* (1833), which is essentially an extract from the former publication, intended for the guidance of those facing cholera in Britain. During his time in Calcutta, Twining established a reputation as a forward-looking practitioner familiar with all the latest developments in European medicine, including pathological anatomy and physiology. He disseminated this information through the Calcutta Medical and Physical Society, of which he became Secretary, until his untimely death in 1835.[57] A review of medical progress in India published in 1837 by Dr H.H. Goodeve of the recently founded Calcutta Medical College celebrated Twining as the most prominent practitioner of recent times, and his *Clinical Illustrations* as 'indisputably the most valuable treatise on the subject hitherto published'.[58]

The importance of post-mortem examinations was emphasized throughout Twining's work. The introduction to *Clinical Illustrations*, for instance, draws attention to the great advantage of being able to examine the state of the internal organs soon after death, before the onset of post-mortem degeneration.[59] His treatise on cholera also began by stating that it was based on extensive post-mortem examinations.[60] He appears to have been greatly encouraged in this line of investigation by two of his superiors at the Calcutta General Hospital: Drs William Russell and John Turner, successively its Chief Medical Officer. Twining wrote of Turner's 'anxiety to facilitate and promote every useful pathological inquiry, and to apply the strictest results of that inquiry to practice'.[61] True medical knowledge, he believed, was only to be gained through the 'laborious and accurate observation of facts',[62] and his observations led him to question a number of widely held views about the causation and treatment of certain Indian diseases. For example, Twining used post-mortem evidence to question the primacy of hepatic disorders as a cause of dysentery. He was unable to find in the majority of cases who died from dysentery – whether Indian or European – any mark of disease upon the liver.[63]

In treatment, too, post-mortem evidence was used to arrive at 'a correct estimate of the confidence justly due to the mode of treatment that had been adopted'. This was especially true of patients who had previously been cured of a different disease from that which had killed them.[64] A couple of examples will suffice to illustrate the way in which Twining utilized post-mortem evidence in his therapeutics. Dissection of patients who had suffered from dysentery revealed clearly to Twining that there was invariably some local inflammation or vestige of prolonged inflammation, such as an inelastic mesentery.[65] In view of these findings he recommended liberal blood-letting – using venesection and leeches – in order to reduce inflammation and the febrile symptoms that accompanied it.[66] For the same reasons, Twining also came to recommend blood-letting in remittent fevers.[67] 'The closest attention to clinical observation, as well as the result of post-mortem examinations,' he wrote, 'convince me that remittent fevers in Bengal are invariably connected with local congestions, which often run rapidly to inflammation.' These local manifestations of fever, he continued, were to be found principally in the stomach, intestines, the cellular structure surrounding the duodenum and the root of the mesocolon; indications could also be found in the lungs, brain, liver and spleen.[68]

But these were general recommendations and Twining believed that they had to be modified according to the condition of the patient and according to race. To an even greater extent than Johnson, Twining maintained that disease appeared differently in the bodies of Indians and Europeans. In the introduction to *Clinical Illustrations*, he informed his readers that each chapter would end with remarks on the 'modifications of disease, to which the Natives of the country are liable'. He explained that

> Such of their maladies as may be reasonably ascribed to high temperature, and the result of inflammation, are generally much slighter than corresponding diseases in Europeans; which is probably in a great degree owing to the peculiarities of their constitutions, adapted to the Climate.

However, he also believed that this less marked tendency to inflammation was also, in some degree, due to their 'habits with respect to food and drink, which must be acknowledged in many respects to be more reasonable than ours'.[69] This same combination of constitutional adaptation and temperate lifestyle also explained why Indians appeared to be exempt from certain forms of fever, such as the common continued fevers of Bengal, in which there was persistent inflammation.[70] 'In the Dysentery of Asiatics', too, Twining claimed to 'observe a disease which was less marked by inflammatory symptoms'.[71]

On account of these apparent differences, Twining felt that it was necessary to modify treatment to some degree. In the treatment of remittent fevers, for which he recommended a combination of copious bleeding, quinine and cathartics in Europeans, he was inclined to be more moderate in the case of Indians. He noted:

> The Natives of Bengal, are very liable to suffer from remittent fever during the rainy season . . . [ordinarily] the majority of cases occurring among Natives who are not in absolute poverty, are usually slight, requiring only a few mild purgatives, and the application of leeches to the temples, in the early stage of

> the disease, and small doses of Sulphate of Quinine in the intervals of the exacerbations.[72]

In other words, bleeding should be local and light in the case of Indians, and both general and local in the case of Europeans, who could be bled by venesection in addition to leeches. When Indian patients had been debilitated by poverty or fatigue, he refrained from bleeding altogether.[73]

It was much the same with cases of cholera: 'When Cholera attacks robust Asiatics, who are living in affluence,' he maintained,

> they very seldom have that form of the disease which is at the commencement combined with pyrexia and inflammation: and that description of the disease which usually affects the poorer natives of Bengal, is still more rarely attended with febrile or inflammatory symptoms.

Post-mortem dissections also appeared to show that 'visceral disorders are seldom found to occur as its sequelae in natives.'[74] The predominance of this 'low' form of cholera among Indians meant that bleeding was seldom required, unlike in Europeans, where inflammatory symptoms were more likely. Rather, according to Twining, 'A tea-spoonful of laudanum with a spoonful of brandy . . . if given at the first moment of attack, very generally arrests the disease instantly.'[75]

Twining believed that there were some constitutional differences between Europeans and 'Asiatics', as he termed the inhabitants of India, but we should not automatically conclude from this that he believed Europeans to be inherently superior. There is no evidence to confirm whether or not he held supremacist views of the kind expressed by some of his contemporaries such as James Ranald Martin.[76] Although he thought in racial terms, Twining was generally complimentary about Indians and sympathetic to their culture and circumstances. In his *Clinical Illustrations*, for example, Twining wrote that 'Some of the habits and customs of Asiatics . . . and some of their modes of domestic management during disease, appear to be worthy of consideration.'[77] Twining also described the native population of Bengal as 'a handsome race' which possessed 'in common with the most distinguished inhabitants of Europe the Caucasian conformation of the head. . . . Their features are regular and well-formed, with an expression of mildness and intelligence.'[78] These comments are suggestive of some kind of racial hierarchy but it seems that some Indian 'races' shared essentially the same features as Europeans, perhaps on account of their common 'Aryan' ancestry.[79] The reference to Blumenbach's system of racial classification also smacks of phrenology, which had become a popular pursuit in Calcutta during the 1820s and 1830s.[80]

The pathological museum

Observations on race and pathology – of the kind expressed by Johnson and Twining – were made with increasing frequency during the 1840s as opportunities for the dissection of Indian bodies increased. Police surgeons, superintending surgeons at

Indian jails, and surgeons at the native infirmaries established in many of the larger Indian towns, routinely dissected the bodies of the poor. The new Medical College in Calcutta (founded 1835) was supplied with 3,500 Indian bodies for dissection between 1837 and 1847.[81] The College also established a pathological museum that drew thousands of specimens from around the country in order that students might learn early in their career to recognize the morbid indications of disease. The majority of these students were Indians, enrolled in one of the Medical College's two classes: the English language class, and the Military, or Hindustani, class, most of whom were destined to become sub-assistant surgeons in the Company's armies. For a brief period, in the 1840s, the College also educated students from Ceylon, whose fees and expenses were paid by the colonial government of Ceylon.

From the foundation of the College, it was envisaged that anatomy should play an important part in the teaching of medical students.[82] Inducing Indians to open up the body was seen as a major step in dispelling ignorance and superstition. For this reason, the first dissection performed by an Indian – which took place at the College in 1836 – was heralded as a major event, and received widespread coverage in the press in India and in Britain.[83] Anatomical teaching was therefore to be 'experimental' and practical, rather than simply theoretical, and the volume of work led the College to employ a European assistant solely to prepare the bodies and clean the dissecting rooms.[84] It is significant that it was still thought inappropriate to engage an Indian for such a task.

This emphasis on practical training and first-hand observation of morbid appearances gradually increased in the first decade of the College's existence. In the early 1840s, it was still felt that students in the Military Class lacked sufficient practical training and knowledge of human anatomy,[85] a criticism which led to all dissections being conducted and supervised by the Professor of Anatomy and his Indian demonstrator.[86] This initiative was accompanied by the publication in 1846 of an *Anatomical Atlas*, prepared by Dr F.J. Mouat, Secretary of the College's Council and of the Bengal Council of Education.[87]

Anatomical tuition proved very popular among students of both the English and the Hindustani classes, and Indian students played an important part in building up the College's museum of pathological anatomy, conducting many of the dissections, and preparing the specimens for exhibit.[88] The museum, which was modelled on the British Army's pathological museum at Chatham (*f.* 1815), was a great advantage to the teaching of medicine in India, since it was difficult to carry out public dissections during the hot season.[89] There was talk of a 'dissecting season' from October to April, in much the same way as the Company's soldiers spoke of a 'campaigning season' over the same months.[90] The exhibits also permitted British surgeons new to India to learn quickly the morbid indications of Indian diseases before they went into the field. They, in turn, went on to contribute specimens to the museum from their stations in various parts of the subcontinent. However, there was initially some reluctance among British surgeons to prepare specimens and in the mid-1840s many aspects of pathology were still not represented in the museum.[91] The absence of these specimens was extremely problematic in view of the fact that the Medical College was refashioning its curriculum in order to obtain recognition from the Royal College of Surgeons of England – which it eventually achieved in September 1845.[92]

The problem of supply stemmed from the fact that surgeons were expected to purchase the alcoholic spirits, jars and other vessels necessary to preserve the specimens. Dr Mouat therefore urged the Government of Bengal to request regimental authorities to send specimens from the military hospitals, 'in which the worst forms of Tropical Diseases are daily witnessed, and which alone, would in a very short time furnish an extremely valuable collection of interesting and instructive cases'.[93] This the government did, and provisions were made for surgeons to draw upon regimental funds for any expenses incurred.[94] However, outside Bengal, there was some reluctance to send pathological specimens to Calcutta because the medical boards of Madras and Bombay were equally keen to develop pathological museums in their own medical institutions.[95] Despite protests from both presidencies, the Calcutta museum took precedence, the aim being to construct a museum worthy of the capital of British India and one that would be of service to all parts of the empire. It was, however, agreed to send duplicates of any exhibits in Calcutta to the other pathological museums.[96]

Within three years, the Calcutta museum had acquired nearly 2,000 pathological specimens.[97] The person coordinating this vast enterprise was Allan Webb, who was appointed Curator of the museum and Demonstrator of Anatomy to the Military Class in 1845.[98] He also held the professorship of Military Surgery, although he appears to have resigned this by 1847, by which time he had been appointed Professor of Descriptive and Surgical Anatomy at the Calcutta Medical College. When given the task of assembling the specimens, he called upon some of the most prominent surgeons in Bengal, including Twining, H.H. Goodeve and his brother Edward (a personal friend), and the up-country surgeon Kenneth McKinnon.[99] Local hospitals donated their collections, which were merged with those of the College, and surgeons from around India and beyond (e.g. the Malay Straits Settlements) sent specimens to the College on a regular basis. The outcome was a museum that exhibited all the chief diseases of India as they appeared in both Indians and Europeans. It provided an indispensable resource for a comparative pathology of the kind begun by Twining.

Like Twining, Webb took a great interest in the racial manifestations of disease and so did his students. Their observations and accounts of dissections conducted by police and jail surgeons were published by Webb in a remarkable and curious work entitled *Pathologica Indica*. This was first published in 1843 – before his appointment to the College – and in a greatly enlarged edition in 1847. *Pathologica Indica* is an extraordinary collage of pathological observations and lengthy commentaries on ancient and modern medical texts, both European and Indian. It was very well received in both Britain and India,[100] exploding the then prevalent idea that tuberculosis and other pulmonary diseases were largely unknown in the subcontinent. Numerous pathological specimens belied the common assumption of Indian immunity to such disease; a view popularized in Alexander Tulloch's highly esteemed military-statistical reports.[101] Webb also drew attention to the high incidence of cardiac disease among Indians, which was responsible for many medical discharges from the Bengal Army. Cardiac diseases had previously been thought to be very uncommon among Indians but Webb believed that they often suffered from them very severely.[102] Whether this predisposition to heart disease was innate or due to the effects of poverty and custom, however, is unclear from Webb's account. In tuberculosis, though, Webb did notice some racial differences in the morbid appearance of the disease. He noted that European children, especially those with very fair skin, suffered from scrofulous abscesses more frequently than the children of other races, although some Eurasian children also displayed them. They appeared to be very uncommon among Indians.[103]

Webb believed that tuberculosis, like many other diseases, was attributable to inflammation and that inflammatory diseases were generally common in the tropics on account of the extreme heat at certain times of the year. Such diseases were common among Europeans and Indians, he believed, but in certain cases they appeared differently, and this could be detected by post-mortem examinations. While he believed that there was a general tendency in 'tropical inflammation' towards 'disorganizing and dissolution' of organs, he concluded that this 'dissolving tendency' was much more prominent in Indians than in Europeans. 'Asthenic pneumonia breaking up all the structures of the lungs, is the commonest form of pulmonic disease amongst Natives,' he insisted,

> And even in the slower progress of tuberculosis, we never find . . . those pauses, nor those indications of arrest, or of limitation, which in Europe, and with Europeans, even here, is common; and which in the case of tuberculous diseases, shew attempts at a favourable conclusion.'[104]

In other words, the ways in which tuberculosis affected Indians and Europeans were not dependent merely upon location: one had to take into account some other factor, such as constitutional differences, to explain the variation.

Conclusion

In this chapter I have developed two interconnected arguments. The first is that the British presence in India provided opportunities for the advancement of morbid anatomy that were not present in Britain itself. The second is that morbid anatomy provided the basis for new ideas of racial difference that began to emerge in British culture in the early nineteenth century: ideas that stressed the stable and hereditary nature of differences between Europeans and 'Asiatics'.

The circumstances under which British surgeons worked in India were not unlike those which produced Parisian pathological anatomy. There was a steady supply of cadavers, an absence of constraints upon their dissection, and a unification of surgical and medical practice. In India, as in Paris, these circumstances led to the refinement of an organ-based pathology into a pathology of tissues, and to attempts – within the controlled environment of colonial hospitals – to correlate post-mortem findings with bedside observation. The observations made in these hospitals – and in post-mortem examinations – became the foundation of medical practice in British India.

In other words, all the classic features of 'clinical' or 'hospital' medicine were present in India well before 1800, providing support for Keel's argument that many features of 'hospital' medicine had evolved prior to the French Revolution.[105] The history of morbid anatomy in British India also supports Warner's contention that the supposedly revolutionary impact of Parisian medicine in England was more rhetorical than real: rhetoric that played up a need for reform and glossed over important developments in an indigenous tradition of morbid anatomy.[106]

In India, many features of clinical practice – including the centrality of morbid anatomy – were more strongly marked than in Britain itself. But this did not mean that it developed in isolation. There were extensive connections between practitioners in India and in Britain, and also with those in other colonies (although there has not been space to explore those connections here). These networks ensured that some of the observations made by surgeons working in India were incorporated into the publications of eminent metropolitan authorities, such as Dr Saunders, who had never visited the subcontinent. Surgeons with colonial experience – and hence with a keen interest in morbid anatomy – also helped prepare the ground for the importation of Parisian ideas. James Johnson is an excellent example of one such surgeon: a man who incorporated Parisian pathological anatomy into the vibrant, 'Hunterian' tradition of which he, himself, was a part. Johnson and Twining are also notable for working out, on the basis on post-mortem observations, the nature of differences between European and Indian bodies. Their work provided the basis for new ideas of racial difference that estranged Europeans from the Indian environment and had profound implications for the nature of imperial rule in India, especially for debates about colonization and acclimatization.[107] The continuing relevance of racial ideas in medicine in British India is evident in the attempt to construct a pathological collection representative of the Indian empire and particularly in the work of Webb, who made use of those specimens to develop theories about racial propensities to diseases such as tuberculosis.

Notes

1 On morbid anatomy in late eighteenth-century Britain see Othmar Keel, 'The Politics of Health and the Institutionalisation of Clinical Practices in Europe in the Second Half of the Eighteenth Century', in W.F. Bynum and Roy Porter eds *William Hunter and the Eighteenth-Century Medical World*, Cambridge: Cambridge University Press, 1985, 207–58; Russell C. Maulitz, *Morbid Appearances: The Anatomy of Pathology in the Early Nineteenth Century*, Cambridge: Cambridge University Press, 1987, 3, 109–16.

2 On Parisian 'hospital medicine' and the emergence of pathological anatomy see: E.H. Ackerknecht, *Medicine at the Paris Hospital, 1794–1848*, Baltimore, Md.: Johns Hopkins University Press, 1967; Michel Foucault, *The Birth of the Clinic: An Archaeology of Medical Perception*, London: Routledge, 1997.

3 Russell C. Maulitz, 'Channel Crossing: The Lure of French Pathology for English Medical Students, 1816–36', *Bulletin of the History of Medicine*, 55, 1981, 475–96; John Harley Warner, 'The Idea of Science in English Medicine: The "Decline of Science" and the Rhetoric of Reform, 1815–45', in R. French and A. Wear eds *British Medicine in an Age of* Reform, London: Routledge, 1991, 136–64; Thomas Neville Bonner, *Becoming a Physician: Medical Education in Britain, France, Germany, and*

the United States, 1750–1945, Baltimore, Md., and London: Johns Hopkins University Press, 1995, 148–52. Warner, however, makes the important point that some British students were visiting Paris before 1815.

4 David Arnold, *Science, Technology and Medicine in Colonial India*, Cambridge: Cambridge University Press, 2000, 58.

5 Charles Maclean, *Practical Illustrations of the Progress of Medical Improvement, for the last Thirty Years: Or, Histories of Cases of Acute Diseases, as Fevers, Dysentery, Hepatitis and Plague, treated according to the Principles of the Doctrine of Excitation, by Himself and other Practitioners, chiefly in the East and West Indies, in the Levant, and at Sea*, London: for the author, 1818, xiii.

6 Susan Lawrence, *Charitable Knowledge: Hospital Pupils and Practitioners in Eighteenth-Century London*, Cambridge: Cambridge University Press, 1996, 309–10.

7 Mark Harrison, ' "The Tender Frame of Man": Disease, Climate and Racial Difference in India and the West Indies, 1760–1860', *Bulletin of the History of Medicine*, 70, 1996, 68–93; idem, *Climates and Constitutions: Health, Race, Environment and British Imperialism in India 1600–1850,* New Delhi: Oxford University Press, 1999.

8 Christopher Lawrence, 'Ornate Physicians and Learned Artisans: Edinburgh Medical Men, 1726–76', in Bynum and Porter eds *William Hunter and the Eighteenth-Century Medical World*, 153–76.

9 Maulitz, *Morbid Appearances*, 138–9; Ruth Richardson, *Death, Dissection and the Destitute*, London: Routledge and Kegan Paul, 1987.

10 See Malcolm Nicholson, 'Giovanni Battista Morgagni and Eighteenth-Century Physical Examination', in C. Lawrence ed. *Medical Theory, Surgical Practice,* London: Routledge, 1992.

11 Lawrence, *Charitable Knowledge*, 308–9.

12 See: John Pickstone, 'Bureaucracy, Liberalism and the Body in Post-Revolutionary France: Bichat's Physiology and the Paris School of Medicine', *History of* Science, 19, 1981, 115–42; Elizabeth Haigh, *Xavier Bichat and the Medical Thought of the Eighteenth Century, Medical History*, Supplement 4, 1984; Maulitz, *Morbid Appearances.*

13 Maulitz, *Morbid Appearances*, 116–18.

14 Quoted in Robert Harvey, *Clive: The Life and Death of an Emperor*, London: Hodder and Stoughton, 1998, 66.

15 D.G. Crawford, *History of the Indian Medical Service, 1600–1913*, Vol. II, London: Thacker, 1914, 391–422.

16 James Annesley, *Researches into the Causes, Nature, and Treatment of the More Prevalent Diseases of India, and of Warm Climates Generally*, London: Longman, Brown, Green, and Longman, 1841, 3.

17 Walter Raleigh, *Observations on Idiopathic Dysentery, as it occurs in Europeans in Bengal, particularly in Reference to the Anatomy of that Disease,* Calcutta: Thacker, 1842, 5.

18 Annesley, *Researches*, 4.

19 Peter Mathias, 'Swords and Ploughshares: The Armed Forces, Medicine and Public Health in the Late Eighteenth Century', in J.M. Winter ed. *War and Economic Development*, Cambridge: Cambridge University Press, 1975, 91–102; Ulrich Tröhler, 'Quantification in British Medicine and Surgery, 1750–1830, with Special Reference to its Introduction into Therapeutics', Ph.D. thesis, University of London, 1978; W.F. Bynum, 'Cullen and the Study of Fevers in Britain, 1760–1820', in W.F. Bynum and V. Nutton eds *Theories of Fever from Antiquity to the Enlightenment, Medical History Supplement*, No. 1, London: Wellcome Institute for the History of Medicine, 1981, 135–48; N.A.M. Rodger, 'Medicine and Science in the British Navy of the Eighteenth Century', in C. Buchet ed. *L'Homme, la Santé et la Mer*, Paris, 1997, 333–44.

20 Bynum, 'Cullen and the Study of Fevers'; David Harley, 'Honour and Property: The Structure of Professional Disputes in Eighteenth-Century English Medicine', in A.

Cunningham and R. French eds *The Medical Enlightenment of the Eighteenth Century*, Cambridge: Cambridge University Press, 1990, 138–64; Lisa Rosner, *Medical Education in the Age of Improvement: Edinburgh Students and Apprentices 1760–1826,* Edinburgh: Edinburgh University Press, 1991.

21 Christopher Lawrence, 'Disciplining Disease: Scurvy, the Navy and Imperial Expansion', in D. Miller and P. Reill eds *Visions of Empire*, Cambridge: Cambridge University Press, 1994, 80–106; Mark Harrison, 'Medicine and the Management of Modern Warfare', *History of Science*, 26, 1996, 379–410.

22 N.D. Jewson, 'The Disappearance of the Sick-Man from Medical Cosmology, 1770–1870', *Sociology*, 10, 1976, 225–44.

23 John Clark, *Observations on the Diseases in Long Voyages to Hot Countries, and Particularly on those which prevail in the East Indies*, London: D. Wilson and G. Nicol, 1773, 134–5.

24 Clark, *Observations*, 135, 205.

25 Clark, *Observations*, 268.

26 John Peter Wade, *A Paper on the Prevention and Treatment of the Disorders of Seamen and Soldiers in Bengal,* London: John Murray, 1793, 117.

27 e.g. Wade, *A Paper*, 47.

28 Wade, *A Paper*, 179.

29 Wade, *A Paper*, 152.

30 Wade, *A Paper*, 91–2, 155–6, 162.

31 Charles Curtis, *An Account of the Diseases in India, as they appeared in the English Fleet, and in the Naval Hospital at Madras, in 1782 and 1783, with Observations on Ulcers, and the Hospital Sores of that Country,* Edinburgh: W. Laing, 1807, 117, 119.

32 Curtis, *An Account*, 130–1.

33 Curtis, *An Account*, 79–80.

34 Curtis, *An Account*, 74–5.

35 Curtis, *An Account*, 130.

36 E. Hay, Calcutta, to G.G. Ducarel, Exmouth, 14 July 1784; L. Archdekin, Calcutta, to G.G. Ducarel, 22 November, 1784, Record of Ducarel Family, D.2091, Gloucestershire County Record Office.

37 William Saunders, *A Treatise on the Structure, Economy, and Diseases of the Liver; together with An Inquiry into the Properties and Component Parts of the Bile and Biliary Concretions*, 2nd edn, London: J. Philips, 1795, 261.

38 Saunders, *A Treatise*, 131–2.

39 William Falconer, *Remarks on the Influence of Climate, Situation, Nature of Country, Population, Nature of Food, and Way of Life, on the Disposition and Temper, Manners and Behaviours, Intellects, Laws and Customs, Forms of Government, and Religion, of Mankind*, London: C. Dilly, 1781, 13. William Falconer (1744–1824) studied medicine at Edinburgh University, where he took his M.D. in 1766; he took a further M.D. at Leiden in 1767. Falconer spent much of his early professional life in the Chester Infirmary, later establishing a successful practice at Bath (among tropical invalids?), where he became physician at the General Hospital. His attainments as a scholar and physician were said to have been of 'the highest order', as is shown by his election to a fellowship of the Royal Society in 1773: *Dictionary of National Biography*, (*DNB*).

40 Saunders, *A Treatise*, 136–7.

41 Alan Bewell, *Romanticism and Colonial Disease*, Baltimore , Md.: Johns Hopkins Press, 1999.

42 Bewell, *Romanticism*, 133–4.

43 'A Sketch of the Life, and Some Account of the Works, of the Late Dr. James Johnson', *Medico-Chirurgical Review and Journal of Practical Medicine*, n.s. 3, 1846, 1–48. Most of the following biographical information is obtained from this source and the *DNB*.

44 J. Johnson, *The Influence of Tropical Climates, more especially of the Climate of India, on European Constitutions; and the Principal Effects and Diseases thereby induced,*

their Prevention and Removal, and the Means of Preserving Health in Hot Climates rendered obvious to Europeans on every Capacity, London: J. Callow, 1815, 22–4.

45 Johnson, *Influence*, 41–2.
46 Johnson, *Influence*, 43.
47 H.H. Goodeve, 'A Sketch on the Progress of European Medicine in the East', *Quarterly Journal of the Calcutta Medical and Physical Society*, 2, 1837, 147.
48 Johnson, *Influence*, 251–64.
49 Johnson, *Influence*, 251.
50 Johnson, *Influence*, 264.
51 Johnson, *Influence*, 265–8.
52 Harrison, *Climates and Constitutions*, 103–4.
53 Johnson, *Influence*, 355–6.
54 Johnson, *Influence*, 336.
55 Robert Knox, *The Races of Man: A Fragment*, London: Henry Renshaw, 1850, 86–7, 107, 215.
56 See Harrison, *Climates and Constitutions*, chapters 1 and 2; idem, ' "Tender Frame of Man" '. John Hunter of Jamaica was no relation to the more famous London surgeon of the same name.
57 Obituary of Twining, *India Journal of Medical Science*, 2, 1835, 376. Twining died after rupturing a blood vessel while assisting an injured man.
58 Goodeve, 'A Sketch on the Progress of European Medicine', 154–5.
59 William Twining, *Clinical Illustrations of the More Important Diseases of Bengal, with the Result of an Inquiry into their Pathology and Treatment*, Calcutta: Baptist Mission Press, 1832, vi.
60 William Twining, *A Practical Account of the Epidemic Cholera, and of the Treatment requisite in the Various Modifications of that Disease*, London: Parbury Allen, 1833, xi.
61 Twining, *Clinical Illustrations*, ix–x.
62 Twining, *Clinical Illustrations*, xxiv.
63 Twining, *Clinical Illustrations*, 3.
64 Twining, *Clinical Illustrations*, viii.
65 Twining, *Clinical Illustrations*, 13–14.
66 Twining, *Clinical Illustrations*, 14.
67 Twining, *Clinical Illustrations*, 625.
68 Twining, *Clinical Illustrations*, 623.
69 Twining, *Clinical Illustrations*, xxi.
70 Twining, *Clinical Illustrations*, 618. This opinion seems to have been generally held, although other writers were careful to differentiate between the anti-inflammatory vegetarian diet of high-caste Hindus and that of Muslims, which more closely resembled that of Europeans. See W.L. MacGregor, *Practical Observations on the Principal Diseases affecting the Health of the European and Native Soldiers in the North-Western Provinces of India; with a Supplement on Dysentery*, Calcutta: W. Thacker, 1843, 34.
71 Twining, *Clinical Illustrations*, 122.
72 Twining, *Clinical Illustrations*, 656.
73 Twining, *Clinical Illustrations*, 657.
74 Twining, *Practical Account of the Epidemic Cholera*, 230.
75 Twining, *Practical Account of the Epidemic Cholera*, 231.
76 Martin accused Bengalis of lacking pride and moral character, and showed contempt for Hindu customs. See James Ranald Martin, *Notes on the Medical Topography of Calcutta,* Calcutta: G.H. Huttman, 1837, 45, 51–2.
77 William Twining, *Clinical Illustrations of the more important Diseases of Bengal with the Result of Inquiry into their Pathology and Treatment,* Vol. 2, Calcutta: Baptist Mission Press, 1835, 420.
78 Twining, *Clinical Illustrations*, Vol. 2, 419.

79 On the Aryan myth in relation to India, see Thomas R. Trautmann, *Aryans and British India*, Berkeley: University of California Press, 1997.

80 Harrison, *Climates and Constitutions*, 118–19.

81 Allen Webb, *Pathologica Indica, or the Anatomy of Indian Diseases, based upon Morbid Specimens, from all Parts of the Indian Empire in the Museum of the Calcutta Medical College*, Calcutta: Thacker, 1848; first published, 1843, 237.

82 On the foundation of the Calcutta Medical College see David Arnold, *Colonizing the Body: State Medicine and Epidemic Disease in Nineteenth-Century* India, Berkeley: University of California Press, 1993, 56–8; Anil Kumar, *Medicine and the Raj: British Medical Policy in India 1835–1911,* New Delhi: Sage, 1998, 19–22; Zaleh Khaleeli, 'Harmony or Hegemony? The Rise and Fall of the Native Medical Institution, Calcutta; 1822–35', *South Asia Research*, 21, 2001, 77–104.

83 Kumar, *Medicine and the Raj*, 24.

84 J.C.C. Sutherland, Secretary-General of the Committee of Public Instruction, to H.J. Prinsep, Secretary to Government in the General Department, 11 January 1836, India (Home Consultations) P/186/71, OIOC.

85 Secretary of the Medical College Council to Secretary of the Council of Education, 16 May 1843, Bengal (Council of Education Procs) No. 4, 23 October 1843, P/15/29, OIOC.

86 Secretary of Council of Education to Secretary of Medical College Council, 27 June 1843, Bengal (Council of Education Procs) No. 4, 23 October 1843, P/15/29; Secretary of Council of Education to Secretary to the Government of Bengal, 29 November 1845, No. 5, 7 January 1846, Bengal (Council of Education Procs) P/15/38, OIOC. The Indian Demonstrator appears to have been Pandit Madhusudan Gupta, who was the first Indian to perform a human dissection at the Medical College.

87 Secretary to Council of Education to Secretary to the Government of Bengal, 1 January 1846, Bengal (Council of Education Procs) No. 11, 21 January 1846, P/15/38, OIOC.

88 Webb, *Pathologica Indica*, xiii.

89 Webb, *Pathologica Indica*, vii, xiii.

90 F.J. Mouat, Secretary to the Council of Education, to F.J. Halliday, Secretary to the Government of Bengal, 1 January 1846, Bengal (Council of Education Procs) No. 11, 21 January 1846, P/15/38, OIOC.

91 Under Secretary to the Government of Bengal to Secretary to the Council of Education, 11 February 1846, Bengal (Council of Education Procs) No. 11, 11 February 1846, P/15/38, OIOC.

92 Secretary to Council of Education to Secretary to Government of Bengal, 22 February 1845, Bengal (Council of Education Procs) No. 9, 5 March 1845, P/15/35; Secretary to Council of Education to Secretary to Government of Bengal, 22 September 1845, Bengal (Council of Education Procs), P/15/36, OIOC.

93 Secretary to Council of Education to Secretary to Government of Bengal, 28 June 1845, Bengal (Council of Education Procs) No. 1, 30 July 1846, P/15/36, OIOC.

94 Under Secretary to the Government of Bengal to Lt.-Col. J. Stuart, Secretary to the Government of India, Military Department, 16 July 1845, Bengal (Council of Education Procs) No. 2, 30 July 1845, P/15/36, OIOC.

95 Mr George Pearce, Secretary to Madras Medical Board, to Chief Secretary to the Government of India, undated, Bengal (Council of Education Procs) No. 1, 17 October 1845; Secretary to the Government of Bombay to Secretary to the Government of India, 30 October 1845 and Secretary of Bombay Medical Board to Secretary to Government of India, Military Department, 13 October 1845, Bengal (Council of Education) No. 7, 17 December 1845, P/15/36, OIOC.

96 Secretary to Council of Education to Secretary to Government of Bengal, 26 October 1845, Bengal (Council of Education) No. 3, 19 November 1845, P/15/36, OIOC.

97 Webb, *Pathologica Indica*, i.

98 Under Secretary to Government of Bengal to Secretary to Council of Education, 19 February 1845, Bengal (Council of Education Procs) No. 19, 19 February 1845, P/15/35, OIOC. Webb was employed on a consolidated allowance of Rs500 p.m. He was one of several new appointments made at that time, including the new Professor of Surgery, W.B. O'Shaugnessy.

99 Webb, *Pathologica Indica*, vii.

100 Dr Mouat described Webb's *Pathologica Indica* as 'a work which has received the highest commendation from eminent authorities in England as a very valuable contribution to the medical literature of this country' (Mouat to Secretary to Government of Bengal, 26 October 1845, Bengal (Council of Education Procs) No. 3, 19 November 1845, P/15/36, OIOC).

101 Webb, *Pathologica Indica*, 100.

102 Webb, *Pathologica Indica*, 66–7, 91–2.

103 Webb, *Pathologica Indica*, 128.

104 Webb, *Pathologica Indica*, 128.

105 Keel, 'The Politics of Health and the Institutionalisation of Clinical Practices in Europe'.

106 Warner, 'The Idea of Science in English Medicine'.

107 Harrison, *Climates and Constitutions*, chapters 2–3.

11 Pharmacology, 'indigenous knowledge', nationalism

A few words from the epitaph of subaltern science

*Projit Bihari Mukharji**

European interest in South Asian flora and its medicinal virtues largely predates colonialism.[1] In the colonial era this interest was, however, radically transformed due to the fundamentally altered field of power relations within which it was implicated. Proximity to the imperial power gave colonial botany an unprecedented authority to describe the botanical resources of the region and alienate them from their social and cultural milieux. A combination of novel figurative schemes and their enabling technologies, underwritten by the imperial hegemony, allowed Indian botany to be recast in a completely new light. David Arnold has recently argued that one of the organizing *topoi* within which these new figurative actions were arranged was the concept of 'tropical India'.[2] Moreover this also allowed for the increasing 'professionalization of nature', premised upon the technology of the 'travelling gaze'. A single roving eye, through the technological innovation of the botanical tour, sought to 'discover' its objects. Instead of collecting information from and gaining access to Indian flora through 'native' intermediaries, the colonial botanists came to locate and map Indian flora in the course of 'botanical tours', without apparently significant 'native' intellectual mediation. Unlike the earlier Europeans like Garcia da Orta or Van Rheede – who had written of their access to the plants within a socio-cultural milieu, the colonial botanists narrated their 'discoveries' in a pre-cultural 'natural' frame. The earlier attitude is brought out in Brian Hodgson's – Joseph Hooker's elderly host and friend in the Himalayas – advice to the latter that it was better to 'explore one district well than to wander'.[3] Hodgson himself had spent a lifetime among Indians, lived with a Kashmiri woman, spoke several Indian languages and yet had not written much, whereas Hooker – who was to become undoubtedly the most influential botanist of his age – produced the definitive classic on Indian botany as a result of a breathless tour of merely two years and only a nodding acquaintance with local Himalayan society. Hodgson stood in putative line with older Orientalists such as William Jones, who combined their interest in the 'natural' and 'cultural' worlds under the rubric of 'natural history'; Hooker, on the hand, like most other eminent colonial botanists, sought to premise his knowledge upon a strict division between these two domains.[4]

We argue in this chapter that this changed view of colonial botany reflected a deeper impulse towards the discursive framing of Indian botanical material in ways which enabled their easy alienation from their local socio-cultural milieux by the removal of the need for local intermediaries. This is not to suggest that colonial botany was able instantly to do away with local intermediaries. In fact it continued to rely on indigenous collaboration till almost the very end of imperial rule. However, its orientation, reinforced by the bureaucratic apparatus within which it functioned, automatically restructured indigenous botanical cultures and enabled its ultimate take-over by the nationalist botanists. By repeatedly collaborating with elite/learned 'indigenous' botanical cultures, it allowed these latter to gain dominance within a pre-existing fractured and plural world of 'indigenous' botany. This learned hegemonic domination in turn empowered the nationalist efforts to further marginalize subaltern botanical cultures.

Politics of names and the early social contexts of Indian botany

Arnold explains that:

> Although in Europe botany had attained a degree of intellectual independence from medicine by the mid-eighteenth century, it still formed an integral part of the education of Company surgeons . . . of the forty-two individuals I.H. Burkhill identified as practising botanists in the period up to 1840, twenty-eight were surgeons, as were roughly a quarter of those active in the second half of the century.[5]

Many Indians trained in western medicine too – such as Iswar Chandra Ganguly, Rameshwar Awasthi and Mohiuddeen Shariff – took an active interest in 'indigenous drugs'.

Matthew Edney has pointed out that practising 'science' emerged among the Anglo-Indians as a way of establishing one's genteel credentials in a society where gentility was not as fixed as in metropolitan Britain.[6] This further encouraged the popularity of scientific pursuits such as botany among those with a rudimentary scientific interest – for example, the early doctors. This medical connection meant that pharmacology became a yardstick for the practice and testing of botanical knowledge. Writing one of the first in a long series of catalogues of Indian medicinal plants and drugs, John Fleming in 1810, for instance, explained that his book was 'intended chiefly for the use of gentlemen of the medical profession on their first arrival in India, to whom it must be desirable to know what articles of the Materia Medica this country affords, and by what names they may find them.'[7] But this laudable object was easier stated than achieved.

With an ever growing stock of plants known to botanists, the persistent impediment to their reliable pharmacological use was how to be certain if the plant described by a previous botanist was indeed the plant at hand, i.e. how to match names and descriptions to the available plants. Reality, be it human or herbal, was and is infinitely varied. Just as two different people, however closely related, seldom look exactly the same, similarly herbs seldom resemble each other completely. This unreliability of the identity of the plants often led to embarrassing results. The report

Table 11.1 A catalogue of books dealing with 'indigenous drugs' published between 1790 and 1869

Author	*Title*	*Date of publication*
William Jones	*The Design of a Treatise on the Plants of India*	1790
Sir William Jones	*Botanical Observation on Select Plants*	1795
Sir William Jones	*A Catalogue of Indian Plants*	1795
Father Loureiro	*Flora Cochinensis* (second Berlin edition in 1793)	1790
John Fleming	*Catalogue of Indian Medicinal Plants and Drugs*	1810
Whitelaw Ainslie	*Materia Medica of Hindoostan*	1813
William Jack	(Died suddenly in 1822, but fragments of his work appeared in Sir W. Hooker's *Companion t o the Botanical Magazine* and John McClelland's *Calcutta Journal of Natural History*)	
William Roxburgh	*Hortus Bengalensis*	1814
William Roxburgh	*Flora Indica* Vol. I	1820
William Roxburgh	*Flora Indica* Vol. II	1824
Whitelaw Ainslie	*Materia Indica* (2 vols)	1826
William Roxburgh (with substantial material from Nathaniel Wallich)	*Flora Indica* Vol. III	1832
Robert Wight and G.A.W. Arnott	*Prodromus Florae Peninsulae Indiae Orientalis*	1834
Robert Wight	*Illustrations of Indian Botany*	1838
John Lindley	*Flora Medica*	1838
J. McCosh	*Topography of Assam*	1837
J.F. Royle	*Illustrations of the Botany of the Himalayan Mountains and the Flora of Cashmere*	1839
D. Butter	*Medical Topography of Oudh*	1839
J.F. Royle	*The Productive Resources of India*	1840
W. Dollard	*Medical Topography of Kumaon and Shone Valley*	1840
Robert Wight	*Icones Plantarum Indiae Orientalis* (subsequent edition in 1853)	1840
W.B. O'Shaughnessy	*Bengal Dispensatory and Pharmacopoeia*	1841
R.H. Irvine	*General Medical Topography of Ajmere*	1841
J.F. Royle	*A Manual of Materia Medica*	1845
J.O. Voigt	*Hortus Suburbanus Calcuttensis*	1845
R.H. Irvine	*Materia Medica of Patna*	1848
Richard Strachey	*Catalogue of Plants of Kumaon, Garwal and Tibet*	1852
J.F. Royle	*The Commercial Products of India and the East*	1854
R.H. Beddome	*Ferns of Southern India*	1863
G. Birdwood	*Vegetable Products of Bombay Presidency*	1865
R.H. Beddome	*Ferns of British India*	1865
Kanny Lall Dey	*Indigenous Drugs of India*	1867
Pierre Edmond Boisser	*Flora Orientalis*	1867
B.H. Baden-Powell	*Punjab Products*	1868
E.J. Waring	*Pharmacopoeia of India*	1868
J. Forbes Watson	*Index to the Plant Names of Indian Plants*	1868
J.L. Stawart	*Punjab Plants*	1869
R.H. Beddome	*Flora Sylvatica*	1869

of the First Indigenous Drugs Committee mentioned that on examining a sample set of squill bulbs obtained from the different Presidency Medical Depots, it was found that, while 'the Madras bulbs . . . all proved to be one or other of the two species of Indian Squills . . . the Bombay bulb No. 9660 which Dr. Parker [said] was formerly used in the Medical Depot [was] not squill at all.'[8] Thirty years earlier Mohiuddeen Shariff – another botanically inclined doctor – writing on the vernacular names used in extant botanical literature, mentioned that useful knowledge was 'blended with great inaccuracy and confusion'.[9] Another Sub-Assistant Surgeon, Iswar Chandra Ganguly, writing in 1842, found faults with W.B. O'Shaughnessy's – one of the leading authorities on Indian botany at the time – description of colocynths.[10] What was remarkable was that this 'confusion' persisted despite the wealth of research and publications on the subject following Sir William Jones's early hesitant 'observations' in the 1790s.

In 1838 the government appointed a committee to investigate the reliability of indigenous drugs. Unfortunately it could not fulfil its mandate through the death or transfer of most of its members, and the secretary W.B. O'Shaughnessy alone produced a report.[11] This report clearly proved that no investigation of 'indigenous drugs' could avoid the problem of names. Paul Carter has pointed out that cartographic and botanical naming were two alternate strands born out of the Enlightenment impulse to appropriate the world as words. Yet while cartography, as Carter brilliantly demonstrates, tends to particularize place names, botany is constantly riven with the wish to generalize and systematize.[12]

Metropolitan botany was torn asunder first by the claims of the Linnaean sexual system of plant classification and then again by the Natural System. In South Asia, however, the contest between Linnaean and the Natural systems was overshadowed by the debate on 'indigenous' names.[13] While early Orientalists like Jones argued for Sanskrit in preference to Latin and other extant vernaculars,[14] later Romantics like W.B. O'Shaughnessy argued precisely the opposite, championing the vernaculars, among which he included English along with Bengali and Hindi. While Jones felt that the contemporary Indian languages would change over time and lose their relevance, O'Shaughnessy argued that the use of contemporary languages would allow scions of the Indian middle classes to become apothecaries and thereby stop the European apothecaries in India from fleecing the masses, as they were doing at the time.[15] Given the plural nature of indigenous botanical cultures, accepting any one language proved difficult. Roxburgh used a 'motley brew of Sanskrit, Bengali, Arabic, Persian, Hindustani and Hebrew', and Francis Buchanan, while paying lip service to Jones's view, could not always live up to his recommendation of Sanskrit.[16]

Despite the obvious differences between them, there were also discernible similarities between Jones and O'Shaughnessy. While Jones relied on Brahmins like Ramakant, Radhakant and Servoru, O'Shaughnessy wanted his work to be useful in producing a class of 'native apothecaries' drawn from 'native' youth who knew Bengali, Hindi and English. He went on to clarify that these youth would be able to combine in their persons the western scientific education and the knowledge of their forefathers. Given his support for this particular class, members of it are quite likely to have been informants for his report. Moreover, clearly, knowledge of English in 1840s Bengal would have been available to the relatively small class of *bhodrolok*. By turning to these informants and ignoring other groups who possessed indigenous botanical knowledge, both Jones and O'Shaughnessy were indulging in a process of selection. As Richard Grove has pointed out, early European botanists such as Garcia d'Orta were more open to the plurality of indigenous botanical intermediation.[17] Though, as we shall see later, Jones cannot be thought of as being totally within the colonial botanical framework, he already shared some of the features that came to be central to later colonial botany. The selection of elite, learned collaborators as representatives of the indigenous botanical traditions created a context for the progressive marginalization of subaltern botanical cultures. The espousal of continuity with earlier traditions of botanical writing on Indian flora by the colonial botanists was thus more mythic than real. Antonio Gramsci's comments on the misplaced continuity that intellectuals at the intersections of a different economic order claim with the intellectual legacies of the previous order are relevant here. Gramsci argues that this misplaced continuity allows intellectuals to think of themselves 'as "independent", autonomous, endowed with a character of their own, etc.'[18] This in turn allows them to overlook their complicity with the existing economic and political hierarchies of domination.

In this chapter we shall focus on one aspect of this discontinuity, i.e. the privileging of elite/learned strands of 'indigenous' botanical knowledge over other strands.

The heterogeneity of indigenous botanical knowledge is most dramatically seen in an anonymous botanical journal from the early nineteenth century, belonging in all probability to Francis Buchanan. On several pages of this handwritten journal we find the same plants classified differently on the same page by an unnamed 'Doctor' and another 'Collector'. There are even notes pointing to disagreements between the two about which plants were related and which were not. Moreover, in most cases the Collector is seen to be proved right, for example in the case of *Sonaphuli*. The Doctor initially classifies five varieties under the separate head of *Nagphuli*, but comes round to agreeing with the Collector that they are all varieties of *Sonaphuli*. Similar disagreements and resolutions in favour of the Collector are also seen in the case of plants like *Gorokha*, *Hidyasaram* and *Sapola*.[19] Unfortunately, however, Buchanan was the victim of bureaucratic politics, and never fulfilled his botanical potential. He and, with him, his attempt to compare 'informants' from different social groups were marginalized.[20] Consequently both W.B. O'Shaughnessy, in his capacity as the secretary of the Pharmacopoeia Committee of the 1840s, and Dr McConnell, as member of the Indigenous Drugs Committee in the 1890s, continued to summon 'better known Kabirajes . . . held in the high[est] esteem' as their sole informants.[21] The question of deciding on indigenous names therefore also involved an act of selection between competing schemes of nomenclature.

Later, as the British administrators in India and the science of botany both grew in confidence, the contours of the debate changed. The language of scientific description was pitted against 'indigenous names' and most books from the second half of the nineteenth century included discussions on the accuracy of the vernacular names given in earlier texts when judged in the light of scientific names and descriptions.

Two discernible camps emerged from this new debate. The first used the insufficiency of 'indigenous names' to draw attention to the 'unreliability of the bazaar', thus expressing the constant anxiety of the educated scientist of being cheated by the 'illiterate tradesman'. This camp called for complete reliance on 'scientific' names alone. The second camp increasingly lost faith in a language of scientific description and sought greater accuracy in vernacular names. Hence while the former camp attempted to completely eradicate the trader intermediaries, the latter camp sought more reliable intermediaries.

Writing the preface to the long-awaited and necessary reprint in 1874 of Roxburgh's classic *Flora Indica*, C.B. Clarke expressed the views of the former camp when he wrote that,

> Considerable assistance in discriminating Bamboos can be got from the dealers in Bamboos, though even in this case the name of the species differs in different districts of the same province . . . the natives of India have no idea of accurately observing anything and the best names that even Roxburgh is able to give for common plants are sometimes only Chota Doodhee Luta (Small White Creeper), Doosera Sag (Another Spinach) and such like. As to the grand Sanskrit names they are still of less value than the vulgar ones, being founded on less actual observation.[22]

On the other hand the Bengali pharmacologist Kanai Lal Dey went on to represent the latter camp when he wrote that,

> Identification will remain a prime difficulty until certain prominent characteristics of each drug becomes established, as no amount of verbal description will enable the non-botanical mind to identify some plants and parts which even in themselves do not invariably present quite the same characters. The ease and cheapness with which almost all the drugs of this country are to be obtained will be facilitated greatly with the help of the vernacular names peculiar to each district, as also with the aid of the professional castes who deal in these substances, the *Musheras* of Central and Upper India, the low caste *Moules, Bediyas, Bagdis, Kaibartas, Pods, Chandals, Kaoras* and *Karangas* of Bengal and the *Chandras, Bhils* and *Gamtas* of Bombay.[23]

The 'indigenous' in indigenous knowledge

A more fundamental issue in the discourse on 'indigenous' drugs was the definition of indigenousness itself. Did it mean drugs available in India, drugs used in indigenous pharmacopoeias, drugs cultivated in India or drugs which had their 'origins' in India? George Watt, for instance, describing his friend Kanai Lal's usage of the term, states that,

> He has rightly recognised that the expression 'Indigenous Drugs' if employed too literally would have excluded a distinct percentage of the drugs that enter very largely into every-day practice. Many of the so-called indigenous drugs can be shown to be introduced plants completely naturalised. Others, such as Cinchona, are cultivated in India, and therefore should find a place in an Indian student's manual. But there is a still more arbitrary restriction forced sometimes on the expression 'Indigenous Drugs' that would exclude from that position all the drugs that appear in the British Pharmacopoeia even although India may be the country of the world's supply. Dr. Dey has not accepted that view, and accordingly deals with all the drugs procurable in India whether they be indigenous to this country or not.[24]

Proceeding further along this line of reasoning, within ten years of Watt's comments, David Prain wrote in the very year when the 'Swadeshi' movement was putting a new premium on what it meant to be 'indigenous', that,

> There is a sense in which except perhaps in the Goghat sub-division of the Hughli District, no species *can* be indigenous in our area [i.e. the districts of Hughli, Howrah and twenty-four Pergannahs in Bengal]; the whole or nearly whole tract consists of land laid down by the great river Ganges or its distributaries . . . however the fact is not altered that a considerable number of species . . . though not even natives of India are established as wild plants in our area.[25]

The ambiguities of the term 'indigenous' reflect a deeper contradiction. To appropriate Carter's elegant phrase, 'reality is a naïve reflection of the language available to describe it.'[26] The polymorphism of the term 'indigenous drugs' in pharmacology clearly reflected the multiplicity of languages and systems of botanical knowledge available in colonial South Asia. If a medicine originally of Arabian origin was used in Unani medicine, for instance, was it going to be accepted as 'indigenous'? To further complicate the picture, what if this plant had at some point been introduced into South Asia, and subsequently grew in the wild? The Europeans were not the first or the only ones to introduce plants into South Asia: Grove mentions for instance that the early Europeans merely grafted onto pre-existing networks of plant transfer in the Indian Ocean.[27] Similarly the Buchanan manuscript mentions that *Jabas* (Hibiscus), though 'lately introduced into Bengal' had been part of the native pharmacopoeia for many years.[28] In an area where several learned and folk traditions thrived and hybridized without giving up their identities, 'indigenous' domains of knowledge proliferated and could not be reduced to any one tradition. John Marshall – who visited Bengal in the seventeenth century – mentioned that the local 'black Portuguese' community of Bengal had developed its own medico-botanical lore. Even the Anglo-Indians (English residents of India) themselves developed their own medico-botanical traditions. John Fleming in the late eighteenth century gives many instances of specifically Anglo-Indian medico-botanical ideas.[29] Clarke and Dey also mention distinctly Anglo-Indian medico-botanical traditions.

Moreover, there were regional variations of botanical names. Regional variations of pre-colonial pharmacopoeias such as the Sanskrit *Nirghantus* and the Persian *Makhzans* were known to have existed. In the absence of any apparatus for centralization, there had never been an attempt to standardize all these regional texts. Uday Chand Dutt, for instance, writing in 1870 mentioned that, '[i]n the North West Provinces the Nirghantu compiled by Madanpala, is generally perused by students. In Bengal, a very superficial compilation, under the name of Rajavallabha, is in currency. In Orissa, a superior work, called Satkantha-ratnabharana, is used.' There were still others such as the 'Dhanwantari Vanaoushada' and the 'Dhananja Padardha Nirghantus' in Telegu areas and the 'Muligai Nirghantu' in Tamil lands, to name just a few. Garcia da Orta had therefore pointed out that 'At Goa, doctors are very little conversant with things in Delhi.'[30]

The phrase 'indigenous drugs' was problematic on at least two levels. First, it was unable to recognize the plural nature of botanical traditions in the region and the multiplicity of systems of nomenclature deriving from that plurality. Second, the networks of plant transfers upon which these older traditions depended for the ingredients of their pharmacopoeias did not always fit precisely with political territories. Plants which grew in other countries had been brought into Indian markets along much older routes and these drugs were often included in indigenous pharmacopoeias. Francois Bernier had mentioned Chinese drugs that came through Nepal and Bhutan and later British observers such as Samuel Turner continued to remark on the Chinese drugs coming to India, yet China was never politically connected to the Indian subcontinent.[31] These transfers depended upon a chain of local intermediaries and the same product often acquired different names when sold by different traders in different areas of the long overland route. Since the original collector was seldom the actual user of the substance, the identities of the substance within their respective classificatory systems did not always match. This meant that the purity of a product used by the 'native physicians' was assured not by its provenance or even appearance but rather through the identity of a dependable chain of intermediaries. In the late eighteenth century, both Roxburgh and Fleming were confounded to find that the Hindu druggists who sold Myrobalan – an important ingredient of several indigenous prescriptions – did not have the slightest idea whether it was a seed, a stem or a fruit. It was only recognized after much effort through reference to an old Persian text.[32] David Hooper, writing in 1903, mentioned that 'native physicians' recognized two different varieties of *Shilajit*, by buying them from different groups of Nepalese and Bhutia traders.[33] The most startling example, however, was the 'Treeak Farooq', long used by South Indian Hakims and mentioned in several English treatises as an 'indigenous drug' and an effective cure for beriberi. When Assistant Surgeon J.G. Malcolmson sought to find the origins of this blackish tar-like substance, the indigenous physicians could give no clue as to the origins of the product, stating for certain only that they bought it through Mughal merchants, who in turn pointed out that they imported it through Arabian traders. On further enquiry, Malcolmson found that the product was after all a patent medicine sold by an Italian priest called John Baptist Sylvestrius on the Rialto in Venice.[34]

The colonial state, with its bureaucratic apparatus and pursuit of fixed names, was not able to accommodate a system of transfers which called the same thing by different names in different areas and yet managed to communicate successfully. Confronted by a plethora of names for the same substance, it often sought to choose those that were in accordance with its own administrative hierarchies. *Cubebs Officinalis*, for instance, was called *Sital Chini* in South India, while the related *Allspice* was called *Kebab Chini*, but the reverse was true in Calcutta. The government hospitals and dispensaries chose the Calcutta usage which caused much confusion in Madras.[35] More dramatically, when the British Pharmacopoeia Committee sought suggestions from the Indian authorities for possible inclusion of an 'Indian and Colonial Addendum', this policy to reproduce names used in Calcutta – the imperial capital – precipitated a political crisis and ultimately scuttled the Addendum project itself.[36]

The shared material context meant that from the later decades of the nineteenth century the same tendencies were also discernible in the Ayurbedic and Unani Tibbi traditions. Horolal Gupto's *Ayurbed Bhashabhidan* (Encyclopaedia of Ayurbedic Names), which was first published in 1296 BS (AD 1888–89) and went into its fifth edition in 1313 BS (AD 1905), mentioned that,

> These days most Ayurbedic texts tend to follow the language in use in Calcutta. This is usually cause for great consternation for the lay practitioner of Ayurbedic medicine. They tend to get their training in one particular district and learn the names of the herbs in that district's language, but then because of various exigencies have to move to another district where the herbs are known by another name.[37]

Similar sentiments were also repeated in the Bengali Unani text, *Makhjaane Masiha* (Guide to the Materia Medica), with the additional problem that Bengali Hakims had to learn most of the names in Persian as well.[38]

Indigenous knowledge and the 'fabulous'

Texts such as Gupto's raise other questions about the nature of the 'indigenous' knowledge that is produced through colonial contact. In the third edition of his text, Gupto included a strikingly 'modern' classificatory system for arranging herbs according to whether they bear flowers, the type of roots, the type of leaves, etc. The herbs are arranged as follows: lists of names in different languages, followed by a physical description of the plant in terms of the type of leaves, flowers, appearance, height, etc., followed by the medicinal and other uses as stated in other texts. Michel Foucault described a very similar plan while summing up the formal organization of the Linnaean 'natural history' texts.[39] In these, the '*Litteraria*', or 'All the language deposited upon things . . . [the] discoveries, traditions, beliefs, and poetical figures', are pushed back to the very end, where 'discourse is allowed to recount itself'.[40] But if Gupto's text formally resembled Linnaean texts, Gupto himself added that,

> The number of genital organs in each flower vary. Some experts on plants have attempted to classify them according to the number of genital organs in each. Even some Aryan seers are said to have done this. Today though such practices are hardly deemed necessary, and hence I too have decided against including them here.[41]

The allusion to a debate between a 'sexual' and a 'natural' system is clearly reminiscent of the debate between the Linnaean and Natural systems in European botany, though equally interesting is the narration of such a debate within a framework of Aryan science. Michael Taussig has drawn our attention to the mimetic gestures which mark knowledge produced through colonial contact.[42] Mutual mimetic 'entanglements' encourage neighbouring colonial traditions to increasingly resemble each other.[43]

Apart from mimesis, active hybridization also recasts 'indigenous' traditions under colonial contact. A classic example of such hybridization is to be seen in Kobiraj Bijoyrotno Sen's lengthy prefatory note to Birojachoron Gupto's highly influential classic, *Bonoushodhi Dorpon*. Sen included in his review of texts he thought relevant to Ayurbedic pharmacy such works as Irvine's *Materia Medica of Patna*, Stuart's *Punjab Plants*, Sakharam Arjun's *Bombay Drugs*, Drury's *Useful Drugs of India*, Waring's *Bazaar Medicine*, Nobin Chondro Pal's *Indian Herbalist*, Watt's *Dictionary of Economic Products* and Dey's *Indigenous Drugs of India*, along with the *Dhonwontori Nirghontu*, the *Rajbollobhiyo Drobyo Gunoh, Modonbinod Nirghontu, Raj Nirghontu*, etc.[44]

Both Gupto's and Sen's texts bring out the impossibility of identifying 'purely indigenous' botanical traditions in a colonial context. This difficulty is most acute in texts and discourses produced by the elite/learned traditions which were exposed to the maximum proximity with colonial 'western' knowledge and texts. Moreover, both claimed that their discourses were 'modern' and 'scientific'. Gyan Prakash has commented on the 'complex strategy of hybridization and negotiation of difference and discrimination, [whereby] science's status as a sign of Western power was instituted and came undone'.[45] Prakash further argues that science lost its 'autonomy and originality' in its renegotiations with the 'traditions' it sought to render 'superstitious' and 'fabulous'. The examples of Gupto and Sen show that the strategies of contestation could vary widely. While the former contested the originality of science by prefiguring contemporary debates within 'Aryan' traditions, the latter domesticated 'western' science within an evolving indigenous cultural context. These differences in strategies of contestation can be evinced through a scrutiny of the ways in which these 'modern', 'rational' texts sought to deal with 'fabulous' and 'irrational' elements within local traditions.

In Gupto's text – which articulated indigenous knowledge within a self-consciously 'indigenous' frame of Ayurbedic tradition – Aegle Marmelos' (Bel) origins are described in terms of the Pauranic story of the Goddess Komola/Lokkhi obtaining a boon from the Lord Mohadeb who had been moved by her devotion to his worship.[46] Thus while the contemporary description and uses it could be put to were updated and so made modern, the 'litteraria' recounted the fabulous origin myths and firmly established the identity of the plant within a recognizably Hindu Bengali cultural heritage. In Mohiuddeen Shariff's text, however – which placed itself more firmly within the European tradition – the fabulous associations of 'Farid Buti' with the local mystic Fareed Shakar Ganj are narrated ironically, without assertion of the author's belief in them but rather as evidence of his thorough knowledge of local lore.[47]

Both Gupto and Shariff, however, shared the impulse to dissociate the plants from the local mythologies that surrounded them. While Gupto's avowed project was to establish a common Ayurbedic (Hindu) idiom which was common for all of Bengal and therefore free of localized, sub-Bengali associations, Shariff sought an even broader idiom that applied to all of India.

It is interesting to compare the narration of the fabulous in Gupto and Shariff with that of William Jones. Jones's *Observations* in many ways functioned within an earlier episteme and its relation to both the 'indigenous' and the 'fabulous' was different. While for Gupto the fabulous serves to 'preserve the true social affinities of the plant names',[48] for Shariff it serves to lend credibility to his own identity; for Jones, on the other hand, the name itself derived from its aesthetic/poetic association with a classical mythic allusion. Jones agreed with the poet Calidas in calling the *Cadamba* the *Nipa* since 'it may justly be celebrated among the beauties of summer',[49] or affirming the name using *Camalata* since 'the plant . . . is the most beautiful of its order . . . its elegant blossoms are celestial rosy red, love's proper hue, and [hence] have justly procured it the name *Camalata*, or *Love's Creeper*.'[50] Jones's mythic recollections thus serve to add to the pageant of colour, sight and smell. To Jones the plants were aesthetic cultural artefacts, and their names added to the grandeur of that perception. In certain ways, Jones's names were thus like Carter's reading of the names in Cook's journals, which attempted to evoke the sensory quality of the perceptions in the observer's mind rather than possess the objects through names.[51] Jones, like Hodgson, saw the plants within a socio-cultural milieu from which they were inextricable. He sought to participate in their splendour through access to the symbolic worlds the plants inhabited, not through their insertion into a vacuous space where they would be defined as solitary objects capable of extraction, acquisition and transfer without reference to the socio-cultural contexts in which they grew. Jones was thus opposed to the universal naming of plants and mused that Linnaeus himself 'would have retained the native names of *Asiatic* regions and cities, rivers and mountains; leaving friends, or persons of eminence, to preserve their own names by their own merit'.[52] Clearly Jones's names were not meant to possess the botanical objects for imperial exploitation.

Despite the difference between them, Gupto and Shariff are both marked by their encounter with the 'cultural authority' of science. Significantly the ease with which

Jones could have rejected the Linnaean names was no longer possible for either Gupto or Shariff, for, as Gyan Prakash put it, science was authorized in the early nineteenth century as a 'sign of modernity'.[53] The divergent responses of Gupto and Shariff also hint at their distinct modernities.[54] While the former seeks to contest the modernity of science by arguing that contemporary debates were prefigured in available traditions, yet at the same time recasting tradition symmetrically to modern science, the latter embraces the modernity of science by critically distancing the tradition he now wishes to modernize through science.

National herbs

Shariff's text predated the rise of formal Indian nationalism and Gupto's text dates from the very first decade of organized nationalist politics. Yet in their own ways, being modern texts, they remain implicated in alternate visions of a state structure. While Gupto's vision is that of a unified and internally homogenized Bengali polity steeped in Bengali Hindu traditions of Tantrism, where products and persons can be moved around internally with ease, Shariff's vision is closer to that of the secular all-India nationalism which would allow federal exploitation of local resources by a scientifically trained middle class.

The 'indigenous drugs' appeared in the nationalist discourse officially in 1894 when owing to the efforts of Watt and Dey the Indian National Congress included the extended investigation and use of indigenous drugs in its demands. In response to this demand the government set up an Indigenous Drugs Committee, which survived haltingly till the 1920s. However, after 1909 when it published its Second Report and called for the establishment of a School of Tropical Medicine to further its mandate, it died in all but name. Later, in 1930, another committee under the nationalist doctor R.N. Chopra was formed, and subsequently yet another one on the eve of independence in 1946. For Chopra, who emerged as the most influential authority on the subject in the twentieth century, the terms of the discourse were amply clear: the nation was impoverished by importing expensive foreign drugs, most of which could actually be grown locally. The solution was thus, according to Chopra, 'state controlled cultivation' of indigenous drugs.[55]

Clearly stating the nexus between nationalism and interest in indigenous drugs, the vastly successful author K.M. Nadkarni, whose first book on the topic was supplied to all government medical stores, mentioned the 'spirit of Swadeshism' in the wake of the Bengal Partition of 1905 as the *raison d'être* of his interest.[56] Nadkarni explained that, like Chopra, it was the drain of 'nearly two crore rupees annually' that offended him most, and started him off on indigenous drugs research. Though the nationalist discourse was framed strictly within an argument for resisting economic waste, the mythical was not alien to it. Instead of the older 'fabulous' myths about plants, the myth of nationhood was now sought. The cover of Nadkarni's influential book therefore depicted *Bharat Mata* (Mother India) holding herbs.

This nationalist mythography posited a common economic interest for the whole nation through its depiction of the nation as an indivisible maternal body. At the same time it challenged the British right to exploit or export these drugs as they belonged rightfully only to the sons and heirs of the mythic Mother India. Vaids, tabibs, doctors and pharmacologists all contributed to the constitution of this national mythography. The economic frame was also used by exponents of different traditions; however, the Ayurbedists sought to argue further that Indian herbs were peculiarly suitable for 'Indian constitutions'. An early version of this argument can be glimpsed in Gourinath Sen's 1877 text *Native Constitution and Treatment*. Binodlal Sengupto's 1879 text *Arya Griho Chikitsha* made a similar claim.[57] From the 1920s, however, it was the economic arguments that came to predominate. This change of emphasis was partly the consequence of the emergence of 'scientific universalism' as the prime legitimator of modernity in the post-First World War era.[58]

The nation and its fragments

This new emphasis underwrote an even more confident marginalization of local and subaltern botanical cultures and interests in the name of science and the nation. While the colonial discourse on 'indigenous drugs' had completely ignored women, turning for its information to a host of male informants and wholly disregarding the existence of any sort of herbal/ botanic knowledge among women, the nationalist project allowed the male bourgeois citizen to appropriate this knowledge by subsuming women within the national maternal mythology. In a gesture reminiscent of Bankim Chandra Chattopadhyay's eponymous heroine Kopalkundola, women who possessed the knowledge of the medical properties of wild herbs now come to use it in the service of the male bourgeois heroes of the piece and eventually be domesticated as obedient housewives, mothers and grandmothers. Nobin Chondro Pal's 1873 publication *Indian Herbalist* and Ramchondro Bidyabinod's *Ayurbed Kusumanjoli* in 1897 both mentioned benevolent mothers and grandmothers who had used their botanical knowledge for the benefit of their sons.[59] Both Pal and Bidyabinod now sought to make this knowledge available to the professional physicians. The proliferation of vernacular journals devoted to medicine also allowed the insertion of this feminine botanical tradition into the professional repertoire through regular columns devoted to 'Garhosthyo Chikitsha' (Family Medicine), 'Bonoushodhi' (Herbal Medicine) and 'Totka' (Simples).

A specially fertile example of the way the national myth allowed the appropriation of feminine medico-botanical traditions and their deployment by professional male nationalist physicians can be witnessed in Moyej Uddin Ahmad's 1931 text. Ahmad wrote in the introduction that,

> I have merely tried to collect and put down in as simple a language as possible those medicines that have been known and passed on amongst old wives. Our mothers like Rani Lokkhibai in the villages know these medicines much better than we do. They always have. I do not wish to encroach upon their eternal right to do so either. I am merely writing about whatever little experience I have of using these medicines in my long medical career.[60]

By identifying all women with the faceless mythic 'Rani Lokkhibai' (Rani Laxmibai, the heroine of Jhansi in the war of 1857), Ahmad can without further qualms or the need for individual acknowledgement appropriate this domain of feminine medico-botanical knowledge for commercial exploitation.

While the labour of women was buried under the mythic dimensions of maternity, the subaltern now emerged as the threatening figure of the illiterate cheat, who through either knavery or ignorance became a threat to life itself. Though the link between dishonest commerce, inadequate education and danger to public health requiring urgent, specialist, 'scientifically' trained supervision of the pharmaceutical trade had already been made by colonial authors, the nationalist discourse elevated it to novel proportions.[61]

The nationalist chemist and member of the Planning Commission in independent India, J.C. Ghosh, forcefully stated the argument in a pamphlet published in 1918. He called for greater collaboration between 'honest capitalists' and 'scientists' in the field of drug research under the strict supervision of the state, in order to 'protect the public from fraud' as well as finally settle the question of the efficacy of indigenous medicine by identifying the 'correct' Ayurbedic drugs.[62] R.N. Chopra's Report of the Third Indigenous Drugs Committee of 1931 made similar recommendations, urging strict controls to be imposed on pharmacists. Illiterate and knavish traders were singled out as an important cause for the decline of 'indigenous medicine'.

The Report's conclusions that most indigenous practitioners had lately taken to buying the herbs from illiterate and unreliable middlemen instead of collecting them personally – as they supposedly once did – was soon accepted as common sense by most. By 1943, Pulin Bihari Sen, historian of Ayurbed and himself a scion of an old *Boddi* family, wrote wistfully that,

> *Shrabonee, Mohashrabonee, Brohmosuborchola, Adityoporonee, Padma, Som*, etc., so many of the medicines mentioned by Chorok, must still be available in India, but we do not recognize them any longer. The names *Rasna, Thogor, Patla, Brahmee*, etc. are used for completely different herbs in the different provinces of the country today. Many a learned *Kobiraj* today lacks the skills or knowledge to identify herbs, instead *the trader's word is considered to be the final authority.*[63]

We have already referred to the existence of the large number of drugs brought from well beyond the immediate local contexts of indigenous physicians well before the onset of colonialism. Samuel Purchas, Francois Bernier, Niccola Manucci and John Fleming all attested to the continued existence of long-distance pharmaceutical trading. Moreover, the redoubtable George Watt had in fact argued in the 1890s that it was 'those in the weekly village markets and fairs who sit by the roadside selling a heap of roots, barks, fruits and flowers' who were the true repositories of indigenous herbal knowledge.[64] The concept of the idyllic village, where the learned physician himself found all his medicines personally from his neighbourhood, was yet another nationalist myth. This mythic past in turn served to legitimize a new national pharmaceutical capitalism.

The two pre-eminent figures of early twentieth-century Bengali pharmacology were arguably the nationalist entrepreneur and scientist P.C. Ray and, somewhat less known, Butto Kristo Paul. While Ray's stature as a scientist and nationalist earned him wide renown, Paul was a humble entrepreneur who gave up the family business in gun-metal (*Knasha*) utensils and broke into the racial clique of the pharmacological business by sheer dint of perseverance and resourcefulness. Though very different in their backgrounds, Paul and Ray[65] have been memorialized in remarkably similar ways. While Ray has been endowed with the epithet of 'Acharya' (Teacher), and his remarkable entrepreneurial exploits narrated through the prism of dedication to the nation, an almost identical trope is to be seen in Paul's biography:[66] he has been called a 'Sadhu' (Ascetic) and his exploits too are shown to be not for the sake of trade, but rather for the nation.[67] It was as if the *taint* of gross trade was unacceptable to the *Bhodrolok* mentality. In order for trade to be honest and respectable, it had to be carried on by 'disinterested' Sadhus and Acharyas. In short, only those were worthy of trade who traded not for a living, but for 'national glory'. This trope then allowed the lowly *Moules*, *Bediyas* and *Koibortos* as well as the host of other localized groups who were involved in the collection and sale of medicinal herbs, to be rendered unreliable and redundant.

The development of chemical substitutes for drugs throughout the early twentieth century allowed for further entrenchment of the pharmaceutical trade within bourgeois capitalist structures of production.[68] In post-independence India nationalist economic planning afforded state protectionism for Indian pharmaceutical capitalists, leading to the emergence of Indian pharmaceutical firms as global players, while ironically its 'marginals' continue to labour under appalling conditions of medical care and lack of access to medicines.[69]

Acknowledgements

I am grateful to Biswamoy Pati, David Arnold, Waltraud Ernst and Monjita Mukharji for their suggestions and inspiration which have contributed immensely to the arguments in this chapter. Whatever inadequacies remain are, of course, mine alone.

* Note on transliteration: The spellings of names of Indian authors referred to in this chapter have been modernized, but they are left as they are appear on the title-page of the books concerned in the notes, to allow interested readers to identify the books concerned in libraries. Since most of the vernacular sources are drawn from Bengal, transliterations have followed Bengali pronunciations in order to avoid generalizations about the whole subcontinent.

Notes

1 See Richard Grove, *Green Imperialism, Colonial Expansion, Tropical Island Edens and the Origins of Environmentalism 1600–1860*, Cambridge: Cambridge University Press, 1995.

2 David Arnold, *The Tropics and the Travelling Gaze: India, Landscape and Science 1800–1856*, New Delhi: Permanent Black, 2005.

3 Quoted in Arnold, *The Tropics*, 208.
4 For a discussion of Hodgson's life and friendship with Hooker, see Arnold, *The Tropics*, 205–11.
5 David Arnold, *The New Cambridge History of India: Science, Technology and Medicine in Colonial India*, Cambridge: Cambridge University Press, 2002, 49.
6 Matthew Edney; *Mapping an Empire: The Geographical Construction of British India 1765–1843*, Chicago: University of Chicago Press, 1997.
7 John Fleming, 'A Catalogue of Indian Medical Plants and Drugs, with their Names in the Hindustani and Sanscrit Languages', *Asiatick Researches*, XI, 1810, 153.
8 George King, *Report of the Proceedings of the Indigenous Drugs Committee of India, from 3rd Jan., 1896–21st July, 1899*, Calcutta: Bengal Secretariat Press, 1896–9, 57–8.
9 Moodeen Sheriff, *Supplement to the Pharmacopoeia of India: A Catalogue of Indian Synonyms of the Medicinal Plant*, Madras: no publisher cited, 1869, Preface.
10 Eshur Chandra Gangooley, *Half Yearly Report for the Year Ending 31st July 1842*, Calcutta: Bengal Secretariat Press, 1842, 52.
11 W.B. O'Shaughnessy, *The Bengal Dispensatory*, Calcutta: W. Thacker, Spink, 1842, III–IV.
12 Paul Carter, *The Road to Botany Bay*, London: Faber and Faber, 1987, 22.
13 One of the reasons for the debate on the Linnaean system may be connected to the way early botanical appointments were made through the personal recommendations of Sir Joseph Banks. For a richly informative discussion of the politics of early botanical appointments in India, see: Ray Desmond, *The European Discovery of Indian Flora*, Oxford: Oxford University Press, 1992.
14 William Jones, 'The Design of a Treatise on the Plants of India', *Asiatick Researches*, II, 1790, 345–52.
15 O'Shaughnessy, *The Bengal Dispensatory*, XV–XXI.
16 David Arnold, *Science, Technology*, 38.
17 Richard Grove, 'Indigenous Knowledge and the Significance of South-West India for Portuguese and Dutch Constructions of Tropical Nature', *Modern Asian Studies*, 30, 1, 1996, 121–43.
18 Antonio Gramsci, 'The Intellectuals', *Selections from the Prison Notebooks* (ed. and trans. by Q. Hoare and G.N. Smith), London: Lawrence and Wishart, 1978, 3–23.
19 European Manuscript No. MSS Eur. 120, Oriental and India Office Collection (hereafter OIOC), British Library.
20 Marika Vicziani, 'Imperialism, Botany and Statistics in Early Nineteenth-Century India: The Surveys of Francis Buchanan (1762–1829)', *Modern Asian Studies*, 20, 4, 1986, 625–60.
21 *Report of the First Indigenous Drugs Committee, Proceedings of the 1st Meeting dated January 3rd, 1896*, Calcutta: Bengal Secretariat Press, 1896.
22 C.B. Clarke, 'Preface to Reprint', William Roxburgh, *Flora Indica or Descriptions of Indian Plants by the Late William Roxburgh*, Calcutta and London: Thacker, Spink, 1874.
23 Rai Kanny Lall Dey, *Indigenous Drugs of India*, Calcutta: Thacker, Spink, 1896, Introduction.
24 George Watt, 'Preface', in Rai Kanny Lall Dey, *Indigenous Drugs*.
25 D. Prain, The Vegetation of the Districts of Hughli, Howrah and the 24 Pergunnahs, in *Records of the Botanical Survey of India*, III, 2, 1905.
26 Carter, *The Road to Botany Bay*, 48.
27 Grove, 'Indigenous Knowledge', 122, 133.
28 MSS Eur. 120, OIOC.
29 For instance, *Andropogon Schoenauthus*, otherwise known as *Juncus Odaratus*, long since rejected by European apothecaries was said to be used by the Anglo-Indians as an 'excellent dilutent in stomach complaints'. Fleming also mentions that this usage was distinct from that of the 'Asiaticks'.

30 Sir Clement Markham, *Colloquies on the Simples and Drugs of India by Garcia da Orta*, London: Henry Southern, 1913, 483, quoted in Grove, 'Indigenous knowledge', 131.

31 Bernier states that the caravans that used to travel between China and northern India through Kashmir had been interrupted even since Shah Jahan's attempted invasion of Great Tibet, leading to that trade being rerouted from through Patna. Among the articles which these caravans brought back from China were medicinal herbs such as Musk, Chinese Rhubarb, China wood and the Mamiron-i-Chini used for eye complaints. Elsewhere Bernier again mentions that Bengal was a source of 'various drugs' for the rest of the Mughal dominions: Francois Bernier, *Travels in the Mogul Empire A.D. 1656–68*, ed. Archibald Constable, Westminster: Archibald Constable, 1891, 425–6; 440; Samuel Turner, *An Account of the Embassy to the Court of the Teshoo Lama in Tibet*, London: W. Bulmer, 1800, 371, 394–5.

32 Fleming, 'A Catalogue', 182.

33 David Hooper, 'Silajit: An Ancient Eastern Medicine', *Journal of the Asiatic Society of Bengal*, LXXII, 2, 1903, 98–103.

34 John Grant Malcolmson, *A Practical Treatise on the History and Treatment of Beri Beri*, Madras: no publisher cited, 1835, 296–313.

35 Sheriff, *Supplement to the Pharmacopoeia of India*, 121.

36 The Indigenous Drugs Committee was initially set up in 1896 owing to the efforts of Kanai Lall Dey and George Watt, and the consequent inclusion of the study of indigenous drugs in the demands of the Indian National Congress: Home (Medical), June 1900, Proceedings 'A', No. 214. National Archives of India, New Delhi.

37 Horolal Gupto, *Ayurbed Bhashabhidan*, 1st edition, Calcutta: no publisher cited, 1296 BS (AD 1888–9), Introduction.

38 For an engaging summary of early twentieth-century efforts by indigenous medical traditions to develop a discourse on 'national herbs', see Guy Attewell, 'Advocating Desi Tibb: Collaborations, Rifts and Hybrid Knowledge in Unani Tibb in Early Twentieth Century India', unpublished paper presented at a Conference on Hybrids and Partnerships, Oxford, 2005.

39 The fact that at least certain sections of Bengali elite society were directly influenced by the work of Carl Linnaeus and his system is directly borne out by the publication of 'A Plea for the Formation of a Linnaean Society in Calcutta', by one Saratchandra Mitra in the *Calcutta Review* of 1891.

40 Michel Foucault, *The Order of Things: An Archaeology of Human Sciences*, London: Tavistock Publications, 1970, 130.

41 Gupto, *Ayurbed Bhashabhidan*, xiii–iv.

42 Michael Taussig, *Mimesis and Alterity: A Particular History of the Senses*, London: Routledge, 1991.

43 On 'entangled histories' see Waltraud Ernst, 'Beyond East and West: From the History of Colonial Medicine to a Social History of Medicine(s) in South Asia', *Social History of Medicine,* forthcoming.

44 Birajacharan Gupta, *Bonoushodhi Dorpon,* Calcutta: SC Auddy, 1908, Introduction by Bijayaratna Sen, 55–64.

45 Gyan Prakash, 'Science Between the Lines', in Shahid Amin and Dipesh Chakrabarty eds *Subaltern Studies IX,* New Delhi: Oxford University Press, 1996, 62–3.

46 Gupto, *Ayurbed Bhashabhidan*, 112–14.

47 Sheriff, *Supplement to the Pharmacopoeia of India,* 110.

48 Grove, 'Indigenous Knowledge', 139.

49 William Jones, 'Botanical Observations on the Select Indian Plants', in *Asiatick Researches,* IV, 1795, 251.

50 Jones, 'Botanical Observations', 249–50.

51 Carter, *The Road to Botany Bay,* 32.

52 Jones, 'Botanical Observations', 231.

53 Gyan Prakash, 'Science Between the Lines', in Shahid Amin and Dipesh Chakrabarty eds *Subaltern Studies IX,* New Delhi: Oxford University Press, 1996, 61.

54 On multiple modernities see Sudipta Kaviraj, 'An Outline of a Revisionist Theory of Modernity', http://www.mit.edu/~shekhar/southasia/kaviraj_modernity.pdf, accessed on 23 October 2007.

55 R.N. Chopra, *Indigenous Drugs of India: Their Medical and Economic Aspects*, Calcutta: The Art Press, 1933, 35–40.

56 K.M. Nadkarni, *The Indian Materia Medica,* Bombay: Bijur, 1927, i–ii.

57 Seema Alavi has described a very similar trend at a slightly later period among Hakims of Awadh. See Seema Alavi, 'Unani Medicine in the Nineteenth-Century Public Sphere: Urdu Texts and the Oudh Akhbar', *Indian Economic and Social History Review,* 42, 1, 2005, 101–29.

58 On the emergence of 'scientific universalism' as a sign and legitimator of Indian modernity after the First World War, see Benjamin Zachariah, 'The Uses of Scientific Argument: The Case of "Development" in India, c. 1930–50', *Economic and Political Weekly,* 36, 39, 2001, 3689–702.

59 Nabinchandra Pal, *The Indian Herbalist or the Indigenous Remedies for Preventing Diseases in India*, Calcutta: no publisher cited, 1873; Ramchondro Bidyabinod, *Ayurbed Kushumanjoli,* Calcutta: no publisher cited, 1897, 29. An especially good example of this framing of women's agency as a source of knowledge of indigenous medicinal herbs as a mythic trace within a masculine bourgeois political economy which almost coincides with the 'nationalization' of 'indigenous drugs' can be seen in a pamphlet published by Lal Mohan Chokroborty, the owner of the immensely successful nationalist pharmaceutical firm of Ayurbedic medicines, *Dhaka Shokti Oushodhaloy*: Lal Mohan Chokroborty, *Paribarik Chikitshaye Grihini,* Calcutta: no publisher cited, 1302 BS [1895].

60 Moyej Uddin Ahmad, *Deshiyo Oushudh Sikhya,* Dhaka: no publisher cited, 1338 BS [1931], Introduction.

61 R.H. Irvine, 'A Short Account of the Materia Medica of Patna', Calcutta: unpublished, 1848, 2.

62 J.C. Ghosh, *Indigenous Drugs of India,* Calcutta: no publisher cited, 1918, 6–7.

63 Quoted in Probhakor Chottopadhyay, *Ayurbeder Itihaash*, Calcutta: no publisher cited, 1370 BS [1963].

64 Quoted in Benoy Bhusan Roy, *Unish Shotoker Chikitsha Byabostha: Deshiyo Bheshoj O Shorkar,* Delhi: International Centre for Bengal Studies, 1998, 81.

65 In Ray's case, though, there is definitely a similar ambivalence between an entrepreneurial impulse and an aversion to it as something petty and unworthy of nobility by itself, in Ray's own self-presentation. For an informative and nuanced account of Ray's life see Pratik Chakrabarti, *Western Science in Modern India: Metropolitan Methods, Colonial Methods,* New Delhi: Oxford University Press, 2004.

66 Once again blurring self-presentation and posthumous memorialization, the 'biography' was almost certainly paid for by Paul's sons.

67 Gopalchondro Mukhopadhyay, *Shadhu Butto Kristo Paul,* Calcutta: no publisher cited, 1326 BS [1919].

68 For details see Projit Bihari Mukharji, 'Medicine and Modernity in Colonial Bengal, c.1775–1930', unpublished Ph.D. thesis, School of Oriental and African Studies, University of London, 2006.

69 See Noam Chomsky, *On India, GATT and Pharmaceutical Patents,* http://www.cptech.org/pharm/noam.html. accessed on 4 June 2007.

12 Creating a consumer

Exploring medical advertisements in colonial India*

Madhuri Sharma

Although there has been a substantial body of writings dealing with the 'professionalization' of medicine in colonial India, medical advertisements do not seem to have attracted much scholarly attention.[1] This was a sector closely associated with drug manufacturers and medical practitioners in twentieth-century India. The colonial context saw the emergence of the print media that disseminated new kinds of information about health, hygiene and medicine to an eagerly receptive public. In fact, advertisements were a particularly active agency that created a consumer for medical products and services across a variety of medical systems. Besides being a form of 'social communication' that offered the people new ways to understand themselves and their needs, advertisements were crucial to the economic functioning of capitalism. As an industry, advertising categorizes people as 'consumers' rather than 'users', and wields considerable power within capitalist society. It conditions marketing practices, helps to sustain the flow of goods and is tied directly to economic structures.[2] Moreover, advertisements are a valuable source for a social historian interested in understanding the prevailing social environment, values and lifestyles. In fact, the products and services advertised indicate, to a large extent, how people lived and/or aspired to live.[3]

This chapter explores the way European entrepreneurs advertised medical products in colonial India. It also assesses the initiatives taken by Indian drug manufacturers to create a space for their products in the market. It is primarily concerned with newspaper advertisements. It focuses on how advertisements drew upon cultural codes to increase the market for medical products and the role they played as a communicating medium, by disseminating knowledge about health and disease. For this purpose this chapter examines medical and health advertisements in the *Times of India*[4] and the *Journal of the Association of Medical Women in India*[5] as well as *Abhyudaya*, the first Hindi weekly established by Madan Mohan Malaviya in 1907.[6]

The beginning

Advertising through letters, news columns and editorial comments is very much a part of the process of communication whereby meanings are exchanged between individuals (advertiser and reader) and between objects and individuals, through the common understanding of a system of symbols.[7] It reflects a particular facet of changing culture in the history of a nation or community.

Although advertising existed in pre-industrial societies in the shape of announcements and proclamations, it acquired its present form and dimension only with the development of modern machine-based mass production.[8] Advertising stepped in to create mass demand and to compete for it. Thus, by the mid-nineteenth century the 'industrial revolution' had altered the relationship between advertisers and consumers. The growth of the modern newspaper marked another watershed for advertising, enabling the manufacturer to place his goods before the eyes of thousands.[9] Early advertisements were very much like announcements, giving factual information such as the availability of a particular item and in most cases indicating its price and the address of the retailer. Later on, sketches along with descriptive details and photographs were also included in the advertisements.[10]

Medicines and health products were advertised regularly. Medical journals contained advertisement for drugs, health food, medical publications, retailers and suppliers of western medicine and surgical instruments and, in turn, advertisements generated revenue for publications/newspapers.[11]

Most advertisements in English dailies were for imported medicines and usually included testimonials and interesting explanations.[12] For instance, Holloway's Pills were advertised in 1858 as

> indispensable to the security and life in the new settlements. Fever and ague, bilious remittent and bowel complaints are the worst enemies the western pioneer has to encounter, and he can only certainly and permanently put them to fight with the aid of this unrivalled cathartic, detergent and restorative.[13]

These early advertisements suggest that advertisers were keen to address the health problems of Europeans in 'new settlements' such as India and Africa. After all, their market was limited to the European population only.

Most of the advertisements were either for tonics or general pills that cured all sorts of ailments.[14] Eno's Fruit Salt was the foremost prescription among the common aids to health recognized in India from 1878[15] while Invalid's Port was the recommended tonic for 'invalids' forty years earlier.[16] Based in London, the Virol Limited Company marketed Virol, a health tonic, in India. The widespread sales return of Virol showed that it was prescribed by reputed hospitals. It seems that it was duly supplied to hospitals and clinics with government support.[17] Dettol, an antiseptic solution, captured the major proportion of the advertising market during the 1940s. The consistency with which the Ovaltine advertisement appeared in the *Journal of the Association of Medical Women in India* shows how it dominated the journal's advertisement space over the 1911–38 period. The Ovaltine advertisement claimed that it was a tonic food beverage which ensured adequate lactation. One finds that European medical products dominated the advertising space in English dailies and journals.

The world of medical advertisements

This section locates the strategies used in advertising by European medical firms to create consumers in India, thereby widening the market for their products. Advertisements in English newspapers and journals restricted the market to the English-literate only. To widen the market and increase the numbers of consumers, European firms also started placing advertisements in vernacular newspapers. European firms worked through codes of local culture and assimilated them to their own symbols so as to draw on features with a universal appeal. They also had the financial resources to flood vernacular newspapers with both visual and print advertisements.

Explicit advertising claims are sometimes repeated so often that they become a part of the audience members' assumptive worlds.[18] For example, Dettol became synonymous with antiseptic solution. Another striking example is Bayer's Aspirin,[19] the advertisement for which stressed its superiority vis-à-vis competitors' products, even though the Bayer product contained five grains of aspirin, the same as those of other companies that manufactured this drug. Consequently, advertisements sought to make 'consumers' out of 'users'. The best example for this is the advertisement of baby food marketed by Glaxo (see Figure 12.1). It heralds the use of 'calendar art' in the print media.[20] The centre of attraction is the image of a healthy

Figure 12.1 Glaxo Baby-food.

Source: Abhyudaya, 14 September 1929

baby boy who looks like a 'white' (British) child. This advertisement shows the eugenic interest of the advertiser, focusing on good mothers for healthy children in order to promote the sale of his product. The consumer was presumed to be a mother attracted by the image of an alert, robust and well-groomed baby pretending to talk on a toy phone; the fact that the infant is a boy was probably expected to have special significance, given the importance of a male child in colonial India. Qualities such as the robustness, intelligence and beauty associated with the ruling race were implicitly 'accessible' to the children of the Indian consumer as well. The underlying logic was that the claims of the advertisement would be accepted and the consumers would choose a product that nurtured the idealized 'fair', 'male' child.

Consequently, besides aiming to sell the products of the entrepreneurs, the advertisements intervened in people's lifestyle. In this particular advertisement the advertiser appears to be 'colonizing the mind' of the mother who endeavours to give the best to her baby.[21] Psychologically, this promoted the concept of the 'ideal mother', who provided the best brand of foodstuff to her child. Thus, the basic aim was to make the parents shift from the otherwise healthy food (viz. mother's milk) that was given to the child, to a marketed product. Moreover, the usage of a catchy phrase '*sanjeevan-tattava-milk food*' (i.e. life-giving milk food) reflects the effort to synthesize Sanskrit and English. A noticeable feature was the positioning of this advertisement, near an article entitled '*Streeyon ka sansar*' ('Women's world').[22]

The incorporation of English terminologies like 'milk food' was intended to create an English sensibility among consumers. It was also expected to 'empower' the consumers and make them feel that they were knowledgeable about the new food products and were capable of selecting the best. Here the English trademark was held out as the guarantee of the genuineness of the product.[23] Along with English terminologies, the incorporation of Sanskrit words like *sanjeevan-tattava* was designed to instil a sense of superiority, in consumers of a product manufactured by a 'superior' race. Through the use of Sanskrit the advertiser sought to establish the 'authority' of genuineness and purity, as it was believed to be perceived by most people. This was necessary since many supporters of indigenous medicines believed and also propagated the idea that European medicines were mixed with alcohol or beef.[24] For instance, in an editorial in *Abhyudaya* Krishan Kant Malaviya pointed out the superiority of ayurveda and condemned the use of allopathic medicines 'from a religious stand point since they generally contained alcohol and other ingredients which are forbidden to Hindus'.[25] Consequently, by using Sanskrit terms the advertisers tried to communicate the notion of 'purity' to express the natural origins of the products and their freedom from contamination with substances like alcohol and beef.

These advertisements also enable us to explore the meanings of stereotypes like 'masculinity' and 'femininity' as they were constructed through these representations, for example by comparing the advertisements for Woodward's Gripe Water and Sequarine health tonic.[26] The advertisement promoting Woodward's Gripe Water portrays a British nurse with a sleeping baby. The nurse signifies tender loving care and affection in supposedly 'Western' society. The very presence of a nurse in the advertisement testifies to the claim it makes. Furthermore, the very trademark of the product seeks to project the so-called authenticity of foreign-made products to the consumer. Comparison with the Sequarine advertisement highlights the dichotomy between the masculine and feminine dimensions. Thus, designed to target women (viz. feminine consciousness), the Woodward advertisement projects a nurturing mother/nurse and infant. In sharp contrast, the Sequarine advertisement in its very depiction highlights the notion of manliness. The Herculean hero holding a snake was supposed to appeal to the male psyche, since men were inevitably the consumers of this product.

Advertisements for Woodward's Gripe Water show a shift in strategy between the 1920s and 1930s. Thus, the advertisement of 1930 uses the image of *Kaliyamardan* – the subjugation of the snake-king, Kaliya, by Krishna.[27] The firm's logo shows a 'white' (British) child throttling snakes, like Hercules, while at the same time evoking the image of Lord Krishna as a baby.[28] This advertisement sought to attract mothers through its reference to the cultural status of baby Krishna in Hindu society. After all, many Hindu families idealized 'baby Krishna' and expected him to be emulated by their children, a feature promoted by the advertisement.[29] Thus, by the 1930s European drug manufacturers were clearly invoking Hindu religious symbols to promote their product. In fact, indigenous images and symbols were supposed to provide an aesthetic touch to the advertisements. This is visible in the depiction of cows grazing in pastures, with rivers and temples in the background. It was hoped that these would enhance the appeal of the product and also widen the market. The Sequarine advertisement also promoted the idea of 'conquest' of evil – viz. illness. The Greek Herculean hero was shown to be capturing and controlling a snake which epitomized evil in the western belief system. It symbolized the efficacy of the medicine that could drive out all maladies. Suggesting the subjugation of illness, this was intended to reach out to large sections of Indian consumers. This advertisement perhaps hoped to promote the notion of a 'universal panacea' for all sorts of ailments.[30]

The trends in advertising examined related to the mindset of European entrepreneurs and their advertisers. Initially the advertisements were limited to some English newspapers and the target audience were European and English-educated Indian consumers. However, as seen, efforts were made subsequently to widen the market for their products and advertisements were also placed in vernacular newspapers. This was also motivated by the competition from indigenous entrepreneurs in the twentieth century. This implied the incorporation of signs and symbols from local or regional culture, including mythological gods and goddesses in a prominent role, in order to reach out to people and create consumers among the village folk as well as urban dwellers. The following section examines the strategies adopted by the Indian drug entrepreneurs to make their presence felt in the market through advertisements.

Indigenous medicine in the public space

Indian entrepreneurs adopted the same communication techniques and marketing strategies. They worked through the codes of local culture, and also assimilated the concept of the 'universal panacea'. Anil Kumar refers to P.C. Ray's problems in selling his ayurvedic preparations, by contrast to the products produced by Bengal Chemical Works. As he puts it: 'P.C. Ray himself hawked them [ayurvedic preparations] in the streets of Calcutta carrying in his folio, sample phials of the syrup of *vasak* and *ajowan* water.'[31] Indian entrepreneurs employed salespersons who attracted the attention of the people through songs or tunes that drew upon oral traditions.[32] For example, Vishwanath Mukherjee in his *Bana Rahe Banaras* refers to a song composed by a Bengali hawker in the streets of Benares:

> *Kaviraj kalipadi de ka aascharya malham jo 101 bimariyon mein fayada pahunchata hai- aawaj lagate huai bagal mein tin ka dibba liye bangali babu tahalte the, aankho mein chasma pahne aur haath mein sirf ek chasma liye – 'ek chasma' kee aawaz dete huai bare miyan kuchh logon ki aanke padhte nazar aate the.*
>
> ('An amazing ointment of Kaviraj Kalipadi De which helps tackle 101 types of ailments', sings a Bengali Babu, who roams on the streets. Another elderly Muslim with spectacles, who carried one spectacle in his hand and who tried to read the eyes of people, shouts occasionally, "One spectacle"').[33]

At times their verbal recitation was accompanied by folk songs such as '*Davayee meri awwal, paisa lena dubble*' ('My medicine is number one and you would get double your money if it does not work').[34] Oral advertisements had their own limitations since the medium of hawking covered a limited area of consumers. In this sense, the development of advertisements in the vernacular print media proved to be a boon for Indian drug manufacturers and indigenous medical practitioners. Indigenous practitioners advertised their skills through the columns of vernacular newspapers, endorsed by testimonials from eminent personalities of the locality. Thus, under the heading '*Kustha Chikitsak*', the house physicians of the Nawab of Murshidabad, Satishchandra Mukherjee and Yatishchandra Mukharjee, endorsed 'Pandit Kriparam' who 'had successfully treated a patient suffering from an old history of leprosy in their presence. He had also treated many other leprosy patients.'[35] Such testimonials also enabled physicians like Pandit Kriparam to regain and revitalize their social status and respectability, which reflects on the importance of elite patronage to indigenous medical practitioners. Besides, it helped to endorse the medical skills of the practitioner solely on the basis of social and cultural norms irrespective of any scientific grounds. But even more importantly, these advertisements served to project how skills developed by the physicians of the royal, elite households were also accessible to all.

In order to prove the authenticity of their product, manufacturers used phrases such as '*lagatar 75 varshon se iske sevan se lakhon aadmi acche bane hain*' ('This medicine has been in use for the past 75 years and has benefited lakhs of people').[36] By associating their medicines with a 'glorious past' and using phrases that indicated how they had been tested over time, such as '17 *varshon kee parikshit*' ('Tested for seventeen years') or '15 *varsh kee ajmayee hui*' ('Tried for fifteen years'), the producers of indigenous drugs tried to legitimize their products.[37]

The effort to catch the attention of consumers coexisted with attempts to provide monetary incentives to attract salesmen or agents. As articulated in an advertisement: '*Vyapariyon ko kaafee kamishan diya jata hai*' ('Distributors are remunerated quite handsomely').[38] This shows the creation of a retail network and the business attitude among Indian drug entrepreneurs. Retail networks helped in the sales of the products. Sometimes medical products were supplied directly to the consumer through parcels, and health advice and consultations were sent through the post. Through advertisements many *vaidyas* and *hakeems* encouraged readers to seek medical advice and treatment by post, sometimes free of cost.[39]

The Indian drug manufacturers of allopathic or indigenous medicine tried various methods to tighten their grip on Indian consumers. For example, to capture the attention of consumers Pandit Rameshwar Mishra of Kanpur created a full-page advertisement in which he explained the efficacy of his drugs. In fact, indigenous practitioners advertised their name and skills by phrasing the title of the advertisement in catchy styles. Examples are: '*Banaras Ke Mashoor Doctor Ganeshprasad Bhargav Ka Banaya Hua Nimak Sulaimani*' ('A Sulaimani salt prepared by the renowned doctor Ganeshprasad Bhargav of Benares') and '*Kanpur Ke Prasidh Chikitsak Pandit Rameshwar Mishra Vaidya Shastri Ke Ayurvediya Aushsdhalaya Kee Sacchi Tatha Anubhut Aushadhiyan*' ('Genuine and authentic medicines from the ayurvedic pharmacy of Pandit Rameshwar Mishra Vaidya, the famous practitioner of Kanpur').[40]

Consequently, it needs to be noted that drugs and medical preparations were advertised in a context that saw competition over the market space, as well as the possibilities of an increasing clientele. Advertisements were often associated with success and popularity which, in turn, ensured the professional success of the *vaidyas* or *hakeems* and sustained their pharmacy. At the same time, one needs to grasp the importance of courting an impersonal clientele and the offers of medical advice that formed a vital part of the advertisements. The following section shows the technique of communication of Indian drug entrepreneurs to prove the efficacy of their product.

Universal panacea: 'Ramban' and 'Sulaimani'

Medical advertisements often used words like 'Ramban' and 'Sulaimani' metaphorically to advertise a sort of 'universal cure'. These words highlighted the efficacy of the product. Thus, the medicine removed the root cause of disease and cured all sort of ailments, like the arrow of Rama (a mythological Hindu god) which swept away all evil.[41] For example, as the advertisement to promote Pransanjeevani put it: '*Kalkatte ke prasidh vaidya Srivaman Das Jee Kaviraj ka sab prakar ke jwar ko ek din me bhagane wala Ramban ausadh*' ('A medicine by the famous Vaidya Shri Bavman Das of Calcutta which, like Ram's arrow, cures all sorts of fever in one day').[42] Similarly, 'Sulaimani' expressed the power of Sulaiman, the Turkish king. Thus, the 'Salt Sulaimani' possessed the power to cure all health problems, like King Sulaiman, who vanquished his enemies. The inclusion of words and terminologies like 'Ram/Suleiman' and '*swadeshi*' or '*desi*' helped to generate religious identities (viz. Hindu/Muslim) and appeal to Indian sensibilities. The effort was to make the consumers feel that they were buying an indigenous Indian product, prepared with locally available raw materials. Consequently, one sees the footprint of the Swadeshi movement on the medical advertisements, which demonstrate broader political shifts.

Indigenous entrepreneurs also sought to draw upon images of traditional healing practices and ingredients. Nevertheless, these were recast within a frame that took into account the changes ushered in by the colonial experience. This was quite clearly reflected in some advertisements, for example those for Amrit Dhara and Piyush Ratnakar. Thus, the advertisement for Amrit Dhara. (Figure 12.2 shows a picture of a lady (fairy), ostensibly adopted from European fairy tales, or a 'pari' from Indian folk tales. She was projected as a pure and pristine being, suggesting freedom from all earthly maladies. The fairy-like lady was named Arogyata Kee Devi, the goddess of health. Earth was represented in the form of a globe.[43] 'Gracing the bottom left half of the framed picture is a terrestrial globe on which are sketched what our eyes have been taught to recognize as India.'[44] Above the globe is a young

Figure 12.2
Arogyata Kee Devi – Amrit Dhara.
Source: Abhyudaya, 22 February 1912

woman with flowing tresses and wings. Clad in western fairy tale outfit, she holds a lamp in one hand, and nectar flows from her other hand. Her body, dress and wings mirrored the outline of the subcontinent as it appeared on the animated globe below. Here one cannot miss the fusion of tradition with modernity. The effort was to highlight the superiority of indigenous medicine using a woman (fairy), symbolizing India, shown pouring nectar on earth. This again reflects the interactions with contemporary nationalism, with Arogyata Kee Devi freeing the world from diseases and paving the way for independence.[45]

Similarly, an advertisement for Piyush Ratnakar shows a pot-bellied English gentleman trying to communicate how 'one medicine worked for eighty types of diseases'.[46] Such advertisements show how European and Indian entrepreneurs incorporated both western and Indian cultural symbols in their advertisements, in order to reach out to the Indian customer.

Another strategy used by indigenous entrepreneurs was to distribute calendars, free of cost, with the obvious aim of widening their market. These calendars contained photographs or pictures of eminent Indian personalities or Hindu gods and goddesses, and publicized the address of manufacturers, distributors and even chemists. They also published religious (Hindu) booklets such as *Ramayana* or *Hanuman Chalisa* to advertise their products, thus exploiting a belief that enjoyed wide acceptance (see Figure 12.3).[47]

One should also mention here the idea of including pictures in advertisements. Thus we come across postcards advertising an ayurvedic oil for rheumatism which displayed *Urvashi*, the famous painting of Raja Ravi Varma.[48] All this clearly shows that indigenous drug manufacturers enjoyed a certain advantage over their European rivals in the sphere of medical advertisements. While they used the same infrastructure of communication to attract consumers as their European rivals, Indian entrepreneurs could create a space for their products by appealing to religious and nationalist sentiments.

Invading private space

Medical advertisements also entered the personal domain in colonial India. One sees this typically in the case of advertisements for aphrodisiacs – hardly surprising in a patriarchal culture that stressed male virility. In fact, nearly every Indian newspaper routinely carried advertisements for various *churans* and potions that promised male potency and male progeny.[49] This was a sector in which Indian entrepreneurs participated and competed with their European counterparts. They prepared ayurvedic medicine to give men vigour and vitality, and to promote its sale they advertised their products through well-known idioms and phrases. For example, a Haridas and Company advertisement incorporated the very catchy phrase: '*Mat kaho ki angoor khatte hain kyonki un tak pahunch nahi sakte*' ('Don't say the grapes are sour if you can't reach them'), a metaphorical reference to sexual impotence because of 'weakness'. Another typical advertisement portrays a man thinking about a woman, and a fox looking at a grape vine, with the following textual matter:

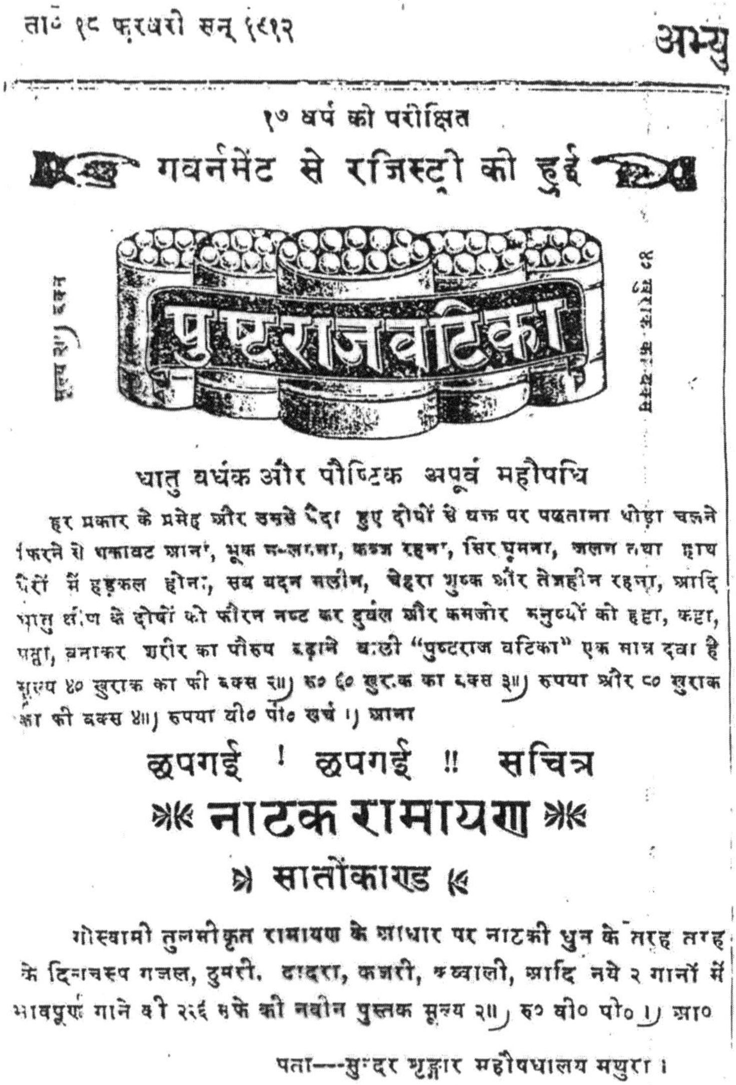

Figure 12.3 Tested for seventeen years, Pustrajvatika (registered).
Source: Abhyudaya, 18 February 1912

Mat kaho ki jeevan niraanand haikyonki uska sukh bhog nahi sakte . . . Aankhe khol ke dava dhoodhon. Tila no. 1-jaadoo sa asar karega. Yeh nason ki kharabi aur guptendriyon ki shisiltha ko door karne ki amogh marham hai. Indriyon mein kafi sakhti aur teji lata hai. Keemat fee sheeshe 15 rupaye, garibon ke liye aadhi keemat-7 rupaye. Saath mein sandipan vati ya navdhatu rogant

> *churan ka sevan sone mein sugandh bhar dega.* . . . Haridas and Company, Mathura.
>
> (Don't say life is boring because you cannot enjoy it. . . . You need to open your eyes to the right medicine. Tila no. 1 will do magic. This is a proven remedy for problems of the vein and the weakness of sex organs. It strengthens and rejuvenates the organs. Price per bottle is Rs 15; the price is half for the poor – Rs 7. . . . It adds flavour to life if taken with Sandipan Vati or Navdhatu Rogant Churan. . . . Haridas and Company, Mathura.)[50]

Advertisements for aphrodisiacs generally used the Sanskrit words *virya* and *vajin*, meaning virility and potency. They often used *virya* as *sukra* – semen – and *vajin* as an adjective, which meant 'heroic' or 'manly'.[51] Advertisers for aphrodisiacs drew upon analogies from the world of animals that were commonly referred to in Indian classics like the *Charak Samhita* and *Sushruta Samhita*. Thus, these advertisements contained references to the stallion (*vajin*), the male elephant (*gaja*), the male sparrow (*cataka*) and the bull (*vrsa*) and the associated male sexual symbolisms[52] – the virile stallion that could copulate many times in quick succession without becoming exhausted; the male elephant that ejaculated abundant semen; the male sparrow that could maintain an erection for an exceptionally long time and copulate with one female bird after another; and the bull that epitomized strength, power and virility.[53] By using these analogies, these advertisements claimed that their preparations were meant to enhance youthfulness, strength, sexual arousal, complexion and voice, and ensure an erect penis and an inexhaustible supply of semen. In an analysis of advertisements for aphrodisiacs Charu Gupta observes that the lion, which was recognized as a symbol of British masculinity, was frequently portrayed subjugated by the virile Indian male.[54] What also needs emphasis is the way these medical advertisements focused exclusively on male desire, remaining completely silent about female sexuality.[55]

During the mid-1930s, the popular press took up the issue of contraception, and information on contraceptives was disseminated through the vernacular newspapers. Methods of contraception and technological innovations were also covered in the vernacular press and were promoted exclusively by the print media through advertisements. Some typical examples can be cited from the *Abhyudaya*.

> *Santan nigrah kee dava*
>
> *Is dava ka upyog karte samay stree sahvas ki manayee nahi hai . . . garbh nirodh ki yeh ramban hai . . . mulya chah maheene ki khurak 1 rupaya 12 aana.* . . . Anglo-Ayurvedic Home, 170, Maniktola Street, Calcutta.
>
> (Contraceptive pills
>
> While taking this medicine women do not have to bother about any restrictions as far as sexual intercourse is concerned. It is the 'Ramban' against pregnancy. . . . A course of six months is priced at Re 1 and 12 annas. . . . Anglo-Ayurvedic Home, 170, Maniktola Street, Calcutta.)[56]

We can cite another typical example:

> *saal dar saal bacche janne se streeyan bahut kamjor ho jati hain. Unki sundarta aur yovan nast ho jaata hai . . . purushon ke liye aamdani kam hone lagti hai jis ke karan parivar ka kharch chlana bhi mushkil ho jata hai. Santan kee jyadati rokne ke liye aap hamse rubber ke bane hue yantra magayen aur sukhmaye jeevan vyateet karen . . . magarmachh ke chamre ke bane hue badhiya yantra . . . prati darjan chah rupaye aath aana . . . dak kharch alag. Note – teen se kam yantra na bheje jayenge, pata* – Central Trading Company, No. 607, Jullundur City.
>
> ('Having babies year after year weakens the body of women. They lose their beauty and youth. . . . A large part of the income goes to bring up children due to which men are unable to bear the burden of family expenses. To prevent frequent births of children you should buy a device made of rubber and lead a happy life. . . . Made from crocodile's leather . . . a dozen cost six rupees and eight annas . . . Postal charges extra. Note: A minimum of three devices have to be ordered. Address – Central Trading Company, No. 607, Jullundur City.')

Here, to promote sales of contraceptives the Central Trading Company used a pedagogical approach, linking the way childbirth affected women's health and appearance, and burdened household expenditure. Besides the male-centric focus that invoked and privileged the appearance of women over their health, one can hardly miss the dimension of sexual pleasure, free from anxieties about pregnancy, advocated in this advertisement.

Concluding remarks

As has been argued in this chapter, advertisements represented an advanced strategy deployed by European drug entrepreneurs to create consumers for their products. For the indigenous practitioners advertisements became a necessity because of the decline of the old patronage system in colonial India. Indian entrepreneurs therefore resorted to using advertisements, adopting this strategy in a context where the medical market pitted them against European rivals. The importance of vernacular newspapers and journals to advertise western medical products hardly needs to be stressed as they made it possible to reach a wide audience. Thus it is hardly surprising that by the 1940s most advertising space in *Abhyudaya* was occupied by European medicines and health products; put another way, 70–80 per cent of the advertising space was monopolized by European medicines in the *Times of India, Journal of the Association of Medical Women in India* and *Abhyudaya*.[58] This shows that western entrepreneurs were able to spend huge amounts on marketing their products – at a level where their indigenous counterparts were not able to compete with them. This ensured the domination of advertisements for western products and boosted their sale.[59]

One of the hegemonic components of medical advertisements for European products was that the consumer was made to feel that a superior system was accessible at a reasonable cost. These advertisements also took into account the colonial experience and drew upon social elements including images of traditional healing practices that were reframed to catch the eye of the consumer.

Bode discusses the syncretic method employed to market ayurvedic and Unani pharmaceuticals: indigenous medicine was usually characterized as representative of 'tradition', and inextricably linked with 'nature'. He describes how advertisements of indigenous products linked 'tradition' with the 'modern' and the 'scientific'.[60] What he does not mention is that this strategy was not monopolized by indigenous entrepreneurs. Interaction with the indigenous order had left its footprint on advertisements for western medical products. After all, as discussed earlier, advertisements promoting European medical products also linked 'tradition' with their modern scientific properties. Consequently, both Indian and European entrepreneurs invoked the past in order to negotiate the medical market of the 'present'. One can also discern attempts by Indian medical advertisements to draw legitimacy from colonial officials. In this sense, these advertisements promoted products that were, perhaps, located not as 'modern' but as new and contemporary. More importantly, one witnesses the creative rearrangement of the 'traditional' and 'modern' in order to reach out to Indian consumers, both 'tradition' and 'modernity' being invoked simultaneously by Indian and European entrepreneurs to project their superiority over each other.

As is amply clear, these advertisements were mainly concerned with the health issues of the upper classes of Indian society. There was not a single advertisement about cholera, plague or the other epidemics that affected large sections of the population. As seen above, medical advertisements were male-centric. Nevertheless, even if in a limited way, some of these advertisements brought issues of health, sex and sexuality into the public domain. A certain transgressiveness is also visible when it comes to locating sex as a pleasurable act even for women, although in a limited sense. These features perhaps marked a significant break with the past. Of course, scholarship needs to be directed at discovering how these medical advertisements impacted consumers. Poets like Akbar Allahabadi provide some clues; as he puts it in a couplet:

> *Tifle mein buu aaye kya maa baap ke avtaar ki,*
> *Doodh to dabbe ka hai taleem sarkar kee.*
>
> (How can one get the essence of the parents in a child,
> When it is fed tinned milk and imparted governmental education?).[61]

* All translations are mine.

Notes

1 David Arnold ed. *Imperial Medicine and Indigenous Societies*, Delhi: Oxford University Press, 1989; Poonam Bala, *Imperialism and Medicine in Bengal: A Socio-Historical*

Perspective, New Delhi: Sage Publications, 1991; Mark Harrison, *Public Health in British India: Anglo Indian Preventive Medicine 1859–1914*, Cambridge: Cambridge University Press, 1994; Andrew Cunningham and Birdie Andrews eds *Western Medicine as Contested Knowledge*, Manchester and New York: Manchester University Press, 1997; Anil Kumar, *Medicine and the Raj: British Medical Policy in India, 1835–1911*, New Delhi: Sage Publications, 1998; Deepak Kumar ed. *Disease and Medicine in India: A Historical Overview*, New Delhi: Indian History Congress and Tulika, 2001; Biswamoy Pati and Mark Harrison eds *Health, Medicine and Empire: Perspectives on Colonial India*, New Delhi: Orient Longman, 2001.

2 N.N. Pillai, *Press Advertising Today: A Study of Trends*, New Delhi: Indian Institute of Mass Communication, 1974; John B. Thompson, *Ideology and Modern Culture: Critical Social Theory in the Era of Mass Communication*, Oxford: Polity Press, 1990; Dileep Padgaonkar ed. *Brand New: Advertising through the Times of India*, Faridabad: The Times of India Sesquicentennial Publication, 1989.

3 Padgaonkar ed. *Brand New*.

4 *The Times of India*, the oldest continuing English daily in India, was launched as the *Bombay Times and Journal of Commerce* on 3 November 1838. A bi-weekly published on Saturdays and Wednesdays, the eight-page, four-column newspaper was more like a bulletin with shipping notices, advertisements of local sales and other commercial news: Padgaonkar ed. *Brand New*.

5 The Association of Medical Women in India (hereafter AMWI) was founded in February 1908 with 124 'fully qualified' medical women as its members. Its main objective was to expand medical work among women in India, to keep members in touch with one another and to access all those interested in women's medical work. This journal was the only medical journal owned by women medical practitioners and it discussed health problems related to women only. The first volume of the journal published by this association (hereafter *JAMWI*) had no contents page or advertisements. It simply started with an editorial section followed by reports from AMWI. It highlighted a few medical cases related to women and also published letters to the editor regarding various medical issues; *JAMWI*, 1 and 5 February 1909, 1.

6 *Abhyudaya* was known as the 'mouthpiece' of Madan Mohan Malaviya. In 1909 Krishan Kant Malaviya became the editor and in 1930 his nephew Padam Kant Malaviya succeeded him. The paper was a weekly, sometimes a bi-weekly and even a daily; it was also published as an illustrated Hindi weekly for a short time. The publication of *Abhyudaya* continued, with a few gaps, till February 1948; for details, see Sitaram Chaturvedi, *Builders of Modern India Series: Madan Mohan Malaviya*, New Delhi: Publications Division, 1996, 27.

7 Meenakshi Gigi Durham and Douglas M. Kellner, 'Adventures in Media and Cultural Studies: Introducing the Key Works', in Durham and Kellner eds *Media and Cultural Studies: Key Works*, Oxford: Blackwell Publishers, 2001.

8 In this section I have drawn substantially upon Padgaonkar's interesting introduction to *Brand New*.

9 Padgaonkar ed. *Brand New*.

10 Advertisements for Amritvatika, Pandit Shivaram Pande Vaidya Kee Jwar Vati, Himtail, Mushki Tambakoo, etc. in various issues of *Abhyudaya*.

11 Advertisements, being one of the main sources of revenue, occupy a substantial proportion of the space in newspapers. Pillai in his study shows that during 1947–51 advertisements took up about 40 per cent of total space: Pillai, *Press Advertising Today*.

12 *The Times of India* (hereafter *TOI*), 25 September 1854, cited in Padgaonkar ed. *Brand New*, 186.

13 *TOI*, 29 January 1858.

14 *TOI*, advertisement of Aprols and Steel Pills, 9 February 1901.

15 Eno's Fruit Salt was a sort of salt preparation meant for digestion: *TOI*, 20 August, 1880.

16 *TOI*, 9 January 1888; at the turn of the century the most popular tonic was Phospherine (1906) and after the First World War, it was Waterbury's Compound (1930).
17 The advertisement for Virol reveals that forty million doses of Virol were prescribed in 3,000 hospitals and dispensaries during 1924: *JAMWI*, XIII,1 February 1925, 4.
18 As for instance Colgate became synonymous with toothpaste, Sunlight with soap and Dalda with *vanaspathi ghee* or hydrogenated oil.
19 Advertisement for Aspirin in various issues of *Abhyudaya* and *TOI*.
20 Popular art, also known as calendar art, was widely circulated in the form of calendars: Erwin Neumayer and Christine Schelberger, *Popular Indian Art: Raja Ravi Varma and the Printed Gods of India*, New Delhi: Oxford University Press, 2003.
21 Here colonizing is not used in Arnold's sense, viz. forced control over the body or mind. Here colonizing does not represent forced action.
22 Shri P.N. Sushil, 'Sharirik Avayon Ke Parivartan Se Garbh Kee Pehchan' (Sex determination through body changes during pregnancy), *Abhyudaya*, 16 April 1931, 21; Shrimati Gayavanti Devi Verma, 'Mahilaon Ka Sharirik Patan' (The degeneration of the female body), *Abhyudaya*, 14 May 1931, 11; Srimati Indira Devi Shastrini, 'Streeyon Ka Swasthaya' (Women's health), *Abhyudaya*, 25 October 1935, 8–9; Srimati Hemant Kumari Devi, 'Mahilaon Kee Swasthaya Raksha Ke Liye Aavashyak Upaye' (Important points for women to keep their body healthy), *Abhyudaya*, 30 November 1936, 21; Kaviraj Sri Brijnandan Malaviya, 'Stan Kee Raksha Aur Upay' (Important points for breast care), *Abhyudaya*, 9 November 1936, 16.
23 The importance attached to English brand names was a feature that was perhaps common to any society colonized by the British.
24 For details see Neshat Quaiser, 'Politics, Culture and Colonialism: Unani's Debate with Doctory', in Pati and Harrison eds *Health, Medicine and Empire*, 317–55.
25 Editorial, *Abhyudaya*, 1 October 1909.
26 These products were advertised in various issues of the vernacular newspaper *Abhyudaya*. The 'Sequarine' health tonic was marketed by Messrs Camp & Co. Ltd.
27 As described: 'Woodwards gripe water keeps babies healthy'; oleograph, *c*. 1930 cited in Neumayer and Schelberger, *Popular Indian Art*, 96.
28 The images used for advertisements do not always reflect the logo/symbol of the firm. Sometimes there were mixed or contradictory messages as well. This can be further explored. At present I am unable to provide examples of mixed and contradictory messages in advertisements.
29 In fact, Marten Bode, 'Indian Indigenous Pharmaceuticals: Tradition, Modernity and Nature', in Waltraud Ernst ed. *Plural Medicine, Tradition and Modernity, 1800–2000*, London and New York: Routledge, 2002, 184–203, also mentions how religious and historical images were used by the industry (Dabur, Zandu and Hamdard) to anchor Indian pharmaceuticals in traditional culture.
30 Advertisement for Sequarine, *Abhyudaya*, 12 April 1913; indigenous terms used as universal panaceas are discussed in a separate section of this chapter.
31 Anil Kumar, 'Indian Drug Industry', in Pati and Harrison eds *Health, Medicine and Empire*, 374.
32 Sometimes these people were not directly employed by the indigenous drug manufacturers/retailers.
33 Vishwanath Mukherjee, *Bana Rahe Banaras*, Varanasi: Vishwavidyalaya Prakashan, 1958, 12.
34 Mukherjee, *Bana Rahe Banaras*. This reference reminds me of a song from the oral advertising culture associated with the Indian cinema of the 1950s – *sar jo tera chakraye . . . lakh marj kee ek dava hai kyun na ajmaye*.
35 'Kushta Rog' (Leprosy), *Abhyudaya*, 1906, 7.
36 *Abhyudaya*, 25 December 1930, 4.
37 Advertisement of 'Pushtrajvatika' and 'Piyushratnakar', *Abhyudaya*, 18 February 1912, 7–8; Bode, 'Indian Indigenous Pharmaceuticals', 192, refers to the association with the

'past' by Dabur, Zandu and Hamdard in their advertisements in order to legitimize their products.

38 Advertisement for 'Pushtrajvatika' and 'Piyushratnakar', *Abhyudaya*, 18 February 1912, 7–8.

39 Advertisement titled 'Muft Ilaj' and 'Vaidya Vidya Muft Hee', *Abhyudaya*, 12 April 1913, 9.

40 *Abhyudaya*, 22 September 1923, 11.

41 Advertisement for the ayurvedic preparation 'Pransanjeevani', *Abhyudaya*, 18 February 1912, 8.

42 'Pransanjeevani', *Abhyudaya*, 18 February 1912, 8.

43 Sumathi Ramaswamy, 'Visualizing India's Geo-Body: Globes, Maps, Bodyscapes', in Sumathi Ramaswamy ed. *Beyond Appearances? Visual Practices and Ideologies in Modern India*, New Delhi: Sage Publications, 2003, 151–90, discovers a national longing for a cartographic form in explorations of the deployment of globes, maps and bodyscapes in patriotic visual practices in colonial and postcolonial India. She shows the varied forms of representation of the globe during the twentieth century. The modern map enables the citizen subject to take 'visual and conceptual possession of the nation space that he inhabits' (152).

44 Ramaswamy, 'Visualizing India's Geo-Body', 155–6.

45 The source here is an advertisement in *Abhyudaya*, 22 February 1912.

46 Advertisement for Piyush Ratnakar, *Abhyudaya*, 18 February 1912, 8.

47 *Abhyudaya*, 18 February 1912, 7; the advertisement for Pushtarajvatika also notified the publication of 'Natak Ramayana'.

48 'Urvashi on Postcard', 1905, cited in Neumayer and Schelberger, *Popular Indian Art*, 52.

49 These trends still exist in India; special potency clinics and virility specialists are found in most cities, towns and villages. Male potency is a thriving industry in India today; for details see Kenneth G. Zysk, 'Potency Therapy in Classical Indian Medicine', *Asian Medicine, Tradition and Modernity*, 1: 1, 2005, 101–18.

50 *Abhyudaya*, 15 May 1939,16. In advertising phraseology '*jadoo sa asar*' represents a 'magic system'. One can also cite the example of doctors like S.C. Verma, Gautam Rao Keshav and Vaman Gopal who advertised their medicines for the health and vitality of men: *Abhyudaya*, 7 September 1930, 4; and 25 December 1930, 4; it is not clear from these advertisements if they were allopathic practitioners.

51 Zysk, 'Potency Therapy', 106.

52 Zysk, 'Potency Therapy', 106–7.

53 Zysk, 'Potency Therapy'.

54 Charu Gupta, *Sexuality, Obscenity, Community: Women, Muslims, and the Hindu Public in Colonial India*, New Delhi: Permanent Black, 2001. It is indeed interesting to note that the symbol of British masculinity was drawn from the colonial Afro-Asian world.

55 Charu Gupta mentions how these advertisements, while they celebrated male sexuality, need to be viewed also as desperate attempts made to allay fears of effeminacy and impotence: Gupta, *Sexuality, Obscenity, Community*, 79.

56 Advertisement for birth control pills, 'Santan Nigrah Kee Dava', *Abhyudaya*, 23 July 1934, 30.

57 An advertisement for condoms in *Abhyudaya*, 8 January 1940, 9.

58 A two-page advertisement for Aspro can be cited as an example to illustrate this point: *Abhyudaya*, 5 February 1940, 18.

59 This is an area that needs a detailed study.

60 Bode, 'Indian Indigenous Pharmaceuticals'.

61 Akbar Allahabadi, 'Sarkari Taleem', *Saraswati*, 26, 1925.

13 Opium as a household remedy in nineteenth-century western India?

Amar Farooqui

This chapter looks at the medicinal or, more generally, non-recreational use of opium at the popular level in western India during the latter half of the nineteenth century. It focuses specifically on indigenous and colonial perceptions of the utility of opium as a medicine. The discussion is based mainly on the *Report of the Royal Commission on Opium* (1895). The voluminous 'Minutes of Evidence' published with the *Report* constitute a rich historical source, which unfortunately has not received the attention that it deserves.[1]

For the purpose of the argument of this chapter what is significant is that the entire exercise of gathering the evidence, especially in western India, reinforced the idea that opium if taken in moderation was not harmful and, when administered regularly in small doses, was actually beneficial. Most of the witnesses (barring a couple of missionary doctors) who testified before the Commission at its sittings in western India held in January–February 1894 at Jaipur, Ajmer, Indore and Ahmadabad spoke of opium consumption in the region as a long-established tradition, both as a social custom and as a popular everyday remedy for a variety of ailments.[2]

The question mark in the title of this chapter is intended to draw attention to the manipulative element in the colonial construction of the popular indigenous discourse about opium. In this construction the perceived medicinal value of the substance was crucial to establishing its relative harmlessness. Further, this relative harmlessness was seen as culture specific. To quote the opinion of Sir William Roberts, the sole medical expert appointed to the nine-member Commission, the higher tolerance that Indians had for opium depended 'on a combination of causes – on race and climate, on hereditary acquisition by centuries of use, on the general prevalence of the malarial constitution and the vegetable nature of the diet'.[3]

Opium was a drug of choice among some sections of western and northern Indian society at least from the later medieval period. The cultivation of poppy, its processing into opium, and the availability of the drug as a commodity prompted the Dutch and subsequently the British to include it in the list of goods for their intra-Asian trade. After the establishment of the British empire in India, opium exports from India to China became a key element of the colonial economy. Significantly, the British had little interest in developing a large market for opium in India. The colonial state concentrated its energies on the export of the drug to

China. There was a tendency to minimize supplies for domestic Indian consumption and to retain inferior sorts of the commodity for the Indian market. In this way the colonial state appeared to have sanitized India, making the drug someone else's problem rather than one that concerned a society that was so deeply involved in producing and distributing it.

It would be difficult to locate even a single sentence in official colonial nineteenth-century recordings of indigenous viewpoints on the opium question that indicate any moral dilemmas. Outwardly there is not the slightest expression of an awareness that opium was hardly a respectable commodity. The opium trade caused no pangs of conscience among, say, community leaders in Bombay who engaged in numerous moral crusades on other issues while simultaneously shipping the drug to China. This cannot be attributed merely to the fact that the use of opium for recreational and non-recreational purposes had a certain level of acceptance among some sections of Indian society; nor to the lack of a western moral critique of the kind articulated towards the end of the nineteenth century by evangelists and anti-opium lobbyists. More than anything, this indifference was the outcome of the legitimizing processes of the colonial state. The legitimacy accorded to the opium industry, together with the sanitization that was implied in not encouraging extensive internal use for recreational purposes, while endorsing consumption by an alien society (reinforced by the image, which persisted into the twentieth century, of China as a strange and distant land), prevented the emergence of a discourse within India questioning the propriety of the enterprise.

It is hardly surprising that the British Government of India was able to marshal sufficient evidence in support of the opium trade when the Royal Commission on Opium toured India in 1893–4. The prevailing common sense about the effects of opium consumption had already been summed up in the entry on the drug in George Watt's *Dictionary of the Economic Products of India* (1892), which stated that 'The bulk of the material evidence goes to support the verdict that it is not more injurious than the moderate use of alcohol, and even its abusive use is less destructive to the victim . . .'.[4] This view was echoed in the testimonies presented before the Commission when it visited western India. Those who spoke of the relative harmlessness (or even benefits) of opium were either themselves consumers or opium dealers, or else were officials of opium-producing territories. The common sense on opium was challenged mainly by missionaries, especially medical missionaries.

Of all the 723 witnesses examined by the Commission in India and Britain, there were fifteen medical missionaries.[5] Some of them, such as Dr William Huntly, presented concrete scientific evidence to show that opium consumption was not as innocuous as was being suggested. Huntly did not argue his case in narrow moral terms, but tried to convince the Commission that the notion that moderate use of the drug did not inflict any physical harm was in fact impressionistic.[6] It was easy to dismiss these views since the missionaries were supposed to be pursuing their own religious agenda. At a more fundamental level representatives of opium-producing areas of western India spoke of the financial losses and economic distress which the cessation of the opium trade would result in. This really clinched the argument in favour of the anti-prohibitionists.

The entire discourse, as John Richards has pointed out in his detailed study of the Commission, was in terms of opium in relation to India and not from the perspective of China.[7] This made the task of downplaying the negative aspects of opium much easier and very little manipulation was required to persuade the Commission that the trade was not really harmful for India; on the contrary, that opium revenues were indispensable for the economy. It is well known that Indian nationalists too in the last quarter of the nineteenth century were not inclined to oppose the opium trade, actually extending tacit support to it. To quote Bipan Chandra, 'a large majority adopted an approach that very nearly coincided with that of the Government of India'.[8] It was felt that if the British Indian Government were to forgo the opium revenue 'for mere sentimental reasons', the shortfall in its earnings would have to be made up by the Indian people. Of course there were some prominent nationalist leaders like Dadabhai Naoroji who consistently opposed the opium trade, 'even though he recognised that most of the other national leaders were not [at] one with him on this question'.[9]

The Commission could afford to maintain an agnostic position on whether the consumption of the drug itself had a destructive impact on Chinese society by obfuscating the issue and focusing on India. Rampant opium abuse was primarily a problem for China and not for India. To add to the overall confusion, there were contradictory scientific views about the deleterious effects of the opium habit. These disagreements did not necessarily represent genuine differences of opinion but were at times the result of deliberate misinformation or suppression of data. The ideological hegemony of western medicine was pressed into service to stifle anti-opium arguments. In a recent study Paul Winther has shown how western science in the colonies persisted with the myth that opium was a cure for malaria even as the notion was abandoned in the metropolis.[10] We shall return to this issue later.

Numerous references in contemporary European texts indicate that the use of the drug was fairly widespread in western India during the sixteenth and seventeenth centuries. Knowledge of some of the properties of the drug, and the quantities in which it could be administered for medicinal purposes or used for recreation without being fatal, was common among several sections of the people. Garcia da Orta, the great sixteenth-century Portuguese botanist who lived in Goa for several decades, gave a detailed description of the drug in his famous treatise, *Colloquies on the Simples and Drugs of India* (1563).[11] Some of the information about the drug that da Orta had access to was obviously acquired through his interaction with practitioners of Indian medical systems. Moreover, opium was routinely used in hospitals, missionary pharmacies and infirmaries throughout the Portuguese colonial enclaves in India during the seventeenth and eighteenth centuries, mainly as a painkiller.[12]

In the nineteenth century imbibing opium as a narcotic beverage was commonplace throughout Rajasthan. The drug was consumed in the form of a preparation known locally as *kasumba*. *Kasumba* was made by dissolving a small quantity of opium in water and then straining the liquid. The preparation was particularly popular among Rajputs, both in Rajasthan and Malwa. Ritual sharing of *kasumba* during festivals and family ceremonies was a social custom among Rajputs as well as other castes of the region.[13] When Maharaja Ranjit Singh on one occasion sent a request to the East India Company for a small quantity of Malwa opium he specially referred to 'opium of the kind that is used by the Chiefs of Rajpootana when they assemble and drink it together as a cordial mixed with water'.[14] Smoking opium, with or without tobacco (tobacco was widely grown in western India), seems to have been introduced relatively late in the region. It is only in the second half of the nineteenth century that we begin to get descriptions of opium-smoking practices.[15]

The pattern of traditional opium use in Malwa, Rajasthan and Gujarat as reflected in statements made before the Royal Commission, was one in which there were three distinct phases of supposedly 'normal' exposure to the drug during the lifespan of an individual.[16] The evidence relates to the last decade of the nineteenth century, but it is unlikely that customary practices had altered significantly during the course of the century. This is obvious from the fact that novel methods of ingestion such as smoking were detested even at the end of the century so that the Commission recommended measures to curb consumption in this form.[17]

Individuals were first exposed to the drug as infants. The practice of administering opium to infants in minuscule quantities, usually till they were three to five years old, was quite widespread, especially in Malwa and Rajasthan. The substance was then withdrawn. The second phase of exposure to the drug, for males in particular, was after marriage (i.e. after consummation of marriage).[18] Consumption of small doses of opium on social occasions by married men in their early twenties was generally acceptable. It is a matter of speculation whether exposure to the drug during infancy allowed young adults to tolerate opium without visible manifestations of negative responses. Subsequently opium was habitually consumed on a daily basis by a sizeable number of relatively older men and women (30–40 years old and above). The quantity ranged from doses of half a *ratti* (a *ratti* is approximately 120 mg) to three *rattis* taken from one to three times a day.[19] This marked the third, and addictive, phase of exposure. These were 'moderate' addicts, many of whom had initially taken to daily consumption for medical reasons and were then unable to give up the drug. It needs to be underlined that opium was looked upon as a common household remedy in western India and it did not require much effort to become a 'moderate' addict.

One of the witnesses who appeared before the Commission, Rao Bahadur Amar Singh of Kota, stated in a response which was quite typical that he had been taking the drug habitually for twenty-five years. He went on to state: 'I took it first to get rid of intermittent fever which would not leave me. The fever left me after I had taken opium for about a twelve-month. Since then I have never left it off'.[20] Amar Singh consumed one *ratti* of opium once a day.[21]

Another witness was asked by the Commission whether the majority of the regular consumers 'take it not for pleasure, but when they get ill or for some pain or disease and afterwards it becomes a habit'. To this the response was that 'Generally it is so. There are exceptions but they are very few'.[22] In other words, we can see a close connection between consuming the drug as a cure for some ailment (most of this being perhaps self-medication, given that it was looked upon as an effective and safe household remedy) and becoming moderately addicted to it if the treatment was prolonged. This differs from the experience of ingesting minute quantities once in a while on social occasions.

The Commission asked a British medical officer who had served in Rajasthan for nearly twenty years, Brigade Surgeon French-Mullen, about the purposes for which opium was used in the region and whether it was regarded as a household remedy. In his reply French-Mullen stated:

> Opium is largely used in bowel troubles of all kinds, in rheumatic pains and neuralgias of all kinds, asthma, chronic cough, some forms of dyspepsia, and so on. I do not think it is much used as an aphrodisiac, but I have known it employed, it was said successfully, to enable the sexual act to be prolonged. It is, I think, *the most widely used household medicine in this province*.[23]

This view was confirmed by another medical officer, the residency surgeon stationed at Indore, who had spent twenty-five years in central India; in his answer to the query 'For what purpose is the opium habit generally commenced?' he noted: 'The purposes for which the opium habit is contracted is to alleviate rheumatic pains; to cure chronic dysentery and diarrhoea; to act as a prophylactic against malarial fever; to cure diabetes; and it is often taken as an aphrodisiac.'[24]

The two officers had more or less the same assessment of the place of opium in the everyday lives of the people except that the latter added diabetes to the list and emphatically stated that the drug was considered to be an aphrodisiac. In passing, one might mention a curious observation made by a senior Anglo-Indian official of the Sindia state according to whom, 'In Malwa it is difficult to digest milk unless opium is taken. I have seen many men look really robust who take opium and who drink milk. They cannot drink milk without taking opium.'[25] One wonders whether this could refer to cases of lactose intolerance, a problem that might have, supposedly, been overcome through opium consumption.

It will be apparent that no independent confirmation was provided of the efficacy or otherwise of opium as a cure for the numerous ailments that were listed. The entire argument was presented in terms of what the indigenous perception of the drug was. A pattern may be seen in the fairly representative examples quoted above. The manner in which the questions were framed and the witnesses nudged to elicit desired answers helped to endorse the view that opium was indispensable to the 'natives' on essentially medical grounds. Infants too were routinely administered the drug for similar reasons. Their parents reportedly asserted that opium 'keeps their children happy and contented, and prevents them from crying, and that it acts as a prophylactic against capillary bronchitis, diarrhoea, and other infantile disorders'.[26] It would not be incorrect to say that a link was sought between regular exposure to the drug during infancy, the capacity to occasionally ingest small quantities on social occasions as an adult, and tolerance for relatively larger quantities consumed either intermittently for medicinal purposes or regularly as a moderate addict.

The flaw in the methodology adopted by the Commission in dealing with medical matters relating to opium was implicitly alluded to by Huntly, the medical missionary referred to above. Huntly had paid special attention to the problem during the course of his work in India. In his lengthy testimony he strongly opposed the view that the opium habit was not injurious to health.[27] With regard to infants being given opium, he drew attention to the danger of poisoning due to overdose (which often might not be recognized or reported), and emphasized that opium made children more vulnerable when they were afflicted with illness.

The exchange between Huntly and the members of the Commission is of some interest and an extract may be quoted to underscore the point that Huntly was at pains to make:

Q: We have had samples of people before us this morning, strong healthy-looking men, who told us they had been using opium, some for 10, and some for longer number of years. Are you as a medical man, to say that those persons are suffering from the habit?

A: I do not see how anyone can say so. My judgement may be flatly contradicted by their own statement whether they are suffering or not. I venture to say and hold that they are suffering.

Q: Do not you think a man knows when he is well?

A: No, I do not think a man does always know when he is well. . . . I do not think we can say that a man is well because he simply feels well.

Q: Are you justified as a medical man in saying that a man in whom you can find no organic disease whatever is not well simply because he is in the habit of taking opium?

A: I never said he had organic disease. How are we to know that a man has no organic disease from his own statement? . . .

Q: I suppose your experience has taught you that opium is a very common household remedy in this part of India?

A: Yes; it is a very common remedy, there is no doubt about that. [28]

As a trained medical practitioner with knowledge of western scientific methods, Huntly was obviously exasperated by the way in which the Commission had approached the problem. The method being followed by the Commission, which had someone of the eminence of William Roberts on it, was unscientific within the framework of standards prevailing in the metropolis in the closing decades of the nineteenth century. Roberts was, to quote Richards, 'one of the best-known clinicians and medical researchers in British medicine at the time'.[29] He was eventually instrumental in drafting the portion of the *Report* dealing with the medical aspects of opium and his conclusions were central to the construction of opium as harmless/beneficial in the context of the periphery.[30]

Yet the statements made about the medical efficacy of opium were never subjected to any scientific scrutiny by the Commission. It was sufficient that at the popular level the drug was *perceived* to be a cure for certain ailments. The indigenous claims about its properties were not tested. Nor was the assumption that people were largely experienced in its controlled use seriously questioned. There was no medical investigation, no physical examination (of opium addicts appearing as witnesses), no statistical compilation of hard medical information, no comparative surveys of patterns of disease and their relation to opium use or otherwise, and no systematic collection of data from hospitals and dispensaries. No women witnesses appeared before the Commission, though it was mainly women in the household who administered opium to infants or older children who might be suffering from ailments. Of course it is unlikely that their experience could have been recorded in the formal, indeed intimidating, setting of the Commission's public hearings.

One aspect of the medicinal use of opium which the Commission showed great interest in was its indigenous reputation as a cure for malaria. Witnesses were repeatedly invited to state their opinion on this. 'What knowledge have you', French-Mullen was asked, 'of the belief of the natives that opium is useful in malarial fever?' His response summed up the understanding of a large number of colonial medical officials serving in India:

> I know it is a general belief amongst natives of this province that those who eat opium are less subject to malarial fever than their non-using neighbours. I cannot vouch for the truth of this belief from my own experience, but I certainly do not wish to declare it un- or ill-founded.[31]

In the final *Report* Roberts made the strange assertion that given the specific pattern of opium consumption in several parts of India, the drug was actually beneficial in combating malarial fevers and even in preventing the disease. This he did by making use of research undertaken in the second quarter of the nineteenth century relating to the possibility of one of the alkaloids contained in opium being a cure for malaria. This alkaloid was narcotine or anarcotine, which is now known as noscapine. Roberts, as Winther has observed, would surely have been aware that this research was outdated by the 1890s. Already by the latter half of the nineteenth century narcotine was no longer regarded as having any significant medicinal properties.[32]

Nevertheless Roberts suggested that opium, due to the presence of narcotine in it, could be used to treat malaria. Since the amount of narcotine found in Indian opium was very small, large quantities of the drug had to be administered, at least sixteen grains but possibly much more over a period of one to three days, for the dose to be effective. This might not be a very serious problem for those who were already accustomed to habitually consuming large quantities of the drug, who in any case would have got some protection against the effects of malaria. As for those who were not adequately exposed to opium, such a large dose would be fatal because of the huge quantity of morphine they would ingest. This problem could be overcome by processing opium for the purpose of extracting narcotine.[33] In either case the efficacy of opium as a treatment for malaria was certified by the Commission, ignoring scientific evidence to the contrary which was available in the metropolis.

This amounted to a subterfuge which allowed popular indigenous notions of opium as a common and innocuous household remedy to go unchallenged. It goes without saying that the virtually unregulated non-recreational use of opium that was being endorsed by the colonial state was quite distinct from the professional medical use of the drug, mainly for its potent properties as a painkiller. The subterfuge served the purpose of developing a discourse about opium in which the drug could be presented as being benign (after all it was a common household remedy) from the perspective of the colonized, and hence morally acceptable.

Notes

1 *Report of the Royal Commission on Opium*, IV–V (*Proceedings*, 'Minutes of Evidence'); VI–VII (*Final Report*), London: Her Majesty's Stationery Office, 1894–95.
2 *Royal Commission on Opium*, IV (hereafter *RCO*, IV).
3 Sir William Roberts, 'On the General Features and the Medical Aspects of the Opium Habit in India', Memorandum I, *Royal Commission on Opium*, VI, 101.
4 George Watt, *A Dictionary of the Economic Products of India*, London: W.H. Allen, 1892, vi, I, 22.
5 John F. Richards, 'Opium and the British Indian Empire: The Royal Commission of 1895', *Modern Asian Studies*, 36: 2, 2002, 395.
6 *RCO*, IV, 58–64.
7 See Richards, 'Opium and the British Indian Empire', 375–420.
8 Bipan Chandra, *The Rise and Growth of Economic Nationalism in India: Economic Policies of Indian National Leadership*, New Delhi: People's Publishing House, 565.
9 Chandra, *Rise and Growth of Economic Nationalism*, 565, 569.
10 Paul C. Winther, *Anglo-European Science and the Rhetoric of Empire: Malaria, Opium, and British Rule in India, 1756–1895*, Lanham, Md.: Lexington Books, 2003.
11 Garcia da Orta, *Colloquies on the Simples and Drugs of India* (trans. by Clements R. Markham), reprint of 1895 edition, Delhi: Sri Satguru Publications, 1987, 330ff.
12 See Timothy Walker, 'Opium in the Portuguese Maritime Empire, 1650–1840', paper presented at the international conference on 'Drugs and Empires', Glasgow, April 2003, 11–12.
13 Elijah Impey, *A Report on the Cultivation, Preparation, and Adulteration of Malwa Opium*, Bombay: J. Chesson, 1848, 8; G.R. Aberigh-Mackay, *The Chiefs of Central India*, Calcutta: Thacker, Spink, 1879, I, lxxvii; C.E. Luard, *The Central India State Gazetteer Series*, V, *Western States (Malwa) Gazetteer*, Bombay: Thacker, Spink, 1908, 15, 89, 119.
14 Letter dated 13 December 1835, National Archives of India, New Delhi, Separate Revenue Branch, Opium Consultations, 12, 1 February 1836.
15 Aberigh-Mackay, *Chiefs of Central India*, I, lxxvii.
16 Based on 'Minutes of Evidence', *RCO*, IV.
17 See Govt of India, 19 October 1895, *Collection of Papers relating to the Royal Commission on Opium*, Calcutta, 1896, 2.
18 Cf. A.P. Hove, *Tours for Scientific and Economic Research, Made in Guzerat . . . in 1787–1788, Selections from the Records of the Bombay Govt.*, new series, XVI, Bombay: Bombay Education Society's Press, 1855, 126–7.
19 *RCO*, IV, 45.
20 *RCO*, IV, 32.
21 *RCO*, IV, 32.
22 *RCO*, IV, 33.
23 *RCO*, IV, 65.
24 Evidence of Brigade Surgeon Lt.-Col. D.F. Keegan, *RCO*, IV, 91.
25 Evidence of Lt.-Col. Sir Michael Filose, Governor of Malwa, Sindia State, *RCO*, IV, 101.

26 Evidence of Keegan, *RCO*, IV, 91.
27 *RCO*, IV, 58–64.
28 *RCO*, IV, 60–1.
29 Richards, 'Opium and the British Indian Empire', 391.
30 Roberts, 'General Features', 99–119.
31 *RCO*, IV, 65.
32 Winther, *Anglo-European Science*, 241.
33 The above discussion is based on Winther, *Anglo-European Science*, 241–2.

Index

Note: n following a page number refers to a note.